# Sons an
# Daughters
## of the World War One Generation

## Volume 2

*"Peace in our time..."*

*Best wishes,*

## Michael Kendrick

Published by Michael Kendrick
© Michael Kendrick 2009

# CONTENTS

# PREFACE

What impresses me about Michael's writing style, whether it is in his books on World War 1 or his poetry, is the warmth and compassion that he captures within the pages. He feels deeply for the people he is writing about, totally understands their hopes, fears, and non-more so than for his grandfather in his excellent: 'Fifty Good Men And True.' His other book on a similar theme, 'Greater Love' also deserves great credit and again displays the courage of the Great War soldiers from his home county.

Within this book, Michael has gone to great length to ensure that the Second World War generation of his area are not forgotten. Sons and Daughters descending from his two earlier books are presented in his own heartfelt manner, and being of their age I can readily identify with them. The scope of the book includes most of the 1939-45 theatres of war, including pilots of the Battle of Britain, the braves of Bomber Command through to the Royal Navy and Japanese Prisoners of War. I spent a considerable time in the Far East during the war and can appreciate how dreadful it was for those prisoners. I know many were from Leicestershire.

I am also pleased to see that Michael has included girls who served during the War, for their role was significant.

For me the book captures some fascinating accounts and the general mood of wartime Britain. It also illustrates the men and women whose devotion and often sacrifice to duty must never be forgotten. Without doubt Michael has made a substantial contribution towards these efforts and for that we must be truly grateful.

Sincerely Yours,

Dame Vera Lynn

# THIS COUNTRY IS AT WAR

In a broadcast from Downing Street: 11.15am on Sunday 3rd September 1939, Neville Chamberlain said:

*"This morning the British ambassador in Berlin handed the German Government a final note, stating that unless we heard from them by 11.00 o'clock that they were prepared at once to withdraw their troops from Poland, a state of war would exist between us. I have to tell you that no such undertaking has been received, and that consequently this country is at war with Germany."*

# DEDICATION

I dedicated my first book: 'Fifty Good Men and True' to my maternal grandfather, Charles Hatter. He devoted so much of his life for the benefit of others; I'd like to think he appreciates my efforts for his generation and now for his children's generation.

'Epitaph For The Few' could not have been written without the support of the late Wing Commander C. F. 'Bunny' Currant D.S.O. D.F.C. and bar, Croix de Guerre. It remains the only anthology of poems written for the aircrew of the 1940 Battle of Britain. It was dedicated to my dearly missed friend.

'Greater Love' was another tribute to those whom served in the War: 'To End All Wars'. It was dedicated to my beloved wife.

With the agreement of my sister, Maureen, 'Sons and Daughters' is dedicated to two people, our mother, Betty, and father, Les Kendrick.

Within the pages of Volume 1, there is a fascinating account of our parents; it could be enlarged to create a book in its own right, but their life's journey deserves to be within the pages of a community with which they belonged. Les passed-away in January 2006; our mother suffers with severe dementia and rests in a local nursing home. God bless them both and may I indulge in thanking them for their efforts in raising a family.

Michael Kendrick
*2008*

# ACKNOWLEDGEMENTS

*Beryl Kendrick, Ted Purver, Michael Kendrick, David Taylor. M.P. (2008)*

First, my eternal thanks to Dame Vera Lynn, who once again spared her time to write the Preface for another of my books; I couldn't possibly write sufficient to thank the leading lady of the Twentieth Century. There are millions of people whom will never forget the warmth and compassion within her voice: 'We'll Meet Again', 'Yours', 'There'll Be Bluebirds Over The White Cliffs Of Dover' and 'You'll Never Know' to name a few of her superb songs.

As with earlier books I'm indebted to the efforts and ability of fine friends, Dennis Baker and Martin Bird, with Martin again displaying the book's contents to the pinnacle of perfection. I would also like to thank my sister Maureen and husband David for proof-reading the text.

The Coalville Times allowed me to reproduce archival photographs to add to the flavour of the time. We will never forget Jack Hussey's: 'The Billet'. That monthly wartime magazine was a unique medium for allowing Coalville and District's men and women, of the armed forces, to exchange personal and general news and photographs.

I thank Hutchinson & Co for a few photographs and maps taken from their 'History of The War' (printed during the war).

My gratitude to the fine folk who contacted me, welcomed me into their homes, and provided me with information that can now be found in this, and volume two, of 'Sons and Daughters'.

My appreciation to North West Leicestershire District Council; I was genuinely stunned to receive a Civic Reception to honour my endeavours over several decades. Thank you, Ted Purver, David Taylor M.P., Christine Fisher, Jim Rowlinson and John Cowley of the Royal British Legion, and everyone that made it possible.

Finally, but never latterly, I am indebted to my dear wife. Beryl, despite ill health insists that I press on with my calling: to record a representation of local men and women for their efforts in world wars.

Michael Kendrick

# FOREWORD

Between 1939-1945 our planet was engulfed in the most colossal and destructive war in human history. The Second World War, as it was known, encapsulated a term now frequently used: Total War. Economies were geared for maximum offence or defence and people, both military and civilian, were involved in a bleak six-year battle for survival. World War 1 vocabulary such as frontline and home front were used, but such definitions became blurred when events occurred with rapidity. German Forces used blitzkrieg tactics to invade northern Europe: the military clashed but home fronts were bombed from the air. The huge swell in the amount of ships for convoy duties: transporting troops, armour, munitions and provisions to support the war effort. Surface vessels like the 'Bismarck', submarines and air forces regularly attacked these vast armadas. In World War 2, nobody was safe, there were no hiding places, and figures suggest sixty million people perished. In reality, that war was an extension of the Great War of 1914-1918:

At 11.00am on 11th November 1918, the guns ceased firing after the most bestial war ever known, particularly so on the Western Front. On 28th June 1919, in the Hall of Mirrors at Versailles, German delegates listened in silent humiliation to terms imposed upon their defeated country. The Fatherland was stripped of chunks of prime industrial land, notably the Saar territory, whilst other areas were shared between the Allies. Significantly, Germany was ordered to pay six billion pounds in reparations for war damage. The army was cut to one hundred thousand, the navy to twenty-four ships and no air force whatsoever; also a proposed occupation of the Rhineland for fifteen years. It was believed that the League of Nations, which formed part one of the above covenant, would prohibit further wars, but the League was 'stillborn'; disinclination of the United States of America to join proved critical.

In 1922, French Premier, Raymond Poincare insisted and understandably so, that France's war damage be paid swiftly, regardless of consequence to the German people. In January 1923, with reparations falling short, French troops entered the Rhineland and expelled nearly a hundred and fifty thousand citizens from their homes, shot hundreds of others and seized many properties. Germany resisted the invasion with an economic strike, which led to their currency (mark) crashing and extensive hunger riots and poverty.

A decade later, relations between Germany and her neighbours had improved, but resentment and bitterness remained. Failings in the League of Nations were exposed on 18th September 1931, Japan invaded Manchuria, a part of China. An appeal was made to the League and they demanded Japan (a member) to remove her troops by November 16th. Japan retorted that she wouldn't tolerate interference and the League backed-down, doing no more than condemn. That decision opened the door for German expansionism, and a certain Adolf Hitler took full advantage of the situation. By 1938, Japan occupied large areas of China and had extracted precious resources to strengthen her economy and war footing.

World War 2 erupted on 1st September 1939 with Germany invading Poland; two days later Great Britain and France, honouring a promise, declared war on the aggressor. Troops of the Russian Soviet Union then marched into Poland on September 17th, and three days later Poland was crushed. Politically, maybe sensibly, the Allies didn't declare war against Russia.

Then came the 'Phoney War': no fighting whatsoever, however, on 9th April 1940, Germany invaded Denmark and Norway to enable it to control the Atlantic approaches. British and French troops assisted Norway but the countries fell a few months later. A B.E.F. (British Expeditionary Force) was sent to France, but Germany mounted a surprise attack in the Ardennes, south of Luxemburg, on 10th May 1940. Holland and Belgium were overrun and the thrust of the German attack was so piercing that, by May 26th, the British and French armies were encircled at the French Channel port of Dunkirk. A third of a million troops were evacuated but little of their capital equipment; on June 22nd northern France surrendered. Adolf Hitler's next objective was to invade Great Britain, aware that the United States could never oppose them without a European base.

Our army was then too weak to resist a sea/air-borne invasion, but first the Luftwaffe, the world's largest air force needed control of the air. In the 1940 Battle of Britain, 'The Few': aircrew of Fighter Command defeated their enemy. It was our 'Finest Hour', the most pivotal battle of the war. Soon to

**11 A.M.
3RD. SEPTEMBER
1939**

WORLD WAR DECLARED OFFICIAL

follow was the Blitz: night bombing of many of our cities, chiefly London, with heavy losses of life, but it failed to conquer the resolve of the British public.

From 1940-May 1943, the Allies fought in Libya against Axis Forces of Italy and Germany. Battles swept across the Western Desert with the Second Battle of El Alamein: 23rd October to 4th November 1942 their turning point. Opposing chiefs, Bernard Montgomery and Erwin Rommel proved inspirational to their troops. Concurrently, the Mediterranean was alight with Greece and Crete falling in 1941; Malta offered unyielding resistance. Germany, with its need of Lebensraum (living space) and hatred of communism, attacked Russia with over three million troops/air support on 22nd June 1941. After three months they were only twenty miles from Moscow, but a decline into severe winter snows caused chaos for the lightly clothed troops and reduced the movement of their armour and provisions. At Stalingrad the Germans lost heavily in all respects: it was a gradual retreat that only ended in 1945!

In the early war years the U.S.A. was neutral, but offered sizeable aid to (which bankrupted) Great Britain in the form of 'Lend-Lease', but matters changed on 7th December 1941. The Japanese, annoyed by strict U. S. A. sanctions preventing them from buying metals and fuels, formulated a plan of revenge. On the above date, without warning, Japanese aircraft attacked America's Pacific Fleet at Pearl Harbour, killing hundreds and destroying eight

battleships and other assets. Four days later, President Roosevelt said: *"December 7th, 1941, a day which will live in infamy"*, and declared war on Japan. Germany declared war on the United States.

Japan advanced in the Far East: weeks after Pearl Harbour they took Guam and Wake Island, and on Christmas Day, Hong Kong. In February 1942 the British base of Singapore Island fell, and in March they invaded Burma. Thousands of allied prisoners were enslaved to construct a 'railway of death' through the Burmese jungle. The Dutch held island of Java capitulated after heavy air attacks and by middle December the Philippines was taken.

In 1942, the Royal Air Force's 'Bomber Command' had the support of the American Air Force (U.S.A.A.F.). Great strides were underway in taking the war to the German homeland: large cities were reduced to rubble in an attempt to crush their war industry. The R.A.F. flew by night while the American aircraft, with superior defences, took to daylight skies. In early 1944, with German Forces in retreat following Italy's surrender, the Allies launched a sea invasion of Anzio between January and May; the battle zones were narrowing. This continued on 'D'-Day, 6th June 1944, when British and American troops invaded Normandy from a vast armada of nearly three thousand ships.

The tide had turned against Germany, and the same happened in the Far East following the near obliteration of the Japanese Fleet by the Americans in the Pacific. The war in Europe ended (V.E. Day) on 8th May 1945, whilst Japan capitulated after Hiroshima and Nagasaki were bombed with atomic devices. Japan surrendered (V.J. Day) on 15th August 1945. Then came the disclosure of the German Concentration Camps, and a little later the 'Cold War', but that is another issue.

The random harvest of World War Two claimed in excess of 50 million lives.

# WELCOME HOME

Kim Kinsey, one time runner-up in the 'Nurse of the Year' award, has a highly responsible position at Coalville Nursing Home. In 2007, driven by worry for her son, Peter: serving in Afghanistan, she wrote and dedicated a poem to parents from all generations that had sons and daughters serving in foreign lands.

Everything seems so loud as I lie awake at night,
Thinking of what I have to do when it gets light.
Slow is the pass of time; again I look at the clock,
As against my window pane bare branches knock.

I toss and then turn, but my efforts are all in vain;
My mind cannot, will not accept that wars are sane!
Come the peeping morning sun and its gentle glow,
While in early rays stark silhouettes begin to show.

Once again I hear the birds singing a dawn chorus:
Is there anything in Mother Nature that's injurious?
A final stretch and placing of hands over my head,
Wonder what are the prospects for the day ahead.

I think of my dear boys: what does the future hold?
Certainly many trials and tribulations as lives unfold.
Far, so far from home fighting other people's crimes.
How can I be of help when they have difficult times?

Life is no heaven, it is never easy: of that I'm sure.
How do we stop pain and will suffering have a cure?
'Hope' is my prime weapon for fighting these fears:
Reports of death and injury bring me close to tears.

You know, a mother's instinct is to protect her child,
Once, not long ago, small, dependent, meek and mild.
How quickly they mature: take destiny in their hands,
And look to the future, making life's long-term plans.

I won't rest until they return home, out of harm's way.
And then, only then, can I hold them tightly and say:
'Welcome Home, Welcome Home!'

*Kim Kinsey*

# JOAN & DOUGLAS ALLEN

**J**oan was born on 1st June 1921 at Hanley, a suburb of Stoke-on-Trent, Staffordshire. Her parents, William James Wilson and Jane Ellen Evans were both born in 1892 at Smallthorne, a small town five kilometres (three miles) due north of Stoke-on-Trent. William, a sergeant in World War 1, spent a considerable part of the war in training infantrymen on Alderney, on the Channel Islands. In his younger years he was a coalminer and later an assistant manager with the Provident Clothing and Supply Company. The couple had one other child, Samuel Evans Wilson: born in 1903. Joan was educated at Hamilton Road Primary School, and until the age of fourteen, at Glass Street Girls' School. Although bright, she was born into an age where a girl's education was secondary to having babies, cooking skills and various homely duties. Nevertheless, Joan attended night classes and developed much sought after secretarial skills. She obtained the position of receptionist with some bookkeeping duties, at The Central Loan Company. This firm, in addition to financial loans were also bespoke tailors; Joan was pleased with her wage of 12 shillings and six pence per week (0.62p).

In 1939, fortune smiled her way when an office-clerk at the Provident Clothing and Supply Company was called-up into the Forces. Joan applied for his position: receptionist/clerk and was employed at a rate of thirty shillings a week (£1.50).

*"In those days it was a good wage; I felt quite rich and was able to treat myself for a time, and life was even better when my boyfriend, Denys Bulmer, asked me to marry him. Denys was born at Hanley on 21st April 1922. As the war progressed the firm began to suffer and I was made redundant: there was no compensation in those days! Denys didn't want me to join the Forces, and so I approached the Labour Exchange for another job. I also had to consider my mother, who at the time was a semi-invalid. In a short time I received notification that I'd been posted to Civil Defence."*

Joan was allotted to the National Fire Service, and ordered to report to Wolverhampton Fire Force 40.

*"I received an eight week training course at Smethwick: five kilometres to the west of Birmingham's city-centre. It was there that I was taught, among other things, how to slide down a pole and to climb up a hosepipe tower. Next came a posting*

*Denys Bulmer and Joan Wilson, early 1940's.*

*to nearby West Bromwich Sub-Divisional Headquarters, and then onto Swan Village, Tipton, about thirteen kilometres (eight miles) northwest of Birmingham. We were located near to the base of a huge gasometer that, I was told, had its top camouflaged to look like a lake with swans swimming on it; I never climbed the meter to see whether that was correct. Very soon I developed a problem: dreadful sinusitis; I think I must have been allergic to the slight gaseous smell that lingered there, and so I asked for a different posting. My qualifications must have been taken into account because I became the company officer's secretary in the sub-divisional headquarters at West Bromwich."*

*Joan's National Fire Service badge.*

As the year 1940 progressed into autumn, and not forgetting the glorious efforts of 'The Few', the national state of affairs remained grave, there was the possibility of a German invasion.

Joan Wilson on parade, second in nearest row.

Joan in the National Fire Service.

*"They were difficult times but we got through. In 1943, we were ordered to Birmingham Fire Station and then dispersed to fire stations in southern England to meet the bombing there. I spent a period at Farnham, only sixty kilometres (thirty six miles) southwest of Westminster, and situated on the Northern Downs of Surrey. London had a very bad time during the 1940/1 Blitz and I shall never forget the night raids that I saw. The enemy was still causing bomb damage, especially around the dockland area, and I recall seeing the distant searchlights, the Ack-Ack guns firing away, the droning aircraft, lots of explosions and the glow from the burning buildings. On a lighter note: one night four of us girls went to the local cinema; it was dark when we took our seats, but when the interval lights came on we realised that it was packed with men in khaki, and we were the only females. All we could hear were catcalls, wolf whistles and lewd remarks: typical lads!"*

Joan had a variety of postings around Reigate and Redhill areas, directly south of London.

*"I had relief postings at Dorking, Epsom, Ascot and Leatherhead. A despatch rider used to take me on the back of his motorbike; I had to cling on for dear life. Quite a lot of the time I worked the switchboard. As fires were reported I obtained their locations, estimated their sizes and alerted fire-crews as to their requirements. The alert came when I pulled a handle referred to as: 'When The Bells Go Down': Tommy Trinder starred in a wartime Fire-Service film of that very name! I recall one night at Redhill whereby I was watching an air raid from the top of a building. The guns were firing away and all of a sudden there was a bright flash in the night sky: an enemy aircraft had been hit and exploded!"*

In March 1944 Joan received devastating news!

*"I received a telephone call at the office to say that Denys had been killed in action. Later I heard that he had trod on a land mine at the Anzio beachhead in Italy. He'd been badly wounded and taken aboard the hospital ship: 'St. David' which was moored just offshore. The ship, clearly marked Red Cross, was blown out of the water by German bombers. Denys was only twenty-one years of age, another tragic victim of war. He had a lovely sister named, Joan. She was a nursing sister and ranked as a captain in the*

*Denys Bulmer was killed whilst aboard the Hospital Ship 'St. David.' The ship had been moored just off the Anzio beachhead when the enemy bombed it. His body was never found.*

*Queen Alexander's Nursing Service. Joan was based in a hospital at Cairo, Egypt, and cared for many, including the El Alamein casualties. I was very upset for days after hearing of his death, but a compassionate local family looked after me: they took me under their wing and were wonderful."*

Denys was wounded at Anzio, which started on 22nd January 1944 with a beachhead invasion from the Tyrrhenian seaboard. A dreadful failure by senior officers to exploit the surprise attack allowed the enemy to regroup, strengthen, and occupy the coastal Alban Hills, thus keeping the Allied troops on the shore for five months. Only when Monte Cassino, a fortified monastery/peak-town occupied by elite enemy troops, fell to the Allies were they able to dislodge the ensnared Germans and march on Rome.

Joan was posted to Hove, near to Brighton, on the Sussex coast.

*"The German fighters had these frequent hit and run raids; they'd zoom in a few at a time, drop bombs, strafe the area with bullets and depart. We never felt safe! An Ack-Ack gun was on the roof of our building, which meant that when we went to the lavatories, which were outside, we had to wear our tin hats because shell casing used to drop everywhere.*

Joan's wartime service came to an abrupt end following a serious injury.

*"I was in Hove. I'd just boarded a double-decker bus and was climbing the rear stairs of the vehicle when it suddenly jolted to a halt. I fell down the stairs and off the open-end of the bus onto my bottom; my head missed the front tyres of a large wagon by two feet! The wagon - driver screeched to a halt and climbed out to comfort me until I was taken to hospital. X-Rays revealed that I had fractured the second lumbar vertebrae: very painful. I was put into a plaster cast and eventually sent home, remaining in the cast for six months. When it was removed I needed physiotherapy three times a week for eighteen months."*

Joan was discharged from the Fire Force and when fully fit went to the Labour Exchange.

*"I started with Brown Brothers at Stoke-on-Trent, a well known wholesale motor factors and was employed in the administration section, mostly dealing with invoices. I met Doug in December 1947 at a dance hall: The King's Hall, Stoke-on-Trent. We became engaged on Easter Sunday, 1948, and tied the knot on the 4th September 1948. The ceremony took place at St. Matthew's Church, Hanley. The church had a corrugated roof and during the service it began to rain very heavily: it sounded just like bullet fire, back to the war-years again!*

*We stayed at the Wyngarth Hotel at Llandudno for our honeymoon and have returned there over the years. The building is still there, but sadly it is no longer a hotel.*

*We thought we had been cursed because soon afterwards Doug's father passed away (April 1949) and then I nursed my mother until she died in 1950."*

Joan obtained a job at Marks and Spencer. On becoming pregnant, and when it began to show, she was asked to work behind the sales floor: it was considered improper to serve customers in that condition! The baby was still-born in 1953: causing much grieving. Her father passed away in 1955.

*"I re-started on a part-time basis as a sales assistant with Marks and Spencer. After a few years I gave birth to Iain on Easter Sunday, 10 April 1955, at Cleethorpes in Lincolnshire. We moved to Coalville in 1955 and our second son, Stephen, was born at Ashby de la Zouch Cottage Hospital on St. Swithan's Day, 15th July 1958."*

They lived at 13, Longcliffe Road, Greenhill, and later on Joan had a spell with the 'Coalville Times': working in their Belvoir Road shop. Next, she worked at Messrs. T.G. Grieve (Coalville needle

*56 Flight R.A.F. Scarborough. Doug is 4th from the left, back row.*

manufacturers), and finally for the East Midlands Electricity Board.

*"I worked in their office in Market Place, Coalville, then the Accounts Department at Shepshed, and finally in the Engineering Department in the same building."*

Joan and Douglas live on the Agar Nook estate: within walking distance of the beautiful Charnwood Forest. Always busy, she has spent the last thirty years involved in raising moneys for Cancer Charities; indeed, Joan and the team she works with have raised incredible sums and deserve enormous praise.

**Douglas** was born on 9th September 1924 at (The) Meir, a southwestern suburb of Stoke-on-Trent, Staffordshire. His father, William Norman Allen was born on 7th April 1896 at Normacot Stoke while his mother, Maud (nee Cooper), at nearby Meir on 8th September 1902.

*"My father helped to build the Meir's private aerodrome and my Uncle Jack and Auntie Kathy Cooper lived in a cottage right on the edge of the aerodrome. I loved the annual air show there; it was called 'Alan Cobham's Flying Circus' and I was fascinated by the assortment of aeroplanes, especially one called the 'Flying Flea'."*

Douglas attended Meir Infant and Junior Schools, and because he was always, by far, the youngest in his class, did very well to pass for Longton High (Grammar) School. If he'd been born two days later (September 11th) he would have been the oldest of the lower class.

At school he displayed exceptional gifts in mathematics and mental arithmetic.

*"I left school at fifteen, nearly sixteen years of age, and became a junior clerk in the sales section of the Gas Board at Longton: dealing with clocking-in/out records and wage sheets.*

*In 1942, I was called-up into the Royal Air Force Voluntary Reserve, and while awaiting a posting I joined the Air Training Corps (A.T.C.) and passed as a glider pilot. Happily it was at Meir airfield. I thought flying was wonderful and couldn't wait for my chance in the bigger stuff. I entered the R.A.F. on 3rd June 1944: service number 1819793."*

*Betty Allen circa 1946.*

*A.C.1 Douglas Allen.*

Nottingham, as a clerk.

*"I had six months of heaven there, wherever I looked there were gorgeous girls, but the civilian billet wasn't too good."*

Douglas then went on a course at Flight Mechanic School, Melksham in Wiltshire and was promoted from Aircraftsman 2 (AC2) to AC1.

*"It was a handy increase in pay from three-shillings a day (15 new pence) to three shillings and sixpence (17½ new pence). I was posted to R.A.F. Jurby in the northwest of the Isle of Man; I spent six months there, but it was now 1946 and the requirement for flight engineers was pretty low. I had a good time there and played football for the R.A.F. During that posting I had twelve leaves: travelling by ferry from Douglas to Liverpool and then by train to Meir."* (He was also a keen cricketer, and loves the sport to this day.)

His next posting was to Burtonwood, just northwest of Warrington, in what is now called, Merseyside, and his final one to Kirkham, between Blackpool and Preston, where he was demobbed on 15th July 1947.

Douglas was five feet seven inches in height (now 2" less) and says that his brother, Kenneth William, is six feet three inches; born on 7th April 1927 and served in the post-war army. It is clear that Doug is very fond of his sister, Betty, who was born on 30th September 1929, and at present is none too well.

On 3rd June 1944, Douglas, as part of 56 Flight (R.A.F.), was at Scarborough Air Crew Reception Centre. The course lasted for six weeks and on making his preferential training choices wrote: *'pilot or flight engineer'.*

*"I dearly wanted to be a pilot and so I was posted to Sealand, just northwest of Chester and not far from the rivers Mersey and Dee: good navigational aids. I was trained on a 'Tiger Moth' and thought I did pretty well, but decided not to say that I was a trained glider pilot, thinking that's where I might end-up. From all of the trainees only very few were selected and to my dismay I wasn't one of them. There was something about my three point landing they didn't like: probably a habit I picked up from glider training."*

Douglas asked for flight engineer training, only to be told there was a large backlog, and so received a temporary posting to Burnham in Buckinghamshire.

The commanding officer, on appreciating his talents, arranged for a posting to the Deputy Provost Marshal's Office on Upper Parliament Street,

R.A.F. Form 2520/25

**RELEASE AUTHORISATION**

PART I
To be completed in Unit except when marked**.

Rank .... AC1 ....     Number 1819793

Initials .... D ....     Surname .... ALLEN.
(Block Letters)

**To be completed at the Dispersal Centre**
{ Release of the above-named airman is hereby authorised as a Class A .... release, and he is relegated to Class G .... of the Reserve. The effective date of release (i.e. last day of service) is 9 . 9 . 47 .... **.

It is hereby certified that the above airman served in the R.A.F. on whole-time service during the following periods:

| From | To |
| --- | --- |
| 22.3.43 | 23.3.43 |
| 3.6.44 | 15.7.47 * |

*(Date of departure from Dispersal Centre)*

He is granted [ 56 ] days' leave on release commencing the day following the date of departure from the Dispersal Centre

*Douglas' R.A.F. Release Certificate.*

*Joan and Douglas on their Wedding Day.*

*His intelligence is above average and we strongly recommend a course in accountancy.'*

His character was graded as *'Very Good'*. A letter written in June 1946 (by V. A. S.) observed from his aptitude tests that he was of 'high order', with 'very high constructive and mathematical abilities that deserves further education'. Douglas continues:

*"The early months of 1947 saw incredibly heavy snow falls; it was very cold and it remained so until April. I remember coming home on leave and in parts around Meir Railway Station, which was in a cutting, the snow was up to my shoulders."*

On demobilisation, Douglas re-joined the Gas Board as a junior clerk; he also attended the North Staffordshire Technical College for two years and ultimately travelled to Battersea Polytechnic for his final examinations: practical and written. Passing, he began employment as a sanitary inspector for the Public Health Department at Stoke-on-Trent.

Douglas' R.A.F. Release Certificate carries a statement by Squadron Leader E. C. Jones:

*'He is a very keen and willing worker and wishes to become an accountant, and has been recommended by the R.A.F. Vocational Advice Service (V.A.S.).*

*"My pay was £405 per annum; I had my own office at Smallthorne and at the time lived with my wife's parents; we were married on 4th September 1948, and had a memorable honeymoon at Llandudno in Wales. Several years later, in 1954, a similar position but with*

*On honeymoon.*

Douglas is the longest serving member of that church congregation: fifty-three years. Early on he was deputy and then Church Warden for three years. Joan, at first with another church, has now attended for decades and been actively involved in many instances. While at the couple's delightful bungalow on the slopes of Charnwood Forest, I admired framed paintings hanging on the walls: Douglas had painted them. The couple's children are in regular touch. Iain lives locally with wife, Sandra (nee Baker), while Stephen married Yorkshire lass, Sharon (nee Sidebottom) and lives at Pudsey, West Yorkshire.

My thanks to Joan and Douglas for the above; I think we can accept them as residents of the area after over fifty years.

*a house attached became available at Cleethorpes in northeast Lincolnshire, and it was there that our first son, Iain, was born. We stayed there for eighteen months until, in 1955, I heard of a vacancy at the Council Offices on London Road, Coalville. My role was that of a Sanitary Inspector in the Environmental Health Department, and I specialised in food control and infectious diseases."*

After a while they moved into 163, Broom Leys' Road, Coalville.

*"Jabez Emmerson, famed as one of the Famous Fifty, lived a few doors away. He used to show Iain and our second son, Stephen, who was born in 1958, his medals. We also knew another of those Fifty, Walter Handford, because they attended our local church: St. David's. I lost my father in 1968."*

# JOSEPH ANSELL

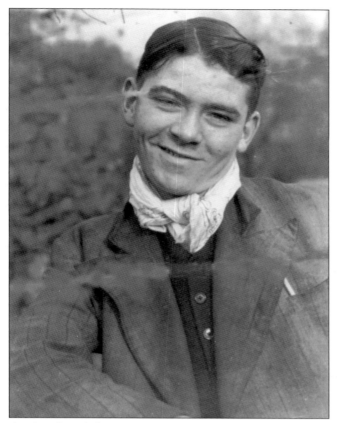

*Joe Ansell aged sixteen.*

*Joe's parents: Fred and Amelia Ansell, 1948.*

I was well advanced into this volume when I rang an old friend, Roy Howe, and asked if he knew of a 'Bevin Boy'. Within minutes he let me have the telephone number of Joseph.

In 1939, 'Joe' lived with his parents in Ferdinand House, Ferdinand Place in the London district of St. Pancras: near to the railway station. His father, Frederick (Fred) had served with a Welsh Battalion during the Great War and had been gassed, indeed, he died prematurely: aged just fifty-three years as a result of scarred lungs. Fred's brother, William, served with the South Wales Borders and was killed at Vimy Ridge. His mother, Amelia (nee Murphy) of Irish stock gave birth to nine children: Frederick (Fred) on 2nd February 1922 at St. Pancras Hospital, Joseph on 27th February 1924, and James (Jim), Florence, Doris, George, Phyllis, Jean and John.

Joe's father worked as a gardener at Regent's Park, but after the early London Blitz he was requisitioned to help demolish the huge amount of damaged and unsafe buildings.

Soon after the start of the war, the eldest sibling, Fred, enlisted for the R.A.F.: more will be written later in this essay. Around the same time Amelia and her two youngest children were evacuated to St. Neots, a small town twenty-eight kilometres (sixteen miles) due west of Cambridge. Then came a period of inactivity: 'The Phoney War', and so they returned to St. Pancras, only to be evacuated again at the onset of the night Blitz, this time to Sileby, a village fourteen kilometres north of Leicester City. Concurrently, four other siblings were evacuated to St. Austell, Cornwall where they remained for the war's duration. Joe and sister, Florence stopped with their father, with Joe: aged sixteen, volunteering as a messenger for the A.R.P. (Air Raid Precaution).

Joe: "*A red brick building was built for the A.R.P. on Harmood Street, in the district known as Chalk Farm: near to St. Pancras. I was out most nights when the bombers were overhead; I was given a bike and I had to relay messages to headquarters as and when required. It was mainly to inform where new fires had started or where emergency vehicles were needed. I saw some sights; I remember going into this bombed pub and trying to help in moving this piano to free a man trapped by it! Alternatively, I was with an A.R.P. man at the top of a building; it was our duty to note where incendiary bombs were falling and inform the firemen by a field line. It was rough stuff what with searchlights, shrapnel falling from the Ack-Ack guns, the roar of the bombers, the explosions, the smoke and the fires made it like daylight!"*

I smiled and said that I came to write about a 'Bevin Boy', and congratulated him on what he achieved in earlier circumstances: his endeavours saved lives and he was a mere teenager.

Joe's father and Florence left London to join the evacuees at Sileby, while Joe decided to remain in London. He later travelled to see them on his birthday in 1941 and they urged him to stay: he acquiesced.

*"I returned with my dad to our London home and took what few of our meagre possessions we could carry and never returned."*

Joe enlisted into Sileby Home Guard and spent training-weekends at Beaumanor Hall, Old Woodhouse, near Loughborough. On leaving school he had trained as a panel-beater, repairing damaged cars, and this skill was utilised at 'Victory Works', Woodgate at Leicester, where he was involved in repairing the radiators of aircraft.

*"We repaired all kinds of radiators from Spitfires, Hurricanes, and all types of bombers. While I was working there I met my future wife."*

He received his 'call-up-papers' and travelled to Lichfield Barracks, but after an interview he was deferred: his job was considered a reserved occupation. About a year later he received another set of papers and asked to report to the Labour Exchange. *"I was seen by the manager there, I knew him because he was a corporal in the Sileby Home Guard; he said he was sorry but there was a need for hands in the collieries, and that I had been called to be a 'Bevin Boy', it was compulsory recruitment!"*

From 1939, many young miners joined the Armed Forces, and in May 1941 an 'Essential Work Order' was applied to collieries to prohibit men from leaving and also employers from dismissing them! In June 1941 an appeal was made for fifty thousand ex-miners to voluntarily return to the industry; this met with little success. In July, a compulsory order was made for all whom had worked in the trade since 1935 to return: sixty thousand were forcibly returned.

All of the above was initiated by Ernest Bevin (1881-1951). He had a prominent career in Trade Unionism (Transport and General Workers Union)

before entering Parliament. From 1940-45 he was Minister of Labour, and further, by necessity, he informed the House on 12th October 1943, that arrangements had to be made for the compulsory conscription of twenty thousand seventeen and eighteen year olds to solve the colliery's labour crisis. The 'Bevin Boys' were not selected, but taken according to a ballot: adjusted from time-to-time, relating from 0-9 on their National Service Registration Certificate numbers. This method of selection ignored various work's experiences, education and physical abilities, yet was considered the fairest means. Hence: though smaller, stockier men were best suited to work in the lower seams, instances arose where teenagers of six feet had to hunch over and accept the consequences.

*Joe Ansell the 'Bevin Boy' in 1944.*

Coal was a necessity, not just for waging war, but also to support the country's domestic and industrial needs. By 1942, forty per-cent of the colliery's labour force was over forty years of age, and increased demands placed additional strains and stresses, such that in 1943, seven hundred and thirteen miners were accidentally killed and thousands injured. It was calculated that every fourth underground miner had either been killed or injured! Clearly, being a Bevin

Boy was no soft option for being in the armed forces. In 1945, five hundred and fifty miners were killed and two thousand three hundred and fifty-three seriously injured.

Mr Bevin told the House on 2nd December 1943, that entrants with no mining experience would receive four week's initial training, both in classes and in underground practices. They would be held at special training centres to be organised by his department in consultation with the Ministry of Fuel and Power. On completion of training they would go to collieries for a further two week's training before working below ground. Also, for at least four weeks after starting underground work, they would come under the personal supervision of an experienced miner.

On arrival the Bevin Boy would observe the pithead, a vast metallic structure with thick steel ropes that grinded up and down and ultimately heralded the cage. Stepping into the cage they'd be taken down, down a deep shaft into the murky black depths of the bowels of the earth; a new and perilous way of life waited!

*"I travelled by train to Doncaster Station and was met by members of the W.V.S. (Women's Voluntary Service) and taken by bus to Askern, a village six miles north of Doncaster. I received my initial training there and was billeted with a Mr & Mrs Poulson of Cemetery Road, Woodlands, near Doncaster. The training lasted for a month. To improve our physical fitness we had to put on boiler suits and hard hats and march the streets, the local lads used to call us Utility Miners! After training we were told what pits to go to and I was lucky because they sent me to Ellistown, not far from Sileby, while some of the lads with me were sent hundreds of miles from home."*

Joe was indeed lucky because whilst working at Ellistown Colliery he met a Mr Toon, who was at South Leicestershire Colliery, the father of Mildred, the girl he took a fancy to while at the Victory Works. The Toon family lived at Markfield, only several miles from Ellistown, and he was invited to lodge with them, and cycled with Mr Toon to the Colliery.

Eventually, Joe became a hewer: drilling away on the coalface; others shovelled coal into tubs and took part in underground haulage by rails, while some loaded tubs into the cage to take to the surface, and reloaded with empty tubs. Another duty was 'stone

dusting': coating surfaces to minimise potential explosive mixture of coal dust in the atmosphere; some did 'water leading' to remove excess water.

Most jobs demanded above average physical strength and effort; conditions were hot, damp, with foul air, poor lighting, and danger from roof collapse, methane gas, and other perilous situations! Conversely came brotherly companionship, always a factor in shared adversity.

*"Mildred and I got married on 29th September 1945 at St. Michael And All The Angels Parish Church, Markfield. (John Wesley, the Methodist preacher used to sermonise there).*

*After the war my wife worked as a machinist in the shoe industry at Airborne Shoes (Anstey) and also at C.W.S. at Leicester. We spent most of our married life, fifty-four years at 3, The Green, Markfield."*

Post-war, Joe remained at the colliery, but in 1950, feeling victimised by a member of the management team he handed in his notice, and rejoined 'Victory Works'. After a short time a vacancy arose at Nailstone Colliery, and he returned to the coalface for many years, only leaving for Bagworth Colliery when Nailstone closed. After damaging neck-vertebrae he retired: aged sixty-three. Joe is well remembered and respected in mining circles to this day.

I mentioned to him that a number of my ancestors were miners, and was delighted to hear that he knew several of the Hatter and Kendrick tribe.

As mentioned earlier, his brother, Fred, joined the R.A.F in 1939. He spent most of his service with Bomber Command in the Middle East, operating either as a tail or mid-upper gunner. Fred was ill fated to be trapped for a time at Tobruk and so endured the Axis siege that lasted from April-December 1941. Later, between January and May 1944, his Liberator squadron was involved in the bombing of Monte Cassino, Italy. This heavily fortified location was defended by elite German troops responsible for delaying the Allied push up the leg of Italy. An old communiqué states: *"The Liberator limped back to its Italy base following a night operation over the Verona marshalling yards, it was holed in 166 places. A shell had burst near to the cockpit smashing the nose of the aircraft and shattering the front and mid-upper gun turrets. The port inner engine caught fire and filled the aircraft with smoke, oxygen bottles burst, the radio*

Back row. Fred Ansell is second left; centre is Lt. Benade of South Africa; next is Flying Officer Peter Raw of Australia. Others are Sgt. Danielles of Southampton, Sgt. K. Brown of Birmingham and Sgt. Breedon of Lincoln.

Sergeant Fred Ansell, R.A.F. gunner.

and intercom smashed, hydraulic pipes shot away and half the pilot's instruments were dead. The mid-upper gunner: Sgt. F. Ansell, of Charnwood House, Sileby escaped injury, as did the navigator: Lt. Benade, while wireless operator, Sgt. K. Brown was wounded in both legs. The pilot: P.O. Peter Raw suffered from frost bitten feet caused by exposure. The bomber circled for forty minutes while the crew lowered the flaps and landing gear by hand winch. As they touched down the tyre of the nose wheel burst while smoke poured from the over-strained engines. The bomb bay was full of petrol and oil from broken feed lines. The nose of the machine was like a colander."

Just after the war, Sergeant Frederick Ansell was demobbed at Syerston, near to Newarke on Trent, and worked in engineering. Marrying Mildred, a Syston (local girl), they had a son, Neil, who lives at Ashby de la Zouch. After serving from 1939-45 without a scratch, Fred was tragically killed on his motorbike just outside the main-gates of Rolls Royce at Mountsorrel, where he was working at the time. Colin, the son of Joe's younger brother, Jim, lives at Goldray,

*Joe and Mildred Ansell in 1997.*

near St. Andrews in Scotland, and is in regular contact with Joe. Colin is fascinated by W.W.1 and regularly visits the old battlefields.

On a lighter note, Joe spoke of when his wife and he were arrested on holiday at Brixham.

*"Two policemen and a policewoman approached us and asked if they could take a photograph of us and them together to send to the Police Force in the U.S.A. We agreed and they said they'd pretend that we were being arrested. We nodded and they took a lovely shot us just in front of a replica of Francis Drake's 'Golden Hind'."*

At a recent special occasion, Joe, with others, received a medallist-badge. David Taylor MP presented them. Nationwide eleven thousand badges were presented to commemorate their brave and sterling efforts during the war.

I left Joe's house in the more characterful part of Markfield, shook hands and agreed to meet again. I have written about a Bevin Boy, an A.R.P messenger and a Home Guard Soldier.

# OPERATION PIED PIPER

The operation began in 1939. With war imminent, arrangements were made to evacuate children from what were considered to be potential sites for aerial bombing, to areas of relative safety. In essence it meant the entraining of boys and girls from major city/industrial centres to rural areas, and for many it proved quite a culture shock. Leicestershire's evacuees were mainly from Birmingham and her environs. It is somewhat ironic that the 1284 AD derivation of 'The Pied Piper' fable relates to Hamelin in Westphalia, Germany. The town was infested with rats until a mysterious piper offered to remove them for a certain sum. The piper played his flute and all the rats followed him to their demise, but payment was not forthcoming. In retaliation, the piper once again played his flute and all the children followed him to a cave: they were never seen again!

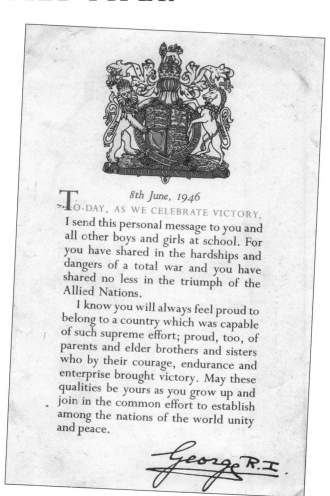

*8th June, 1946*

TO-DAY, AS WE CELEBRATE VICTORY, I send this personal message to you and all other boys and girls at school. For you have shared in the hardships and dangers of a total war and you have shared no less in the triumph of the Allied Nations.

I know you will always feel proud to belong to a country which was capable of such supreme effort; proud, too, of parents and elder brothers and sisters who by their courage, endurance and enterprise brought victory. May these qualities be yours as you grow up and join in the common effort to establish among the nations of the world unity and peace.

*George R.I.*

*A message from King George.*

# JOHN DOUGLAS BACKUS

J ohn Alfred Backus was born at Leicester in 1883, and for most of his working life was a skilled tonsorial: a hairdresser. He married local girl, Elizabeth Eld, and the couple settled at 14, Greenwood Road, Leicester, having two sons, Lesley: born in 1911 and John Douglas (Doug) born on 30th January 1923. Both sons attended Leicester's Green Lane School.

*Edward Chapman, wife, Lizzie, two sons and Lilian. Circa 1930.*

*Doug Backus in 1943.*

Doug assisted his father in the city-centre shop at 392, Humberstone Road, and became a skilled hairdresser, with the shop also serving as tobacconists. His call-up papers arrived in 1942, and being a hairdresser he was allocated to the Royal Engineers; his daughter, Susan asks: *"Was this typical Army logic?"*

Before his call to the Colours he was dating Lilian Chapman, the daughter of Edward 'the colonel' Chapman, that wonderful World War 1 'Tigers' veteran who features so strongly in my earlier book: 'Greater Love'.

Sapper John Douglas Backus, service number: 4868936, was trained in various mechanical skills, but above all others he received specialist training in the extremely dangerous art of detecting and destroying land mines.

Susan: *"Only in his latter years did father talk about his war service. He said that early on there was a shortage of equipment for detecting mines, and so he mostly had to use a bayonet and hands to remove them."*

*John and Elizabeth Backus. Circa 1940's.*

*George, Clarence, Norman, Lilian, Jack, Reg and Ted Chapman (brothers). Circa 1942.*

*The wedding of Doug Backus and Lilian Chapman. The elderly lady is her grandmother. Her mother, Lizzie (nee Osborne)'s mother. 3rd September 1943.*

Whilst on leave, on 3rd September 1943, he married fiancée Lilian Chapman at St. Mary's Church, Humberstone; they knew that their future held perilous possibilities, but they were devoted to each other and that was all that mattered: 'Que sera, sera!'

Doug followed a period of hectic training because his unit was scheduled for an impending invasion, namely: 'Operation Overlord'. Early morning:

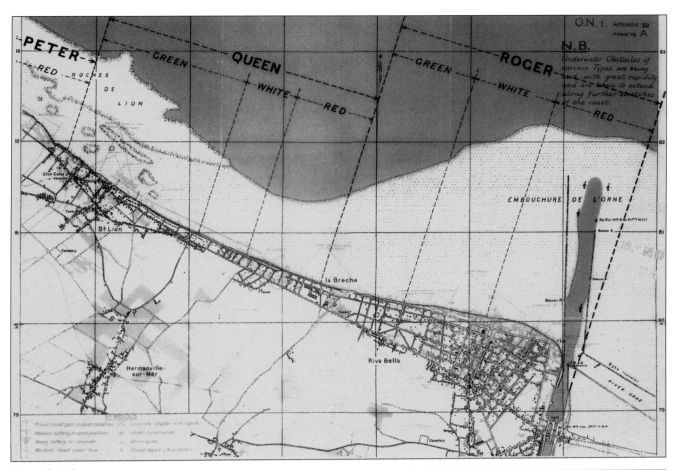

Sword Beach

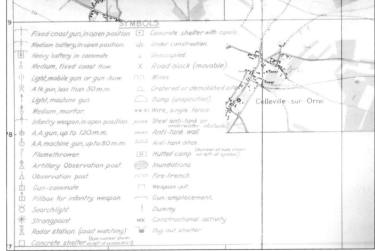

Sword Beach symbols

approximately 6.00am, on 6th June 1944, his team, with equipment, was at the front of an L.C.T. tank-landing craft approaching 'Sword Beach.'

Susan: *"In the craft a young man was standing next to my father, and asked whether he thought there would be any Jerries waiting for them. Father, who was also scared but trying not to show it, answered that his guess was as good as his team-mate, to which the lad looked dead scared. When the large doors of the landing craft lowered the young man received a serious, possibly fatal bullet wound. As the first tank left the L.C.T. my father jumped onto it and thankfully made it to the beach, however, the tank commander took a sniper's bullet and died instantly, and so father jumped into a shell hole. When the opportunity arose the team started clearing the mines, and as they worked their way up the beach they left a white taped pathway for the infantry to follow. I am very proud to say that after the initial battle, father and five others cleared the whole of 'Sword Beach' (see map). They were always in demand during the allied advance, but an occasion arose whereby they reached a farmhouse. Finding it unoccupied they discovered a sow and a litter of six piglets; one of the team was a pre-war butcher and so they enjoyed pork all of the way to Germany."*

Susan has every right to be very proud of her father's achievements. The task they undertook was extremely treacherous, to say the least, and whilst doing it they had to accept the risks of sniping and shelling. What brave men!

Doug spoke of the restricted number of tall-hedged lanes: 'Bocage' in the Normandy battle, and how the enemy kept them pinned within a perimeter for about

Leslie Backus with son Don and daughter, Julie. 1940's.

Doug Backus in 1944.

twelve weeks. (See Harry Wortley's memoirs in Volume 1.) After the breakout, Field Marshal Montgomery advanced steadily into Belgium and succeeded in capturing the vital port of Antwerp. With the port being on the Scheldt estuary, the allies needed to capture both banks of the river before the port could be used, thus ensnaring the German 15th Army in the Low Countries. The objective was not achieved and so an even more ambitious plan was written, which could possibly be a step too far!

17th September 1944 marked the opening of: 'Operation Market Garden', an attempt by Allied airborne troops to cross the Meuse, Waal and Neder-Rijn rivers in Holland. The American 82nd targeted Nijmegen, the American 101st went for Eindhoven and the British 1st Airborne to the vital bridge at Arnhem. The key to victory was the necessity to capture and hold the Arnhem bridgehead; this would expose the north German plains to a mighty attack and shorten the war by months. History shows that the operation was poorly planned and the 1st Airborne at Arnhem was heavily outnumbered by elite enemy troops. The paratroopers fought with great valour, but

the objective was: 'a bridge too far', and the tragic episode meant that of the nine thousand airborne troops dropped, fewer than two-and-half thousand escaped. It was a good idea by Field Marshal Montgomery, but the very first time during his long career that he threw caution to the winds, the result was disastrous!

Susan: *"Father was involved in the advance to try to reach Arnhem, but they could only get as far as Nijmegen. He said the roads were too narrow and so constrained and restricted the advance. While at Nijmegen, he spent some time on guard-duty on the Bridge. My father and his pal, Tom, began a conversation with a paratrooper from the 82nd Airborne. Before their drop they had been stationed around Leicestershire, notably Quorn. The American produced some photographs of his homeland and also one of his girlfriend from Leicester: imagine the surprise when the girl was none other than Tom's sister-in-law."*

Doug took his hairdressing kit with him and the officers regularly asked for a trim: 'A short back and sides, sir?' His 'salon' was usually located in a

*Lilian Backus with daughter, Susan. 1952.*

*Susan and Trevor Backus in 1953.*

sheltered part of a damaged ruin.

*"Sometimes it could be dangerous, risking life and limb when cutting an officer's hair!"*

Following Doug's demobilisation, he and his wife: with baby Trevor, born 7th March 1945, moved into a 'Prefab', viz, a newly erected prefabricated house on Rockingham Road, near Wicklow Drive, Leicester. It was there that Susan was born on 3rd January 1948. Later, they acquired a new council house at 46, Westmeath Avenue on the Goodwood Estate at Leicester. In 1946, Doug, to utilise his expertise gained with the Royal Engineers, joined Adcock and Shipley, off the Humberstone Road (Bridgeport Textrion). He was employed as a mechanical engineer and remained there until his retirement aged 65 years. Periods of sadness followed the death of his mother, Elizabeth on 17th September 1962, aged seventy-nine years (1883-1962) and father, John on 22nd June 1972, aged eighty-nine years (1883-1972). Both are listed in the Book of Remembrance at Leicester Crematorium.

Following his mother's death, Doug and family moved to the parental home: 14, Greenwood Road,

Leicester. He loved his sport and he was devoted to Leicester City Football Club: Filbert Street. In the 1960's he enthused about manager Matt Gillies taking them to Wembley on two occasions, then again in 1969, and almost winning the league and cup double in 1963.

*"Father believed in keeping himself smart; he had to be presentable, even if it was just to pop to a local shop. He also liked music and another big love was for cars. His first was a Ford 8, there followed a Morris Estate with wooden trimmings and then a Triumph Coupe. Being an engineer he kept his cars in immaculate condition. My son, Thomas, had father's last car: it was a Nissan Sunny and it had lots of extra light bulbs, fuses, etc. He was always taking things to bits and then putting them together again!"*

Doug kept in touch with his wartime friends by joining the Normandy Veterans' Association (N.V.A.) and this was highlighted on attending the Fiftieth Anniversary of the 'D'-Day Landings in 1994, with the Queen being present. (The author took great interest in the televised version).

Leslie Backus served bravely with the 'Desert

*Edward Chapman with Susan and her future husband, John McGrenaghan.*

Rats' in Africa and Normandy during World War 2; he too was a member of the Normandy Veteran's Association: Branch 46. Les died on 22nd July 1998 aged eighty-eight years. Susan attended the funeral service at St. Bartholomew's Church at Quorn on July 30th. His funeral was at Gilroes Crematorium.

Douglas Backus passed away on 5th January 2004; just missing the Sixtieth Anniversary he eagerly looked-forward to. At his Gilroes Crematorium funeral service were representatives of the N.V.A. Part of the service reflected his wartime experiences, the Last Post was played, the Reveille and Lawrence Binyon's: 'Ode For The Fallen' was read.

Trevor Backus continued the Army tradition by enlisting in 1963, and served three years before marrying 'his sweetheart', Ann. The couple live on Carlton Drive at Wigston Fields, and he takes great pride in taking care of his father's medals.

Susan: *"My mother is not doing too badly although her mobility is very poor and has no speech. When I show her the photograph albums she is all there and delights in seeing them."*

Doug had trained as a hairdresser, and, if not for the war, he no doubt would have taken over the running of his father's business following retirement. Like most

*Nijmegen Bridge in the 1990's.*

people who served their King and Country, he appeared to be just an average guy, but clearly, below the surface was a man of extreme bravery. I doubt whether one per cent of the population would possess the nerve to defuse explosive devices, knowing that you could be within seconds of being blown to oblivion.

My thanks to Sue McGrenaghan, who like her brother, Trevor, is so proud of her father and very pleased that he will now be remembered within the pages of this book. Edward 'the colonel' Chapman would also have been delighted.

# 6th JUNE 1944 'D'-DAY

Grey, depressive clouds survey our enormous invasion fleet.
A gloomy, treacherous and turbulent sea rolls and swells.
A gale howls within my ears; sea-spray cascades on my face.
An air-armada cruises over us and England is sleeping.

Naked fingers 'anchored' to the wood of our landing craft.
Wood that grew on sunny days of peace to reach maturity.
What if we fail? Do they know at home what is happening?
We are so afraid, but not forlorn, as England sleeps.

Brown army uniforms are damp from nervous perspiration.
Helmeted figures lunge forward with violent seasickness.
An instant roar as a massive shell fragments a nearby craft.
Human debris is shed to the gale, as England sleeps.

We all took those peaceful days of the past for granted.
If I survive I will surely saviour every moment of my future.
Did I stroll down country lanes amass in spring blossom?
My fiancée waits, but will I return? Let England dream.

Not sweet aroma of honeysuckle: the pungency of cordite.
How could I live and not appreciate the quality of life?
Those who are fatally wounded will not appreciate dying!
I can see the Normandy coast and England is sleeping.

We're almost there, "Steady Lads", shouts the officer.
Shells explode and bullets further ripple the sea's surface.
"Get Ready men"; the ramp drops and we jump to our destiny.
Men are falling to my left and right; let England sleep-on!

**Michael Kendrick**

# DENIS WALTER BAKER

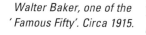

Walter Baker, born on 5th November 1889, was educated at the Coalville British School, London Road Baptist Chapel, and the Wesleyan School on Belvoir Road. He mastered Pitman shorthand and typing skills by the age of twelve, and soon taught adults at night school. He was also a gifted pianist and organist. On leaving school he became a costing clerk at nearby

*Walter Baker, one of the 'Famous Fifty'. Circa 1915.*

Stableford's Wagon Works and trained as a draughtsman.

In August 1914, he enlisted into the 1/5th Leicestershire Battalion and was one of the 'Famous Fifty'. An officer noted his sharp-mind and administrative skills, and on 1st April 1915 sent him to Aldershot to study military techniques, before further training in the Army Service Corps, London. He was posted to the 52nd Lowland Division (half of whom fought in France in 1914) and involved in the Division's logistics for embarkation to the Mediterranean.

Walter served as a staff sergeant under the command of Sir Ian Hamilton: leader of the Dardanelles' Campaign, and assisted with the December 1915 evacuation plans. The finest aspect of the Campaign was the brilliantly thought-out and executed evacuation plan.

On being evacuated to Egypt, he first fought in defending the Suez Canal and then driving the Turks back through Sinai. Conditions were so bad that Walter contracted malaria and dysentery. In 1918, and just when they were about to enter Jerusalem, they were transferred to Flanders: having been away from England for the whole time. He was in the Arras Sector of France during the German's Spring Offensive, but obtained furlough to marry Fanny Kirkland Price on 5th June 1918. Returning to the Arras Sector he was eventually demobbed in March 1919 and rejoined Stableford's. For his outstanding four and a half years of military service he was awarded a Meritorious Service Medal and a Mention in Despatches.

With ill fortune, in 1927, just as Walter was to take charge of the costing office the firm went into receivership, however, by the time Walter and Fanny moved into their family home, 182, Forest Road, Hugglescote, he had become the Assistant Relieving Officer for Ashby de la Zouch District.

*King George VI Coronation 1936. From left: Mum, Aunt Ethel, Uncle Albert Hull, Aunt Lizzie (nee Price), Aunt Edna Hull (nee Price). Front: Denis, Uncle Jack Price holding Derek Hull, Alan and Uncle Harry Ratciffe.*

The couple had two sons, Colin Price Baker, who died in childhood and Denis Walter Baker on 4th October 1930. In October 1933, Walter was appointed Deputy Registrar of Births and Deaths, then Deputy Registrar of Marriages.

*Denis Baker and Alan Ratcliffe in 1936.*

Denis Baker and his Dad, Rhyl, 1936.

Denis Baker, Dad and Mum, Rhyl, 1938.

There follows Denis' wartime memories as seen through the eyes of a 'frontline' youngster.

He was at Bridge Road School, when, a class at a time was sent to the Baths Hall to collect their gas masks (civilian respirators). Denis:

*"After the masks were placed under our chins, they were strapped to the head, and soon we found that if they were loose around the neck we could create rude noises, what fun! Dad, a street warden, had a mask with a central valve and that could make even better noises!"*

At first some of the younger children disliked them: having a feeling of suffocation!

Denis was a member of a gang that included cousin, Alan Ratcliffe at 180, Forest Road: Harry Ratcliffe married his mother's sister, Ethel. Also, cousin, Derek Hull at 178: Derek Hull married his mother's sister, Edna. Alan's granddaughter, Alice Ratcliffe wrote: 'The World War Lie' for Volume One. Another gang member lived almost opposite: Denis:

*"Sheila Wortley* (see Volume One) *was real tomboy and was as good as us at climbing trees, scrumping apples, 'spirit rattling' of front-doors with lengths of wool, etc."*

Denis began to collect cigarette (fag) cards that provided information on how to make sandbag defences, bomb and gas-proof shelters, how to extinguish incendiary bombs, taping of windows to

Alan Ratcliffe, Ruth and Roy Skelcher and Denis. 1940.

stop shattering in bomb blasts, and choosing a refuge room at home, etc.

*"I was inspired by all this knowledge and helped in sticking brown paper strips onto the inside of our*

windows; *following this came a black insulating tape that created a mock leaded-light affect. Finally, 'Woollies' started to sell rolls of a thin transparent plastic material that was patterned with a stained-glass affect. It took me ages to remove the tape and fortunately no further fashion trends were set!"*

After the cinema showed trenches being dug, the gang, including Sheila, set about digging their own on Scotland's brickyard.

182 Forest Road, Coalville where Denis spent his war years.

*"At the Rex Picture House we also saw how to make bunkers and command posts and old sheets of corrugated iron came in very handy, after all we were on the frontline. We also made our very own armaments: broom stales and unwanted pieces of wood from Grudging's Wood Yard fashioned us with superior Bren guns and the very best automatic fire rifles. Sometimes we had to defend our position from the 'Oxford Street Gang', but we made sure that our grenades (brick ends) fell well short of their infantry attacks."*

The civilian population had been told that the bomber would always get through, and steps were taken to eliminate all forms of exposed light from dusk to dawn. Blackout covers were made from roofing laths, felt, and hooked to the outside window; fine in summer but heat trapping during summer months, and some replaced them with thick, black fabric curtaining.

The first batch of Birmingham refugees, three hundred and forty-one children and teachers, arrived at Coalville Station by a special train at 11.15am on Friday, 1st September 1939. Eventually, seventy-five thousand children left that city for foster care in Leicestershire.

*"A large group of children came along our road, some weeping, especially when they were separated and taken to different houses. Mum went out and was told that they had twins that didn't want to be separated. Mum agreed to foster the girl, Ruth Skelcher, while my aunt, next door, took in Roy. I found it odd to have a foster sister and wasn't used to mixing with girls except the girls in our gang."*

With rationing, it was human nature for people, when possible, to hoard tinned foods: the likes of fruit, meat pastes, fish, various preserves and bags of sugar, etc. When it was heard that a shop had received a certain rationed item, then queues quickly developed; children becoming 'queue-deputies' until a parent arrived.

*"So long as I got my ration of sweets I was happy; on Saturday mornings I'd stand outside of Joblings on Belvoir Road to collect my share. Families had to make do; most grew their own vegetables and many kept pigs, chickens and rabbits. Mums made food last longer, for instance mine added cornflower and milk to butter to make it a thinner spread."*

Ironically, human nature often meant that most tinned stores were not used until presented at 'Victory in Europe' street parties. As the war progressed to 1940/1, the folk of northwest Leicestershire heard more of the bombing of various cities and towns of Great Britain.

*"Dad was a street warden and sometimes, on moonlit nights, I'd go and stand with him on Forest Road Bridge and watch the hundreds of enemy bombers roar over Bardon Hill. Dad counted them, assessed their movements, and went home to telephone the information to headquarters. I've still got his old telephone to this day. The aircraft noise was terrific, and they used the Hill as a compass point and adjusted their bearing for Coventry, Birmingham, Nottingham, Derby or elsewhere. Searchlights crossed to and fro and later anti-aircraft barrages. The sky would light up where raids were taking place. Coventry was a bad night! If it was a Derby raid their*

Ack-Ack was very loud; Dad said they had some six-inch Naval guns, and the following day we would see bits of shell-casing (shrapnel) over Coalville's streets. We kids used to collect it, also bits from incendiary bombs!"

With Walter being the area's Relieving Officer, he was entitled to a petrol ration for his car; travelling to bomb damaged areas, especially Birmingham, to arrange re-housing, etc.

"Once, during a lull in the blitz, Dad took me to see his sister, my aunt Maud, who lived near to the B.S.A. works in Small Heath. We weren't to know there had been a raid in the night. I couldn't believe the scene: dozens of barrage balloons, buildings with roofs missing, walls collapsed to expose rooms and furnishings, fires and smoke, glass, firemen's hoses across roads and bodies here and there. Until then the war was exciting, but this opened my eyes to what it actually meant, and could understand Dad's reluctance to talk about World War 1! Auntie Maud was quite cheery, her house was intact, and after obtaining water we had a cup of tea, but it was getting dark when we left. Vehicle headlights were very limited during the war, mere ruler slots of light through a blackout: useless!

As we left the sirens started and we heard the Ack-Ack and bombs exploding! It was a close brush with the enemy and a long inky-dark journey home."

When Coalville sirens sounded an alert it was time to take cover 'under the stairs'.

"My friend, Bill Platts, told me that a field at nearby Sinope took several thousand incendiary bombs, and the huts of his father's chicken farm were destroyed, evidently they thought they were Nissan Huts. Another night, Dad rushed in the back door and yelled for us to lie flat on the floor; almost simultaneously we heard the whistle of bombs and then an almighty blast that threw us along the hall into a heap! Dad said that a passing steam train had emitted sparks just when enemy planes were overhead; he heard one begin to dive and its stick of bombs detonated from the Convent field to Coalville Park. We lived opposite to Convent Drive and so took the blast but the windows held out. (Sheila Wortley recalls that night). Next morning produced great excitement as we investigated the damage. The field had two craters and damaged hedges; the rail track by London Road

Cemetery had a crater (see Geoffrey Boot's account); a wall blown out of Mr. Brown's (dentist) house, and a wall destroyed in Coalville Park. Only later was a large unexploded bomb removed after it had buried itself; boys had found it while using the crater as a hideout. It had fallen on the far side of the park and near to Whitwick Colliery's powder magazine; it's best not to think of the probabilities had it exploded! Some time later a massive bomb fell on Mr. New's farmyard on Owen Street, and once again the town was fortunate it didn't explode (see Raymond Cross and 'Satan Bomb'). Once defused it was put on show in the foyer of the Rex Picture House and folk were invited to buy an old sixpence savings stamp to stick on it with the ruse that it was going to be dropped on Germany."

In 1941, Denis passed for Ashby Grammar School, which his cousin Alan already attended.

"Almost daily, the teachers kept us informed about how the war was progressing in the Western Desert and then Singapore. Before 'D'-Day we guessed that an invasion of some kind was about to happen because there were so many American soldiers around. We often hitched lifts on their lorries and we'd be given various luxuries such as delicious tinned fruitcakes, etc, and I gave lots of 'Camel' fags to Dad. In June 1944, I was woken-up by hordes of aircraft flying over and heard about the invasion; fewer Americans were around."

Earlier, in 1942, Denis had joined the Hugglescote Scout Troop and his first encampment was in the fields of Gopsall Hall. He loved it, particularly cooking on the campfire (the author also enjoyed this role in the scouts), but his peace was soon to be disturbed.

"The bugle call had just woken us from a deep sleep in our bell-tents when we heard a powerful purring noise. Our patrol leader screamed at us to take cover in the nearby wood; we saw the underbelly of a German fighter as it flashed by and then the chatter of machine-guns as it attacked the incumbent military in the Hall. I don't think anyone was hurt but it was a bit of a shaker for us all!"

Several enemy aircraft were shot down over the district, and as word got around they became attractions with children bicycling for miles to see them.

"I remember seeing a Dornier 215 near to Lount, and another one came down near to the monastery. We

*Denis Baker in 1944.*

*couldn't get too near because soldiers guarded them. Also, we'd cycle late in the day to Castle Donington to watch our Lancaster bombers taking off; as soon as they became airborne their wings used to rise about six feet and we were told that when the bombs were released the wings would judder and bounce to their normal incline. We'd also cycle there at the crack of dawn to see them returning, and some were in a bad way."*

On the European Front the news improved daily apart from the setback of the 'Battle of the Bulge', but with the Russians advancing on the Eastern Front and the Japanese retreating island-by-island in the Pacific the end was in sight.

*"Mr. Ramsell, one of our teachers, told us that the Germans had capitulated and that we were to be given a day's holiday. Street Parties were arranged and pre-war stocks of fireworks put on sale at Champions shop on Forest Road.*

*It was a very happy occasion and the evening fireworks were spectacular, but most of the service men were yet to return and the Japanese war to be won!"*

Atomic bombs dropped on Hiroshima and Nagasaki resulted in the end of the World War.

*"Everyone went to the cinema regularly to watch films about the war. The Nazi concentration camps*

*and the Holocaust were beyond belief, and the bestial treatment by the Japanese to our prisoners really disturbed me! I was inspired by heroic stories of airmen in the Battle of Britain and Bomber Command, the Artic and Atlantic Convoys, the Desert Rats, etc."*
From 1939-45, Walter bought his son a collection of magazines giving an outline on the various campaigns: The Battle of Britain, German And Italian Aircraft, Roof Over Britain, The Eighth Army, Target Germany, Mediterranean Fleet and Front Line, The Air Battle of Malta, and so on, and Denis still has them in excellent condition.

By 1945, Walter was Registrar of Births Marriages and Deaths for Ashby de la Zouch and district, and also their Relieving Officer. Life had been very challenging for him, particularly his efforts with the latter relating to the heavy movement of evacuees. Since the end of the Great War he had suffered recurrent bouts of malaria: spending days in bed with severe pains and fever! More recently he was having periodic fainting bouts, and specialists diagnosed myocarditis (heart disease). It was during the dreadfully long and cold winter of 1947, following an attack of pneumonia that further weakened him, that he quietly succumbed after a determined struggle, aged only fifty-seven years!

For many years he was Deacon and organist for Coalville's Ebenezer Baptist Chapel, and closely associated with such friends as my grandmother's folk (Palmers). A packed Ebenezer Chapel paid their respects to a very fine man.

Denis met his future wife, Gwenda, a Swannington lady, through an Ebenezer connection and they married at the aforementioned Chapel on the snowy Easter Day of 16th April 1955. The couple lived at 182, Forest Road until in 1979; following the passing of Gwenda's parents they moved into that house with its lovely rural setting.

Gwenda was born on 31st May 1931 and suffered poor health. Gwen:

*"Whenever the sirens sounded in the evenings my parents and I used to go to bed. On some occasions I'd cycle on what was no more than a 'fairy' bike with my parents to Castle Donington to see aeroplanes. I attended the Griffydam Schools before going to Coalville Grammar and remember being given a gas mask. What I remember most about the war years was*

Denis and Gwenda Baker in 1995.

the comradeship, people looked out for, cared and helped others."

After Grammar school Denis was employed by Fisons, formerly 'British Chemicals and Biologicals' at Loughborough. He studied Chemistry for three half days a week and Saturday mornings at Loughborough College. Denis qualified, by taking examinations at London, as an organic chemist with a B.Sc. after his name. He left Fisons to take a post at Aldermaston until joining Precision Rubbers (soon to be taken over by Dunlop).

"I worked in the Polyurethane Division of Dunlop at Leicester, but had a problem with some chemicals and so I was given a car and travelled extensively as the technical manager of the tyre products. Finally I taught for twenty-three years, until my retirement, as a lecturer at Coalville Technical College."

Denis and Gwenda had two children. Ian was born in 1957; is married to Helen and has James and Lesley-Anne at university. Gary, born in 1960, was tragically killed in a motor accident in 1979; he was on a motorbike and travelling to work at Precision Rubbers at Bagworth.

Denis is well known and respected in the district for his local historical knowledge and the many books that he has produced. I am proud to be a distant relative of his through the Palmers.

Recently, Denis was selected as a 'Community Hero' and taken to 10, Downing Street by his MP: David Taylor, in recognition of his tremendous work to record and promote local heritage.

Many thanks to my dear friends, Denis and Gwenda Baker.

*Denis knew of many locations where bombs were dropped. On the evening of 22nd November 1940, around 10.30pm, a Dornier bomber dropped bombs on Loughborough, but was then damaged by anti-aircraft fire. The doomed aircraft hit three fences and came to rest one hundren yards from the village school of Burton on the Wolds. The petrol tank ignited and the Dornier exploded sending huge sheets of flame into the air, these could be seen from Quorn.The Luftwaffe airmen are buried at Loughborough Cemetery. On 16th December 1940, a bomb exploded on Main Street, Woodhouse Eves. The lady who lived in the nearest cottage to the explosion, a Miss Ground, said that she heard the aeroplane and the bomb as it came whistling down.*

The day after the bomb, clearing the rubble. 17th December 1940.

A modern photograph of the scene.

# HORACE BIRD

Horace aged seven.

Horace was born on 29th April 1922 in Bull Row in the village of Swannington. He grew up in happy surroundings with brother, Sidney (Sid) and sisters: Lena, Eva, Olive and Daisy. His sisters recall warm memories of their childhood together. With little money about in the 1920/30s, their mother used a large bunch of red-berried holly instead of a Christmas tree, and draped the large pictures that hung on the wall with shawls of paper garlands. The sisters say that they were all particularly fond of the festive period.

Horace grew up in Swannington and was known to get into a bit of mischief; he also had a good business brain. His son, Martin:

*"The Fountain Inn had a tennis court where the present back garden is situated. He and other children would wait for balls to be hit over the netting and then charge the players a penny for each ball returned! He also loved bonfire-night, and once, he and a pal loaded a big old lock with bangers; when they exploded it blew the lock off the door and into the road. Dad collected bunches of watercress from the fresh springs found in the valley and sold them to villagers, also he delivered flowers to help local nurseryman, Ernie Thurman. Like all kids he adored iced-cream and it was to his great benefit that farmer, Bert Adcock used to make it."*

Paul Clark was a little older than Horace, and they were close pals; he owned a record player and amplifier and soon Horace joined him in a love for music and dance. They organised dances at Swannington Institute and travelled to Swadlincote Rink to listen to the top bands of the day: such as Victor Sylvester.

On leaving the village school, Horace worked as a brickies' labourer for local builder, Albert Robinson, and remained in this job until being called-up into the Army. He was selected for the Royal Artillery and sent to Lark Hill in Somerset for training.

Gunner (later Bombardier) Horace Bird, service number 1133192, was in 'A' Section of 'C' Troop, 8/12 Battery of 2nd Medium Regiment, Royal Artillery: (now referred to as the Regiment). Earlier in the war, in 1940, the Regiment fought in France, indeed some of the personnel that Horace joined had escaped from the beaches of Dunkirk.

As the Eighth Army drove Rommel's *Afrika Corps* across North Africa: winning an eventual victory in the spring of 1943, it was planned to strengthen their numbers for the invasion of Italy. With this in mind, 2nd Medium Regiment departed from Liverpool on 15th December 1942. The convoy stopped at Freetown before arriving at Durban on 17th January 1943, thereon to Bombay, and up the Persian Gulf for a period at Basra in Iraq (15th March 1943.) The final journey up the Red Sea took them into Egypt and onto Alexandria. Martin:

*"During his time in North Africa, my dad said that the Egyptians were not friendly and that they very much sided with the Germans. Shops would not sell our soldiers any goods so they had to bribe locals to do the shopping for them. Also, dad was a keen boxer,*

Horace Bird's boxing cups, both inscribed Gnr. Bird R.A. of the United Services Boxing. Alexandria, M.E.F. 1944.

*and when he was at Alexandria he boxed for the United Services Boxing team and won two trophies: both feature in this book.*

After operations in Italy, details which follow, the commanding officer of 2nd Medium Regiment: Lt. Colonel L. H. Harris wrote the following:

'*Having chucked close on 150,000 well directed shells at the German Army, and received some of theirs back too, we are now breaking up and returning to our homes and families. Many of us in the long years in front of us will look back with pride on our achievements in Italy. We will remember the suppressed excitement we all felt on going into action for the first time at Sessa; the shelling we endured at Cassino, Arezzo and many other places; the great night of the 11th May 1944: the dash past Rome with the long advances and quick actions; the mud and discomfort at Sassaleone; the mad dash to the Po and across it and finally the Armistice and relaxation.*'

Most of the Regiment's personnel arrived at Taranto on the '*Princess Kathleen*' on 21st December 1943, with the equipment following a few weeks later.

The men had a good Christmas with beer available and plenty of vino, but after those cheery days there

came almost continuous hard fighting and toil right up to the Swiss frontier. In late December, they moved a short way to a tented camp where the conditions were described as rainy, cold and uncomfortable. The Regiment was split into: 4/7 Battery with 5.5 inch guns and 8/12 Battery with Horace and 4.5 inch guns. In late January 1944, the Batteries arrived near *Lauro* and *Fasani* in southwest Italy. The conditions were appalling, heavy rain and the roads, already churned up by heavy traffic, were deep in mud, but eventually the guns opened up and fired at least 120 rounds. As part of 10 Corps, their Front stretched from the mouth of the River *Garigliano* to a few kilometres inland. The river had been crossed in places but fighting was in progress to capture other bridgeheads. Because of the atrocious conditions and mountainous, dangerous heights, signallers from the Regiment found it difficult to climb to their forward observation posts (and so direct the gunfire). What these brave men could take in the way of equipment and provisions was always minimal. Our gun detachments worked with feverish haste, and within the first week over 12,000 rounds were fired at the Germans, but this slowed to 4,000 per week for the rest of the month. With such heavy firing there was a regular need for calibration checks to ensure accurate fire from the guns, also much work was needed on the gun pits as water constantly seeped into them.

During the coming weeks the *Garigliano* Front developed into a slogging match between the opposing guns. Because of the damage the artillery can inflict

*A 2 Medium Regiment gun pit near Pietra Colora.*

upon armour and troops, opposing batteries seek each other out with just one aim: to exterminate the other!

As spring arrived so conditions improved, and the Regiment was posted to *Casanova* on March 29th. This was situated off Route 6 between the villages of *San Vittore* and *Cervaro* and generally overlooked by the enemy from *Monte Cairo* and the infamous monastery on *Monte Cassino*. 8/12 Battery was positioned a kilometre from the road and so working parties had to carry heavy timber, steel platforms, etc, prior to the guns being located. Besides each gun pit were the dugouts of the subsections: complete with fire, kettles and other comforts. Horace was now a bombardier and responsible for his own gun and gunners.

From April 3rd, their followed six weeks of static warfare with counter battery fire again a main feature. With an American unit nearby, arrangements meant that return fire often constituted sixteen heavy guns, sixty-four medium and twenty-four Field guns; this meant that when the Germans sent thirty shells they would receive a barrage of four-five hundred! It is written that the enemy artillery was a troublesome menace with all guns subjected to two heavy concentrations of fire and regular harassing fire.

As summer approached precautions were taken against flies and mosquitoes: with stagnant pools of water sprayed and fly-proof latrines used. In May 1944, preparations for the coming attack against the German's *Gustav Line* were made, and gun holdings were increased to six hundred rounds per gun. The Regiment was to support the attack of 6 AGRA, from 13 Corps, the 6th Armoured Division, 8th Indian Division and 1st Canadian Armoured. At 22.55 hours on May 11th, a clear starlit night, all that could be heard was the song of nightingales; five minutes later all hell descended on the *Cassino* Front as six hundred guns let fire. A veritable roar reverberated through the valleys, plains, and all around gun-flashes lit up the night to the brightness of day. It is written that those who witnessed the barrage would never forget it! By the following morning it was clear that the Germans were putting up a fanatical resistance and that the allied infantry were having a hard time, especially in the area of the monastery, and most nights the Luftwaffe attempted to bomb allied positions. Canadian Sherman tanks crossed the River *Rapido* on the second day, and some of the Regiment's signallers went aboard for forward observation. The Americans, on the coastal sector advanced and reached the *Gaeta* peninsular. On May 18th, the Regiment crossed the *Rapido*: with 8/12 Battery in action near to *Cassino* itself. The enemy's famous Line was soon to be broken and the advance would take the Regiment beyond *Rome* and to within twenty-four kilometres of *Bologna.*

The Regiment was pleased to leave this sector: talk was of a smell of death and scenes of desolation! The Americans in the south linked up with the *Anzio* bridgehead troops, and on June 2nd, the Regiment moved thirty kilometres through *Ceprano* to the outskirts of *Frosinone,* which had been captured. The Germans withdrew fairly rapidly to the north of *Guarcino,* but held positions in the mountains on either flank, with their snipers proving active. News came through that the Allies had entered *Rome.*

Leaving on June 5th, the Regiment travelled along Route 4, and next day took up a position near *Monterotondo,* northeast of *Rome.* By 23.30 hours, 8/12 Battery had fired over 470 rounds, with the enemy returning a heavy barrage to both Batteries.

On June 12th, the 2nd Medium Regiment travelled to a concentration area under 6 AGRA, and near to *Belvedere*: a village a few kilometres from the *Tiber.* The route took them through *Rome* and they enjoyed what was described as a private victory march through the city with streets lined with crowds. Six days later they moved north to *Viterbo* and deservedly had a life of leisure for twelve days, with swimming in *Lake Bolsena.*

Switched to support the 6th Armoured Division, whose objective was *Florence,* the Regiment was ordered into action near the village of *Riccio,* and then onto *Montecchio,* where they endured heavy shelling before returning fire. The same sequence of events occurred at *Castiglione,* and after a furious final day, June 15th: during which 2,300 rounds were fired; the battle of *Arezzo* was won. Two days later 8/12 Battery moved through *Arezzo* to a position three kilometres further north, but the enemy, who held the high ground, overlooked them. That evening the Battery was subjected to a heavy, sustained barrage by the German artillery, and many charges were hit and set alight. Amidst many instances of personal bravery and dedication to duty, several gunners were badly wounded with Gunner P.J. Turner killed. 8/12 location was untenable and at 03.00 hours they were withdrawn to Arezzo.

On July 29th, the Batteries were posted to *Ponsacco* on the *Pisa* Front with no specific orders other than to support the whole frontline: the war had entered a static phase. Deep and secure gun pits and command posts were dug together with foxholes and bivvy holes. One evening there came a very heavy downpour and all watercourses became raging torrents; the guns sat in three feet of water and many items, including kit and equipment were simply washed away. By late August 1944 they were based near *Pontassieve,* and were lucky that the Batteries had mine detectors because several had to be cleared from their immediate area. The enemy continued to retreat while the Allies' policy was not to launch a major attack but to maintain a steady pressure. During this period the Batteries were kept moderately busy; 8/12 Battery spent quite a time by the river at *Pontassieve.* Next a period whereby the Germans speeded up their withdrawal, and the Regiment looked upon digging gun pits as somewhat futile, but invariably found that when pits were not dug they were needed and vice-versa. On September 26th, they had a frightening trip over a three thousand feet pass: the road being cut out of the rocky mountainside and in some parts there were sheer, unguarded drops. 8/12 Battery moved its guns on to the slopes above *San Benedetto* and provided support for the infantry attack, and on October 2nd they fired 90 rounds per gun in only three hours. The weather during this period was very wet and this together with the mountains slowed down the Allies' attack. On November 11th, the Batteries took a welcome rest at *Leccio*

On November 29th, the Regiment was in the most bleak, barren and desolate valley in the *Apennines*: the *Sillaro Valley.* The gun positions were a vast sea of mud: from twelve to eighteen inches deep. On that evening they followed Route 65 over the *Futa* Pass, which could only be described as a rough, slippery, exposed and highly dangerous road. During those cruel winter months little firing was done, and with each gun detachment having a communal tent, the gunners did their best to remain cheerful: improvisation for comfort always the key. The conditions hindered the movement of supplies to a great extent.

Shortly before Christmas it began to freeze and snow fell, however this was something of a relief because it froze the clinging mud and enabled greater mobility for men and machines.

8/12 Battery had Christmas day off; 4/7 had Boxing Day, but then the frosts became more severe, the

*Horace Bird witnessed this scene. Dictator Benito Mussolini attempted to escape the Allies by hiding in a German convoy headed toward the Alps. Partisans stopped and searched the convoy at Dongo. They found him, thinly disguised, in the back of a truck. The partisans took him prisoner and he was later joined by his mistress, Clara Petacci, at Mezzegra. They were executed on April 29, 1945, and their bodies were hung at an Esso gas station in the Piazzale Loreto in Milan.*

lowest recorded temperature was 24 degrees of frost. Sacking and straw was tied around the recuperater systems of the guns and, additionally, charcoal fires lit underneath at night. Nissen huts were issued to each troop but they proved difficult to erect in the fierce winds. On 4th March 1945, 'C' Troop left the inhospitable *Sillaro* Valley and moved to *San Clemente* with orders to fire at the enemy's rear. The area was a welcome sight: pleasant mountain scenery, green fields and spring flowers.

With the spring offensive, the Batteries' volume of fire began to increase. 8/12 Battery had a position on the road to *Pietra Colora* with an observation post on *Mont Grande d'Aiano*. At 08.30 hours on April 14th, came the drone of large formations of fighters and fighter-bombers, and at 09.45 hours the artillery guns opened with a roar; the push for the central sector of the Italian Front had begun. The Batteries' main task was to support the 10th Mountain Division, and their guns remained very busy for five days, an average of 1,000 rounds per day. The great advance took the 2nd Medium Regiment over the River *Po* and into the foothills of the Alps. On 27th April 1945 they travelled to a position near to *Somma-campagna*, to the east of

*The thankful people of Florence gave these badges to the Allied troops in gratitude for their liberation.*

*Verona*, and it was there that the last rounds were fired. 'C' Troop did the firing at maximum elevation to an enemy column moving north along *Lake Garda*. On May 1st, 8/12 Battery arrived at *Magenta* and were welcomed in the Market Square by cheering crowds: rightly so!

A postcard of the ship that Horace sailed on to Italy. He has made some notes on the back.

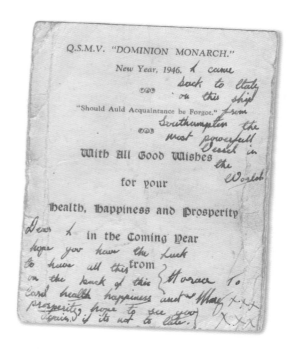

The Regiment returned to England and after a brief return to Italy on the 'Dominion Monarch', Horace was demobbed and warmly welcomed back to Swannington. Martin:

*"Dad said that the American soldiers were on much better pay than them, and also had far more provisions. A good line in business: he was selected to take bottles of Scotch Whiskey (highly prized by the Yanks) and get the best barter going in exchange for food."*

May Horton.

Horace met May Horton: a nurse at Ashby de la Zouch Cottage Hospital, and they married in 1954 at

Horace and May's Wedding Day, 1954.

Christ Church on London Road, Coalville. They lived at her parent's house on Oxford Street in Coalville; Horace worked at Whitwick Colliery. He was very involved with the Royal British Legion and became the Standard Bearer for Swannington Division; later, as a Standard Bearer he represented the Legion at the De Montfort Hall in Leicester.

Horace loved a flutter on the horses, and when fellow miners arranged a trip to a race meeting he was always one of their number. He must have been a good judge because Martin told me that it was exciting to awake the day after a meeting because there were presents for everyone.

Horace retired from Whitwick Colliery in 1982. In February 1983 he lost his beloved wife, May, but he was a strong character and rallied the family for a nostalgic 'war review' trip to Italy. They visited Sorrento, Pompeii, Capri, Cassino, and other places familiar to Horace. *"Dad recalled so many events from*

*Horace Bird, kneeling, presents the standard.*

My thanks to Martin Bird (Birdhouse Design Limited) for all the above information. Martin, a good friend, has been an enormous help to me in producing the five books that bear my authorship; I am forever indebted to him for his assistance.

*the war years: it was like a running commentary."*

After a few years, Horace made friends with Ada Hatter. Ada had lost her husband, Bernard Hatter (nephew of Charles Hatter: one of the Famous Fifty) and they moved in together. They enjoyed a hectic social life and had many holidays including trips to Thailand and Malaysia. In 1997, Ada was diagnosed with a terminal illness. Martin:

*"It was Ada's wish to remain at home and she was lovingly cared for by Dad with the help of Macmillan nurses until her death ten months later. My Dad's care for Ada was an inspiration to us all; it was for twenty-four hours a day, every day!"*

Horace was a very popular man and his many friends were most supportive, and he in turn helped them by doing jobs around the home for friends, family and neighbours.

He continued his membership with the Lone Ranger Country and Western Club in Coalville, and took to the dance floor every Monday night with a variety of willing partners. Martin:

*"He hated missing a good old dance on a Monday night."*

Horace Bird: the ex Bombardier, passed away on 10th August 2002. He is buried with his wife May, in Broom Ley's Cemetery, Coalville.

*Horace with son, Martin, 1960.*

*Horace pictured with his sisters. Standing with him at the back is Daisy (Smith). Front from left: Eva (Brooks), Lena (Holland) and Olive (Croson). Circa 1999.*

# LESLIE BISHOP

*Boy sailor, Les Bishop, circa 1937.*

*Les Bishop, circa 1937.*

Leslie was born on 25th August 1920 at the historical town of Market Bosworth, and spent his childhood at Nailstone, a homely village three miles to the north. He lived with his mother, grandfather and uncle Stan. His uncle was only a few years his elder and they grew up more like brothers. Les received his primary education at the local school and later at Ibstock Secondary School. In his early teenage years he helped a local farmer; he enjoyed farm-life and throughout life adored the outdoors, and spent an age in his beloved garden. Initially, he was employed as a brick/pipe hand, possibly at Ellistown, but upon reaching the age of nearly seventeen his desire was to see more of the world.

On 22nd November 1937, he travelled to Devonport, on Plymouth Sound, and enlisted into the Royal Navy. He signed for twelve years: service number SSX 23703. His Certificate of Service describes him as a little over five feet six inches tall, blue eyes, fair hair and fresh complexion. His training began with the substantive rank of 'Boy 2', serving on 'Wildfire', and progressed to

'Boy 1'; on his eighteenth birthday he qualified as an ordinary seaman after spells on 'Drake 1' and 'Cardiff'.

He was drafted, on 28th July 1939, to the battle/cruiser H.M.S. 'Repulse', and achieved the rank of able seaman. The elegant, mighty warship was 794 feet long with a 90 feet beam and a displacement of 32,700 tons. It boasted six fifteen inch guns in two double turrets forward and one aft, with a secondary armament of twelve four inch guns. Built at John Brown's Clydebank Yard, she possessed a top speed of thirty-two knots, and was the sister ship of H.M.S. 'Renown'. They were launched in August and September 1916 respectively. Both ships had been refitted and modernised, nevertheless, the depth of deck armour was below those of Thirty's construction, while the anti-aircraft power consisted of only eight hand-operated high angle four inch guns and two sets of eight barrelled two-pounder 'pom-poms'. By 1939 each ship was planned to possess a crew of sixty-nine officers and a thousand, two hundred and forty petty officers and ratings.

*Elizabeth Read before meeting Les Bishop, circa 1938.*

*Les Bishop, circa 1939.*

Shortly before the outbreak of war, after a whirlwind romance, Les married Elizabeth Read at Christ Church, Coalville. Lizzie, as she was always known, continued to live at her parent's home on Hermitage Road, Coalville. Les returned to the

'*Repulse*' that, in the first days of the war, was on 'Northern Patrol', defending the seas between Scotland and Iceland from German vessels trying to break into the Atlantic. In November/December 1939, captained by E.J. Spooner, she sailed as heavy escort with trade convoys, and also escorted five liners carrying twenty thousand Canadian 1st Division soldiers to England.

On 2/3rd April 1940, an R.A.F. reconnaissance flight radioed news of a gathering of German warships in the North Sea. Developments saw *Marine Gruppen 1& 2*, with *Kriegsmarine's* powerful battle cruisers '*Gneisenau*' and '*Scharnhorst*', and heavy cruiser: '*Admiral Hipper*', with four troop-laden destroyers, steaming north. The fleet left *Schillig Roads* at twenty-six knots and formed their largest Naval Force of the War. Meanwhile, other *Marine Gruppen's* landed troops as part of a pre-emptive invasion of Denmark and Norway during the small hours of 8th/9th April 1940. On the afternoon of April 8th, twenty-four Heinkel 111 bombers raided Scotland's Scapa Flow Naval Base. Their plan was to destroy the 'Home Fleet', but it had left the previous day and they lost four aircraft to the guns of 111 Hurricane Squadron. It was at 21.15 on April 7th, that the Fleet, including H.M.S. '*Rodney*', H.M.S. '*Valiant*', H.M.S. '*Repulse*', two cruisers and ten destroyers departed in stormy weather from Scapa Flow. With other squadrons involved, H.M.S. '*Repulse*', a cruiser and four destroyers swiftly forge ahead to quell the Navy's fear of an enemy battle cruisers break-out into the North Atlantic; thus creating havoc to British convoys. German reconnaissance spotted the Navy off Bergen, and resultantly *Fliegerkorps X* despatched forty-one Heinkel 111 bombers and forty-seven Junkers 88 fighter-bombers. The anti-aircraft fire was good but a destroyer was lost and two badly damaged; four enemy aircraft were shot down, but other air attacks followed. To the north, off Narvik, the '*Renown*', with nine destroyers, bravely attacked '*Scharnhorst*' and '*Hipper*': enemy capital ships.

The weather was bad with heavy seas and snowstorms; '*Renown*' opened fire at 18, 000 yards: a broadside which damaged '*Scharnhorst's*' superstructure, and she retired from the battle. Simultaneously came reports of an enemy ship landing troops at Narvik. The news was incorrect, within the

*H.M.S. 'Repulse' in 1939.*

Fjord was a flotilla of at least six large enemy destroyers, refuelled and spread within various feeder fjords. Also they had posted 'U'-Boats in Vestfjord to warn of approaching enemy forces. 'Repulse' was one of the ships to blockade Narvik's West Fjord. Luckily the 'U'-Boats, due to the blindingly thick snowstorm, failed to spot the arrival of five British destroyers commanded by Captain B. A. W. Warburton-Lee. At 0510 on April 10th, the destroyers steamed down the narrow waterway and unleashed torpedoes. One hit the enemy flagship's magazine and it blew-up; another had numerous fires, a third ship split in half. A sea mist rolled in to hinder operations and so Warburton–Lee decided to depart at fifteen knots. Suddenly, three enemy destroyers appeared from another fjord and opened fire, and then two more appeared and pounded the flagship: killing Warburton-Lee and destroying the ship. Another ship was sunk while a third was badly damaged. Captain Warburton-Lee was posthumously awarded the Victoria Cross.

The second battle of Narvik occurred on April 13th, whereby the enemy was overcome. Three days later, 'A' and 'B' Companies of the 1/5th Leicestershire Battalion left Aberdeen on anti-aircraft cruisers: H.M.S. 'Carlisle' and 'Curacao' for the four hundred mile (640 kilometres) trip to Aandalsnes, Norway. On April 18th, 'B' and 'C' left on 'S.S. Sunniva' and 'St.Magnus', and faced a very rough North Sea and 'U'-Boats; one of the convoy: S.S. 'Cedarbank' was torpedoed and sunk. (See James Lock).

'Repulse' returned to 'Northern Patrol' duties. In May 1941, as part of the Home Fleet, she was involved in chasing the German battleship: 'Bismarck' and heavy cruiser: 'Prinz Eugen' after they left the Baltic to attack Atlantic convoys. On May 24th, H.M.S. 'Hood' and H.M.S. 'Prince of Wales' exchanged fire with the enemy. 'Hood' sank after enemy shells hit her magazine (inadequate deck armour), and 'Prince of Wales' was damaged. Three days later 'Bismarck' was sunk, only tired engines and lack of fuel prevented 'Repulse' from taking part in the finale, much to the disappointment of the crew as it docked in Newfoundland

In August, 'Repulse' underwent a small refit at Rosyth, while her new captain: W. G. 'Bill' Tennant, was told that she would be one of the first for the new 'Eastern Fleet'. On August 31st she left the Clyde and sailed for Singapore, and at the same time was senior escort for Convoy 'WS 11' that carried troops and equipment for the Suez (via the Cape).

Japan's naked ambition and aggression in areas of China and Mongolia, and support for her Manchurian interests, with Russian friction, created unrest in the West. The Land of the Rising Sun's expansionism required vast quantities of oil (eighty per cent from America), rubber, tin and aluminium-ore from Southeast Asia. The United Nations condemned Japan's brutality, and, in the summer of 1938, America placed 'moral embargos' on trade with Japan, followed by severe restrictions on petroleum. Relationships deteriorated!

With the European War raging in favour of the Axis Forces, Japan exploited the situation and hoped to grasp the mineral rich colonies of Britain, France and Holland. British Intelligence suspected as much, and so her Singapore Naval Base appreciated the timely arrival of the new Eastern Fleet; codenamed Force Z and commanded by Admiral Sir Tom Phillips. Alongside 'Repulse' was Britain's newest battleship: H.M.S. 'Prince of Wales', and four destroyers: H.M.S 'Electra', H.M.S. 'Express', H.M.S. 'Vampire' and H.M.S. 'Tenedos'.

'Prince of Wales' was built by Camel Laird at Birkenhead and launched on 3rd May 1939. A magnificent ship of the King George V class, it had ten fourteen-inch guns, four twin 5.25-inch turrets mounted on each side of the main deck, and six sets of eight barrelled two pounder pom-poms, a 40mm Bofors gun and other light guns.

On 2nd December 1941, Force Z steamed under the huge defensive guns on Blakang Mati Island, into Keppel Harbour and anchored at Singapore. Large crowds cheered as the ships' complement stood on the decks while bands played various naval themes.

Next day's newspaper hailed 'Prince of Wales' as H.M.S. 'Unsinkable', and Britain hoped that enemy spies would note their arrival and deter or delay Japan's ambitions.

Force Z should have included the aircraft carrier: H.M.S. 'Ark Royal', but regrettably she was torpedoed by 'U-81' just off Gibraltar on 13th November 1941. A replacement, the newly built H.M.S. 'Indomitable' hit a reef during fog off Kingston Harbour, Jamaica. She was speedily repaired in America but arrived too late to participate in subsequent actions. This lack of air cover was to prove a pivotal and decisive factor!

Captain W. G. 'Bill' Tennant of 'Repulse' was very popular with the crew; a Greenwich Staff College man and fifty-three years of age. As beach master at Dunkirk, he was one of the last to be evacuated and his crew warmly called him 'Dunkirk Jo'. The ship was well disciplined and happy and everyone felt proud to sail on such a formidable ship; special pride was taken in the accuracy of her main armament: '- -could straddle any battle practise target at 26,000 yards!' Most of her crew were regulars, unlike the crew the 'Prince of Wales', with a good proportion of 'war service only' men. Les Bishop was to say that the crew was told not to be concerned for any future conflict, because the Japanese fleet was absolutely useless: 'a lot of rice paper and string!'

Admiral Sir Tom Phillips, aged fifty-three, and a former Vice Chief of the Naval Staff, had been a naval officer for thirty-seven years. Concerned that both of his capital ships might be destroyed in Singapore harbour, on December 3rd, he sent 'Repulse' to Darwin in Australia for a few days; she was escorted by the destroyers 'Vampire' (Australian) and 'Tenedos': the crews were delighted and Australia's fears concerning national security were allayed.

At 07.49 on 7th December 1941, Japanese aircraft bombed the U.S.A.'s Pacific base of Pearl Harbour, on the Hawaiian island of Oahu. Yet, it isn't generally known that at 00.45 on that morning, troops and equipment of General Yamashita's 25th Army stormed ashore on the beaches of Kotah Bahru, in northeastern Malaya. Concurrently, the Imperial Japanese Navy placed minefields to the south and deployed ten submarines to intercept Force Z if it entered the invasion area. That night, searchlights revealed twelve enemy aircraft at a great height and directly above Force Z; the worst was feared: anti-aircraft guns opened fire but no bombs fell, luckily for them, they'd fallen on Singapore city.

At 17.10 on December 8th, Force Z left Singapore. Led by 'Vampire' they passed over the harbour boom and steamed for the South China Sea with the plan to intercept further enemy troops-ships off Kota, Bahru, Patani, and Singora. At 22.53, Admiral Phillips heard that no air cover was possible, obsolete though it was, due to the loss of Kota Bharu airfield. However, he proceeded, partly knowing British troops were fighting frantically in that area and because visibility was poor: heavy rain and low, thick cloud. Ordinary Seaman H. J. Hall of 'Repulse' later said that there was a funny 'buzz' around the ship, a feeling that this was one trip the ship would not return from.

On December 9th at 13.45, Captain Masao Teraoka of 'I. 65' (30th Submarine Flotilla) spotted the Force, unbeknown to Admiral Phillips. At 17.00, in brighter weather, three Japanese Aichi E13A observation seaplanes were spotted. The Admiral decided that having lost the advantage of surprise, he'd return to Singapore, but to confuse the enemy he ordered Force Z, with the exception of 'Tenedos', to follow the northerly course until nightfall, and only then to steer south ('Tenedos' was low on fuel). At midnight, he was told that enemy landings were taking place at Kuatan. Believing these landings could result in the loss of Singapore, he took a strategic gamble and steamed to challenge the enemy's sea-borne plans; he also knew that Japan had a large bomber force at Saigon.

At 02.20 on December 10th, the Japanese submarine 'I.58', led by Lt. Commander Sohichi Kitamura, spotted and reported the British squadron's location in the South China Sea. He fired a torpedo at 'Repulse' but it missed! At 06.30 the lookouts on 'Repulse' spotted an aircraft low on the horizon; it could not be identified but remained out of fire for thirty minutes. Admiral Phillips maintained radio silence.

At 04.55, a reconnaissance unit of nine Mitsubishi 96G3M2s (two 50 kg bombs) took off from Saigon (French Indo-China: now Vietnam). Next, from 06.25 to 08.00, thirty-four of the same aircraft took-off (one 500 kg or two 250 kg bombs per aircraft), and fifty-one Mitsubishi Navy Type 1 G4M1 Torpedo attack aircraft: part of the Japanese XX11 Air Flotilla. In the interim, Admiral Phillips arrived at Kuatan to find no sign of an invasion. The enemy, as a diversion to attract Force Z, had sent a minor incursion to surprise raw Indian troops of the 22nd Brigade; a few shots were fired. Around the same time a message came from 'Tenedos' telling him that she was under attack from Japanese bombers.

At 11.07, Force Z sighted enemy aircraft: the Admiral maintained radio silence. The naval guns: Oerlikons, Bofors and 5.25 cannons opened up, but reports said that the flak failed to deter the enemy pilots. First, 'Repulse', steaming at twenty-six knots, took two bombs: killing a number of marines below deck and producing a long narrow plume of white smoke. The second wave targeted 'Prince of Wales': nine aerial torpedoes were dropped and one hit her port side: damaging the rudder. A thirteen-degree list soon developed and many anti-aircraft guns were left without power. Further torpedoes hit the battleship: two to the bows and one to the stern. Captain Tennant of 'Repulse' was about one mile due south of the flagship. An officer on 'Repulse' said: "The aircraft then circled us like Red Indians about to attack a Wagon Train'. 'Repulse' adopted a zigzag course at (twenty-five knots) as fifteen Mitsubishis machine-gunned her superstructure, killing many. The aircraft then released their torpedoes, and observers praised the expertise of Captain Tennant for steering his ship: every one from two squadrons missed the target. At noon, during a lull in the action, it was clear that the 'Prince of Wales' was badly crippled while 'Repulse' refitted for another attack. The weather was very hot with minimal cloud cover. Captain Tennant asked his signal office as to what message the Admiral had despatched; on hearing none had been released he sent his own without consenting the flagship. It took just six minutes for Singapore to decode the message! Within thirty minutes eleven Brewster Buffaloes of Australian 453 Squadron took-off from Sembawang for the one-hour flight to their position. Irishman, Tim Vigors, a Battle of Britain pilot, led the Squadron and was annoyed that he had not been kept informed of developments.

Survivors from H.M.S.' Repulse'.

'Repulse' on fire in the South China Sea.

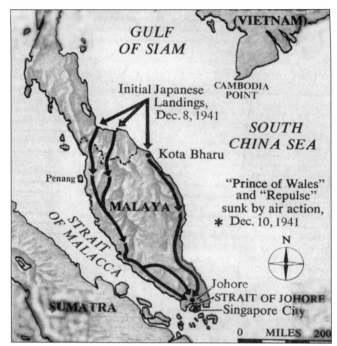

Location of 'Repulse' and 'Prince of Wales'.

'*Repulse*' closed in on her flagship to offer help, but at 12.20 spotters saw a formation of aircraft to the east. Twenty-six Mitsubishis with Model 2 torpedoes gradually lost height and took-up torpedo runs for the '*Prince of Wales*': struggling at fifteen knots. Some aircraft came to just over five hundred yards before releasing their 450lb warheads. Within five minutes at least four of the six torpedoes released shook the ship: she was doomed! The attack then moved to '*Repulse*'; she was only hit by one torpedo after valiantly manoeuvring from at least sixteen! Water poured into her bulge and she began to list, but counter-flooding removed this threat, but a further nine aircraft shaped to attack from various angles. The guns of '*Repulse*' shot down two before three torpedoes hit her port side. Aircraft then released bombs from high altitude; at least two hit the battle cruiser with one penetrating the armour and killing hundreds of wounded men in the cinema flat.

For any navy, air support is an imperative: after battling for three hours: H.M.S. '*Repulse*' keeled over onto her back and eventually sank beneath the waves at 12.33. The '*Prince of Wales*' survived for fifty more minutes before she too rolled over and went to her grave. Admiral Phillips never attempted to leave the bridge and went down with his ship; his last thought may have been that aircraft could never sink a modern battleship! As the destroyer escort picked-up survivors from the oil-ridden sea it is written: '- *decks slippery with blood, the sea of custard consistency due to oil and amass with floating bodies!*' 843 sailors died, and the loss of the two capital ships was the death knell for Malaysia and Singapore. There were 1,285 survivors from a '*Prince of Wales*' total of 1,618, while only 796 remained from a '*Repulse*' complement of 1,306. The enemy lost three aircraft.

Captain Bill Tennant belated distress call meant that eleven Buffalo fighters arrived just in time to see the '*Prince of Wales*' final stage of buoyancy.

They sank at seventy nautical miles southeast of Kuatan in eastern Malaya (see map). Flight Lieutenant Tim Vigors said he'd never forget the bravery and high spirits displayed by the sailors as they bobbed around in the oily sea. He remained over them until his fuel register forced a return to base: "*They were waving and putting their thumbs up, they were amazing!*" Able Seaman Les Bishop was one of those men. Les' daughter, Elaine explains:

"*My dad said that he was not a strong swimmer and he spent four hours in the sea before he was rescued by a Chinese Jung, which was later captured by the Japanese. Many years later he watched and relived the experience in a poignant television programme which showed footage of the 'Repulse' and sailors fighting for their lives in the cruel sea.*"

Captain Bill Tennant, the senior surviving officer said: "*The officers and ship's company were magnificent throughout the ordeal; in some cases I had to order men to leave their guns and save themselves as the ship was about to sink!*"

A Royal Naval analytical enquiry stated that Captain Tennant and the crew of '*Repulse*' never put a foot wrong. It continued that their ship was poorly armed with anti-aircraft fire, and that having fought to the end, it had simply been overwhelmed. Admiral Bill Tennant, justififily promoted to Vice and Full Admiral was involved in the 'D'-Day landings.

The '*Prince of Wales*' had a short history; apart from being damaged by the '*Bismarck*' (See George Hemsley in Volume 1), she had taken Prime Minister Winston Churchill to Maine, where, with President Roosevelt they had drafted the terms of the Atlantic Charter.

After the fall of Malaya came the capitulation of Singapore on 15th February 1942; as for nearby Sumatra, the Japanese copied their German allies by using airborne troops to capture part of the southern section of that island.

Les' Service Record shows that he served with '*Sultan*' until 4th March 1942, and onto '*Drake 1V*' (for missing personnel). He was classed as a Japanese prisoner-of-war on March 5th, and spent a period in Changi Gaol.

*Pankalan Balai Camp in Sumatra.*

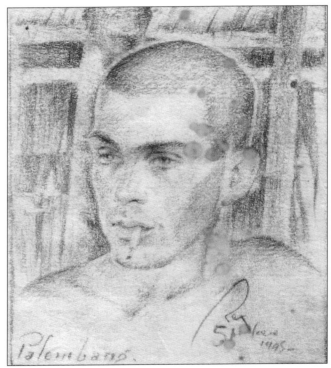
*A sketch by fellow P.O.W. Rex Spencer of Les at Pankalan Balai Camp.*

*Within the hold of the Hell-ship.*

Elaine:

"*Dad never spoke of his time as a POW on the island of Sumatra, but from what I can gather there were many hardships and atrocities.*"

Les, in the first weeks, would have worked at Singapore, what with warehouses to be filled or emptied, supplies to be unloaded at the docks and bomb rubble to be shifted (see Les Kendrick in Volume 1). In 1942, he was taken in the hold of a 'hell-ship' the five hundred kilometres to Pankalan Balai Camp, Palembang on Sumatra. At the camp, in the early days, two R.A.F. men tried to escape by seizing a plane on a nearby aerodrome; they were caught, returned to the camp and beheaded in front of all the prisoners! Elaine:

"*I know mum was most upset when she received a dreaded telegram notifying her that her husband was:*

'Missing - presumed dead'. Mum wouldn't accept he was dead and worried her family and friends by repeating that he'd soon be coming home."

Les, like his compatriots, was a slave labourer: working from dawn to dusk! His rice diet kept him alive, but only just and many succumbed to an early death. P.O.W.s were subjected to beatings, and a host of tropical illnesses such as Dengue fever, beriberi, dysentery, malaria, tropical ulcers, cholera, etc. Les filled in bomb-craters, perhaps slaved at the oil wells, worked on the fertile land, prepared a landing strip for aircraft, but the worst job lasted for twelve months and began in the spring of 1944. They, like their fellow prisoners on the Burma/ Siam 'Railway of Death', built a railway line to run inland from Pakenbaroe on the northeast coast to meet existing lines. The construction of the railway passed directly under the equator and was built by five thousand POW's. The terrain may not have been as bad as the Burma/Siam railway, twenty per cent died, but a hefty twelve per cent perished. The enemy used the railroad to transport troops, coal and food. To supplement their diet the men would eat snakes, cats, dogs, birds, rats, etc: anything to maintain life. See Les as sketched by fellow POW Rex Spencer while at Palembang POW Camp: southwest corner of Sumatra.

An incident described by fellow Palembang Camp prisoner, Ivan Gray (R.A.F.) is as follows:

'There were times when we got terribly depressed, but amazingly, when at our lowest, something or someone lifted us from our doldrums.

One evening we were returning to camp, tired, hungry, dejected, with spirits and morale almost at breaking point after toiling all day with pick and shovel in the scorching sun. To add to our misery we walked into the full force of a tropical storm: thunder crashed, lightning flashed in the angry black sky and rain beat down relentlessly on our poor emaciated bodies. The ground beneath our feet turned into a sea of glutinous mud, and it squelched between our toes and I felt at my lowest! We were soaking and almost out-on-our-feet when some of the lads started singing: 'Pack up your troubles in your old kit bag, and smile, smile, smile!' It was unbelievable, the singing got louder, and everyone joined in. The Japanese guards looked on in wonder, I'm sure they thought we had gone stark, raving mad. At that moment, I believe, they knew they could never break the indomitable spirit of the British serviceman. We marched into our camp absolutely soaking wet but with our heads held high!'

Elaine: "Mum was proved right, but when dad returned home in December 1945, after nearly four years away, he weighed just six-half stone: so weak he needed help from the road to the pavement."

Les' discharge papers state: 'rather emaciated', but he was still pronounced A1 fit! Elaine:

"A bitter blow awaited dad on his return to England: his mum had died without knowing whether he was dead or alive! So, naturally, when Lizzie gave birth to me, their only child, it was a very special event. I was born on 20th November 1946."

As a regular sailor he'd have been expected to enrol into the 'Royal Fleet Reserve', doing so at Devonport on 24th April 1946, and remaining until 24th August 1950. He also spent a period with H.M.S. 'Defiance' until being transferred to the 'Royal Navy Emergency Reserve' on 21st November 1954. Les received a 1st class 'good conduct badge' on 25th August 1941 and through his career his character was graded as 'very good' and efficiency as 'satisfactory'.

Les Bishop's Certificate of Service.

In civilian life he worked in engineering and at various local collieries until 1953. In that year Les and Lizzie became tenants of the 'Royal Oak' on High Street, Coalville. The name was appropriate and so was the position, nearly opposite to the Clock Tower Memorial.

*Les and Lizzie at a Licensed Victuallers' Association event.*

"*Dad and mum lived and worked at the 'Royal Oak' for twelve years and were a very popular and highly respected landlord and landlady.*"

Les, a fine man, became frail in his latter years but retained his mental strength and never allowed the torture and suffering of his earlier years to embitter him.

"*Dad was very pleased when a consultant at Leicester Royal Infirmary, on reading his medical history, said: "Well, Les, you're a tough old stick."*"

After six years of nursing his beloved Lizzie, he died suddenly at home at 'Peggs Grange', Hugglescote in April 2005: aged eighty-five years.

Elaine is married to Martin Bartlett. For readers of 'Greater Love' they will know that his step-grandfather was William Ogden Hoden and his grandmother, Ellen. His father: Harry Bartlett was as a pharmacy assistant at Restalls Chemist at Ibstock, enlisting into the Royal Army Medical Corps in 1939. He trained at hospitals at Taunton and Birmingham before a posting to the Bone Hospital in North Africa. Late in the war he was discharged following a major operation on a kidney. Harry was stores-manager at Forest Road Garage, Coalville for fourteen years and held a similar position at Ford Motors, Coalville. He and his wife, Olive, had a son, John and a daughter, Ann. Harry died in 1981, aged eighty years. Martin did his National Service in Malaya during the troubles with communism. He and Elaine live in the Broom Leys' district and have two sons: Joe and Jon, and a daughter, Hayley, also three grandchildren: Jade, Chelsea and Jacob. The sons had a wreath made into the shape of '*Repulse*' and laid it on their grandfather's grave in Broom Leys' cemetery.

Many thanks to Elaine and Martin for sharing their memories with me.

*Elaine stands alongside a painting of her fathers ship.*

*Elaine and Martin remember Les.*

# HERBERT ERNEST BLACK
## 'One of the Few'

*Sergeant Pilot Bert Black in 1940.*

It was a sunny, autumnal day in 1999 when I travelled across Charnwood Forest; the leaves were tinged with delightful tones of crimson-red and golden-yellow. As I approached the Broom Leys' neighbourhood of Coalville, I stopped at a cosy looking bungalow and was soon welcomed indoors by a dear old lady: Mrs. Gwendoline (Gwen) Annie Black. Gwen had a lively, intelligent mind, just as you would expect from a retired headmistress. Dotted around her lounge were several photographs, two of which particularly caught my eye: a young man wearing the uniform of the Royal Air Force. His name, naturally, was Herbert (but from now will be Bert) Black and Gwen and he were married for just one hundred and thirty-four days. There follows one of the most tragic episodes of World War 2: one that could feature within any book. I recall Gwen pointing to a portrait of her husband:

*"Bert was painted by George A Campbell; he also painted Pilot Officer Keith Gilman that appears on the front cover of: 'The Battle of Britain, Then and Now', by Winston G Ramsey."*

I nodded; I possess the book but Gwen modestly refrained from saying that she wrote the Foreword. Gwen whispered: *"Every morning I look at Bert's photograph and speak to him."*

The earthly bond may have been broken for almost sixty years but an eternal bond of love remained intact. Both were born in the cataclysmic year of 1914, and the reverberations of that world conflict would touch their lives, and many others, two decades later!

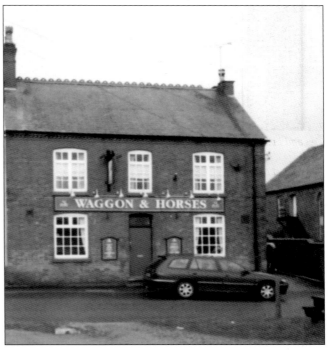

*The Waggon and Horses.*

Bert was born on June 12th at the village of Measham. He moved to Ibstock as a youngster when his father, Herbert (to distinguish father from son), a foreman in the shoe industry, took over as landlord of 'Waggon and Horses'. Herbert took over after the death of his mother-in-law, Eliza Adcock. This was nothing new to him; his parents managed the 'Flying Horse' and 'Hastings Arms' at Ibstock and the 'Victoria Hotel' at Coalville. In the 1930s, Herbert was a Bosworth Rural and Ibstock Parish Councillor and the village's first sub-postmaster. Bert's mother, Mary Elizabeth (nee Adcock), gave birth to Mary Elizabeth (Maisie) on 10th June 1917, but lamentably died on 1st January 1922, aged just thirty-seven. Herbert remarried to Alice Upton and half-brother, George Norman (known as Norman) was born 3rd September 1925; a daughter: Clarice, who died at two weeks of age in 1932.

Ernest Cuthbert (1887-1927), an Ibstock master-butcher was Gwen's father and Esther (nee Clarke), gave birth to Gwen on 8th August 1914. They lived on High Street where Ernest owned a shop and slaughterhouse, but when he died, Esther took Gwen, sisters Dorothy, Marjorie and brother Harry (born 26th January 1925) to 129 Melbourne Road, Ibstock. Gwen:

*"Little boys and girls don't usually befriend each other, but we had an understanding very early on: we were good friends. Bert was a clever lad and he won a scholarship to Dixie Grammar School, and I obtained a scholarship to Coalville Grammar School. He used to bicycle to that famous school at Market Bosworth; it was famed by Dr. Samuel Johnson, an usher there in the early eighteenth century."*

Both were confirmed at the same ceremony in St. Deny's Parish Church, and when Bert joined the Boy Scouts (becoming Scout Master), Gwen a brownie and Girl Guide. They were inseparable: a rare bond between intelligent and like-minded young folk. Bert, a fine student was particularly gifted at sport, and Gwen proudly recalls him playing for the Dixie's cricket team: *"A gifted batsman with good eye/ muscle co-ordination."*

Bert, circa 1930.

The latter quality was an essential ingredient for enlisters into the R.A.F., but Gwen was no slouch and equalled him: they represented Leicestershire in the same mixed-hockey team, and Bert was centre forward for Coalville's side. They became very much in love and local folk knew that they were destined for marriage. Gwen: *"On Sunday afternoons Bert had a Bible Class while I was a superintendent at the Sunday school. We met afterwards and strolled together hand-in-hand down to a brook, then across the fields to a knoll that was*

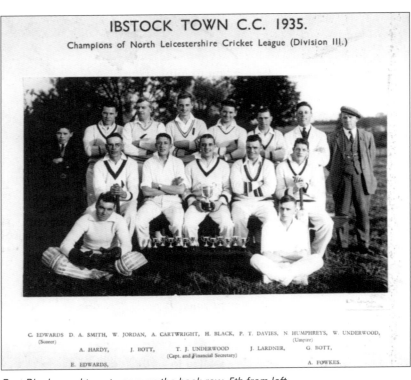

IBSTOCK TOWN C.C. 1935.
Champions of North Leicestershire Cricket League (Division III.)

C. EDWARDS, D. A. SMITH, W. JORDAN, A. CARTWRIGHT, H. BLACK, P. T. DAVIES, N. HUMPHREYS, W. UNDERWOOD,
(Scorer)                                                                                    (Umpire)
A. HARDY,    J. BOTT,    T. J. UNDERWOOD,    J. LARDNER,    G. BOTT,
(Capt. and Financial Secretary)
E. EDWARDS,                                          A. FOWKES.

Bert Black, aged twenty-one; on the back row, 5th from left.

*called: 'Happy Land'. It was our special place."* Gwen qualified as a teacher. Bert studied at Clarke's College, Leicester, passed examinations and became a 'Weights and Measures' inspector at Coalville.

Sergeant Bert Black; circa 1937.

His daring spirit propelled him to joining the R. A. F. V. R. in 1937: service number 740749. Initial training was at Peterborough and then onto Desford: flying Tiger Moths. Gwen:

*"When he was at Desford (twelve kilometres west of Leicester) he would often fly over our village and flip his wings. He said that flying was a different world, and that I could not even imagine what it was like to go belting around the sky. He said that one day we would fly together, but the outbreak of war settled that, at least for the time being we thought. Two old friends from Coalville Grammar knew Bert, that is Les and Pete Ball: they were grand lads, bright, breezy and fun loving."*

In late 1939, he received his 'silver wings', and as Sergeant Pilot H. E. Black was posted to France in the spring of 1940, joining 226 Squadron: Fairey Battle fighter/ bombers. This two-seater aircraft had a maximum speed of two hundred and fifty-seven miles per hour and had moderate success bombing invasion barges, but was no match for Germany's latest fighter: the Messerschmitt Bf109! Bert's Aunt Edith was married to William Nicholls and their son, Cyril, was a good friend to Bert. He sent this letter to his cousin at 17, Broom Leys' Avenue, Coalville. I am grateful to his son: Chris for publication.

The R.A.F. Station
Benson
Oxford
12/3/40.

*Dear Cyril,*

*I suppose Gwen has confirmed your worst fears about this place, Fairey Battles. It appears that these are the aircraft I am destined to fly. From enquiries I have made the only comforting thought about this is that they are only used for patrol work now. I have another blow for you too. No flying for a fortnight. No Sir! Fourteen days of concentrated lectures first, you know how that will suit me. Still, I'm not going to work too hard on them come what may. The Station is fairly comfortable but the nearest town is 13 miles away (Oxford). There is a cinema at the village of Wallingford, which is quite reasonable. The course is expected to last nine weeks.*

*Yours sincerely, Bert.*

*Bert's cousin, Cyril, 1st July 1928.*

On 10th May 1940, German Forces invaded the Low Countries. The Luftwaffe, the world's largest airforce, had three and a half thousand aircraft;

*A Fairey Battle as flown by Bert in France.*

confronting them was our Advanced Air Striking Force. This consisted of ten squadrons of Fairey Battles, two of Hurricane fighters, two of Blenheim bombers, four of Lysanders (reconnaissance), and later two more Hurricane Squadrons. Also were the French L'Armee de l'Air, and a small Low Country's contingent. Bert's airfield was just outside of Rheims in northern France and the Squadron was led by Wing Commander S.L.G. Pope D.F.C. A.F.C., a fighter pilot from World War 1 and nicknamed: 'Poppy'. On May 10th, at dawn, the Luftwaffe attacked 226's airfield: sixteen high explosive and seventy incendiary bombs fell, luckily with little damage to personnel and aircraft. The allied squadrons flew daily sorties but were overwhelmed numerically and technically and suffered severe casualties. On May 13th at 10.20am, seven Fairey Battles of 226 Squadron took-off to destroy an armoured column at the road-junction of Boeimeer-Rijsbergen, in southern Holland. They had a Hurricane umbrella protection from 56 Squadron that flew from R.A.F. Martlesham Heath, Suffolk, but unable to spot the enemy dropped their bombs on a factory at Boeimeer. Heavy ground fire was reported. Next day, at 3.00pm, they took-off with other like squadrons to attack German Army units making rapid advances near Sedan. Heavy casualties were reported from Bf 109 attacks and anti-aircraft fire (flak); yet, British fighters proved their worth with sizeable victories.

Up to 21st May 1940, the air battles followed a similar pattern. Other Hurricane fighters came to support B.E.F. troops as they withdrew to the Channel ports. The ferocity of the air-war can be assessed statistically with the R.A.F. claiming nearly five hundred victories, but admitted to half that number in losses; they could never win a battle of attrition! The R.A.F. did carve out a brilliant chapter in the Battle of France with names such as Dennis David, 'Dickie' Lee, and Peter Prosser Hanks becoming fighter aces.

Nevertheless, the German advance was inexorable and by early June 1940 the R.A.F. was compelled to return to Britain. Bert flew from France, and later onto Desford. Gwen: *"On his way home from France, in mid-June, he circled a number of times over Caldecote Road School in Leicester, where I was teaching. I was so thrilled to know that he had survived over there, it was a very difficult time for all of them and I was so worried!"*

Before going to France, they had discussed a date for marriage, but thought it wise to leave it until better times; some folk believed the war could be over by Christmas. At 7.00am on 17th June 1940, Bert threw a handful of gravel at Gwen's bedroom window to awaken her.

*"There was a pitter-patter on my bedroom window. I was a bit concerned but on peering out I saw Bert standing there with a beam on his face. He told me to get dressed quickly because he had arranged to pick up a special marriage licence from Leicester: we were married at St. Deny's Church that very afternoon!"*

Gwen smiled as she recalled spending the remaining four days of Bert's leave at the 'New Bath Hotel', Matlock in Derbyshire. *"The weather was beautiful,*

*we strolled in woodlands and along rivers, and spoke of our future together: I was so pleased to be referred to as Mrs. G. Black."* The Coalville Times of 21st June 1940 reported on the wedding.

*Bert and Gwen's Wedding Day.*

In the early summer of 1940, Great Britain braced herself for an anticipated German invasion. Folk were fearful, aware that the B.E.F. had no option but to destroy their capital equipment at Dunkirk, but top military officials knew that the Luftwaffe would have to eliminate Fighter Command before mounting an invasion. The Royal Navy, although powerful was vulnerable to 'U'-Boat and Junkers 87 and 88 dive-bomb attacks. Bert told Gwen of the forthcoming air war and, following his Fairey Battle experiences in France, applied for a transfer. Gwen: *"Bert told me about his air battles in France. He couldn't believe the speed and savagery of the enemy fighters, and said that many of his fellow pilots had been killed, and that he was lucky to be alive! He thought his best chance of survival was to get on level terms regarding speed: he would apply for a posting to Fighter Command."*

The monumental and pivotal Battle of Britain

Hurricane fighters as flown by Bert in the Battle of Britain.

raged mainly over southern Britain and broadly lasted from July 18th to the end of October 1940. On September 2nd, Bert was posted to 32 Squadron at Acklington (thirty-five kilometres north of Newcastle-upon-Tyne.) The Squadron had fought fiercely early in the Battle and was taking a rest and refit. Later that month, Bert was transferred to 257 Squadron, rejoining former 32 Squadron ace-pilot, Flight Lieutenant Peter Brothers (later Air Commodore P. M. Brothers. C.B.E. D.S.O. D.F.C. and bar.) Gwen: *"A great friend of Bert's during that interlude was Sergeant Pilot Henry 'Olive' Hoyle. He survived the war and left the R.A.F. as a flight lieutenant in 1946."* Flying from R.A.F. Martlesham Heath, just northeast of Ipswich, Bert was in the thick of the Battle that ultimately secured the freedom of our country, and more! He was in the dogfight when Peter Brothers shot down two Dornier 17 bombers on the tempestuous September 15th (later commemorated as Battle of Britain Day.) Again, thanks to Chris Nicholls, I print a letter from Bert to Cyril:

'257 (Burma) Squadron.
R.A.F.
Martlesham Heath,
Suffolk'
4-10-40.

Dear Cyril,

Thanks for letter of 5th September, which I received at Acklington. Since then I have had a further move round as you know, and generally speaking I have been pretty busy.

Yes, I am very satisfied here in many ways. The pilots are a jolly good set of chaps and the billets and Mess are O.K. Compared with Sydenham this is luxury. Of course it has been a busy time, and I've been on duty much more since I've been in fighter command. As I told you when I last saw you, I was

quite content to sit around at Belfast and have an easy time; but I was very peeved by the way we were bull-shitted around. However, I was not letting that worry me unduly; I must confess I'm really much more suited here.

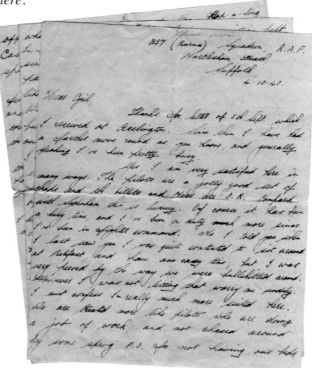

Letters from Bert to his cousin, Cyril.

We are treated more like pilots who are doing a job of work, and not chased around by some sprog pilot officer for not having our beds rolled-up by 7.00am. The C.O. is a grand guy and flat out for getting on with the job and looking after his squadron too. I was hoping that when I wrote to you I would be able to say I knocked one down; I've delayed answering for that reason. This squadron has had a most unusual run of luck. We have done lots of patrols without making any interceptions, and it has not been for want of looking. We are vectored by an Operations Room, all the chaps in our squadron are just bursting to find some Jerries and have a crack at them, and we never see a thing. I suppose it is one of those unexplainable coincidences. If we were trying to keep out of the way we could not manage it better, but believe me the blokes here are new to this squadron and the boot is on the other foot and very much so! I suppose I am the exception, I look as hard as the rest, but I am a patient man, and can wait with more philosophy. The first time I went up with the squadron we were imbeaggled. We were climbing up in tight formation, being vectored smack *into the sun. We were being led by another squadron when we were pounced on out of the sun. Our C.O. shouted 'split up' and you've never seen such a double shuffle. I did a steep turn and tried to follow my section leader and look for Jerries at the same time. One minute the sky was full of planes, next minute there only seemed to be me. I stooged around for some time trying to find a machine to have a crack at but I only saw Hurricanes. I thought, well, I can't go back from my first scrap without firing my guns, so I flew around until I seemed to be the only one left and then went back. I saw several parachutes floating gently to earth. When I got back eventually the others were just beginning to think I had been shot down as I was so long after them. The pilot officer who was No2 in my section was shot down but baled out O.K. (I was No 3). Our C.O. shot a 109 down so we were a draw. I found that I was not the only one who had returned with a full ammunition belt. In fact only two people had fired. I've since learned that these Me109s are very partial to sitting up top, swooping down like a flash and diving away like stink. We can cope with them in a dogfight, but they are much faster than us and can out-climb and out-dive us as easy as a wink. I found that out the next time I was imbeaggled. We were six to twelve when they swooped but they snooped our tail-end bloke and off they came down (he baled out O.K.). This time I saw them but I thought they were Hurricanes at first sight as they came in from the port beam. I whipped round towards them and saw the big black crosses as one of them turned. He was in range when I saw him and I thought 'I'm after you' and belted after him. But he stuck his nose down and so did his pals and went away like a streak of dripping. They went straight back home like sand off a shovel. But next time Hop-a-long-Cassidy ain't having nothing on me for speed of draw.*

*As I say I've done quite a few patrols. I've done them over London and the Thames Estuary, and I've done them over convoys, but I can't send you the news that you are looking for.*

*You will notice that the squadron is the 'Burma' Squadron. This is because Burma has contributed £130,000 plus to the kitty to provide us with aircraft. You will be pleased to know that I am due for six days leave in about one months time.*

*Yours sincerely, Bert.'*

(Author: Flight Lieutenant Peter Brothers was acting C.O.) Sergeant Pilot H. E. Black was finally posted to 46 (Uganda) Squadron at R.A.F. Stapleford Tawney (an airfield between Chigwell and Ongar, northeast of London (Section E). He kindly volunteered for the October posting to allow two Polish pilots, who were close friends, to remain together. The weather was influencing the air battle's intensity, however, there were still some moderate raids and night bombing, especially of London, was increasing. At 11.00am on October 29th, two enemy fighter 'Staffeln' (Squadrons) attacked our airspace; Spitfires fought them off. Concurrently a bomber 'Gruppe' attacked the Charing Cross Station area; Air Vice Marshal Keith Park, Commander-in-Chief of 11-Group, scrambled five squadrons of Spitfires and four of Hurricanes (including 46) in anticipation of a massed enemy attack. Heavy formations of bombers, with a cover of one hundred Messerschmitt Bf109s crossed the Kent coast at Deal.

In the scramble Bert was not flying his usual Hurricane: later saying it was like driving someone else's car. He roared down the runway and made precious height; 46 Squadron attacked the enemy at twenty-two thousand feet, with the Spitfires diving from 'out of the sun' at thirty thousand feet! A savage dogfight took place and the R.A.F. fighters were victorious, but both sides suffered significant losses. In the melee over Ashford in Kent, a Bf109 fighter pilot raked Bert's aircraft with cannon shells. His right leg received a mauling, his left leg lesser so! The aircraft trailed smoke and the cockpit burst into flames! After what must have felt perpetuity, he freed the jammed cockpit-hood, undid his straps and allowed the air pressure to suck him from the inferno while the Hurricane rolled onto its back and spiralled to earth. A pilot's worst nightmare is being cremated alive! From such a great height it takes a parachute some fifteen minutes to descend: an interminable time when so horrendously burnt, but his drop was watched over. Gwen: *"Although in great pain, my husband told me that he was aware of two Hurricanes circling and covering his descent, because during this period some of the enemy machine-gunned our pilots whilst parachuting."*

Bert's Hurricane crashed without causing harm at Hothfield Park near to Ashford. Meantime, Gwen had just arrived at home from teaching at Leicester. She was excited, it was half term and she was to travel to Abridge, a village near Stapleford Tawney, to see Bert. The couple had only been together for sixteen days since their marriage five months earlier. Gwen told me she was packing and humming merrily when the telephone rang: "*I was asked to travel to Ashford Hospital with all haste. I caught the earliest train from Coalville, changed at Leicester and London, and recall urging the train to travel faster. I took a taxi to the hospital and as soon as I saw my beloved I knew it was serious; his injuries were severe! I sat by his bedside and whispered to him that I would not leave his side. Bert's spirits were immediately raised and over several days he told me of the fateful action. I was by his side for virtually all that time: eating alongside him. He was on heavy morphine and sometimes rambled and often repeated: "The boys followed me down, Gwen, they followed me down!*"

The Coalville Times of 8th November 1940 stated that Sergeant Pilot H.E. Black was lying critically ill in hospital in the south of England, having been wounded in action. Gwen added that after a few days his right leg was completely amputated, and a day later most of the left. His facial skin was badly charred, apart from where his goggles and mask protected him, but still the doctor's prognosis was good. His sister, Maisie, visited him during this time, but couldn't stay for long because she was working in the post office. Gwen:

"*As Bert deteriorated he said he didn't want to live and felt that he would be a burden to me. I assured him that I would never, ever leave him. Gradually I watched him weaken: we shared some precious words until finally on November 9th, ten days since I arrived, he slipped away.*

*As he did so enemy bombers droned overhead and bombs exploded in the near distance, but I was unmoved and unconcerned. There were fifty raids whilst I was there. The people of Ashford couldn't have been kinder to me when they realised that my husband was a fighter-pilot: they held those boys in such high-esteem!*"

Gwen insisted that the authorities allow her to bury her husband at their home church. His body was transported by rail to Coalville Station, but en-route his carriage was wrongly shunted to a siding, and he arrived a day late. The funeral of November 13th was postponed for a day, and sadly, the employer's of Bert's half-brother, Norman, would not allow him to take another day off work, and so was absent from the service at St. Deny's Church, Ibstock. Five months earlier at this church Bert and Gwen had taken their marriage vows. Gwen:

"*There was an R. A. F. presence at the church and so many people, so much compassion, it really helped me a lot. I obtained some red roses: they signified my dear love and devotion. It was Remembrance Week and all around folk were wearing poppies. They were also recalling a loved and respected friend who attended their church.*"

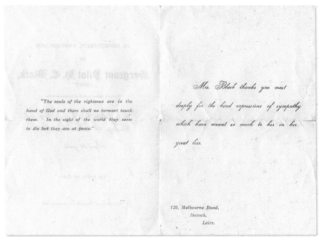

*The Memorial Service for Bert Black.*

The Coalville Times reported: '*Crowds of sympathisers lined the streets of Ibstock as the cortege wound its way to the Parish Church for the funeral. Many tributes were given to the former Scout Master and Leicestershire hockey player.*'

For a while Gwen was inconsolable, the couple

loved children and they'd planned to raise a family when the future was less uncertain.

Gwen and close friend, Frances (fiancée of Jim Bowler), shared the pain of losing loved ones.

The Coalville Times of 22nd November 1940 reported:

'The annual Remembrance Service was held on Sunday afternoon, when the church was packed. This service was also a funeral service in memory of Sergeant Pilot H.E. Black. Members of the Home Guard, ARP, WVS, British Legion, AFS and Girl Guides attended. Alderman J. T. Jacques and Mr. J. V. Measures read the lessons and Mr. J. H. Harratt (Commander of Ibstock Home Guard) read the names of the fallen from the last war. The Reverend M. R. Newberry gave the Service.'

A moment of cheer occurred for the Black family when in January 1941, Bert's sister, Maisie married William (Bill) Bancroft, son of Mr & Mrs J.W. Bancroft of Ravenstone. Steadily, Gwen improved and decided to continue with her teaching career, inwardly conscious that she would never marry again.

Norman Black at R.A.F. Cardington, near Bedford in 1944.

She devoted her life to caring and teaching school children, and became extremely successful, with several headships in her long career. Gwen displayed a warm facial glow as she spoke of her invitation to the unveiling of the 'Battle of Britain Memorial' by King George V1 at Westminster Abbey.

"I had a ticket indicating that I was a Battle of Britain widow. On arrival, two, yes two pilots escorted me to my pew so that I didn't walk alone. That, together with reading Shakespeare's

'We few, we happy few, we band of brothers', beneath the Memorial Window, reminded me of Bert's words: "They followed me down, Gwen!" From then on I knew I was not alone!"

Bert's grave and headstone in St. Deny's Church, Ibstock.

I mentioned that her husband's grave was very well cared for, and that poppies appear on 9th November (with others on Remembrance Day). I repeated that Bert is remembered all year round; she smiled and before leaving I spotted a familiar scene: a framed print of Eynsford village in Kent. Gwen said that Bert often flew over the village and thought that it looked so beautiful from the air. I replied that my wife and I know Eynsford well, and that it is just as heavenly at ground level. Gwen nodded: "You understand, Michael, don't you?" I smiled and felt good inside, saying that I'd keep in touch and visit often. The autumnal sun was still shining and the sky an azure blue, "Good flying weather," I quipped. "Michael, I still miss Bert terribly, but if he was destined to die in the war then he died as a result of doing a job he loved. I am very proud of him!"

I regularly visited Gwen; I arranged for her to become a non-paying member of the Battle of Britain Historical Society (B.O.B.H.S.), and published many

*St. Deny's church, Ibstock.*

*Gwen Black: the middle years.*

| R. ADCOCK. | C.E. BELCHER. | A.E. GIBSON. |
| A. ALLEN. | H.E. BLACK. | G.E. GREASLEY. |
| V. ARMSTON. | L. BURBANK. | E. J. GRAY. |
| R. BADCOCK. | A. COCKBURN. | I.W. HARVEY. |
| C.H. BAILESS. | A. COOPER. | G. HAWTIN. |
| R.H. BAILISS. | H. EGGINGTON. | R.J. HODSON. |
| E.A. BALL. | J.C. FINCH. | R.E. HOLLAND. |
| H. BARNEY. | H.A. FLETCHER. | T.T. HOPKINS. |
| | H.S. FLETCHER. | |

*Ibstock War Memorial. H.E. Black is remembered in the centre row.*

*Norman Black, Maisie and Gwen in 1984.*

an article to keep Bert's memory alive. She was delighted when I arranged for Air Commodore Peter Brothers, whom flew with Bert, to write how much he rated Bert's contribution to the war effort. Then, the B.O.B.H.S. was raising funds for a 'Monument for the Few' to be erected on the Victoria Embankment, London. I paid a subscription so that the name 'Herbert Black' could be engraved on that Monument. He and all other names of 'The Few' are etched in stone, and Prince Charles unveiled it in 2005. It is a superb and fitting Memorial to a Band of Brothers!

Gwendoline Annie Black became increasingly frail and entered Ashby Court Care Home at Ashby-de-la-Zouch: passing away on 28th July 2004. Theirs was a marriage arranged in heaven and are now together for eternity. God bless them both. This essay goes some way to ensure that Gwen's name is also remembered: a very dear and caring lady. I gave her a copy of my poem: 'The Fallen Few of 1940', signed by Peter Brothers, and said that from that date the poem would be dedicated to her husband. In 2006, my anthology entitled: 'Epitaph For The Few' was published and one of the poems was, of course, 'The Fallen Few of 1940', dedicated to Flight Sergeant H. Black.

## The Fallen Few of 1940

*We must n'er forget the fallen five hundred;*
*They sacrificed their young lives for you, you.*

*Leather jackets, fur-lined boots, scarves and goggles;*
*Afraid, yet in aerial combat they conquered fear, fear.*

*A fated sky aflame with wreckage and smoke-trails;*
*So sad is an arena of sky with touches of blue, blue.*

*'Neath green turf they lie or at rest on a Channel bed;*
*Always to remain in our memory so very dear, dear.*

*Gwen's niece, Eileen Hall, 2008*

*Gwen's brother, Harry Cuthbert and wife, 2008.*

The story doesn't end there. On Wednesday 15th October 2008, at The Dixie Grammar School, a special remembrance service was held for 'old boy' Bert. A plaque presented by the Battle of Britain Historical Society, was unveiled by Gwen's niece: Eileen Hall of Coalville, with headmaster John Wood and B.O.B.H.S. member, David Knight, flanking her. Physics teacher, Philip Hamson spoke many fine words honouring the

*From left: Sue Nicholls, Chris Nicholls, Ann with Alexander and Michael Nicholls.*

sergeant pilot, and the school's orchestra played military airs and hymns. Harry Cuthbert, who 'gave-away' Gwen on her wedding day said: *"Bert was a friendly, sociable, sporty young man; he was about five feet nine or ten and of medium build, and as far as alcohol was concerned he only enjoyed the odd pint of cider. My sister Dorothy married Norman Dunicliffe and had a son, John, and Marjorie married Brad Barnet and had Elaine."*

The Lord Lieutenant of Leicestershire was present, as were members of the school's Cadet Force, The Royal British Legion and Central News Television.

The letters sent by Bert to his cousin, Cyril Nicholls, are so precious.

Cyril married Madge: Winifred Madge Carter, who often spoke of Bert flying over his home and waggling his wings. Their eldest: Christopher is married to Susan while Michael is their other son. Bert's younger half-brother, Norman Black married and had two children. Norman passed away on 29th September 2006. Their daughter, and Bert's niece, Ann has two grown-up children: Emma and Ashley (with two children apiece). She also has a young son, Alexander. Bert's sister, Maisie, married Bill Bancroft who is now in his nineties and lives at Ibstock; Maisie passed away in August 1996. Their marriage was blessed by the birth of Margaret, who gave them grandchildren: Paul and Peter. Sadly, Margaret passed away in March 1994, aged just forty-seven years. Bill is now a great grandfather

Many thanks to all of the above mentioned folk who have contributed, particularly Ann.

*Gwen Black*

# JAMES BOWLER

*Jim Bowler at Sywell in October 1939.*

James (Jim) Bowler was the son of James and Laura Bowler of 100, Blackwood (Road), a pleasant location on the Charnwood side of Coalville. Born: 1920, and educated at Coalville Grammar School, he became a clerk at Cliff Hill Granite Quarry. He spent part of his life at the 'Bull's Head', an oak-beamed public house on the Charnwood heights in the miniscule hamlet of 'Abbot's Oak'. The lofty situation allows the hostelry to claim being the highest in the county. Jim, handsome, sociable and with a sense of humour, enjoyed bicycling along the undulating forest lanes, hike the meadowland, climb yon peaks, camp in woods and looked forward to an adventurous future. By 1938 a 'certain girlfriend' was very much on his mind. Jim was friendly with Bert Black; the latter enlisted into the R. A.F.V.R. in 1937, and raved about the joys of flight. Bert's girlfriend, Gwen Cuthbert, had studied to become a teacher, and her friend, Frances, followed the same route.

Frances: born 1921, from Ibstock, was Jim's 'certain girlfriend'.

In 1939, Jim volunteered for aircrew service with the R.A.F. He was accepted and ordered to take the train to Sywell, an aerodrome six kilometres northeast of Northampton. On the same course were two well-known brothers, Les and Peter Ball, both friends of Jim from grammar school days. All three passed the course. In March 1940, he was posted to No8 F.T.S (Flying Training School) Montrose on Scotland's northeast coast, and then from July- September to No 20 (O.T.U.) Lossiemouth, up on the Moray Firth to refine his piloting skills. Frances:

*"From the earliest Jim fancied being a bomber pilot, sharing the aeroplane with a crew. The R.A.F. could tell which men were most suitable for fighters or bombers. He was so happy with his silver wings and during his postings always sent me a regular supply of letters; he loved writing. We had several days together in late June: we were very much in love, and Vera Lynn was singing her enchanting: 'We'll Meet Again!'"*

Before his posting to Newmarket in Suffolk, the devoted couple announced their engagement.

Sergeant pilot James Bowler joined 99 Squadron, equipped with Vickers' 'Wellington' Mk1c twin-engined long-range bombers with Bristol Pegasus engines: his aircraft: R3167. To write that this posting could be dangerous would be an understatement! The aircraft's maximum speed was two hundred-fifty mph and cruised at two hundred thirty-two mph; the power operated nose and tail gun turrets offered some protection against the enemy fighters. Jim wrote to Frances from Newmarket on **Tuesday 24th September 1940:**

*'This is more or less to tell you of a major flying episode! No doubt you have heard on the wireless today about the biggest raid of the war upon Berlin last night. We were there, dropping 500lb bombs and a six-hour delayed one, at one o'clock this morning: we left at 9.30pm last night and landed at 5 o'clock this morning to the accompaniment of German bombs dropping around the aerodrome! So while you were asleep (presumably) darling, we were trekking 1,200 miles or more to Berlin and back. We're now working fine as a crew, Frank Swalton and we five pals. Ted, the navigator took us dead on to Berlin over cloud, and Jake Linton, the wireless operator- he's only nineteen- gets us home like a veteran on the radio. I'm*

Hut band: Jim on the rear right. Montrose, April 1940.

The gang at Arbroath Abbey. June 1940.

hoping to become captain after about five more trips; it all depends on the report that Frank gives the CO when he is due for his rest. We bombed Berlin from about 13,000 feet. There were flares from other kites all over the place, scores of them on the job, and coming out we were chased by two fighters, but managed to keep them off and got rid of them.

The temperature was minus 10 degrees and I was thankful for my Irvin-suit: fur lined jacket and trousers

(£24 a time). You'll guess that I am pretty tired after only three hours sleep, but I'm dosing down early tonight and everyone has all day off tomorrow. I asked to go home for a day but it was impossible, worst luck, and I'll just have to wait for ordinary leave.'

On **Monday 30th September 1940:**

'Darling, on Saturday night we went to Hanau, near Frankfurt in the Ruhr, to bomb a munitions factory. The trip was about 900 miles. We were up from

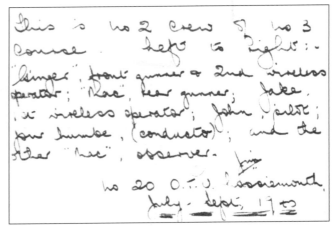

Left: 'Ginger' Dick, Ali MacNab, Jake Linton, John Pascoe, Jim Bowler and J. McKinley. July-September 1940 at Lossiemouth.

Postcard telling of the kites they fly!

Sergeant Pilot Frank Swalton.

10.30 pm to 4.30am Sunday, and landed in semi-fog. I was almost too tired to eat my meal when we landed!

Next trip you will be crossing off the teens darling, and before you know it you'll be off double figures and onto singles. We aren't operating so often just at present, there's no moon out. We may be billeted in big houses in the town before long, we flying crews, although I'd rather be where I am for the winter.

Frank had to make a press statement about our trip to Hanau, and though I didn't hear it I'm told that it was given out on the wireless. He seems to think we're pretty good for a fairly new crew throughout, particularly as both Mac, Jim Mackinley and 'Ginger' Dick, the gunners, never make a murmur when Ack-Ack is bursting all around us. Jake, our 19-year-old wireless operator, makes us really proud of him; he sets courses home and whatever we ask him for, like a veteran; and all the way out he listens in to German transmitters and checks up on our position. Ted (I might as well mention everyone) navigates us fine and bombs well, so we're happy all round. We were fired at all the way to Hanau and back, especially over Cologne coming back, so I had plenty of practise jinking. That was Frank's 23 trip. He wants to stay on operations rather than going to an OUT, thinks it's an easier life!

*Frances and Jim in June 1940.*    *Frances and Jim in September 1940.*

*P.S. I realised an ambition last Friday, to fly a Wimpy (Wellington) as me the only pilot on board. I went to Mildenhall to fetch our new aeroplane, 'B' for Berty, on my own. I flew back with 12 passengers on board: 4 officers and 8 airmen. Felt like an airliner pilot! Bragger.*

Flight Sergeant Frank Swalton, of Collyweston near Grantham, was an experienced pre-war pilot; it was usual to accompany a novice on early flights to offer reassurance. Frances:

*"On one occasion I caught the train to Newmarket. I stayed in a small guesthouse close to where Jim was based. We chatted about old times and our future life while leaning on a little bridge. It was a lovely week but I shed more than a few tears on leaving!"*

Trips were thick and fast. Jim wrote that he went to Berlin on Friday night, 4th October 1940, ominously stating that it was *'bad over there, caught in searchlights with 'Berty' taking fifteen hits to the body'*. He wrote: *'On Monday night, October 7th, we flew to Boulogne.'* He joked that when he returned from France (*at 10.00pm a nice change*), but said the weather was filthy, and that his aircraft was the only one in the squadron to get through and bomb the target. On **Thursday 31st October 1940** he writes:

*'We were up at the house when some 'flying pencils' (Dorniers) made a daylight attack on the aerodrome, so we naturally dashed out to watch the fun and games. When we saw their machine-gunners firing tracer bullets all over the show, and heard them falling on the*

*Alistair MacNab; rear gunner.*    *'Ginger' Dick; front gunner, aged nineteen.*    *Roy Gordon.*

'B' for Betty at Newmarket.

'B' for Betty ground crew.

road, we started sheltering against a wall, dashing from one side to the other like idiots! We were down by it when one of them dropped a big stick of bombs quite close to us, so we promptly raced across a boneyard and some fields to see if we could be of any help: no-one was hurt, though two houses had very close shaves. One of the bombs fell about 20 yards from that little stone bridge we used to go to, in the middle of the road! Some of the bombs hit the aerodrome and one of the bombs made an enormous crater smack in the middle of the racecourse: in front of the grandstand! There was racing here yesterday on the other course, so we went to watch and saw Gordon Richards win the Cesarewitch. He is a jockey, not a horse, if you have heard of him, and he wasn't doing the running himself either (that's beaten you to it!) It's a queer game, the horses dash around a track miles away and all you see of them is when they come up to finish past the stands. Mad, I call it! You should hear the bookmakers shouting one another down with the odds they're offering, just like Coalville market! Will break, wardens are bawling outside about our blackout.'

Jim piloting' B' for Betty. Taken by the co-pilot.

On **Sunday, 10th November 1940**, he is more reflective in his attitude towards the war: 'Yesterday we had a little minor excitement after hearing Jerry overhead during the afternoon. He started dropping bombs by guesswork though the clouds, and they were quite near too, so we bolted down to the air-raid shelters for half an hour. He must have been scared to come down below the clouds. When the squadron operated last Friday night they were after cellar at Munich where Hitler was supposed to be having a big pow-pow.

Fletcher and his crew didn't come back, but don't worry they only ran out of petrol and went down in the sea near Hastings. Coastal Command picked them up all sound and safe; we're expecting to see them tomorrow. Hope my last letter didn't make you feel dismal, darling. I don't know what was biting me when I wrote it, I'm sure. I love you just as much as ever, but sometimes the war makes everything seem so unreal compared with peacetime days, with hardly ever seeing you at all, and I all have to represent you are letters. I suppose when it's all over I shall be able to settle my mind properly once more and my life will revolve around you, instead of around you and aeroplanes and bombs as it is doing at the moment. May the time soon come when I shall have something better to do in my life than destroy things, though I don't mind in the least destroying what we are fighting against. I think I told you that now there's only Mac, Ginger and me left of the original No2 crew of Lossiemouth. All being well John, Ted and Jake will be by the Mediterranean Sea by the time the week is out. Our new navigator seems like a good lad, but I'm not very keen on the wireless operator. He may be OK but if he isn't we'll soon have him swapped."

Bombs exploding in the distance during a raid on enemy territory, 1940.

Other bombs exploding.

On **14th November 1940,** he lets slip information that Frances had already told me. Frances:
*"Without any senior personnel knowing, Jim managed to slip me into a Wellington bomber and I had quite a flight. Very exciting, I had better not say any more, but it is true."*

Jim's letter:

*'B' for 'Berty'*(R 3167) *has not yet been over your place* (Ibstock) *and the one you flew in never will either! Last night we went to Berlin again for the third time. All was fine going out and over the target but coming back we ran into snow and had to fly blind. However we found our coast OK and set course for home, still in snow, and then ran into a lot of static electricity which made the front guns and propellers go blue and look weird and threw the instruments haywire, finally burning the wireless set. We got completely lost, but eventually came to what seemed a very big place and looked round low, hoping to see an aerodrome. To cut a long story short we were on our last drop of petrol and all had to do the wisest thing possible, leave the machine by parachute. I was in the seat at the time and wanted Frank to go first, but as captain he naturally insisted on being last, and persuaded me to set an example to the others. We all went through the bottom door by which you entered, and went out at 3,000 feet into the snow clouds, and gosh what a queer sensation it was. This was at 1.10am this morning, after 8 ½ hours in the air. I just dived through and got clear of the machine, pulled the ripcord and in a second or two got a terrific jolt, then was swinging down in dead silence through snow. I didn't see the ground until about 200 feet up, and a few seconds later landed on my back with a terrific bang, seeing stars, and the next thing I knew was being dragged across the field I landed in at about 20mph*

*and helpless to stop myself. Finally the silk hit a hedge and I was shot head first into it. Then I detached the silk, was violently sick (shame) and staggered into some one's back garden where I could get no answer to my knocks. Sorry darling, but I just can't carry on tonight. I feel ill and pretty well all-in. I'll carry on tomorrow.*

### Friday 15th November 1940.

*Well, I feel a lot better now after a normal night's sleep. To continue the narrative, I staggered on a little further, knocked at another house and stood waiting in the snow, listening to a dog barking inside. Then a quavering female voice asked who was there. I told her that I felt very ill and was in a shocking state, but she wouldn't trust me and wouldn't let me in, so I thanked her for her hospitality and staggered further on to a pillbox at the side of the road where there were soldiers. After making sure who I was, they phoned the commanding officer at Heston aerodrome, half a mile away, and he fetched me in his car and put me to bed in his pyjamas. So, we're in London!* (Heston is four kilometres southwest of Ealing.) *He was a fine fellow and took everything out of my hands and within half an hour I knew all the others were safe, though we were spread over 10 miles.*

*'B' for 'Berty' had hit a house in Hampton Court and was burnt out. Two people in the house had a miraculous escape. Mac and I have been to see the wreck and ruins, yesterday. I've never been so pleased in all of my life as I was when I knew everyone was safe. Mac landed on the edge of a gravel pit full of water at Hounslow and just missed drowning; Frank landed in a garden near the house; our new wireless-op landed in a road; our new navigator landed on the hospital he's in, walked off the roof and sprained his ankle. But we got the biggest laugh over Ginger, he*

landed in a tree in Hounslow military barracks, and hung there for two hours in the snow! He bawled out for help, a soldier thought he was a Jerry and called out the guard. First they fetched out a ladder, which was too short, and the next thing Ginger heard was the Fire Brigade clanging its bell, and finally they got him down a fire escape and he spent the night in a hospital there. We got back here last night in two staff cars sent down for us, and in the morning we're fetching a brand new 'B' for 'Berty' over and I hope she lasts a long time. I'm OK now apart from bruises and a stiff neck and shoulders.

P.S. I'm not in the least superstitious but it's interesting to know it was my 13th operation, on the 13th of the month!'

The exchange of letters continued and after the shock of losing his aircraft and suffering from slight concussion, Jim appeared to take on a new lease of life.

**Tuesday 19th November 1940.**

'I suppose this will sound rather a tame letter after the last. Hope you were thrilled because I can assure you that I was when it all happened. We've been interviewed quite a lot by the 'big boys' of the R.A.F. and told them what we did. They were all delighted to know that we were all safe and didn't care a toss what happened to the machine. You should see the new 'B' for 'Berty', which we have now, the other was a 1c, but this one is the very latest, 1d with two extra guns just in case they are needed. We should have operated in her tonight, but the wireless wasn't quite ready so we were scrubbed. Our crew are now members of the 'Caterpillar Club'. There are no membership privileges: membership means that you have saved your life by parachute. We shall have a little solid gold caterpillar brooch with our names on from the Irvin Parachute Co. The idea of a caterpillar comes from the silkworm caterpillar 'whose life hangs by a golden thread', as they put it.'

### On **Sunday 24th November 1940**:

"We took new 'Berty' on her maiden operation on Friday night and should have gone to the Rhine, Germany, but Mac had some trouble with the rear gun turret just after take off. Rather than go through enemy fighter zones we went to Ostend and bombed the docks there. Our substitute navigator was a young pilot officer on his first trip, about 6 feet 7 inches tall, but he did some wizard bomb aiming and we started some

glorious fires with incendiaries. When the navigator moved past me to do his bombing I saw his head go past and looked down two minutes later and saw his legs just moving after him. True!

In contrast to the previous trip there was not a cloud between the earth and the moon, beyond that I can't vouch for, and everything went perfectly. Hardly half a dozen shots were fired at us, not many searchlights were out, and the moon lit up the target like daytime. I said we went on Friday night; actually we took off at 3.00am on Saturday morning and landed at 6.00am.

Frank has been selected to represent the squadron by his looks and has got to go to sit for an oil painting for the Air Ministry. You should hear what he is saying about it. Quite a good choice, I think, don't you?

I'm going to write a letter to the parachute firm after this to get our little gold caterpillars I mentioned. Ginger is dying to get his; he really is an excitable sort of lad. Our navigator who was hurt has returned to us today. He's hopping about with a stick and has one foot and ankle in Plaster of Paris. He seemed pretty shaken, too, by his experience. He told me he was as sick as a dog over his navigation table after I told him to put on his parachute and take off his flying helmet. Poor little blighter, no doubt he will be going on a long leave. I almost wish I had broken a leg! Some dirty 'souvenir hunters' at the hospital in which he has been taken have stolen half his clothes, all his money, his watch and his flying boots.

Well darling, once this month is over, and that won't be long, it will soon come round to Christmas. It would be marvellous if it happened, but I'm afraid it's not even worth hoping I shall be at home for it. That glorious week we had together here might have happened a year ago, so long does it seem since I last saw you. However, it should be our ordinary turn soon, and on that reassuring note I think I may as well close down for tonight. Cheerio, dearest, write as often and as much as you can. Your *ever adoring, Jim.*'

All of Jim's letters carry cross-kisses, this one carried twenty-three, the most! At 11.00pm, Monday, 25th November 1940, 'B' for 'Berty' raced down Newmarket runway and took to the stars, circuiting to await the remainder of 99 Squadron. They had been briefed beforehand to expect a lot of Ack-Ack over their target, Kiel, a port on the Baltic Sea in Schleswig

*Jim Bowler in June 1940.*

Frances (then Davies) was widowed for a second time in the early 1990s. She was living on Valley Road, Ibstock and the last time I saw her she was in poor health. Frances:

*"I did marry later on and I was very happy. I have wonderful children and grandchildren, but you can never forget your first love and you never lose that feeling of being left behind. After Jim went, I often thought that he might have been captured and put in some POW camp. I still miss him dearly, you never forget!"*

Jim, handsome, sociable and with a sense of humour, enjoyed bicycling along the undulating forest lanes, hike the meadowland, climb yon peaks, camp in woods and looked forward to an adventurous future. By 1938 a 'certain girlfriend' was very much on his mind.

Frances was Jim's 'certain girlfriend'.

Rest in peace.

Holstein, northern Germany. 'Berty' gained height, the moon was waxing; the navigator was busily checking his course and speaking by intercom to Jim, who acknowledged. Ginger checked his forward-guns with a short burst, as did Ali MacNab in the rear. Time dragged: then over the target at sixteen thousand feet; finger searchlights beamed with great intensity; anti-aircraft guns filled the sky with exploding shells! The bomb-aimer called to Jim: *"Steady, steady, left a bit, steady, bombs gone."* 'Berty' climbed as the bombs lightened the aircraft then a sickening roar from the starboard engine! Jim instantly put the aircraft into a shallow dive to fan out the fire, and headed north towards the North Sea and hopefully escape the coning searchlights and the biting flack.

The raid was a success, with 'B' for 'Berty' successfully dropping bombs on warehouses, petroleum tanks, railways networks and shipping at Germany's vitally important port.

Wellington bomber 'B' for 'Berty' (R1176) was last seen in a blazing vertical dive, plunging into the sea several miles off the German coastline. No survivors. Only the dear memories of loved ones survived.

# ANNE & TOM BRADSHAW

*Seated are Anne's parents William Ranyard and Florence Cooke. Her Grandfather, William Cooke is on the rear right. 1922.*

I had just completed a presentation regarding: 'Local Heroes', when I enquired if anyone in the audience had served in the Auxiliary Territorial Service in World War 2. I was compiling this book and felt more female accounts were essential to display the excellent role they had performed. Anne nodded but said she was a Yorkshire lass, but had lived in Leicestershire for over fifty years. I said she could just about claim to be a native of these parts, and am I pleased because the following essay is breathtaking.

**Anne's** storyline starts with some of her prose, it reveals a lot:

*What is love that it should be as changeable as the weather?*

*Is it joy or is it pain, or is it both together?*

Anne's mother, Florence, was born at Sheffield in 1896, the second child of William and Emily Cooke; first born was Willy and the third, James, died aged two in a motor accident. William was employed as a council-bailiff, with Emily a nurse. When Florence was eighteen years she met James Hull, and they married in early 1914: with both families disapproving. Five months later, James (Jim) was born and in 1917 a daughter, Audrey. In 1918, the family hoped to dispel all of the War's sad tidings, but in 1919, thirty-two years old James Hull died in the influenza pandemic. Florence was still estranged from her husband's parents, but her parents had accepted the situation and helped: two young children and no income! Sadly, in 1920, six years old Jim ran-off to his elderly paternal grandparents, and they arranged for two aunties to care for him. Subsequently he passed a teaching certificate and a doctorate in psychology from Manchester University. In 1962, married with a son, and suffering from a lung complaint, he was advised to live in Switzerland where the air could ease his condition. Before leaving he met his mother for the first time in forty-two years. He taught English language and never returned to England, dying at eighty-seven years of age.

Florence, at first heartbroken by Jim's departure, joined 'Robert Brothers', a departmental store in Sheffield, first as an assistant and then a buyer in the soft furnishing department.

Anne's father, William Ranyard, was born near to Boston, Lincolnshire on 11th October 1894: one of five children. His father, William (senior): a farm labourer, and mother, Charlotte, wanted a better life and so moved to Sheffield. Tetley's Brewery hired him as a drayman: a team of horses pulled his cart as he delivered barrels of ale to public houses and hostelries. His household adhered to the strict Anglican values of hard-work and clean living; he played the Church organ and Charlotte was a Sunday school teacher. Not atypically, their strong-willed son rebelled to the lifestyle, and in 1915, he volunteered for Kitchener's Army. He joined the Transport Corps, becoming a driver/mechanic: honing his skills on a variety of vehicles on the Western Front. His three sisters often wrote to him (he was their hero) and kept his return letters for over fifty years.

Discharged in 1919, William returned to Sheffield and quickly used his skills to obtain the position of chauffeur to steel magnate: Mr. Robson. He met Florence Hull (nee Cooke) in 1921, romance blossomed, and they married on 2nd January 1922, living in Duncan Road, Crookes: Sheffield. His family was disgruntled, with plainly dressed sisters perhaps jealous of his wife's fashionable clothes and adoption of five years old Audrey (Hull). This was the environment that Anne was born into on 27th January 1926; also she contracted scarlet fever and diphtheria within the first four years of her life. In 1933 a brother, Ted, was born.

Her father worked long hours in establishing his own garage, and the family lived in eight different houses around Sheffield.

In the 1930s, Audrey attended a commercial college and was employed in a secretarial job in the city centre, while her mother's health was poor. Anne recalls:

*"It did not mean much to me when people spoke of war clouds gathering, I was more worried about mother's health. Father worked long hours, by then he had a large garage with a petrol forecourt, three mechanics, and a secretary running his office. Soon the secretary was to ruin my father's life and ended with my parent's divorcing."*

Ted started to school and became a handful, too much so for Florence's poor health and she reluctantly allowed her husband's sister, Charlotte, to bring him up: he never saw his mother again, with history repeating itself. Anne:

*"Just after the war started, Audrey joined the Women's Auxiliary Air Force (W. A.A. F.), and I felt that my family had fallen apart. On 21st June 1941 she married a rear-gunner who had many trips over enemy occupied Europe with Bomber Command and was fortunate to survive.*

*I tried to visit Ted, but it made him unsettled, and so I was asked not to visit again. Years later I heard that they feared I might persuade him to return to our mother, and father very much wanted him under his wing."*

Life was difficult for Florence; in quick succession she'd lost her husband, son and home (in her husband's name). Florence and daughter, Anne, returned to a three-story house at Crookes, but events continued to conspire against her! Anne:

*"I was a film buff and loved watching young stars like Mickey Rooney and Judy Garland, and often stayed in the cinema to watch the film for a second time. One afternoon in December 1940, while watching Judy Garland in: 'The Wizard of Oz' the air-raid sirens started. We were advised to proceed to the*

Anne, Ted and Audrey Ranyard. Christmas, 1940. Anne has written: 'To Daddy with love'.

*shelters but if you wished to stop the film continued; I liked the escapism and so stopped, coming out in the dark, with no trams, no buses. It took me fifteen minutes to walk home in total darkness; it would not be safe to do so today. I arrived to find my home had been reduced to rubble, together with many others! I must have been in shock, just thirteen years old and I cannot recall what happened next, but remember being told that mother was in hospital."*

Anne received no help from her grandparents and so sought her father. He just sent her to various friends, the last being a retired business colleague, Mr. McDonald. He decided to move with his wife, and Anne, to his brother's farm at Thorpe Arch, near Wetherby, twenty kilometres (twelve miles) northeast of Leeds, Yorkshire.

*"It was one of the happiest periods of my life. Mrs. McDonald was like a mother: teaching me to cook, make butter and jam, to sew (in later life it framed my career), etc. With living on a farm we had no food shortages, as we had in Sheffield, and living in the countryside was far safer from air raids. One night I was taken to a barn where I held a lantern as a foal was born, it was magical. I was asked to name her, and on looking to the stars I instantly decided to name her: 'Starlight'. I also bottle-fed an orphan lamb that I called: 'Bunny'. Mrs. McDonald encouraged me to travel into Wetherby to meet other young people, I recall the film: 'Dangerous Moonlight', it was enthralling. I went dancing at the Masonic Hall and walked the three miles back to the farm: never any danger in 1942/3. The McDonalds had to move when I was seventeen, and so I decided that rather than wait to be called-up, and perhaps work in a munitions factory and have my skin turn yellow, as with some local girls, I would join the Auxiliary Territorial*

*Service (A. T. S.). On 31st December 1943 I reported to Pontefract Barracks, twenty kilometres (twelve miles) southeast of Leeds for six weeks of basic training: service number W/293532. We had to drill every morning and the weather was bitterly cold, but I loved every minute of army life; having to keep myself smart and to accept discipline was just what I needed at that time. I met Anne Sherry (a friend for life) and we had lots of fun together."*

*Anne Bradshaw, aged eighteen years,*

When the time came for Anne to decide which A.T.S. branch to follow it took little deciding: 'The Transport Corps', remembering details from her father's garage and the workings of farm tractors. Anne went to the Central Driving School at Camberley for intensive training, not just in driving but also for vehicle maintenance. Passing out she was posted to Worksop, twenty-five kilometres (sixteen miles) southeast of Sheffield.

*"There was a fleet of lorries, I drove a three ton Bedford lorry transporting ammunition from storage bays in Sherwood Forest to Edwinstowe Railway Station. Italian prisoners-of-war did the heavy lifting and we worked long hours, but the comradeship was wonderful and the discipline sharp.*

*Anne Bradshaw, aged nineteen years,*

*We had to be at base by 22.00 hours with one late pass a week until 23.30, and if we were late we were up before the duty officer!"*

Anne says that in the early stages some of the ammunition went to Quorn/Woodhouse Station for storage in Charnwood Forest, and that it became obvious that the amount sent to the south coast meant something was imminent: it was: 'D'-Day, 6th June 1944!

*"Our social life was good, a lot of time was spent in the N.A.A.F.I. but we also went into pubs and had many a sing song around a piano (my first time was in 1944). We had ten shillings a week (fifty new pence), and having to be back at base for ten was fair because roll call was at 06.30 and duty started at 07.00. In winter weather it took us longer to get started, but father tipped me to grease the stops after draining the night before (no anti-freeze), also fill the radiators, crank start the engines (no starter motor/heavy going). At 07.30 we picked-up the Italian labourers from their P.O.W. camp and drove into the Forest. We took packed rations with us, they had little taste, but no worse than the stodgy food we had to eat from our cookhouse; I think the Italians received better food than us!"*

Anne had an opportunity to drive her lorry into Sheffield and decided to stop at her father's garage. He was amazed that she could control such a large vehicle, and pleasingly took her address and said that he would write. Several months later she received a letter inviting her to his wedding to secretary, Mary Hodkin, twenty years his junior. Anne accepted: she dearly longed to see her brother, Ted, who was then thirteen years old. Three years later, Ted joined the Royal Navy and had a very successful career. They wrote but it was thirteen years before they met again.

*"I was at Worksop when the war ended: tears of joy, great excitement and celebrations. Many girls were posted elsewhere but I volunteered for overseas service; it was agreed but I would have to wait for one year. I was posted to York, and then to Beverley on detachment as a staff car driver. On a daily basis I drove, in a small private utility car, my commanding officer to a transit camp at Hull; during the day I was the only female with four hundred men! In the evenings I had the use of the car. While at Hull I'd do maintenance work on the car: wearing overalls and army boots while greasing the underside of the car, etc. I was under the car when I felt a kick and a voice told me to get on parade; the duty sergeant had mistaken me for a soldier. When he saw me he was speechless, the date was 27th September 1945. It was his birthday, and he must have thought I was a present, his name, Tom Bradshaw. I had never met anyone like him before; he was a great storyteller, some sad, some hilarious, but after a difficult period as a German prisoner-of-war was a little tentative regarding a relationship. He had a deep religious conviction that helped him survive the war, and I admired and respected him, we just enjoyed our time together. When I was posted back to York we met at weekends, but then in April 1945, and with mixed feelings, my posting for overseas came up. Tom was demobbed in May and returned to Northumberland and I was posted to Bad Salzuflen and Bad Oyenhausen in Germany, the headquarters of the British Army of the Rhine; could there be any future for us together?"*

Anne says that Germany was in a terrible state with extensive bomb damage, and could not believe that families were living in houses fit only for demolishion. Being in Germany was not easy for Anne; she had fallen in love with Tom, and was delighted on being posted to an administration position at London to await demobilisation. Whilst there she heard of a scheme to retrain ex-service people, and so took the opportunity to enrol for a course at Newcastle-Upon-Tyne: near to Tom.

*"I caught the Newcastle train and on arrival I saw Tom waiting for me, as arranged, under the clock. It was very emotional and Tom asked me there and then to marry me; I blubbered something like: 'all in good time we have so much to talk about!' The date, 24th February 1947, and the weather was very cold."*

Anne stayed at Newcastle's Young Women's Christian Association (Y.W.C.A.) and studied tailoring and dress making: teacher training optional.

At weekends, Tom attended Rutherford College to attain a surveyor's certificate in mining; he lived at New Hartley: twenty kilometres to the northeast, and involved a bus journey. They were separated for quite a time because the winter of 1947 saw heavy snow, but they later spent precious moments together, and arranged their marriage for 24th January 1948.

*"I wrote to father to invite him but received no reply; after a lot of detective work I located mother at Totley, Sheffield. She had remarried a man twenty years her junior, our meeting was emotional and she willingly agreed to attend my wedding."*

With no houses to rent they lived with Tom's mother: Elizabeth Bradshaw and hoped a colliery house would become available. They married at New Hartley's Roman Catholic Church, and A.T.S. friend, Anne Sherry was one of the bridesmaids; Ted Charlton: best man.

*"At the reception a waitress said a gentleman was waiting outside to see me; it was my father, but when he saw my mother he stormed out and I didn't see him again for fifteen years. Tom and I had a decade of happiness in that small mining village, everyone knew everyone else, but I was told that women were expected to be homemakers: husbands went out to work. In summers Tom played cricket and I helped with the teas; winters saw him playing football and I washed the kit: and we were big Newcastle United fans. I threw myself into my hobby, sewing, and volunteered to teach girls my skills at their Youth Club."*

While at Elizabeth's house it became apparent she was ill; she'd had a hard life, widowed, brought-up two children of her own and six stepchildren, and more! Anne had a great respect for her Christian beliefs and nursed her until she died on 30th January 1950, aged

Audrey Ranyard weds Sgt. Brian O'Connor.

Audrey and Brian cut the cake.

sixty-six years. Tom inherited the house: an elder brother had died at seventeen.

*"We had three children, the first was Barbara, then Stephen and finally Susan in 1955. The local collieries were being run down and so Tom looked elsewhere; in 1957 he accepted the post of a planning engineer for the East Midland's Coalfields."*

At first they lived at Whitwick but eventually settled in a bungalow on the lower slopes of the Charnwood Hills, near Coalville. The children were growing-up and Anne began studying at the local college, obtaining various certificates in dressmaking, teaching, etc, and taught art at various schools. The larger family was also doing well. Barbara, a successful fashion model had toured the world with her job, married Malcolm in 1976 and gave birth to Nolan, Edward, Sarah and Kate over a fourteen-year period. Stephen married and had five children, Paul, Claire, Laura, Emily and Edward. Susan married Jerry and had two children, Nicola and Bradley. Anne's elder sister, Audrey served with the W.A.A.F's from 1939-45, becoming a sergeant. She married Brian O'Connor on 21st May 1941. Brian was in R.A.F. Bomber Command and flew many missions over enemy territory: suffering with his nerves after the war. After the war they lived in India, having three children: Michael (now in Holland), Robert (living with his wife and Family at Felixstowe) and Christopher (living in Australia).

Brian O'Connor became an executive with an oil company and all three sons were sent to Taunton Boarding School for their education. Audrey used to travel to England and stay with friends or bed and breakfast to visit them; she now lives in Felixstowe. (See photo).

Anne's younger brother, Ted, and his wife live in New Zealand.

**Tom** (Thomas Bryan) was born on 27th September 1918 at New Hartley, a village that lived neath two giant shadows of grief. First, back in 1862, it lost an entire generation of men-folk when one hundred and ninety-nine fathers and sons died in the 'Hartley Mining Disaster'. They were entombed at their place of work: Hester Pit; a fallen beam blocked their exit and for five days the nation held its breath as relief teams tried to reach them. All of their number was found dead in the pit, it was likened to a 'vast Golgotha'. Secondly, the Great War had just finished and many locals failed to return from fighting for King and Country.

In 1909, Tom's future father, Michael Bradshaw, was left a widower (from Hannah) with six children ageing from two to fifteen. He asked the local church for assistance, and as a result Elizabeth Tivenan arrived as a live-in housekeeper. Born in 1884 at nearby Sunderland, she was an assistant teacher at a convent.

Living conditions for the village community were frugal: two bed-roomed colliery cottages, shared outside earth-toilets, no bathrooms: only a zinc bath in front of an open fire, and only women did the household chores. When the men finished their shift they came home in a filthy state; wives would 'dad' (beat) the dusty clothes and prepare the food on an open fire range. After three years Michael and Elizabeth married and their first-born was Joseph in 1914. Later that year, Michael's eldest son, John, joined the Royal Navy Reserve, and Michael enlisted into the Northumberland Fusiliers, leaving his wife alone with baby Joseph and five stepchildren. Times were hard, but she had a religious determination and a deep faith.

On 9th July 1917, Stoker John Bradshaw, service number 7835S, and twenty-one years, died when: H.M.S. 'Vanguard' was torpedoed in Scapa Flow,

*Elizabeth Bradshaw with her husband, Michael in uniform, with seaman, John and baby, Joseph, Agnes and Richard. Circa 1916.*

Orkney Island, Scotland. He is remembered with honour on the Chatham Naval Memorial. Devastatingly, Private Michael Bradshaw, service number 340225, of the 22nd Tyneside Scottish Battalion, Northumberland Fusiliers, died on 22nd March 1918. He is listed, with honour, on the Arras Memorial, France.

*Tom Bradshaw, aged twelve years, is seated on the middle row, second from the right. A league-winning season 1926/7.*

Elizabeth was one month pregnant when she lost her husband: Tom was born in September 1918 and so

he never met his father! She was left with seven children to feed and care for, fortunately the older boys: Austin, Owen, Michael, and Dick were soon to leave school and earn wages from the colliery.

The General Strike of 1926 and the Thirties' Depression produced desperate times, almost inconceivable to present day folk, but Elizabeth insisted on the family attending Sunday Mass and somehow they survived. Austin married Annie and lived at Seaton Sluice, having three children, John, Owen and Colin. Owen married an elder lady, Nellie, and ran the King's Arms at Cowpen; Nellie died in 1970 and Owen in 1976. Dick moved to London, joined the Royal Navy, married Irish girl, Kathleen, and later worked on the railways. He died in 1965.

In 1931, in the cruellest of circumstances, Elizabeth's eldest son, Joseph, suffered kidney damage when a fairground swing hit his back. He suffered for a year but died aged seventeen years in 1931. He'd passed for Morpeth Grammar School but funds disallowed this; Joe was also a brilliant footballer.

Her second son, Tom was called-up into the Army on 15th February 1940, service number: 4459703, and posted to the 6th (Territorial) Battalion of the Durham Light Infantry. In early 1941, while based at Cullumpton, Devon, and engaged in military exercises on nearby Dartmoor, he heard that the youngest of his father's siblings, his stepsister, Agnes, had died from kidney failure. He received a few days compassionate leave to attend the funeral, but had to take his full kit with him in the event of embarkation. Agnes' husband, Arthur Watkins, asked his mother-in-law to care for children: Bill, three years and Joe, three months; Elizabeth obliged and so brought-up a total of ten children, without complaint, little money or masculine support. Anne: *"Mother-in-law seldom had new clothes, never, ever had a holiday; her life revolved around New Hartley's 'Our Lady and St. Joseph Church', and her family."*

*Tom Bradshaw of the Durham Light Infantry.*

On 21st May 1941, Tom sailed from Liverpool, and Anne can recall that many years later they stopped for a short time at Durban, South Africa. Anne:

*"He loved the ocean voyage and decided that one day he would repeat the journey in happier circumstances. We did so together about forty years afterwards."*

Tom's Army records shows that he spent approximately four months in Cyprus, three weeks in Palestine, three months in Iraq and five months in Egypt/ Libya with the Durham Light Infantry, part of the Eighth Army: the 'Desert Rats'. See *'A Dedication to the Desert Rats'* within this book but briefly: General Rommel, on 26th May 1942, after Stuka dive-bombing British positions launched a major offensive in Libya to capture Bir Hakeim, on the southern end of a British minefield. He sent his Afrika Korps to bite into the British positions while also making a holding attack from south of Gazala to the Trigh Capozzo. Rommel's objective was Tobruk; the battle raged for several days until his attack was repulsed with heavy loses.

The 'Battle of the Minefields' frothed into June, with success following failure for both sides; mighty tank battles took place. On June 17th, after four days of fighting, General Ritchie withdrew his forces to the Egyptian frontier while Rommel manoeuvred the main thrust of his attack towards Tobruk, which fell four

days later after desperate fighting and air-attacks. Thirty three thousand British and South African prisoners were taken and a wealth of supplies. By 23rd June, the battered Eighth Army had taken new defensive positions by Mersa Matruh, and had a new leader in General Auchinleck. He started a further withdrawal to El Alamein, but Rommel, seized the initiative and moved swiftly to trap large numbers of British troops in Mersa Matruh's fortress, while others were killed or captured by Axis troops. Italians captured Sergeant T. Bradshaw's unit on 27th June 1942, and they were shipped to Bari on the southeastern Asiatic coast of Italy, and imprisoned at Camp PG70. A telegram advised that he was missing: presumed killed-in-action. You can imagine the heartache, and the twinkle of relief when, several months later, he was classed as a P.O.W. When Italy and the Allies signed an Armistice in September 1943, Tom was entrained, with others, into cattle trucks for a six-day journey into Germany. There were sixty men per truck and the sanitation was appalling, as was their only daily meal: soup. A large part of their journey was spent in railway sidings, so as not to hinder the movement of enemy troops and equipment.

*Tom Bradshaw at Stalag 1VB.*

Their incarceration continued in Stalag 1VB, until on 23rd April 1945, the twenty thousand inmates were liberated as four Russian cavalrymen rode into the camp at 07.00hours. They announced that units of the Red Army had linked with Americans and that they were free! There came great cheers, some tears, much shaking of hands, and once again time for looking to the future with optimism. A few days later, while

*An England 11 at Stalag 1VB. Tom is seated far right.*

*Church Service at Stalag 1VB.*

*Concert at Stalag 1VB.*

hunting for food outside the camp, Tom found a Swastika flag (see colour secion). Eventually, Tom returned to England and was awaiting demobilisation in a transit camp when he met Anne.

Tom made the best of his long imprisonment. He played football when the opportunity arose and helped with several stage productions to cheer the inmates.

His Christian faith helped him enormously but on his return he remained mentally scarred for a number of years. Anne:

*"Tom often said that he only survived because of the Red Cross parcels (see photo). For years after the war he could get quite depressed at times, finding it difficult to trust people, he was never sure of their intentions but gradually improved. He was a member of the Stalag 1VB Association and we attended most of*

*The grim interior of Stalag 1VB.*

*A German officer receives a salute at Stalag 1VB.*

*the re-unions at Edinburgh and Birmingham. Whenever a close friend from those days passed away he did not like to discuss it, it must have hurt his feelings, and if he heard the song: 'We'll Gather Lilacs' he had to fight not to shed a tear. Apparently they used to sing that song during bleak times at Stalag 1VB to improve their morale. My dear husband, Thomas Bryan Bradshaw, passed away on 14th February 2006, aged eighty-seven years with the Service being held at the Holy Cross Roman Catholic Church at Whitwick. I'd like to finish by saying what a remarkable woman Tom's mother was; she received no rewards on earth, perhaps she will receive them in heaven. I do know for certain that I thank her for giving me her son, a man of great integrity, honesty and a committed Christian."*

Tom was always very moved with the sentiment and lyrics of: 'We'll Gather Lilacs' from 'Perchance To Dream', by Ivor Novello.

### We'll Gather Lilacs

*'Although you're far away, and life is sad and grey, I have a scheme, a dream to try.*
*I'm thinking dear of you, and all I meant to do when we're together, you and I.*
*We'll soon forget our care and pain, and find such lovely things to share again.*

*We'll gather lilacs in the spring again, and walk together down an English Lane,*
*Until our hearts have learned to sing again, when you come home once more.*
*And in the evening by the firelight's glow, you'll hold me close and never let me go,*
*Your eyes will tell me all I want to know when you come home once more.*

*We'll learn to love anew the simple joys we knew, and shared together night and day.*
*We'll watch without a sigh, the moments speeding by, when life is free and hearts are gay.*
*My dream is here for you to share, and in my heart, my dream becomes a prayer.*

*We'll gather lilacs in the spring again, and walk together down an English Lane,*
*Until our hearts have learned to sing again, when you come home once more.*
*And in the evening by the firelight's glow, you'll hold me close and never let me go,*
*Your eyes will tell me all I want to know when you come home once more.*

The song was also a favourite of my parents, Betty and Les Kendrick. It was only after I had spoken to Anne that I realised they had known my parents for decades. I may have met them when they listened to my parents sing old classics at a public house at Newtown Linford; the foursome also played lawn bowls together for Coalville Town.

This account is quite breathtaking and very satisfying. It displays how decent people battled against all of the diversity and sadness that life can muster, and yet, retain their Christian faith. Very many thanks to you, Anne.

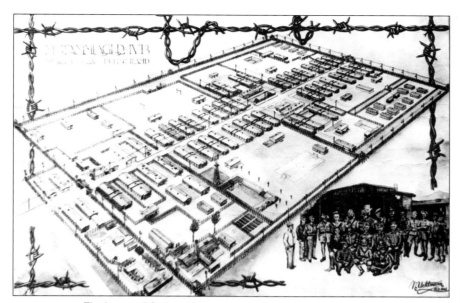

The layout of Stalag 1VB.

Tom Bradshaw in light suit with P.O.W. friends.

Centre rear, Tom and Anne Bradshaw with P.O.W. friends and wives.

Stephen Bradshaw aged ten and Susan aged six, 1961.

Barbara, aged thirteen years.

# THOMAS HAROLD CATLOW

*Thomas Catlow in 1924.*

Thomas Harold Catlow has always been called Harold, possibly because he was named after his father, Thomas (Tom) Lord Catlow. The latter man was born on 24th January 1889 at 22, Mantle Lane, Coalville. He worshipped at nearby Christ Church, attended the Bible Class and was taught by the Reverend Hoskins. A good sports-person, he played football for the church team, alongside goalkeeper: Walter Handford and Edgar Ewart Boot, indeed those three lads later became three of the town's 'Famous Fifty' during the Great War.

When Tom left school he undertook a blacksmith's apprenticeship at Stableford's Wagon Works, almost adjacent to where he lived. In August 1914, he was encouraged, with others at the Works, by Boer War veteran and territorial soldier, James Roland Hill, to volunteer for the 5th Leicestershire Battalion. Tom was one of just twenty-two survivors, albeit a bad wound ended his service days and he spent the rest of the war working in a munitions factory at Nottingham. He married Edith Maud Thirlby, and their marriage was blessed with two sons, George, born in 1917 and Harold on 16th February 1920.

(George was the manager of Bloor's Butchers Shop at Coalville for many years.)

The war wound prevented a return to blacksmithing, and with jobs very scarce, he succeeded in obtaining employment as conductor for Midland Red Buses: a steady and reliable income. From 1936, they lived happily at 197, Thornborough Road, Coalville, with the two boys attending Bridge Road School, and Harold also singing for Christ Church choir. Tom retired at the age of sixty-eight and passed away at Tillson House Care Home on 22nd January 1978. Harold was in the same school-class as my father, Les Kendrick, indeed they were close rivals: especially at hurdling, both being excellent all round athletes. He left school in 1934, aged fourteen years, and was contacted by ex-schoolboy chum, Jim Cooper, who was working at Ellistown Colliery. Harold recalls:

*"Jim was in our class, he later became a surveyor, but at the time he said that the colliery needed an errand boy, a general run-about. Times were bad in the Depression, a job was a job, and so I took it. I must have proved worthy because at the tender age of fifteen I was made an office boy and put on the staff: a junior clerk in the Wages and Land Sale Office."*

*From left: Harold Catlow, Ted Willett, Jim Cooper and Audrey Marsden. Circa 1937.*

Harold, always keen to learn, involved himself in colliery health and safety matters and passed examinations in First-Aid practices. Safety was an important work aspect, and as such lots of practise and teamwork was required. Various competitions were arranged against other colliers from Leicestershire and Derbyshire. A 1936 photograph shows Harold with Jim Cooper, Aubrey Marsden and Ted Willett, in a field near to Ellistown Colliery, displaying a rescue procedure to an on-looking crowd. They finished with a well-earned second place.

In February 1940, he was asked to present himself at Ulverscroft Road, Leicester, for a medical examination, which he passed with flying colours: A1. In April 1940 he was called-up and given the service number 7379261.

*"I was very lucky, someone must have taken note of my first-aid knowledge, because I had to report to the Royal Army Medical Corps (R.A.M.C.) at Leeds. I had thirteen weeks of basic training, and then intensive medical lectures in Beckett's Park, a former Methodist Teacher Training College; it was well equipped with lecture rooms, sports grounds and swimming baths. We slept on a bare floor!"*

Harold eagerly absorbed the various procedures involved in frontline care: field ambulance responsibilities, onward to casualty clearing stations and then base hospitals.

*"I soon passed the first examinations as a nursing orderly class three, my pay increasing by nine old pence to two shillings and nine old pence per day (nearly fourteen new pence). After the course we were marched into a field and names were called-out; they soon made four companies until only six of us were left."*

He went on courses at Birmingham, Macclesfield and Warrington and promoted to corporal.

Subsequently, in late 1940, and as a sergeant, he was posted to Walton Hospital on Rice Lane at Liverpool, and witnessed the devastation the famous port took from the Luftwaffe.

*"The hospital was the largest in north-western England and full of lovely nurses, and one in particular caught my eye, and my ear, she had a lovely Welsh lilt to her voice. Walton is only a few miles inland from Bootle Docks, and so you can imagine it was a lively spot with German bombers a constant threat, bombing most nights that I was there. Casualties came streaming in and we did our best to help before sending them to other hospitals before other victims arrived: it was hectic to say the least. The military had two wards of thirty-five beds each, and occasionally I was allowed into the operating theatre, I learned a lot."*

Catherine Owen in 1938

Catherine Owen in 1940. Photograph taken at Regent Studio, 45 Lime Street, Liverpool.

Harold tells me that after a work-shift he would leave the hospital and often struggle to find his bearings, such was the severity of the surrounding bomb damage.

*"I recall seeing a land mine hanging by its parachute from the apex of a building, if it had fallen and detonated we would all have been killed! Smoke and rubble were everywhere, even churches suffered, and one was left as a monument to the dead of those times. Some nights I would go to the cinema, and if a raid started we were told that it was safer to remain where we were; many's the night I've slept in a cinema."*

There were good times in what Harold considers: 'The Capital of Wales'; it takes a lot to put a happy-go-lucky Scouser down, and he was falling for that Welsh nurse named Catherine Owen.

*"There are a lot of Welsh and Irish folk at Liverpool. I used to go and watch Everton Football Club, it only cost six old pence to get into Goodison and the famous Tommy Lawton was playing for them; I saw him when he was on his way to his wedding!"*

*The home of Catherine Owen, Ty Newydd Cottage at Llandigai.*

Catherine Owen was born on 6th July 1920 at Aberffraw, a village on the western coast of the island of Anglesey, Wales. A wonderful childhood of fresh sea-air and good food; in 1928 the family moved to nearby Bangor, a town just the other side of the Menai Bridge. The family lived in a beautiful house, 'Ty Newydd Cottage', Llandigai on the Penryn Castle Estate (see photograph). Catherine, a caring person and a Girl Guide in her teenage years, developed a yearning for nursing, and in 1938 left home and travelled to Walton Hospital for training. Two years later she was to meet her future husband.

Harold's next posting was to the Duke of Westminster's Eaton Hall at Chester. The Hall was used as a military rehabilitation centre, and several professional footballers assisted with the various exercises. When possible, especially for weekends, he travelled to Liverpool to see Catherine. Following this came a return to Leeds to stay in a building utilised as a holding company to await embarkation, and then passage to the 47th British General Hospital (one thousand four hundred beds) on the Duke of Richmond's and Gordon Goodwood's Estate at Chichester, near to the race-course, prior to a posting overseas.

*"It was early 1942 and we were destined for Singapore, but it was cancelled when the Japanese Forces captured the island. Later we boarded a night train to Sheffield where I recall being given green mugs to drink our tea, the train continued to Liverpool docks. We saw this large grey ship, and talk about security, a docker shouted that we were off to India. However, the ship was not quite ready for sailing, and so we were sent to some barracks at Everton. Quite a number in our unit were from the Liverpool area, and they asked if they could make one last trip home before sailing. It was against the rules, but we were given permission and so I was able to see Catherine for a couple of hours: I did not see her again for four years!"*

It was April 1942 when the 'Capetown Castle' sailed for Glasgow to join a large convoy with a strong escort consisting of battleships, cruisers and destroyers.

*"The convoy was attacked on several occasions and we lost a number of ships during a nine week period. We stopped off at Freetown and again for a few days at Durban in South Africa. We were welcomed at the dock by a lady singing for us; she was dressed in all white clothing, and apparently had made this a custom for some time for arriving troops. A nice gesture.*

*The locals were very friendly and we received lots of fresh fruit, although we slept without covers in a large park, having been told it wasn't the rainy season."*

The convoy steamed northwards to arrive at Bombay on the western coast of India, then entrained

*Sergeant Harold Catlow in India. July, 1942.*

*Sergeant Harold Catlow, Calcutta, 1943.*

to Mhow in the Central Provinces of India, a trip of some five hundred & thirty kilometres (three hundred & twenty-five miles).

"*The weather was very hot and when one of our lads took a shower, it was simply a shower head connected to an exposed large tank full of rainfall, he yelled in alarm because the water was so hot from the sun's rays!*"

Harold's final posting in late 1943 was to Calcutta in Bengal Province: the northeastern section of India and close to the Burmese border. It was a train journey of a thousand-eight hundred kilometres (eleven hundred miles):

"*Very hot and seats like park benches, and the latrines indescribable. The Law Courts became the surgical block/administration centre; the Davidian School for casualties suffering from mental problems such as shell shock, etc, and Loretta Convent at Sealdah for tropical diseases such as: sandfly fever, dengue fever, smallpox, malaria, cholera, etc. It became known as the 47th British General Hospital, India Command.*"

During this time Harold kept in touch with two of his cousins: Angela and Jon Rex Witham, and sent letters and cards, and once a beautiful doll for Angela. (See William Lock) The storm of battle raged in Burma, with fiercely fought campaigns like Imphal and Kohima. Casualties arrived in small hospital ships that steamed across the Bay of Bengal and up the River Hooghly into Fort William, Calcutta.

*Mhow railway station, 1943.*

*A familiar scene for Harold, Mhow.*

*A Christmas Card sent by Harold to his cousins; Angela and Jon Rex Witham, September 1944.*

"*There was a constant stream of allied casualties into our Base Hospital and I saw and learned an awful lot during that period. With being in contact with so much illness, I too went down with a variety of tropical diseases, but rapid treatment soon restored me to fitness. I made a lot of friends during my posting in Bengal and Assam.*"

When the Far Eastern War finished, the servicemen gradually returned to Great Britain; some by sea and some by air: Harold was by the latter, in a small thirty-two seater, Dakota, with a relatively limited flying duration. The pilot stopped-off to refuel at: Delhi, Karachi, Baghdad, Palestine, Tobruk, Sardinia, and finally we arrived at an R.A.F. base in Oxfordshire.

"*Palestine was at the time of the Jewish claim for an independent homeland; there was a lot of gunfire there and I was quite concerned, fortunately we survived. Eventually we landed at Oxford and I was able to take my first leave in three-and-a-half years! To finish my service I was posted to the Royal Herbert Hospital at Woolwich: a hospital given to Miss Florence Nightingale by Lord Herbert. I was made a staff sergeant and chief clerk before I was demobbed in July 1946, after over six years service for my King and Country.*"

Harold clutched his belongings as the train entered Coalville Railway Station, walked to his parent's house and recommenced his peacetime life. He returned to his pre-war job at Ellistown, and over the years achieved success and promotions in central wages/quotas, coalface costings, various figures, etc. "*While abroad, Catherine and I exchanged letters, and in one I asked her to marry me; I was delighted when she accepted, although the mail was worryingly variable, sometimes going months without mail and then six letters arriving at a time!*"

*Harold and Catherine's Wedding Day.*

Harold and Catherine married on 14th July 1947 at St.Tegia Church, Llandegia at Bangor.

"*It was a lovely ceremony and eventually we returned to Coalville and lived in rented rooms at first. During this time we had twin boys, Peter and David, born on 16th October 1948. Shortly afterwards we moved to 35, Oxford Street at Coalville. I had a good and steady job and had some lovely holidays, we had a very good family life. After the boys grew up my dear wife spent many years nursing in the neighbourhood; whenever we went shopping at Coalville everybody seemed to know her: she was very well liked and respected. We had a wonderful life together and toured lots of countries, especially after I retired when I was sixty-two years old."*

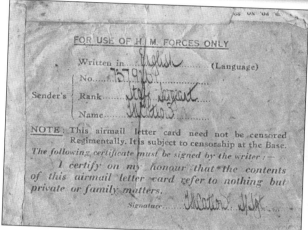

Peter and David Catlow, circa 1954.

Catherine, always a gentle and warm-hearted lady, became ill and entered the Leicester Royal Infirmary, finally being transferred to nearby Glenfield Hospital.

The ex: nurse passed away on 13th December 2002, aged eighty-one years.

Harold reflects on his war-service:

*"Despite difficult times on many occasions, we often were on the go for twenty fours hours without a break, I was fortunate to be in an atmosphere that I enjoyed, and that helped to pass the time. Incidentally, I met very few locals during the war."*

Author: Harold Catlow and my father, Les Kendrick, followed amazingly similar pathways in life. At school they were in the same class, both exceptional athletes: excelling at hurdles and they were also choirboys. They spent periods living at Liverpool and Leeds, both sailing from Liverpool to the Far East. Les was captured at Singapore while Harold's trip to the

Harold and Catherine, circa 1964.

same destination was cancelled when it succumbed to Japanese Forces. Harold assisted the casualties of battle while serving near to the Burmese border; father laboured on the Burma/Siam Railway, and they both retired at sixty-two years of age.

Harold's younger cousin on his mother's side is Angela Lock (nee Thirlby); during his time in India he wrote to Angela (see photograph) and also brought some little Indian dolls for her. My thanks to Harold for his help and supplying such a moving account.

# THE CAVENDISH FAMILY

The name, Cavendish, is of Anglo-Saxon origin and recorded in the 1086 Domesday Book as '*Kavandisc*', deriving from the Olde English '*Cafna*', with '*Caf*' meaning bold and daring. Perhaps, to an extent bravery is inherited, for the above family displayed that noble quality in abundance during two World Wars.

*Private Charles Cavendish, 1914.*

Charles Cavendish, born 14th October 1885, at 21, Crescent Street, Notting Hill, Kensington, London, was the son of Alfred and Mary. Alfred, a boilermaker working for the railways relocated to Coalville. In 1901, when his parents returned to London, Charles asked to stay and was adopted by William and Georgina Barton, Baxton's Row, Hugglescote. William, a forty-three years old collier lived with wife, Georgina, thirty-six, and their adopted niece, Anne Allen (Barton), aged four. Charles worked at South Leicestershire Colliery and stayed there until 1914. Around 1905, he married Jane James of Silver Street, Whitwick; Jane's parents were Charles James, born 1859 in Steventon, Oxfordshire and Harriett James (1861-1908) at St. Martins in Shropshire; Jane had a sister: Elizabeth (later Hill), born 1883 in Hengoed, Shropshire. Charles and Jane lived on Pares Hill, near to Whitwick parish church; later they moved to 84, Ashburton Road, Hugglescote. They had five children: Victor Charles Ernest, William, Charles Gordon, Joseph Herbert and the youngest Edward.

In August 1914 Charles joined the Fifth Leicestershire Battalion: one of the 'Famous Fifty'. He was wounded with the Battalion at Ypres, and after recovery was allocated to the Fourth (1/4th) Leicestershire Battalion. While on the Somme he received a shrapnel wound to the head and was in hospital for seven weeks. After home leave, he returned to the frontline in France. Around this time his wife fled to Nottingham, deserting him and their children. She couldn't take the stress of bringing up five young children, and aware that her husband could be killed at any time. In times of crisis fine people step-in and single Anne, the Barton's niece, looked after three of his children: Victor, William and Charles, while his sister-in-law, Elizabeth Hill, took in Joseph and Edward. The latter two grew up alongside their cousin, Annie Hill, at Vicarage Farm on the Leicester Road, Whitwick.

In October 1917, Charles was seriously wounded in the chest: spending six months away from the frontline and on returning was gassed, finally being killed by shellfire near to the La Bassee Canal on 2nd July 1918.

*Ernest and Cissie Wedding Day, 19th May, 1934. From left: Joe, Anne Allen (Barton), Annie Hill, Mrs. Georgina Barton, Ivy, Edna (Bill's first wife), Gordon, Bill, It was Anne Barton who brought up Ernest, Bill and Gordon.*

**Victor Charles Ernest Cavendish**. Called Ernest, the eldest son, was born on Pares Hill, Whitwick, on 14th August 1908 and in 1916, together with two brothers, was brought up by Anne Allen (Barton) at Hugglescote. He attended St. John The Baptist Church School and upon leaving became a miner at Whitwick Colliery, remaining there for his working life. On 19th

May 1934, he married local girl, Cissie Beenie, at Christ Church, Coalville, and they had one child, Susan: born 31st January 1944. They lived on Hermitage Road at Whitwick, and he served in the Coalville Home Guard in the early years of the War. Ernest died on 8th April 1991, aged eighty-three years and rests in Broom Leys' Cemetery alongside brother, Joseph.

**William Cavendish.** Bill was born on 3rd January 1910 on Pares Hill, Whitwick. With his elder brother, Ernest, and Gordon (below) he was brought-up by Anne Allen (Barton) at Hugglescote, and attended the Parish Church School. Pre-war he worked as a hosiery knitter at Forster, Clay and Wards of Frog Island, Leicester. In 1937 he married Eliza (Betty: nee Jones), and their firstborn was, Brian: on 27th February 1940, whilst living at 21, Danvers Road, Leicester. Bill was called-up in 1940 and after training at Glen Parva Barracks, South Wigston, Leicester, boarded a ship to join the 1st Battalion of the Leicestershire Regiment.

The Battalion had been fighting a rearguard action against Japanese Forces on the Malayan peninsular since the night of 10/11th December 1941. Bill's ship was over-powered by a Japanese naval vessel before arriving at Singapore, thus spending three-half years as a POW. He slaved on the Burma/Siam 'Railway of Death', and never fully recovered from this ordeal. After the war he returned to his earlier job at Leicester. To his delight his wife gave birth to a second son, Graham, on 5th October 1946.

First born, Brian married Carol and they had one child, Richard James Cavendish, born on 23rd April 1966. Brian is a hairdresser and lives on Ashby Road, Coalville. Graham is a policeman and he married Lesley (nee Rumberlow), and they have two sons: Adrian and Gavin, the latter serves with the Royal Navy. Bill died in March 1966: aged only fifty-six years: a late victim of the 'Railway of Death'. He rests in Gilroes Cemetery, Leicester.

**Charles Gordon Cavendish**. Gordon was born in 1912, also on Pares Hill, Whitwick, and brought up by Anne Allen (Barton) at Hugglescote, etc. He moved to Leicester and employed as a dairyman for Kirby and West until being called-up in 1940, and subsequently posted to the 2nd Battalion of the Leicestershire Regiment. In February 1941, he was one of Field Marshall Wavell's thirty thousand men in the Middle

East that routed the 10th Italian Army at Beda Fomm in Cyrenaica: one hundred-ninety kilometres south of Benghazi. In Europe, Axis Forces overran Yugoslavia in under a week, and an April 23rd armistice between the Greek-Albanian Army and the Axis Forces meant Albania fell and then Athens on April 27th. Two days later allied troops, whilst enduring heavy air attacks, were evacuated by the Royal Navy from the Greek mainland and taken to Crete, the largest of the Greek Islands. Crete was of strategic importance, and Winston Churchill was determined to make the island a second Malta. Crete had evacuees of thirty thousand British and Commonwealth men plus ten thousand Greek troops, and among their reinforcements was the Tigers' 2nd Battalion, with Gordon Cavendish a despatch rider/ infantryman, arriving at the port of Heraklion on 15th May 1941. Shortly after arrival they were attacked by Messerschmitt 110 fighters, indeed, by that date the Luftwaffe had air superiority, and such occurrences, especially by siren-screaming Stuka dive-bombers, were a frequent feature. On May 20th, after 'the softening-up', Junker 52s aircraft dropped elite German '*Fallschirmjaeger*' paratroopers on several parts of the island.

*German paratroopers over Crete.*

They met fierce resistance with hand-to-hand fighting! Also, the Germans twice attempted sea-borne invasions but on both occasions were thwarted by the Royal Navy. Enemy troops finally captured Maleme airfield and so were able to reinforce their numbers by air. As a result, on May 28th, the allies' situation was untenable and they evacuated by sea. During this campaign nearly four thousand allied troops were killed and twelve thousand taken prisoner. Enemy losses were six thousand (about half of the 7th Air Division) and over two hundred aircraft. The Royal Navy lost heavily in men with Luftwaffe dive-bombers sinking the cruisers: 'Gloucester' and 'Fiji', and destroyers: 'Greyhound', 'Kashmir' and 'Kelly'; the latter captained by Lord Louis Mountbatten. Many of the 'Tigers' were aboard the cruisers: 'Orion' and 'Dido', and were in need of recuperation on arriving at Alexandria. (See Mathew Richardson's: 'Fighting Tigers' for more information.)

After agreement between Mussolini and Hitler, the German 'Afrika Korps' was formed, and placed under the command of General (later Field Marshall) Rommel, arguably the finest military leader of his generation. For what followed please read in this book: 'A Dedication to the Desert Rats'.

*Desert Rats under shellfire.*

Conditions in the Western Desert were exacting with soaring daytime heat, freezing nights, sand storms, lack of food and water and plagues of flies that cultivated dysentery. On occasions hot, bone-dry winds breezed across the blistering Sahara Desert to dehydrate the troops: men drained radiators from damaged vehicles to satisfy their thirsts.

After El Alamein, 4th November 1942, General Montgomery advanced fourteen hundred miles in ninety days: sixteen miles a day in a most difficult terrain and climate. On 2nd February 1943, artillery fire was exchanged a mere twelve miles from the Tunisian border. On February 15th, Ben Gardene, with its large airfield was taken as the Allies made for Medenine. On March 20th, the Battle of Mareth ultimately led to British and American troops converging to encircle the 'Afrika Korps': they

surrendered in May 1943. (See Peter Moore's account in Volume One). It is a small world: during Gordon's service in the Western Desert he met his brother, Edward; both brothers acquitted themselves very well during a great deal of action, and the family are naturally proud of this. After the war Gordon returned to Kirby and West and married Leicester girl, Edna May Frearson in 1946.

They spent most of their married life at 23, Wilmington Road, Leicester, and had two children. John was born on 10th March 1947 and Ann on 10th September 1949. Gordon passed away from a heart attack on 11th July 1960: he was just forty-eight years of age.

*From left: Bill Cavendish, Joe, Edward, Gordon and Ernest. Circa 1938.*

**Joseph Herbert Cavendish.** Joe was born on 26th May 1913, a twin birth with Edward (dying at birth). In 1916, he went with new brother, Edward, aged one, to be brought up by his mother's sister: Elizabeth and her husband, William Hill, who managed Vicarage Farm on Leicester Road, Whitwick. Joe also grew up with cousin, Annie, attended the local Church School and later became a driver for Whitwick Quarry.

On 6th June 1938, at St. George's Church, Swannington, he married Ivy Elizabeth Peace: born 22nd December 1914, daughter of Levi Peace: born 1882, a collier and Ann Elizabeth Peace: born 1880. Ivy met Joe when she worked as a fettler (tidying the kilned bricks) at Lount Brickyard. Joe and Ivy lived in rented houses at Swannington, Greenhill Road, and 220 Bardon Road, Coalville.

Joe enlisted into the Leicestershire Regiment on

*Right: Ivy Peace at Lount Brickworks, 1931.*

*Joe and Ivy, circa 1935.*

*Ivy Peace, 1931.*

27th June 1940. He trained at Glen Parva Barracks, South Wigston, Leicester: service number 4864029; and was posted to the 1/5th Battalion, his father's old battalion, soon after their evacuation from Norway: (See William Lock). The Battalion regrouped and refitted at Hawick in the Scottish Borders, and deployed to Carrack-Fergus Castle, Belfast, Northern Ireland and began as an officer-cadet training unit; it was here that Joe joined them. During the 1940 Battle of Britain he said he'd like to train as a fighter pilot. His son, David, continues:

*"Dad told me that he arrived at this building to have various tests, and as you passed a test you moved up the building, and on arriving on the top floor you were presented to an 'Acceptance Board'. He managed to get to the top floor and impressed them but just as they were about to accept him they noticed that he had missed one test: just a formality. Dad had the test and couldn't believe it when they said he was colour blind, he could not distinguish between red and*

Joe Cavendish in 1940 with the 1/5th Leicestershire Battalion.

Joe, front-centre with friends, 1943.

*green! On returning to the Board they told him that he could not train as a fighter pilot, but could try for a glider pilot. In pains of disappointment he turned them down and returned to his old unit."*

In June 1942 the Battalion travelled to Wrotham in England: twelve kilometres north of Tonbridge, Kent. From 18th March 1943 to 3rd January 1946, Joe served as a regimental lorry driver/mechanic (RASC Wing 148 PRE, OCTU TRG EST.), and was promoted to lance corporal on becoming a driving instructor.

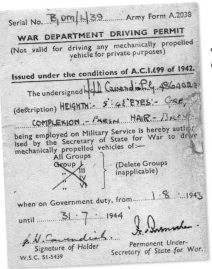

*Joe's War Department Driving Certificate.*

He travelled extensively around southern England carrying all kinds of munitions and supplies. Joe also witnessed much of the enemy's air offensive, and saw the damage left by bombs, V1s (doodlebugs) and V2 rockets.

On joining the Army he wrote in his common prayer book: '*He entered the fight against the oppressors of small nations in memory of his father, who was killed by them in the Great War 1914-18.*'

Joe was demobilised at Wrotham on 2nd January 1946; returned to Vicarage Farm, and that is where daughter, Kay was born on 24th April 1945. The threesome lived at Spring Hill Farm for a time and David was born there on 30th October 1948. Kay recalls:

*"We loved the open-aired life at Spring Farm; it was in the wilds, had no electricity and we relied on paraffin lamps for light and an open range for cooking. We used a pump to draw spring water and the toilet was an old earth type: a bit frightening if you had to go at night with owls hooting and foxes trotting around! We often stayed there and I recall collecting stacks of bilberries. In the summer especially, visitors called at the café alongside our home and sit out at the trestle table or in the rock tors that were all around.*

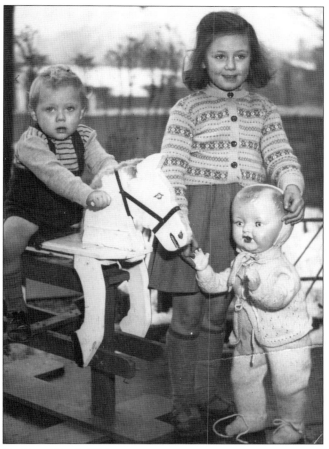

*David and Kay in 1951.*

*David and Joe at Blackpool. 1955.*

*David and I are so sad that nothing is left: all covered with quarry waste, but not our memories!"*

In late November 1949 Joe placed a deposit and bought their first house: 40, James Street, Coalville, and Ivy made it into a cosy home; nine years later moved to 36 in the same street.

He had a variety of jobs after leaving the quarry: delivering coal to power stations and heavy industrial units for Whitmore's and Hickin of Leicester Road, Whitwick, and later delivering bricks for 'Beanies'. Finally he drove lorries for A.R.C., Shepshed, until retirement in 1959.

In the early years of marriage, Ivy nurtured Kay and David, but once they attended Belvoir Road School she helped with the family's finances. David recalls:

*"Every Monday morning, after being taken to school, mother caught the bus into Leicester and collected items from a hosiery factory for domestic sewing and returned them the following Monday. Later she was employed in the dye-house at Clutsom and Kemp Ltd, Coalville, retiring in 1959."*

After Bridge Road Secondary School, Kay became a machinist at Everlastic Ltd: manufacturers of women's swimsuits and underwear, near to the Dumps at Whitwick (now demolished). On 8th November 1962, she married John Massey and they had three children: John: born 23rd November 1962, Andrea: 9th November 1963 and Darren: 23rd March 1966. Kay has since remarried to Roy Elston: 26th May 2001.

*Daughter Kay with her mother, Ivy in 1986.*

David attended Bridge Road School and then moved to the old grammar school building (converted into a secondary modern) on Forest Road. On 28th August 1971, he married Freda May Richards at

Hartshorne Parish Church, Derbyshire. Freda: born 11th May 1948 at Ashby de la Zouch Hospital, grew up at Woodville, Derbyshire, later moving to Hartshorne, near Burton-on-Trent. Freda worked for a well-known biscuit manufacturer at Ashby de la Zouch before joining a local retailer. Their son, Mark Andrew Cavendish: born 28th January 1974 is a career soldier with the Army: R.E.M.E., and marches at Coalville on Remembrance Day.

He married Lindsey Pike at Stow Market on 6th May 2006 and they have one daughter, Kerys: born 15th October 2006 at Ipswich Hospital. David and Freda's daughter, Lisa Marie: born 14th November 1978 and educated at Coalville's Belvoir Road, Bridge Road and Castle Rock Schools and Nottingham University. Lisa took a four-year training course and now teaches at South Wigston. Joe passed away on 6th May 1991, aged seventy-eight years, and rests at plot 86A, Broom Leys' Cemetery: alongside his brother, Ernest. Ivy departed her life on 6th February 2000, aged eighty-five years.

**Edward Cavendish.** Always called Ned, was born on 14th January 1915, and as a one year old was brought up with brother, Joe, by his mother's sister: Elizabeth and her husband, William Hill at Vicarage Farm, Whitwick, etc. On leaving school he became a miner at Snibston Colliery, but aged eighteen years he decided to be a career soldier and joined the Royal Artillery. His nephew, David says:

*"His World War 2 service is something of a mystery. He said very little about his experiences and never even bothered to send for his medals until 1979. They (see colour section) show the 1939-45 Star, Africa Star, Italy Star, and Defence Medal. We do know that he trained as a parachutist and worked behind enemy lines against the 'Afrika Korps', but when his medals arrived an S.A.S. emblem also accompanied them. He wore it on his jacket pocket"*

Colonel (later: Sir) David Stirling founded the S.A.S. (Special Air Service) during the Desert War in 1942. It was very much a hush-hush team of elite troops that developed into a model of excellence for Special Forces worldwide. His conception was for small, highly trained teams to work under-cover behind enemy lines. The men had to pass austere selection tests, be super-fit and self-motivated: there was no officer-rank hierarchy, and members addressed

Jack 'Busty' Cooper.

each other by first names. Rommel referred to Colonel Stirling as the 'Phantom Major'. In 1942, the fifth man to join the S.A.S. was Jack 'Busty' William Ewart Gladstone Cooper. Born in 1914 at Newton Burgoland he became a collier, but not for long, he enlisted into the Army as a regular and served with the 40th/20th King's Hussars and the 9th Lancers. While in North Africa he volunteered for 'hazardous duties', passing tests to join a first batch of seventy-five men selected as paratroopers. He then volunteered for 'especially hazardous duties' and passed arduous mental and physical tests to become the Fifth man to join the S.A.S. The ethos of the Service was clear; they wanted superbly trained and very fit soldiers, but not thugs! In the Western Desert, Edward and Jack took part in numerous raids and escaped death on many occasions, the nature of their tasks resulted in heavy casualties.

It was Jack who drove the first jeep into Benghazi after its fall; his passenger was Colonel David Stirling. Jack also saved the life of a drowning man by pulling him out of the sea by his hair; his name was Norman Holmes of Ibstock. He was married to Pat and I recall he had a daughter: Marilyn Brownlow. Later, Jack lived at Ibstock, died in 1995 and rests in the churchyard; his headstone bears the double wings emblem of the S.A.S.

The S.A.S. played a key role in September 1942 with 'Operation Agreement', whereby a small team of the aforementioned together with Royal Marines and Highlanders stormed Tobruk. The intention was not to retake it, but to get in, cause as much disruption and destruction as possible, then get out! The Operation was successful, but the outrageous cunning of the S.A.S. was noted. Their incursion into Tobruk was by driving enemy trucks and pretending to be prisoners-of-war under escort.

The ribbon on Edward's Defence Medal symbolises his service with the Royal Artillery during the during the early war years; it is likely that he was involved in Anti-Aircraft duties.

In the Desert, Edward would have been involved in many raids, such as plundering enemy munitions, petrol dumps, airfields, etc, and so played a specialized role for King and Country in various theatres of war from 1942-45; only modesty prevented him from disclosing details. I feel it is best to honour his wishes.

In 1946, Edward left the Army and returned to Coalville. A few years later he moved to Leeds, and at 'Club 101': an ex-servicemen's club, met Esther Foster (born 13th March 1915), a girl from Wednesbury in Warwickshire. They had two children: Brian Charles Cavendish, born on 29th July 1950 (dying on 2nd November 1994 after a car accident) and Melvin: born 8th July 1952 and who still lives at Leeds, and married to Irene.

Edward returned to Coalville in 1955 and rented a house in James Street, four doors from his brother, Joe. He became a miner at Snibston Colliery, and then in 1959 moved onto Rugeley Colliery in Staffordshire, before returning to Leeds, where he spent the remainder of his life at 15, Wellington Gardens, Bramley. He worked as a porter and then as a male nurse, spending many years working in a central Leeds hospital. 'Ned' died on 29th July 1985, aged seventy years: his ashes were scattered on Sharpley Rocks, overlooking the beautiful open countryside where he grew up; Esther died on 15th October 1998, aged eighty-three years.

Many thanks to my good friend, David Cavendish. David proudly possesses his grandfather's military bible, and has every right to be proud of his family's efforts for King and Country.

# JOSEPH WILLIAM COLLIER

Readers of 'Greater Love' will know of George Smith, a soldier with the 1/5th Leicestershire Battalion. He married Jane Snow (nee Collier Mackie) at Holy Trinity Church, Loughborough on 15th November 1919. Her first husband, Frederick Snow (senior) of Woodhouse Eaves, was killed in France on 11th April 1917, and she was left with Frederick (Junior): born 1913, Gladys: 1914, Ivy: 1916 and Winnie: 1917.

Jane Collier Mackie: born 1894, and Joseph William Collier: born 1905, were brother and sister, the name Mackie having been dropped after Jane's birth. In 1842, the Mackie family lived at Kings Newton, a hamlet near to Melbourne, Derbyshire, and the Colliers at Church Gresley, twelve kilometres southwest of Melbourne.

William Joseph Mackie (1842-1898) married Mary Collier on 23rd February 1862; Joseph worked at Wragg's Pipe Works at Woodville: a village six kilometres northwest of Ashby de la Zouch, while Mary was a domestic servant and daughter of William Collier. The couple's first son was Edwin Collier Mackie (maternal grandfather of Malcolm Smith in 'Greater Love'), other siblings were: John William: born 6th December 1863, Annie Elizabeth: 1869, Joseph: 1871 and Arthur: 13th August 1878 (died in infancy).

In 1881 the family lived in Grenville Street, Woodville. Joseph, a foreman with Wragg's (a firm still works the site using local clay for pottery, piping, bricks.) also had his two eldest sons as potter-apprentices. In 1891, Edwin's first wife, Ann: nee Woodward, died of typhoid leaving him with three children: Edwin William Collier Mackie aged six, Mary: four, Emma: two. In 1893, Edwin married again, to Elizabeth: nee Podmore, and their first child, Jane Collier Mackie (as mentioned above) was born in 1894, followed by John in 1895, Annie in 1900 and Joseph William: whom died in infancy.

**Edwin's three eldest daughters: Mary, Emma and Jane were all widowed in World War 1.
Our subject, the second son of Edwin and Elizabeth was also named Joseph William Collier, and he was born on 6th February 1905 at Hugglescote, and possibly attended St. John The Baptist Church School, where many of the 'Famous Fifty' were educated. From 1919, he had various jobs, mainly labouring and

*Joseph William Collier. Summer 1925 at Colchester.*

driving, however, on 12th March 1924, he travelled to Loughborough to join the 1/5th Territorial Battalion, Leicestershire Regiment. He enjoyed military life so much that on 28th August 1924, he went to Glen Parva Barracks, Leicester, and enlisted as a regular soldier with the same Regiment: service number 4853043. He signed for seven years with the Colours and five as Reserve. His Regular Army Certificate of Service tells us that he was nearly five feet eleven inches, of fresh complexion, blue eyes and dark-brown hair. Part of his training was at Colchester (summer 1925): a picture shows him on horseback, but on 28th November 1927, he was posted with the 1st Battalion to India. In 1928 they were based at Argaum Barracks at Kamptee; tactics and equipment had changed little since 1918, and in the barracks elderly females and children pulled ropes to operate swinging punkahs. The troops had a headdress of large solar pith topis with an all round brim of one-and-half-inches, and whenever possible the soldiers stayed indoors when the sun was at its highest. The sergeants were mostly veterans from

7th Platoon, 1st Battalion of the Leicestershire Regiment at Amritsar, India. Circa 1928.
Private Joseph Collier is second from the left, standing on the second row.

1914-18 and they passed on experiences to younger men; in 1931, the Battalion moved to Ambala. At this time, the troops maintained law and order by imperial policing, and quashed the occasional tribal disputes: Indian soldiers had served Great Britain with bravery and loyalty in the earlier war. Sport played a prime role in life, and the Battalion was top flight in competitions involving football, rugger (with ex-Leicester Tiger: Fred Drummond), boxing, hockey and cross-country running.

canvas-encampments, barracks, rich ranges of forested mountains, football matches and railways sidings. He writes place names such as Amritsar, Kalka, Agra, Delhi, Ambala, Kamptee and Taj. His Battalion also served at Multan, Jubbulpore, Razmak and Jhansi on the northwest frontier, where it remained until World War 2; prior to this time it lost much of its backbone to the Army's expansion at home, their numbers being replaced by militia.

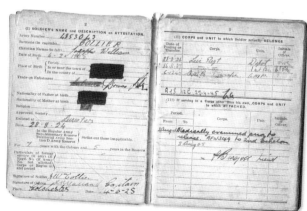

Joseph Collier's paybook.

Friends of Joseph Collier in India. Circa 1930.

As I look through Joseph's album I see many photograph: mostly without reference, shots of friends,

Joseph was in India for four years and 139 days and at some stage became a Regimental Policeman (this would be of extreme value at a later date). His commanding officer's assessment was: *'Very Good. Clean and honest, hardworking and reliable. Did well on Regimental Police.'*

*The Wye family photograph that was carried by father. Trooper Harry Wye in the Great War. From left: Albert, Lucy (wife), Phyllis, Margaret and Elsie with Raymond in front. Circa 1916. Elsie married Joseph Collier.*

On 7th April 1932, at Lichfield, Private Joseph Collier signed to transfer from Regular to Reserve status; he had been with the Battalion for seven years and 223 days. On returning to civilian life he was employed as a cinema projectionist, but little is known as to which 'picture houses' he worked. He married Margaret Edith Wye (born 1910), a tall, attractive lady from Loughborough. Her father owned a greengrocer shop at 3, Wards End in the town; the family living above the business, with Margaret also working at the nursery garden on Westfield Drive. A 1916 photograph shows the family, and on the back is written: '*Love and kisses from us all, and we want you to come back to us some day, Luce*. (Lucy his wife). He in turn writes just below this: '*If anybody finds this one, please return it to Mrs. Wye at 3, Wards End, Loughborough, Leicestershire.*' Happily he returned a few years later to take care of his family.

Joseph and Margaret moved to a house on Main Street, Normanton on Soar, a village four kilometres northwest of Loughborough. They had three children, John Barry: born 28th February 1936, Phillip (Pip) David: born 29th April 1938 and Margaret (Peggy) Elizabeth Ann on 18th November 1941.

On 1st September 1939, his reserve status having passed, he re-enlisted, and although retained by the Leicestershire Regiment, was drafted to a Regimental

Police Force and as such was a member of the British Expeditionary Force. (B.E.F.)

The B.E.F.'s first landing was on 4th September 1939 with the General Headquarter initially at Le Mans. By 11th October, one hundred-fifty eight thousand troops with equipment had arrived. The troops disembarked at Cherbourg while the equipment was taken to Brest and Nantes. Private Joseph Collier left for France on 5th October 1939; there was always the worry of 'U'-Boats, indeed, on September 17th the Aircraft Carrier '*Courageous*' was torpedoed in the Bristol Channel: five hundred & fifteen men lost their lives. While Poland was putting up a valiant but impossible fight against German and Russian Forces, the B.E.F. settled to a defensive war around the Maginot Line, dealing with isolated attacks. On October 14th the battleship '*Royal Oak*' was torpedoed in Scapa Flow with eight hundred & ten deaths; there was also an air raid on the Firth of Forth. It was a

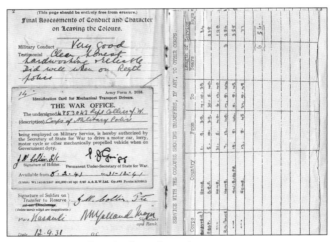

*Joseph Collier's Regular Army Records.*

bitterly cold winter and a period referred to as the 'Phoney War', although fighting took place in the Saar-Moselle region, southeast of the Duchy of Luxemburg. Joseph spent this time in the fortified zone between St. Omer in the north to Valencia in the south; he helped to keep the roads clear for troop movements and maintained the good conduct of British troops. From April 1940, developments began: Germany invaded Denmark and Norway, the Luftwaffe raided Channel convoys and southern England, and then, on May 10th, the invasion of the Low Countries: with paratroopers having a key role. Luxemburg fell, Holland in just five days, and units of the B.E.F. advanced to counter the offensive in Belgium;

precisely what the enemy wanted and they outflanked the Allies with a surprise attack through the Ardennes. General Rommel's 7th Panzer Division spearheaded one thousand-eight hundred tanks across that remote forestland: considered impassable! They reached the Meuse from Liege to Namur on May 14th. Concurrently, Army Group A's main Panzer formation broke through at Sedan; French troops counter-attacked but their efforts were ineffective. B.E.F. troops defended stoutly at Louvain, Liege and elsewhere, but to no avail. Germany's huge deployment of armour/storm-troopers and aircraft surged rapidly southward and westward, and by May 28th the Germanic flood had engulfed Holland, Belgium and France north of the Somme, with Bologna and Calais in their control.

Joseph would have served as both a policeman and soldier during the retreat to Dunkirk, which followed a corridor covering old W.W.1. battlefields. (See map re: Frederick Snow).

The naval evacuation began on the 27th (Belgium capitulated on May 26th) and lasted until June 3rd, with the Royal Navy losing eight destroyers in this period. On the 26/27th only 8,000 soldiers were evacuated, May 28th: 19,000 men, 29th: 47,000 men, 31st: 68,000 men and when the last ship departed the total stood at 224, 585 British and 112,546 French and Belgium troops. The factor for the increase was the introduction of 'small boats': coastal steamers, pleasure boats, yachts and other civilian boats. Most could get close to the beaches, and so allowed soldiers to wade-out to them. British naval guns shelled enemy artillery locations and R.A.F. fighters intercepted the Luftwaffe deep in occupied territory, and so limited their effectiveness over the beaches. The stoic effort of French troops in restricting the enemy's advance was vital to the overall total, though Hitler stopped the movement of his Panzers.

Joseph patiently waited his turn in the enormous queues near to the mole (pier) as ship after ship took aboard troops. They had to scatter frequently as enemy aircraft targeted that area and many men lost their lives. Joseph's son John Collier recalls:

*"Father said that he spent three days digging holes in the sand to provide some sort of protection. He was eventually evacuated by one of the larger ships via the mole on May 30th."*

*The Dunkirk mole (pier) is on the left. 1940.*

*Troops queue at Dunkirk beach: 1940.*

During this evacuation most of the heavy weapons and transport had to be left behind, leaving Great Britain highly vulnerable to invasion. Prime Minister Churchill said: *"Wars are not won by evacuations."* The King's words: *"A success greater than we had ever dared to hope."*

Joseph came ashore at Dover, Folkestone or Margate and entrained to a military venue for regrouping, followed by a spell of home leave: he had been in France and Flanders for two hundred- thirty-eight days. During this period of leave he made the 'black-out boards' that can be seen on a photograph taken in March 1945.

The Wehrmacht conquered northern France between 10th May to 22nd June 1940: forty-two days; losing twenty-seven thousand men, the Allies five times more, mainly French. Germany learnt from the stalemate of the earlier war and devised plans for a 'lightning war', possessing superbly trained troops with better quality equipment and more of it. Understandably, France tried to forget the 1914-18 war on their homeland, and compared to Germany had achieved little in military development: ie, a bastion defensive set-up such as the Maginot Line could never survive a war of mobility. The B.E.F. were ill equipped, they too neglected their armed forces until it was nearly too late, especially with armour; also French/Allied co-ordination and co-operation was not at its best. France was annoyed by the British evacuation: hoping to fight alongside them, but if so the result would have been a disaster! The B.E.F. troops let no one down; they were undoubtedly brave and from 6th June 1944 displayed their admirable qualities to the full!

On 7th December 1940, Joseph was transferred from the Leicestershire Regiment to the Corps of Military Police (C.M.P.), and remained with them until demobilisation. He set a trend that was passed to his next generation. He attended a course on Provost Duties from 7th December 1940 to 3rd February 1941, and a refresher from 28th November 1942 to 12th December 1942.

His early duties were at Leeds: his billet, with others, was with a Mrs. Craven at 36, Bagby Road in the city. His notebook describes policing at various railways stations, etc, where he questioned, took details and arrested those who were 'Absent Without Leave' (AWOL), and other fascinating cases. He was a 'paid lance corporal' from 3rd February 1943.

From 31st January 1944 to 23rd February 1944 he attended the Southern Command Vehicle Maintenance

*Lance Corporal Joseph Collier MP, 1942.*

*Lance Corporal Joseph Collier's Royal Military Police notebook.*

School (Sandbanks Hotel, Bournemouth). I read his handwritten pages/drawings of this time and admit to bemusement by such technology as magnetos, voltage regulators, etc. There followed a trip to Scottish Command for a Vehicle Waterproofing Course; there was also a 185 (HQ) Provost Company War Course.

On 18th August 1944, after three days of embarkation leave, Joseph was posted to France; he was involved in driving duties and on 20th April 1945 received promotion to corporal.

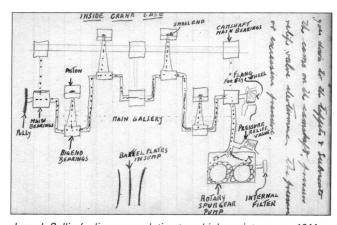

*Joseph Collier's diagrams relating to vehicle maintenance. 1944.*

"*Father said that when he was based at Antwerp he was sitting in the cabin of his lorry when there was a tremendous explosion. He said it was a V rocket and that the force of the blast-wave blew him from the cabin.*"

He must have experienced and seen much of war-torn northern Europe.

On 27th July 1945, while at Antwerp his officer's appraisal:

"*During the time that this NCO has served under my command, he has proved himself to be a good,*

Corporal Joseph Collier at Antwerp in April 1945, C.M.P.

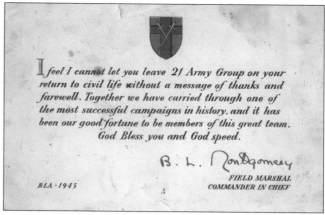

I feel I cannot let you leave 21 Army Group on your return to civil life without a message of thanks and farewell. Together we have carried through one of the most successful campaigns in history. and it has been our good fortune to be members of this great team. God Bless you and God speed.

B. L. Montgomery

BLA · 1945

FIELD MARSHAL
COMMANDER IN CHIEF

Thanks from Montgomery.

John, Phillip and Peggy in March 1945 at Normanton on Soar.

Joseph's wife Margaret Collier in March 1945. Note blackout boards by the windows.

reliable soldier. He is honest, trustworthy and willing."

Joseph was discharged at No3 Military Dispersal Unit, Northampton on 8th October 1945, with official release on 27th October 1945. In the war he served a period of six years and fifty-six days: a total military service of thirteen years two hundred seventy-nine days.

Joseph returned to Normanton to continue his happy marriage and civilian life. In 1950, the family moved to 'The Ferns', 30, Main Street, Long Whatton: six kilometres northwest of Loughborough. Here, he bred pigs, cockerels, geese, and also started working for the brothers Reginald and Vernon Harlow, of Harlow Ltd, Long Whatton. Not only did he drive to cities such as Hull and Grimsby to collect timber, but assisted with the construction of horseboxes, trailers and other farming assemblies. Later, Brush Electrics of Loughborough employed him as a driver for internal deliveries and then in their packing department. Margaret, always busy, commendably spent many years working as a home help.

Eldest son, John Barry Collier (half inch short of six feet) was serving an apprenticeship at Brush 4 Electrics when conscripted. His National Service, number 23385122, began on 4th April 1957 with the Royal Engineers, but soon transferred to the Royal Military Police. On 29th August 1957 he was awarded the 'Certificate of Merit' from The Depot and Training Establishment, Royal Military Police, Inkerman Barracks at Woking:

*'L/Corporal Collier J.B. was considered, to be the most efficient member of his squad at the completion of his recruit training.'*

Corporal John Collier on patrol.

During his National Service, John saw action in Cyprus. After two years with the R.M.P., on 2nd April 1959, he was tempted to become a regular, but decided in favour of his trade, having completed his apprenticeship prior to call-up; also his wife, Delia was pregnant. John had an outstanding career as an electrical engineer, and the job took him around the world. The couple live at Loughborough. Delia (nee Barker) was born at Long Whatton and lived at 'The Oaks' and recalls her father digging an underground bomb shelter with a concrete roof: *"We sheltered down there and, even though I was a little girl, I remember seeing searchlights and hear bombs exploding. I also remember the Women's Land Army working in the*

*fields and buying stuff from Mrs. Carlew in the village shop. We didn't have a lot but how we enjoyed Paradise Field, it was just behind the school, we played games there, and in the autumn we picked lots of berries."* (See Olive Poole in this volume).

MELVIN COLLIER

Melvin Collier.

Their son, Melvin Collier, once of the Boys' Brigade, continued the family's military tradition when he was sixteen years old by joining the Lifeguards of the Household Cavalry Regiment. He was in the Press when, as one of twelve trumpeters, they played a fanfare on the steps of St. Paul's Cathedral: this at the wedding of Prince Charles and Lady Diana on 29th July 1981 (see photograph). He began playing the trumpet at the age of twelve, was a member of the Leicestershire Schools' Orchestra and received further training at the Army School of Music. He has featured many times in the Queen's 'Trooping of the Colour'. His sister, Wendy, breeds and trains mountain dogs while brother, Adam, is in finance.

Melvin can be seen between Diana and her father. 1981.

*Philip Collier of 5 Dog Company, C.M.P. 1960's.*

Joseph's second son, Philip (Pip) was called for National Service in February 1960, service number 23764335. After two weeks at Catterick Camp in Yorkshire he followed the family tradition, was transferred to the Corps of Royal Military Police, and was trained at Inkerman Barracks, Woking. Lance Corporal Philip Collier, at six feet four inches tall, served with 5 Dog Company, Melton Mowbray Camp at Singapore, Malaysia. After completing two years of service, he returned to his trade, and with his wife, Carol, moved from Loughborough to Dunstable to work in the Design and Management Department of Vauxhall Motors until retirement.

John's sister, Margaret (Peggy) Collier married Michael Brooks; their only son, Paul Brooks, joined the Royal Navy, and during a period of around twenty years achieved the rank of Petty Officer (mechanical), and served aboard Her Majesty's diesel and nuclear submarines.

The grand old soldier, Corporal Joseph William Collier: Dunkirk veteran, passed away on 22nd December 1972; his wife, Margaret joined him in 1995.

Many thanks to John and Delia Collier for their help and information, also Malcolm Smith.

*Left: Lance Corporal John Collier C.M.P. 1957. Above: Life Guardsman Melvin Collier leads a mounted parade in London.*

# FREDERICK THOMAS SNOW

Readers of 'Greater Love' and Joseph Collier will recall Frederick Snow (senior). He was employed by the Herrick family of Beaumanor Hall, Old Woodhouse, and lived at nearby Woodhouse Eaves. He married Jane (nee Collier), sister of the aforementioned Joseph Collier, and had four children, Frederick (Fred) Thomas Snow: born 1913, Gladys: born 1914, Ivy: born 1916 and Winnie: born 1917. Frederick Snow (senior) was killed on 11th April 1917, whilst with the 8th Leicestershire Battalion, and rests at St. Leger cemetery. At the time of his father's death, Fred was living with his mother and sisters at 4a, Pleasant Place, Factory Street at Loughborough. On the 15th November 1919,

Jane Smith (nee Snow), 1930.

Jane Snow married again; her husband was George Smith, who had fought throughout the Great War with the Fifth (1/5th) Battalion of the Leicestershire Regiment. The ceremony took place at Holy Trinity Church, Loughborough. George was twenty-four years of age with Jane one year older. George adopted Jane's four children and brought them up as his own. He was known as Dad to ultimately seven children, and was never referred to as 'step-father'. To begin with, they lived at 7, Wellington Street, Loughborough and it was there that Jane gave birth to Edna May in 1920 and George (junior) in 1926. They then relocated to a newly built council house: 152, Derby Road, again Loughborough, where Malcolm Smith was born in 1932.

Fred Snow, in 1930, aged seventeen, enlisted as a regular soldier and soon joined the 1st Battalion of the Leicestershire Regiment; possibly just missing being reunited with his Uncle Joseph (just eight years his senior) in India. It is thought that his uncle may have spoken of his experiences and recommended life there. Fred married a woman named, Barbara, while his Battalion was based at Jubbulpore, and they had a child that sadly died in infancy.

From 1937, Regimental Headquarters began recalling some non-commissioned officers from India to help form the backbone of a new battalion: the 2/5th. Fred was among their number, but his wife refused to return with him, believing her future lay in India with her family. He divorced her on the grounds of desertion. Malcolm Smith, Fred's half brother (a term unheard of in the family), corresponded with Barbara during the war years when she was as a nursing sister. The last time he made contact she was serving in the household of the Maharajah Sultan of Mysore.

The 2/5th Battalion was raised in 1938 after a decision to double the size of the Territorial Army, bearing in mind their immense contribution in the Great War. The Battalion consisted of 'C' Company from the 1/5th Battalion, with fresh drafts and volunteers, and was based at the Magazine Barracks, Leicester. Visits to Glen Parva Barracks saw Aubrey Moore M.C., recalled after serving as an officer with the 1/5th Battalion during the Great War: see 'Greater Love'. Extra training was on Leicester City's Filbert Street Football Ground and Leicester's Welford Road Rugby Ground. At first the commanding officer was Major Guy German, but he was transferred to the 1/5th, replacing the famed 1914-18 veteran, Claude Barratt V.C. (A surgeon who joined the R. A. M. C.). Major (later Lieutenant Colonel) Kenneth Ruddle commanded the Battalion that left Leicester Railway Station for Southampton on 26th April 1940. It was part of the 139th Brigade, 46th North Midland Division and its objective as part of B.E.F. 2 was to support the earlier Expeditionary Force in France. At night they steamed to Cherbourg, then entrained to Rennes in Brittany and a further eleven kilometres west to l'Hermitage Camp. At first, in beautiful weather, they helped the Royal Engineers, whom were busy constructing six-half miles of full gauge heavy railway track to feed a Base Ordnance Depot. They were told that for every nine weeks: six would be on the railroad and three spent in training, but after just seventeen days they received orders to move to the Front. As it was for his uncle, Joseph Collier: also in France, on 10th May 1940, waves of German infantry with tank and air support, blitzed their way into Holland and Belgium, and by the 15th had broken through the French Line. So serious was the situation, that on May 13th, General Lord Gort V.C. ordered the raw, relatively untrained, unprepared, ill-equipped 2/5th Battalion from Leicestershire, twelve-hour notice for possible frontline duties.

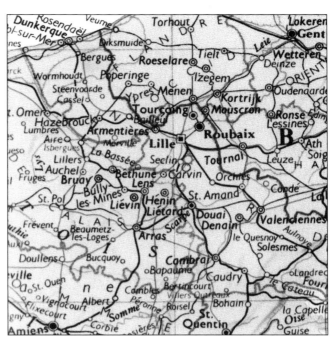

The corridor of withdrawal to Dunkirk. Douai is south of Lille.

*Sergeant Frederick Snow. 2/5th Battalion Leicestershire Regiment. 1940.*

With Sergeant Frederick Snow in the 2/5th, was Jack Smith of 'Volume 1', and their journey bisected the Great War battlefields of northern France and Belgium. The B.E.F. had no option but to withdraw when outflanked by an enemy with more tanks, artillery and superior co-ordination within their Forces; generally the French were disorganised and poorly led. The withdrawal followed a corridor to the Channel coast: the southern section of which was continually attacked by enemy armour. On May 17th, the Battalion was close to the Belgium border: near to Seclin, and then marched to Renaix (see map). Their first duties were to guard and keep the roads clear and also to

undertake anti-sabotage tasks. It was to prove a thankless mission. The serious circumstances bred a general drought of information, which caused a lack of co-ordination. Also, it wasn't easy to shepherd nervous civilian refugees aside to allow drained, battle scarred allied troops to pass, particularly when regularly targeted by enemy bombers and fighters from an apparently unhindered air force. Most of the British 1st Division passed along this route and many of their drivers were unclear of their destination. The men of the 2/5th performed especially well! The Battalion was ordered, on May 18th, to withdraw from Renaix: partway by truck but also a forced march of forty-five kilometres (thirty miles), sometimes along uneven cobbles. On May 19th they arrived at Toufflers with blistered feet and low on food, and next day marched to Lesquin, and on the 20th to Emmerin. Whilst there, Brigadier Chichester-Constable instructed them to move to the forward areas the following day, their task, as part of a new defensive force, was to guard the southern flank of the withdrawing B.E.F. On May 21st, they marched to Bois de Flines, living off the land and moving closer to the fighting. Next day they arrived in the area of Marchiennes, and took up a defensive position alongside the River Scharpe (see Douai on map), guarding bridges and other crossings. By May 23rd, enemy troops had occupied Abbeville and cut the Somme Line, also the Luftwaffe was bombing Boulogne, Calais and Dunkirk. On May 24th, due to a faltering frontline, they were directed to Carvin. Battalion troops lined the River Escaut, and received orders to defend a crossing point on the Canal de la Haute Deole, near to Pont-a-Vendin. The Battalion had to spread its Companies thinly: stretching over eight miles, with only French and Senegalese troops in support, and their morale was poor due to language problems and mutual distrust. On the night of May 25-26th, during a fierce thunderstorm and British barrage, large numbers of German troops were spotted massing on the other side of the canal; soon their artillery opened up a barrage. **Captain Geoff Gee led his Company (and other officers likewise) into slit trenches near to a colliery slagheap. At about 10.00am the barrage stopped and thirty 'shrieking' Stuka dive-bombers descended upon them; heavy shelling and machine-gun fire followed this, also an assault crossing along the length of the Battalion's front. With only rifles, Bren-guns and anti-tank guns, they were overwhelmed by superior numbers and withdrew by stages, but hundreds were killed, wounded or taken prisoner. However, Fred Snow, Jack Smith and others escaped across open country, mainly men from Captain Gee's 'B' Company. About forty men took cover that night in a house at Seclin; next day they slaughtered poultry to roast and Private Foulds, of Woodhouse Eaves, milked a cow. The following morning, upon hearing gunfire, left to march to Lille and in the evening passed blazing villages that turned the sky red.

spoke of his capture, the canal, and of a farm where he and other prisoners had their first decent sleep for ten days. Dick was imprisoned at Stammlager XXA camp. The escapees filtered their way towards Dunkirk, joining an exodus of nearly half a million troops seeking salvation. They entered many villages and towns with familiar names from 1914-18; it must have seemed ironical to RSM Edwin Ross DCM, and RQMS Joe French DCM, as both were Great War veterans. Arriving in the suburbs of Dunkirk, they saw colleagues dismantling huge quantities of lorries and armoured vehicles. Military police were seen using pickaxes to pierce engine sumps and then running the engines until they seized-up. Fred, without knowing, perhaps one was his uncle.

A small group from the Battalion, under the command of Major K. Symington, was ordered to defend a blockade at Couderkerque, while others were also drafted into the rearguard: 'They Shall Not Pass' was the byword and the evacuation was code-named: 'Operation Dynamo', all planned in the Casemates within Dover's chalk cliffs.

The centre of Dunkirk was in chaos; it was being shelled and bombed and there were lengthy queues of troops wherever one looked. There were appalling sights of dead and dying soldiers lying on roadsides and nearby dunes, with no escape from enemy fighters and bombers. Soldiers felt that the R.A.F. was letting them down, but this was an erroneous belief; our fighters were engaging the Luftwaffe inland, and but for them the situation could have failed. Dunkirk's oil tanks were burning: enormous black plumes of smoke could be seen from southern England! Lieutenant Richard Everard said that men on the packed beaches cheered when six Spitfires flew over, the first they had seen in fourteen days. The Lieutenant and some of his men reached the mole and crossed on the Channel steamer: 'Canterbury'.

*Rear left: Corporal Dick Vincent with other 2/5 Battalion prisoners at Stammlager XXA camp.*

After the Channel crossing the remnants of the Battalion were taken to a staging camp; firstly they only numbered ninety men: more arrived later.

A one time next-door neighbour and friend of the author's, Corporal Dick Vincent, wasn't fortunate; he

Apart from those mentioned, Lance Corporal Ronald 'Clem' Webster of Coalville was also evacuated. Clem

Troops wade out into the Channel. 1940.

Huge queues cover the Dunkirk beach. The mole
(pier) is on the left.

Coalville soldier Ronald
'Clem' Webster of the 2/5th
Leicestershire Battalion.

swam out to the 'little boats' and was machine-gunned by enemy fighters during the process. Maurice Cornfore, of St. Saviour's Road, Coalville was also an evacuee and returned to France on 'D'-Day 1944; he also fought in Italy and Germany. An old friend of the authors: Gordon Elliot from Earl Shilton was evacuated to Folkestone. He served with the R.A.M.C. and witnessed some alarming scenes.

**Geoff's brother, Harry, lived at Old Woodhouse for many years. Their family owned the Leicester shoe firm of Stead and Simpson.

Malcolm Smith recalls seeing his half-brother soon afterwards:

*"I recall walking with Mum in Nottingham in early June 1940, and seeing this bedraggled group of soldiers. Mum shouted: "There's Fred!" She dashed into the middle of the road and embraced her son: a survivor from the beaches of Dunkirk. Mum was doubly lucky as her brother was also evacuated."*

Fred asked to join the Army Air Corps (A.A.C.) as a trainee glider pilot. He was accepted but failed to qualify, and so he immediately enlisted into the newly formed, elitist Parachute Regiment, where he swiftly received promotion.

Sergeant F. Snow participated in the 'D'-Day Landings of 6th June 1944; rather, paratroopers were taken by glider or parachuted behind the enemy's coastal defences the night before.

This allowed them to capture or destroy bridges, strategic positions or ammunition dumps; so delaying or denying the enemy from supporting their frontline. Malcolm:

*"My brother was passionately proud of being in the Paras and remained with them till war's end. When his battalion returned from Normandy they were in barracks at Tilshead, on the Salisbury Plain. My parents and I travelled to see him, and we were introduced to the officers and NCOs. It was very evident that Fred was highly thought of and very popular. I too was made much-of, in spite of many of those men having arms and legs in plaster. We had lodged at a nearby cottage, and one day Fred called in a army truck; being a nosy thirteen year old I went to look it over, but taken aback to find the rear full of German prisoners: all officers. One of them saw my fear/shock and so took off a winged cap badge and handed it to me: I have it to this day. Later in the war (almost certainly the Arnhem Campaign) I recall coming home from school to see Mum in floods of tears: she'd received notification that Fred was missing in action. She no doubt thought fated: to loose a son in warfare, just like she lost his father in an earlier war. I swore that I would kill every German I met! It transpired that he was in hospital with a severe head wound and suffering from memory loss. He recovered but the physical scars remained: losing most of his scalp."*

Malcolm says that Fred was very much the no nonsense regular soldier; he was still serving when Malcolm was doing his National Service and based near to Aldershot.

"*I was about to go abroad and received an order to report to the orderly room. I was shown into the Company Sergeant Major's office to find my brother chatting to him. Afterwards I was told that Fred simply walked into the office had demanded to see the CSM, thereto he said his kid brother was in the camp and wished to see him.*"

While Malcolm was in Korea, he received a letter from his brother asking him to remember him to a Regimental Sergeant Major: they'd served together in India during pre-war days.

While Fred was serving in post-war Germany, presumably, he failed a medical examination; and was reposted to a Worcestershire Battalion, but disliked it and so retired from the army in the late 1950's. Fred served Crown and country for nearly thirty years: in the Far East and on the battlefields of northern France, Belgium, Holland and Germany. It was men of his ilk, and his uncle, that enabled our island race the opportunity and freedom that we have to this day! His late father would have been very proud of him.

Malcolm has the last word: "*My brother returned home and lived for a time with Mum and Dad. He had several jobs and eventually bought his own heavy-goods-vehicle, which became his livelihood until retirement. In his later years he lived with his wife, Elsie, at West Bridgford, a suburb of Nottingham. When Fred passed away in 1988, aged seventy-five, a number of his paratrooper associates attended his funeral, which was accorded full military honours.*"

While Fred was with the B.E.F. in France he must have considered the possibility of visiting his father's grave, but realistically it could never have happened during such troubled times. In later years Malcolm performed that duty for him.

Malcolm's uncle, Bill Smith, served with the Royal Marines and was involved in the Dieppe raid and later in northern Europe. Another paternal uncle, Frederick Smith served with the Grenadier Guards in Europe whilst another, Sydney Smith, was an engineer at Brush Electrics of Loughborough and he received a handwritten letter from Baden Powell congratulating him on the formation of the first scout troop in Loughborough.

Many thanks to Fred's half brother: Malcolm Smith, cousin to John Collier.

# CLEMENT J. W. CULLEY

*Rear left: Sergeant Clement Culley, rear centre: Flight Sergeant Siddle. Circa 1943.*

latter taking eight hours and fifteen minutes and with a claim for a Messerschmitt 109 fighter. I turn the neatly and boldly written pages of Clement's Log Book; red indicates raids whilst black represents training flights, etc. Red: 6th September 1943, it is recorded that the damaged Lancaster 'U', flown by the now promoted, Pilot Officer Siddle, crashed on return landing after bombing Munich. Red: 23rd December 1943, Lancaster 'R' was operating over Berlin; six days later they returned to the capital city with yet another consignment.

Clement was born on 14th August 1922. His family home was on Marshgate Lane, Stratford, in London E15, and this is where he lived with his parents, brother, Tony and two sisters. In the early 1940's he enlisted into the Royal Air Force and requested to be aircrew, possibly as a means of retaliating against the Luftwaffe's aerial bombardment of his hometown and other cities. He asked to be trained as an air-gunner and applied for the highly dangerous position of tail gunner: open to volunteers only! At No3 Air Gunnery School he obtained a 72.3 percent pass mark, which included using tracer bullets fired for a beam, under tail and quarter attack. He also attended No4 Radio School and qualified as an excellent wireless operator, so good in fact that this was to be his future role in Bomber Command.

His early months of training was in a Wellington bomber, usually flown by a Sergeant Siddle, and this involved mock high level bombing, night flights, formation flying, etc, to allow the crew to bond into an able and confident team. After a spell on a Manchester bomber they finally completed their training on the legendary Lancaster heavy bomber.

The team was allotted to 'B' Flight of 9 Squadron, based at Bardney: sixteen kilometres (ten miles) due east of Lincoln. Six days later, just after sunset, they took off in Lancaster 'U' for a raid over Hamburg; Clement was the wireless operator and the round trip took an arduous and hazardous five hours-twenty minutes. There followed yet another raid on Hamburg and then flights over Mannheim and Nuremberg, the

*Clement Culley*

The principal task of Bomber Command was to obliterate the enemy's war manufacturing capacity: capital war items, weapons, equipment and munitions! Another function was to lessen the population's willingness to wage war. Post-war, this became a contentious issue with the politically correct and pacifist fringe, but it must be stated that from the moment Hitler swept through most of Europe, Bomber Command was Britain's only means of countering Germany's aggression, and their role was supported by the nation's majority. Sadly, and regrettably, but those who live by the sword, die by the sword!

In the war's early days, especially, it was recognised that high level bombing was notoriously and widely inaccurate, often several miles off target. This resulted in thousands of civilians losing their lives, and consequently many key targets left undamaged. As a result, on 5th July 1942, Arthur Harris, Commander in Chief of Bomber Command, appointed Group Captain Donald C. T. Bennett to take charge of a Force consisting of five Squadrons: 7, 35, 83, 109, and 156. The conception was based on 'elite raid leaders'; a selection of experienced, efficient aircrews to specialize and spearhead R.A.F. bomber fleets over enemy territory. Identifying the targets was vital: they would drop coloured flares and/or 'gel bombs' (that produced vivid white flames), marker bombs, incendiaries, high altitude sky flares for use above clouds, etc. They were named the Pathfinder Force (PFF), and steadily the standard of bombing precision improved; from the onset the bravery of the aircrew was immense. The Force grew in size commiserate to the success obtained!

The quality of Pilot Officer Siddle and his crew had been noted, and in early 1944 they were transferred to 'B' Flight with the famed 83 Squadron. Warrant Officer Clement Culley had become a Pathfinder and the Squadron was based at Wyton, just east of Huntingdon in Hertfordshire. In the spring of the same year they moved to Coningsby, twenty-six kilometres (sixteen miles) south east of Lincoln.

Due to the additional dangers therein, all PFF members were volunteers and primarily the most experienced and capable aircrew of Bomber Command.

At least three members were awarded posthumous V.C.s: Ian Bazalette, Edwin Swales and Robert Palmer, the latter being trained at Desford, and we will never forget Leonard Cheshire.

On 16th February 1944, Lancaster 'N' was over

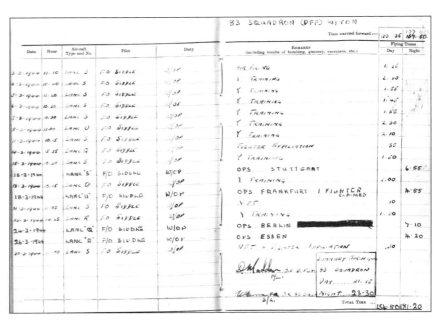

*Clement Culley's Log Book.*

*The two markers of 'A' show where the Pathfinders target indicator bombs have been dropped. Numerous sticks of incendiaries can also be seen burning.*

Berlin, and they claimed two fighters shot down during a seven hours-forty minutes mission. Three days later they highlighted targets over Leipzig. Clement saw action over Berlin, Leipzig, Stuttgart, Frankfurt, Essen, La Chapelle, Schweinfurt, St. Medard, Toulouse, Brest, Pas de Calais (Flying bomb platforms), and Kiel. The targets were sites such as ball-bearing works, railway yards, oil refineries, bridges, etc. There followed targets:

1st June 1944   -   Saumur Railway Bridge.
5th June 1944   -   La Pernelle Flak Guns.
6th June 1944   -   Caen Railway Bridge.
10th June 1944   -   Orleans Railway yards.
21st June 1944   -   Wesseling Oil refinery (near Koln).

Of particular note is the evening raid of 5th June 1944 with Clement's Lancaster 'S' involved in the bombing of the anti-aircraft (flak) guns at La Pernelle; the following day came the second front with the invasion of Normandy ('D'-Day: viz Destination Day). And so it continued, the unceasing endeavours to improve precision and techniques led to even greater stress being placed upon the crews.

*Adeline tries on Clement's uniform. 4th September, 1947.*

*Clement Culley, circa 1945.*

*The farmhouse for 'Home Farm' where Clement, Adeline and Brian lived.*

Whilst in the R.A.F., Clement met Adeline Pepper, originally from 'Bybrook Farm' in Swithland, near to Woodhouse Eaves, Leicestershire, but in 1930 the family (she had two brothers: Bryan and Norman), moved to 'Home Farm', 30 Soar Road in Quorn (Quorndon). Clement and Adeline married on 6th July 1946.

On leaving the R.A.F. in early 1948, Clement had the following flying hours in his Log Book: Daylight: 359 hours forty minutes. Night: 385 hours fifty minutes. A grand total of 745 hours and thirty minutes, or 31 days and 1hour thirty minutes. Analysis shows that Clement spent 245 hours and 25 minutes (or ten days, five hours and twenty-five minutes) in Lancaster bombers over enemy occupied territory. Bravery, endurance, resilience, composure, stress!

Clement and Adeline lived at 'Home Farm' with

Brian: born on 17th April 1947. Adeline's brother, Bryan Pepper still lives in the farmhouse, with Adeline just a few doors away.

For many years Clement worked at Rolls Royce and later owned an antique shop on Station Road, Quorn. The old Pathfinder passed away in 1982; his brother, Tony Culley was Chief Flight Control Officer at Gatwick Airport during his working life.

Brian Culley owns the award winning fish and chip shop in Quorn (the old antique shop) and he and his wife have two sons, Jon and Stephen.

Air Chief Marshal Sir Arthur 'Bomber' Harris died on the 5th April 1984 aged ninety four years, while Australian, Don Bennett died on 14th September 1986, his seventy-sixth birthday. Even after sixty years the arguments continue about the ethics and efficacy concerning aerial bombing, not just of Germany but

Brian Culley in his award-winning fish and chip shop The photograph on the wall above him is of his son, Jon, who has just caught a whopper!

Clement and Adeline Culley during their middle years.

also the nuclear devices dropped by the U.S.A.F. on Japan. Judgement is always polarised as indeed the deeds, with the German campaign starting in 1940 and the Japanese ending in 1945. It is easy to pass a retrospective comment; I believe that only the individuals who made the decisions at the time can have the final say. Both men believed that bombing shortened the war and thus saved lives in the long run.

Rudyard Kipling sees and writes it to perfection:

Oh, it's Tommy this an' Tommy that an'
Tommy go away.

But it's 'Thank you Mr Atkins'
when the band begins to play.

Its Tommy this an' Tommy that and
'Chuck him out the brute.'

But it's 'Saviour of his country'
when the guns begin to shoot.

Then it's Tommy this an'
Tommy that and Tommy 'ow's yer soul?

But it's thin red line of
'eroes when the drums begin to roll.

History shows that fighting forces are revered when they succeed in their task of saving or winning a battle, but condemned when there has been severe loss of life.

It is possible to name the remainder of Clement's crew, but not to identify their faces; Clayton Moore was one of their number, as was flight engineer: Reginald Mosley, bomb aimer: Alan Machin, Dick Jones the mid-upper gunner, and Dick Lodge the navigator.

My thanks to Brian Culley and his mother, Adeline. Clement will now be remembered.

Just off Station Road at Quorn can be seen a plaque: *'This avenue of trees was presented to the village by F. A. Stenson esquire, and is dedicated to the many United States of American Forces who were based in this Parish during the 1939-45 War but did not return from their missions. This stone is from the damaged church at Nijmegen, the scene of one of their paratroop engagements. May 1952.'*

# JAMES HATFIELD D.F.M.

*A young John Hatfield.*

James, called John in later life, and throughout what follows, was one of four siblings to James and Margaret Hatfield of Waingroves, a small mining village that lies about a mile from the town of Ripley in Derbyshire. The eldest son, George, born in 1910, spent about five years in the wartime Royal Air Force, mostly at Aden. Second son, William, born 1914, spent all of his working life, as did his father, in the Gas Industry, which had been the traditional occupation of the Hatfield family for three/four generations. The youngest sibling, Marjorie, the only girl, was born in 1928, while John was born on 1st February 1921. John's early education was at the village school: strong in its emphasis on the three 'R's and little else. At the age of eleven he was transferred, along with others, to Codnor Central School, two miles south of Ripley. It was a progressive establishment, ahead of its time, with science on the syllabus, a subject in which John had a keen interest. Aged fourteen he started work, also in the Gas Industry, as a technical assistant and commenced part time studies in chemistry at Derby Technical College. By seventeen he had passed the preliminary examinations and had embarked on a course leading to

a degree, however, war clouds interfered with this schedule. His perception of the future was perhaps implied when he volunteered to assist the local defence group, filling sand bags and assembling civilian gas masks. Then came Sunday, 3rd September 1939. John recalls:

*"Chamberlain announced that we were at war with Germany. I said nothing but was excited; mother was upset, but lads of my age had heard of the Great War: trenches, mud, rats, shells and the great songs: 'The Long, Long Trail a Winding' & 'Keep The Home Fires Burning'."* Life changed rapidly: windows had blackouts fitted, ration books issued, cinemas closed, church bells remained silent (unless the Germans invaded), signposts removed, place names painted over, etc. John's bus-trip to Derby College took longer, with windows locked and covered, interiors filled with smoke. However, all were eclipsed in January 1940:

*"January was very cold with skating on ponds and Butterley reservoir: life seemed exciting. Suddenly, unexpectedly, our father died, just fifty-four years of age! I was devastated, lost interest in studying and suffered a severe influenza attack. I stayed away from college until the departmental head persuaded me to continue."*

Later in September, John answered a newspaper advertisement for young men to train for flying duties. He travelled to Cardington, Bedfordshire, and was interviewed by a panel of officers who said they were satisfied by his knowledge of trigonometry, vectors, etc, and was provisionally accepted for training as 'aircrew' (actual 'trade' not yet advised), and then sent home pending further communication. He was recalled to Cardington only a few days later and informed that he would be accepted for training as a pilot.

*"I officially joined the R.A.F. on 10th October 1940, a cold, misty day. At Cardington I entered a Nissan hut and was allocated a steel-framed bed and three straw packed 'biscuits'. On top were three army blankets and two sheets. I was given a Form 1250, a blue Identity Card, and two identity discs to wear around my neck, one reddish, one grey, one impervious to water and one (a tacit message here perhaps) to fire. Together with a uniform, cutlery, a mug encrested R.A.F., webbing, injections/ vaccinations, I emerged as AC2 James Hatfield, service number: 1196249."*

While awaiting training, John was posted to the R.A.F. Regiment at Cottesmore airfield, Rutland, where a squadron of *Hampden* bombers was based. He, along with his new mates, was put on airfield-perimeter guard duty.

*"We were billeted in half-built houses smelling of damp sawdust and plaster. Plumbers hammered away and we were miles from a mess hall. At night we were driven to a remote timber hut where a corporal and six of us guarded the aerodrome for two hours on-four hours off."*

Off duty, John and friends visited Oakham, finding a pub landlord who tolerated thirty minutes to drink half-a-pint each.

Returning they got lost and arrived at camp at 02.00, greeted by a duty sergeant not best pleased. Then a posting to Morecambe, Lancashire; billeted in a cheap boarding house with rooms stripped of all fittings and furnished with steel beds. At four to a room, theirs opened onto a hall damp from spray. John was introduced to gymnastics, parade drill and rifle drill using Lee Enfield 303s of First World War vintage.

*"We had allowed twenty rounds each: half for a good grouping, the rest for rapid-fire. I was suitably impressed with the angry recoil and barrel temperature after firing twenty bullets."*

Next to Stratford-upon-Avon where John recalls appalling meals, and wondered whether the tea was bromide-laced to reduce sexual desires, or just tasted that way. Finally to No6 Initial Training Wing at Aberystwyth, a holiday resort on the west coast of Wales.

*"We were billeted in the 'Belle View Hotel', rooms stripped bare. We learned navigation, meteorology, signalling (Morse and lamp), and aircraft recognition. I had two unpleasant and foolhardy experiences with river and sea stunts, but joy in a spring afternoon hike over Cader Idris and excitement of seeing a German Dornier bomber at two hundred feet scurrying across the Bay. And guard duty on cold moonlit nights, with the sound of the sea washing the pebbles on the beach."*

John, now promoted to Leading Aircraftsman (L.A.C.), was next posted to the R.A.F. centre at Wilmslow, near Manchester, with many other young men aspiring to aircrew, all identified by a white flash on their caps. Futures were decided here: forms stating which Elementary Flying Training School to attend. Until then, training was mostly in Britain. However, larger numbers of aircrew were needed, and the Air Ministry looked for facilities in the U.S.A. Later, John was one of the first five hundred to cross the Atlantic (8,000 up to closure in 1944) for training under the new 'Arnold Scheme'. The trainees entered the U.S.A. as civilians, and wearing grey flannelled civilian suits. The U.S.A. was officially 'neutral'.

(**About 4,000 entrants ultimately received silver U.S.A.A.F. (United States Army and Air Force) 'Wings' at conclusion of their training, of which about 2,000 were subsequently killed in later training or in action.)

*"It is difficult to describe the enormity of the venture. To us America was like another planet, what with Hollywood, the Wild West, High Society glamour and Bing Crosby."*

Leaving Greenock Docks in mid-May 1941 aboard 'Britannic' of the Cunard White Star Fleet, they were escorted by H.M.S. 'Rodney', a powerful battleship with four attendant destroyers. Two days later a violent storm blew up.

*"It was fierce with rolling hillocks of blue/black sea tipped with white spray. 'Rodney' was indifferent to the swell: big and solid, while the destroyers fussed about us like porpoises."*

They never tired of seeing 'Rodney', that leviathan in her stewardship, but suddenly she and three of the destroyers turned ninety degrees and headed due north.

The departure was a result of 'Bismarck', a German pocket battleship, that was reported to be on the loose in the North Atlantic and heading in *Britannic's* direction. In the ensuing naval encounter H.M.S. 'Hood' was sunk, only three crewmen from fourteen hundred surviving. Later seaplanes torpedoed 'Bismarck' and 'Rodney' helped sink her, two thousand German sailors dying. Recent correspondence enabled John to discover that Ludovik Kennedy (now Sir) was an officer serving on one of the destroyers escorting 'Rodney'.

*Britannic* steered southwest as a means of avoiding 'U'-Boats.

*"The course took us to the Azores and after nine-ten days at sea we landed at Halifax, Nova Scotia. We*

ASHDOWN
AVEBURY
MARLBOROUGH
WILTSHIRE SN8 1RF
TEL/FAX: (01672) 539274

J. Hatfield
124 Meadow Lane
Coalville
Leics. LE67 4DP

1 June 2001

Dear Mr Hatfield,

Many thanks for yours of 20 May which I read with great interest. I was in
one of the destroyers escorting you. But according to my records the ship
you were on was the *Britannic* and not the *Georgic* which was also at sea at
the time being protected by Captain Vian's Tribal destroyers which were
detached to attack the *Bismarck* during the night with torpedoes
unsuccessfully.

With all good wishes,

Yours sincerely,

*Ludovic Kennedy*

(Sir Ludovic Kennedy)

*A letter sent to John Hatfield by Sir Ludovik Kennedy.*

All eyes were on these boys who paraded in Tuscaloosa yesterday. This picture shows part of the group of Royal Air Force pilots being trained at the Air Corps Training Detachment in Tuscaloosa. Stores closed and bands played a sthe city welcomed the British and Canadian fliers.
—Staff Photos.

*entrained for Moncton, New Brunswick, about one
hundred miles away and likewise to Toronto, another
eight hundred miles, and once there we were taken to
a large Royal Canadian Air Force reception centre:
the Manning Depot."*

Arrangements were in hand for transportation of
the cadets to the southern States of the U.S.A. with
John's group scheduled for Tuscaloosa, Alabama. See
photo of itinerary.

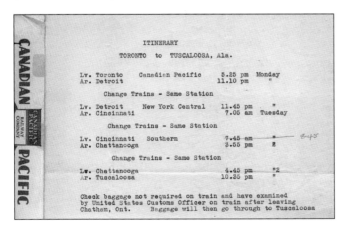

*"Our Flying School was a civilian organisation.
Already stationed there were fifty American cadets
about five weeks ahead of us in instruction. We had a
parade through town, and, for this occasion only we
were allowed to march proudly, if uncomfortably, in
R.A.F. uniforms.*

*The crowd was large, the atmosphere electric, and
it was a very hot June day. I have the newspaper
cutting of us standing at ease whilst listening to
various orations."* See photo.

The first five of ten weeks involved basics of
flying, the remainder with relevant techniques and
experiences. The training aircraft was a Boeing
'*Stearman*' *PT17*, a sturdily built bi-plane. John
comments:

*"I returned to Tuscaloosa in 1991. Back in 1941
the locals were very charitable and kind; but now only
one aged lady could recall the British boys that made
such an impact on their town. I saw the large arched
hanger, but most other buildings had gone. I almost
'heard' the engine sounds of our youth and the
flapping of the lazy wind sock by the control tower."*

Next, 'Gunter Field', a U.S.A.A.F. Station near to
Montgomery, capital city of Alabama, for another ten
week course. This was followed by 'Maxwell Field'
for the final ten weeks of advanced training on a single
wing A.T.6 '*Harvard*'. Towards the end of the course
they flew '*Harvards*' armed with a machine-gun and
practised aiming for a ground target. During a night
cross-country flight, John lost two of his friends when
their aircraft crashed.

On 7th December 1941, a surprise Japanese air
attack on the U.S.A. Naval Base on Oahu Island,
Hawaii, in the Pacific, resulted in over three thousand

military personnel being killed and a large section of their Pacific Fleet destroyed. 'Pearl Harbour' brought the U.S.A. into World War 2 with the Japanese becoming allied to Germany.

*"We completed the course in January 1942, and at graduation our sterling silver Wings were presented. When pinned to our jackets we felt enormously proud of our achievements, but we quickly acquired the famous embroidered R.A.F Wings and sewed them to our jackets."*

After six months away they returned to Moncton Barracks, New Brunswick, and winter had truly arrived in Canada:

*"Glistening snow two feet deep, yard long icicles hanging from gutterings. Billets with yellow lights shining through triple-glazed windows in the double insulated walls. It was a Dickensian scene and typical of many Christmas cards."*

When they finally arrived at Halifax harbour, ships were arriving festooned in inches-thick- ice: rigging and hand railing looking like glass. They sailed in late January 1942 aboard the Dutch liner: SS 'Volendam'. On 1st February 1942, John's twenty-first birthday, they were in mid-Atlantic when at 22.00 hours alarm bells sounded and the ship's engines stopped.

*"The ocean was still and in full moon it looked like a pool of mercury, no ripples, no swell. All was quiet. After ten minutes a deafening explosion rent the air; it was not a torpedo explosion, just an over enthusiastic gunner on the five-pounder situated on the ship's stern."*

Back in England, John was posted to No12 Advanced Flying Training School at Spitalgate, near Grantham, Lincolnshire, training on twin engined 'Oxfords'. He once flew over his village at one thousand feet and saw his mother, who waved a towel, at which John waggled his wings with glee. Training continued all summer; dense morning mists often concealed the airfield, testing all the pilots' skills and bravery. Sadness was never far away and two of John's friends were killed. In mist one struck the mast of a ship in Grimsby harbour and the other grafted itself to a hillside.

Passing out 'above average' he was posted to No15 Operational Training Unit, Harwell, Oxfordshire for training on a Wellington 1C bomber aircraft. John's crew was: an Irish front-gunner, two Scots, one a rear-gunner from Glasgow, the other a radio-operator from Aberdeen, and a navigator from a southern county, all sergeants.

*"The Wellington 1c seemed large and heavy, but the power of the two Pegasus engines provided that awesome feeling of at last piloting a real aircraft. We did a lot of night flying and simulation bombing."*

On completion of training, in August 1942, two newly commissioned pilot officers were added to the crew, one as captain and the other as navigator. Although always causing a little friction, the modified crew were posted to an operational squadron in the Middle East, and on September 18th flew to Portreath, Cornwall, prior to the flight to Gibraltar.

*"On the 19th we roared down the runway and levelled at two thousand feet. After an hour the starboard engine's oil gauge commenced wobbling. We set course for Portreath and jettisoned guns, ammunition, and anything else to hand. After earlier rehearsals we all knew precisely what to do. Excess fuel was dumped and minutes later the captain gave the well practised order: 'Dinghy, Dinghy, whilst the radio operator transmitted an S.O.S. and we took to our ditching positions. As trained, the pilot allowed the tail wheel to touch the sea first and then the aircraft jolted to an almighty stop within feet. The bottom of the aircraft was torn out and the sea flooded in like a tidal wave. We were momentarily submerged, and on surfacing saw the dingy inflate with carbon dioxide. We were safely down but the wireless operator was floating in the sea, barely conscious, with a head wound caused by the crash. Jumping off the wing into the sea I doggy-paddled him towards the dinghy where he was pulled aboard. Five minutes later our aeroplane sank into the Bay of Biscay. The sea was very choppy and white-capped waves crashed into our dinghy. The wireless operator, bloody, but by now conscious slowly recovered. We were all shocked and extremely cold, having dumped most of our clothing and now attired only in shirts and trousers. Our S.O.S. had been picked up and after five hours were collected by a high-powered launch from Air-Sea Rescue on the Isles of Scilly. Official rescue procedures recommend a drink of hot sweet tea, but the captain of the launch managed to persuade us to sample his bottle of rum and we were quite happy when we made St. Mary's."*

(** In 1995 John revisited St. Mary's and found a crew

*The rescue launch R.M.L.542.*

*The quayside at Hughtown, Scilly Isles.*

member who was involved in that very rescue during the War; he very kindly gave John a photograph of the launch RML 542 (see photo.)

After a week's 'Survivors' Leave' they were posted to O.T.U. at Moreton-in-Marsh and took charge of a new Wellington. In late October the same crew flew again to Portreath, and on November 21st set course for Gibraltar. After six hours flight they found the Rock hidden by a thick fog. Ground Control advised they fly onto Port Lyautey in French Morocco, which they duly did. On landing they were told by an American Ground Controller not to vacate their aircraft or risk getting shot; the Vichy French were causing trouble and the Americans were using the landing strip as a no-go area.

Ultimately they were taken to an American destroyer moored in the port, well fed and allowed a blissful sleep before flying back to the Rock. Once there, they were delayed by bad weather; the captain considered it too dangerous to fly and complications set in. John heard that the captain and navigator were flown back to England: no explanation was given other than to pack their kit and board a ship bound for Glasgow.

*"We were the only non-civilians on board and received excellent treatment. A good deal of Strauss was played on the Tannoy system and the only sad memory was later hearing that our Wimpy, taken over by a new crew, had malfunctioned on take-off and crashed into the sea, killing all!"*

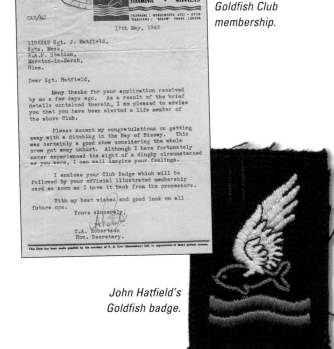

*Goldfish Club membership.*

*John Hatfield's Goldfish badge.*

*John Hatfield.*

Docking at Glasgow on December 23rd, the four received separate orders to attend different O.T.U.s. John and the front-gunner spent Christmas Day with the Glaswegian family of the rear-gunner, whereas the radio-operator set off for Aberdeen. Good-byes all round!

John, again as captain, descended on Moreton-in-Marsh, No21 O.T.U., and recommenced in February 1943 with a new crew.

*"The wireless operator was an ex-London policeman who had been awarded the George Medal for bravery during the Blitz. The navigator came from Lincoln. The bomb-aimer/front-gunner from Chesterfield and the fifth member was a very young rear-gunner."*

The team bonded very well and after three months, mid-May 1943, they flew from Portreath to land at Ras El Ma, then in French Morocco. It took eight hours of flight, mostly over sea, and proved wearying. The following day they flew east for seven hours along the Mediterranean to Castel Benito, and then a two-hour flight to El Gardabia and 104 Squadron.

*"We believed this was to be our ultimate destination, to assist 104 Squadron in bombing Messina on the big toe of Italy. But no, after a few days in the desert we were posted to India: Burma was hotting up."*

with thatched roofs, and the whole almost surrounded by woodland and palms.

John's first war operation began with an experienced pilot in command, when a bridge was attacked at low level with 250-pound bombs. Standing alongside the captain, he had a ringside view of what was happening, a view second only to that of the front turret-gunner, who could be heard firing bursts into the smoke below, *'retaliating to heavy machine-gun fire coming towards us'*, he assured the captain! A target on Ramree Island was next attacked, also at low level, and left ablaze.

John, now as captain, and crew, were next turned loose on a series of coastal patrols and long flights inland over the Burmese hills and jungle. All such flights, whilst not exposed to enemy gunfire, required placing faith in two engines. If they failed, the choices were ditching in hostile waters or crashing into the dense jungle, where no prisoners were taken!

Night flying had its own nightmares. The latest (as in the 1940s) navigational aids, radar, etc, were unavailable in this theatre of war operations, and

إلى كل عربي كريم

السلام عليكم ورحمة الله وبعد فحامل هذا الكتاب ضابط بالجيش البريطاني وهو صديق
لكافة الشعوب العربية فنرجو أن تعاملوه باللطف والاكرام . وأن تحافظوا على حياته
وفي من كل طارئ. ونأمل عند الاضطرار أن تقدموا له مايحتاج اليه من طعام وشراب . وأن
ترشدوه إلى أقرب معسكر بريطاني وسنكافئكم مالياً بسخاء على ماتسدونه اليه من خدمات .
والسلام عليكم ورحمة الله وبركاته .

القيادة البريطانية العامة في الشرق

To all Arab Peoples - Greetings and Peace be upon you. The bearer of this letter is an Officer of the British Government and a friend of all Arabs. Treat him well, guard him from harm, give him food and drink, help him to return to the nearest British soldiers and you will be liberally rewarded. Peace and the Mercy of God upon you.

*The British High Command in the East*

John Hatfield's copy of what was nicknamed 'The Goolly Chit'.

They flew to Cairo, a trip of five and a half hours, spent two days there, which included a visit to the Pyramids, and then onto Habbaniya in Iraq and Aqir in Palestine. The next stop was Bahrain, all camels and minarets in the grey sand and searing heat, and an eight-hour flight to refuel at Sharjah in Arabia before touchdown at Karachi, India.

*"In early June 1943 I flew our Wimpy for nine hours to Jessore in Bengal (now Bangladesh) and joined 99 Squadron. It was to be our home for the next year. We began to settle in and in the evenings listened to scratchy records of Vera Lynn."*

The airfield was a concrete strip of about a mile long and a collection of crumbly red brick buildings

navigational skills in 'dead reckoning' and 'astro' were essential.

*"My first two night operations were in mid-August 1943; the primary target was, Taungup, the secondary, Akyab. Both were obscured by ten-tenths cloud. Six hours night-flying on instruments in cloud with intermittent sleet was very tiring, and ice on the leading edges of the wings made the controls heavy and sluggish; carrying two tons of heavy-explosive around was no one's idea of evening entertainment!"*

A week later came an identical trip to prevent a build up of Japanese troops.

A supernumerary navigator on that trip wrote to John many years later: *'Wretched weather conditions*

*Left: Sergeant Pilot James Hatfield and his crew.*

*meant that we were cut off from a clear run to base. Brilliant lightning flashes lit us up, and the vicious air currents tossed our Wimpy this way and that and the compass was useless for a while, for our skipper (John) it must have been a very dicey situation. We were lost. After a period of looking down, a break came in the cloud and I recognised land; we headed west as quickly as possible to avoid the cloud-shrouded mountains!"* John adds:

*"The violence and duration of those storms was nothing like we have in Great Britain. It was helpful being an economical pilot: my fuel consumption was near two miles a gallon, sometimes a little more, my best: 2.15."*

(Sgt. James Bowler, whose essay appeared earlier, flew in 99 Squadron. He was killed on 25th November 1940 and lived a few minutes walk from where John has lived for years.)

The dryer season approached and John flew the five hundred miles East over the Chin Hills towards Mandalay, the targets being airfields and ammunition dumps on the riverside docks at Sagaing. His bombs stirred up many an enemy nest with explosions and massive oily fires.

*"The Chin Hills rise to eight thousand feet, and flying in cirrus cloud over them often resulted in ice on the wings, thus a loss in airspeed and height. Often craggy tops were only a few hundred feet below us. After a night's raid, and as we approached base, which was often blanketed in dawn mist, my trusty navigator would stand on the step alongside me and say: "E.T.A. four and a half minutes", to which I would somewhat nervously add that I was on my last reserve tank; and sure enough he would be right. We were home safely, again!"*

Most of the crews suffered greatly from serious stomach disorders and skin infections, but just had to tolerate the problems despite the Medical Officer's best efforts, constantly assailed by a variety of relentless microbes and parasites.

The food was in short supply and pretty awful, and it was essential to be very careful what fluids were drunk: adding purifying tablets to water altered the taste from swamp-like to essence of chlorine. Malaria wasn't too much of a problem but dengue fever was, the symptoms being similar to influenza and left the victim debilitated for several days. Impetigo was common, with John having blisters on the face that scabbed and ruptured to ooze puss. Sufferers were liberally anointed with Gentian Violet, but flying, having regard to an oxygen mask, was impossible under such an affliction.

In October 1943, with the monsoons nearly finished, targets were the Japanese airfield at HeHo and marshalling yards at Sagaing, near Mandalay.

*"There were lots of searchlights but we gave them a stick of bombs. Each Wimpy carried 4,000 pounds, a mixture of 250 and 500 pounders and incendiaries. In early November, Thetabyin took a pasting before we returned to long distance coastal patrols again."*

During one such patrol John's 'Wimpy' developed propeller trouble and he had to ditch into the Bay of Bengal. He knew what to expect from his Bay of Biscay experience:

*"Following the initial impact the nose of the aircraft settled deeply into the water. Strapped in the cockpit I saw the surface three feet above me: bright green with flashes of light, bubbles and sundry debris. Nothing happened as I tugged at the harness release toggle, it was jammed! I felt weary after the labours of trying to keep the aircraft airborne and accepted that my end was to be a watery grave. In the event the radio operator dived down and with powerful muscles freed me from the harness, grabbed my collar and pulled me to the surface where the other crewmembers were already in the dinghy. The Wimpy still lies at 20.45 North by 92.12 East, or what is left of it."*

They could do little more than sit in the dinghy and hope, and after three hours heard a high-flying single-engined aircraft. By good fortune it was a Hurricane of the Royal Indian Air Force and the pilot spotted them, a chance in a million! He circled several times, wagged his wings and flew off. A torpedo boat of His Majesty's Indian Navy was nearby and after acknowledging the Hurricane's message motored at full speed for an amazing rescue.

*"Just after being picked up, a Wellington roared towards us at a height of no more than fifty feet and wagged his wings with gay abandon. It was Colin Lee, a close mate from our 99 Squadron who had been sent out to search for us."*

Around this time the Supreme Allied Commander of South East Asia, Lord Louis Mountbatten, visited the Squadron. John said:

*"Everyone lined up looking their best. He inspected us, smiled aristocratically, and occasionally stopped to have a few words with an individual. It was good for morale because the Forces in this theatre of war were largely forgotten, we were second fiddle to overcoming the European problems!"*

In late November the Squadron bombed targets at Rangoon, a long 'hairy' trip. One aircraft failed to return. December saw further raids on HeHo, a Japanese fighter airfield. It was cratered, and then another target at Wuntho received the same treatment. In the same month further night raids on Prome and Sagaing, with the constant worry of the Chin Hills, together with raids on several other Japanese airfields and dumps, often well equipped with searchlights.

*"Their searchlights improved and one night their master-beam caught me and other lights beamed in: we were well lit up. I banked violently and escaped, but for a few minutes my night vision was hopeless, a little worrying when over the target and with other pilots stooging around and possibly just as blind."*

(**Just after John had left 99 Squadron two aircraft collided over the target; the crews baled out into the jungle, never to be seen again. During this raid a Zero fighter badly shot-up one of the Wellingtons; a machine-gun bullet passed through the top of the wireless operator's leather helmet but didn't even graze his scalp.)

*"We received 4,000 pound bombs, named 'cookies' in November and dropped them on ammunition and fuel dumps, the aerial photographs taken showed an awful lot of smoke."*

On the evening of Christmas Day of 1943 they flew over the Hills and bombed ammunition dumps around Mandalay, creating havoc. They took leave whenever they could, usually in Calcutta, but twice to Darjeeling, about four hundred and forty kilometres (300 miles) north of Calcutta. Once John tried horse riding: not to his liking, finding it uncomfortable, tiring and excessively dangerous. Oh, for the wings of a dove, but not so for the shoes of a stallion!

In mid-January 1944 he was promoted to Flight Sergeant, long overdue. It had been delayed, and indeed, on 24th January 1944 the Air Ministry commissioned him as Pilot Officer.

In February, another V.I.P. visited them: an American, Major General Howard C. Davidson, Air Commander, Strategic Air Force, Eastern Air Command. His task was to find out how the British were busying themselves in their flying missions.

*"He arrived at our Jessore airfield with a retinue of white-gloved aides. We were already scheduled to bomb HeHo airfield again that night. We learned he wanted to join us on this raid, and amazed when hearing that I had been selected as his courier. It was light when we left with a 3,000-pound bomb load, a mix of 250 pounders and incendiaries, but when we arrived it was dark over the target. The weather was good but we had been warned about night fighters. The Major General occupied the second pilot's position: he didn't want to miss a thing, and even lowered himself into the bomb-aimer's position to see whether he could detect anything at ground level. The raid went very well with a lot of damage despite some nuisance from fighters. Our V.I.P. was impressed and sent me a letter, which I still have. I felt quite proud, as did our squadron commander."*

The next evening, 5th February 1944, John had a 4,000-pounder 'Cookie' to deliver to the airfield at Aungban; only a few had been dropped on Burma.

*"The bomb was big, fat, blunt nosed, over eight feet long by two-and-half feet in diameter. It was necessary to modify the bomb bays and discard the bomb doors to fit it in, causing drag and reduced airspeed. It was set to explode on impact so causing maximum surface damage. The tremendous flash was recorded on the aerial photograph. However, we had to land at Chittagong after six hours flight as we were low on fuel."*

Airfields became main targets, and on February 20th, John, as pathfinder on a raid on Taungup, first located, not an easy task, and then dropped twelve parachute flares and added six 500 pounders. 99 Squadron plastered the airfield and, later, the squadron commander warmly congratulated John. They were slowing the enemy's attack but not stopping it, and soon the Japanese would be hammering on the gates of Imphal, the door to India. Allied strategy was a 'Maximum Effort' raid to slow this Japanese advance. *"99 Squadron had two flights each of eight aircraft, the same as for 215 Squadron, who shared our airfield. We were always low on spares and other supplies but by super efforts the ground crews managed to get thirty-two Wellingtons serviceable for this special event.*

*I was second in the take-off queue, and as we gained height my rear gunner watched the third aircraft coming down the runway. Suddenly, it veered left, the port undercarriage collapsed and it ground to a halt amid dust and smoke. Then a crimson flash as ruptured fuel tanks released their contents and dislodged bombs exploded; the blast waves shook our aircraft. Below followed bright flashes as Photoflashes exploded: white smoke, then black and flames.*

*Ground Control ordered me to continue with the mission: there was precious little chatter over the intercom!"*

Returning several hours later the wreckage was still smouldering, but 'Maximum Effort' had been put on hold due to a largely unserviceable runway. The accident, almost certainly due to a tyre burst, left Bengalis combing the long grass to collect human and aircraft parts.

In May of 1944, 99 Squadron was involved for the first time in carpet-bombing. Tight formation flying was crucial; when the formation leader opened his bomb-doors the rest had to follow in unison. Thus the shower of bombs, usually 250 pounders, fell within a one thousand-metre square or so. This tactic slowed the enemy down, yet still they pushed on towards Imphal and Kohima.

*"The enemy surrounded the British and Indian Forces for the historic 'Siege of Imphal', with all supplies for the beleaguered troops having to be flown in. 99 Squadron was given the task of transporting 250 pound bombs from an airstrip at Kumbiagram into Imphal. The airstrip lies about eighty kilometres (fifty miles) east of Imphal and had no facilities other than*

Bombing of Ningthoukong on the 9th May 1944.

*the concrete airstrip, deep in thick red mud on both sides. The bombs, stacked like big, fat slugs glistened in the pouring rain as armourers, stripped to their waists, struggled to load sixteen bombs into the Wimpy bomb bays. The bombs were for the use of 'Hurribombers': Hurricane fighters equipped to carry a bomb under each wing to strafe enemy positions. Flying through the downpour was deadly, and to this day I marvel how aero-engines survived when flying through what appeared to be a sheet of water.*

*We flew to Imphal; it lies in a depression amid surrounding hills. We would take off, carrying armourers as passengers to do the off loading, and keep pretty low to spot key navigation points, and then climb slowly as the ground rose towards the hills. We were advised to watch-out for fighter resistance, but perhaps the atrocious weather kept them grounded. This was not always the case, however, as one of the crews was sadly to discover later. The weather failed to curb the aggression of the enemy's machine-gunners in the woods below, as attested by the two crews I spoke to at the time. After crossing the high ground I reduced power and made the decent to the airstrip, always aware that Zero fighters might be about!"*

These were all daylight flights; the turn round was as quick as possible and so the engines were not turned off. During this off-loading the enemy mortars and artillery pounded the area. A variety of books are available on the subject, and it is thanks to the bravery, skill and team work of all the men involved that the infantry won through in what was a dire situation.

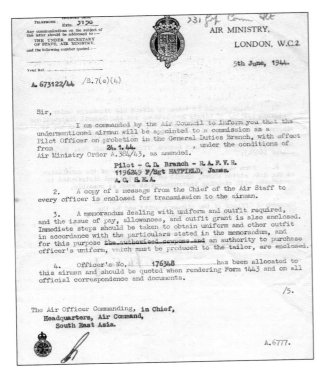

*A letter dated 5th June 1944 confirming John's promotion.*

Imphal ended John's operations over Burma and around this time he received a telegram congratulating him on receiving the Distinguished Flying Medal (D.F.M.).

*"In a year with 99 Squadron I flew twenty-two day and thirty night sorties in a 'longish' tour. Particularly stressful was when the enemy Ack-Ack was quiet: we then knew that night fighters were around, and it was like sitting in darkness knowing that a knifeman could pounce at any moment! Together with the elements were the distances flown on sorties. The 'round' Rangoon trip for instance was 1300 miles, excluding any diversions. All this on just two engines; we prayed they kept turning for eight hours and more. On occasions they didn't, and flying home on one engine was not always successful, and very dodgy when it was. We owed a lot to those who serviced our machines with limited resources and under terrific heat and disease. Despite the weather, dysentery, prickly heat, food shortage, the loss of friends and homesickness, there was a wonderful spirit between us all."*

Just after leaving Jessore, John heard of the death of their squadron commander, decorated with the D.S.O., D.F.C. and a hero of Bomber Command in the European theatre.

*"He was ferrying bombs to Imphal and was downed by a Zero fighter near to the Chin Hills. We heard they were taken alive but did not survive. One of the squadron leader's crew was Remmy, a good pal."*

John was now posted to: 'Communication Flight 231 Group', based at Alipore near Calcutta, and teamed up again with Colin 'Lofty' Lee D.F.M. John's job was to transport passengers/ information to various airfields scattered over Bengal and Assam.

During this posting John flew the two-engined American *Expediter,* the single engine high-wing *Argus*, a single engine *Proctor,* an Anson bomber, a *Harvard* and a *Hurricane*.

The war was going badly for the Japanese, in Burma, the Pacific and in their homeland, and in August 1945 two Atomic bombs ended the worldwide conflict. At the end of August, John, with a navigator, was detailed to fly three senior military types and Navy officers to recaptured Akyab. He took an *Expediter* and set off for the flight of over 300 miles.

*"We were nearing Maungdaw when large raindrops and hail hit us. All I could see was dense yellow-green cloud. We were soon in the middle of it and sight of the ground was lost. I banked to stay out of the worst, but it was endless and as black as night. The compass was spinning and in seconds we'd lost two thousand feet.*

*We didn't want an argument with hills to the east and the other direction took us to the Bay of Bengal, of unhappy memory. We tried to calm our passengers who were airsick and alarmed. I turned onto a reciprocal course intent on finding north and return to Chittagong, but it was equally bad; the storm had us in a pincer movement! I tried steering in the rough direction of Akyab and to gain height, but there was a violent downdraught. Air currents lifted, dropped and swivelled us from side to side, my artificial horizon 'toppled', the cockpit was filled with a flickering half-light and flashes of lightning were continual, and detonations of strikes were like cannon. If we had not been strapped in we'd have been tossed into the far corners of the craft. We were totally lost and our altitude was varying by hundreds of feet: possibly false readings. I could barely hear the engines! I felt that the aircraft couldn't take much more, and in desperation decided to head seawards and ditch, but which way was seaward? Then the blackness started to ease and I spotted a gap in the cloud just below; a circular hole, like the entrance to a tube with a rim of black boiling smoke, and unbelievably, we were over the concrete runway of Akyab. I went into a near vertical dive and as I did so the hole started closing like the iris of a camera. Pulling back the throttle we lost speed and then I lowered the undercarriage. I was still exceeding the safety limits but the drag slowed us down as I approached for a landing. With flaps now fully down I hit the runway and a deluge of water shot up like a bow-wave, struck the underside of the wings and made a sound like a beating drum. I was aquaplaning on the wet surface with a howling crosswind determined to push us off course. After what seemed like an age we came to a halt. I didn't taxi to a dispersal point, just switched off the engines and we looked at each other without saying a word. The passengers left with a sickly half-smile knowing we had escaped with our lives! The weather eased and we waited in the Control Tower whilst our aircraft was examined. It was in reasonable condition but the fuel tanks were virtually dry. The navigator and I prepared to return to base, but not before one of our passengers, a naval officer, said that the trip had been 'hairy but interesting'. We flew back to Alipore in the dark."*

John was next posted to No77 (Transport) Squadron, based on some desert land some way outside Karachi, the other side of India. He was ferrying troops at twenty-four a time from Karachi to Chakulia via Delhi in a Dakota 1V. Each trip took eight/nine flying hours and was routed over Agra.

Christmas 1945 and John, now a Fight Lieutenant, regularly checked the Mess Notice Board to see if his 'Demob Number' had come-up; it did in February 1946. He was now aged twenty-five years.

*"I obtained clearance signatures, etc, and found myself, on 22nd March 1946, at Lynham, England. My joy was tempered by feelings of bewilderment and insecurity. In sunshine I briskly walked across the airfield. Two young W.A.A.Fs in new uniforms tipped an inexpert salute. I was happy to be coming home but had doubts as to what my future held. I stopped at the gateway and looked at the Nissan huts, the smoky cookhouse chimney, the gaunt hangers and the redundant barrage balloons. With the next step I had left the R.A.F. apart from the memories. It all started on a cold, misty, autumnal day; now it had finished on a warm, sunny, spring day. I suppose that is how all such little histories should start and finish."*

My thanks to John for a remarkable account of life above the jungles in the Far East War.

# WILLIAM JAMES HILL

William has always been called Jim, while his father, James Roland Hill, as Roland. The latter gentleman cut a distinguished figure every Remembrance Day whilst leading the procession to Coalville's Clock Tower Memorial. Roland's story is in 'Greater Love'; born on 14th January 1880, he served with the Leicestershire Volunteers during the Boer War, and more impressively with the Fifth (1/5th) Battalion of the Leicestershire Regiment in the Great War. He helped to train the 'Famous Fifty', and on 1st January 1916, at the Battle of the Somme, saved the life of Captain Ward Jackson, by carrying his badly wounded officer back to their frontline. For this bravery he was awarded the prestigious Distinguished Conduct Medal.

*Jim Hill, aged one month, with his mother, 1916.*

Roland married Elizabeth Ann Horton on 8th April 1901 at Christ Church, Coalville, and lived at 26, Melbourne Street in the town. They had six children: Jack born in 1901 then: Leonard, Frank, Marjorie (Madge), Thomas (Tommy) and finally Jim on 5th October 1916.

In 1918, he returned to his job at Stableford's Wagon Works, and moved to 301, Ashby Road, Coalville: this is where Jim Hill grew-up. They were mainly happy years, but blemished in May 1927 when brother, Tommy, was killed on a motorbike. It was a loaned bike, and on this first journey died opposite to Broom Leys' School, aged sixteen years!

Roland Hill, a brave, honourable man, also received a certificate from: 'The Royal Humane Society' after diving fully-clothed into Stableford's pond, in an attempt to save a man who succeeded in committing suicide. Jim recalls:

*Roland Hill in 1914, 1/5th Leicestershire Battalion.*

*"Mother was a devout Christian and she brought us up that way. We attended Christ Church several times on a Sunday, and my brothers were members of the Church Lads' Brigade. I sang in the choir and knew every hymn in the Ancient &Modern and Psalms and Canticle, still do. My sister played the organ at the Sub-Church of All Saints. We loved our Madge; at a time she was poorly, her nightgown caught fire and she received bad burns."*

*1922. The Hill family from rear left: Jack, Tommy, Marjorie, Len and Frank. From front left: Roland, Jim and Elizabeth.*

As for Jim's siblings: Jack spent his entire working life in various collieries. An excellent vegetable gardener he passed on his skills to Jim, who in turn excelled in this category. Jack showed immense courage in rescuing a child that had fallen down a water-well; the well was opposite to the 'New Engine' public house at Peggs Green. Len, originally a collier, joined the Lancashire Fusiliers in the Twenties and spent an age in India. Mobilised in 1939, he remained in England during the war years, and later became head-gardener at Markfield Sanatorium. His marriage produced brothers Peter and David. Frank left the coalmines to join the Post Office and was often seen at the top of telegraph poles, especially correcting matters around Charnwood Forest after snowy weather. A fine cricketer: a founder member of Broom Leys' Cricket Club. Madge was a tailoress: employed by, 'Hart and Levy' at Leicester and then 'Thornloes'. Jim's life altered significantly when he was eleven years:

*"I passed for Broom Leys' School and found the discipline strict. The teachers wore black gowns, and we had lots of homework. I enjoyed arithmetic and read well: my bookcase contained Robinson Crusoe, Coral Island and ten volumes of 'Peoples Of All Nations', etc. While I was there I became addicted to rugby and gave it my all: becoming captain of the School's Fifteen. I was strongly built and a fast sprinter, tackled freely and in my last year won the Victor Ludorum in 1930."*

*Jim Hill with the Victor Ludorum.*

Jim's science master was none too pleased when he blew-up part of the school's science laboratory while testing the uses of sodium; however, Miss Blayney was delighted when Master Jim Hill topped the class in English literature: Jim still adores poetry.

*"I left school at fourteen. After a short time in the electrical trade I was offered a position of office junior with a well-known hosiery company at Leicester. I was very happy there."*

Aged fifteen years, he joined Coalville Rugby Club, and eventually played with many 'Old Boys': most players came from Broom Leys. Jim says that his game developed under the guidance of 'Mr. Rugby', viz: Mr. A. G. Ball (see the Ball Brothers in Volume One).

In 1932, he made a few appearances with the First Fifteen; the Coalville Times wrote: '*He filled his position with great credit for one so young, a strong runner and determined tackler, he has a great future.*' Jim was a first team regular at seventeen, and soon the captain asked him to take place kicks and penalties to the right or left of the posts up to the touchline. Scoring in most games he once kicked six penalties, that against Nuneaton Town.

*"Kicks in front of the posts were Jack Ball's domain. I was on the right wing, and Jack was my inside man: a very intelligent player. We'd a good understanding of the scissor movement; that tactic split many opposing defences."*

Jim thought that with the right coaching he could have made a name for himself in athletics. Twice a week he trained with his club and twice under his own initiative.

*"I massaged calf and thigh muscles every night with 'Elliman's Athletic Rub' before jumping into bed. I never pulled a muscle but it made my bedroom stink, but Mam never complained. After away games we'd stop there for a meal and a drink, and for home games we'd go to the Fox and Goose for a sing-song and a few pints of ale."*

Jim was a keen cyclist: a member of 'Reynard Wheelers' (now Coalville C.C.), and on some weekends cycled long distances, sleeping at Youth Hostels. Occasionally he would take a week's trip to places as far afield as Snowden, and around North Wales: totalling hundreds of miles. He also cycled to work at Leicester five days a week, thirty miles per day.

No one can catch Jim Hill as he sprints for a try. Circa 1936.

"*After home games we'd often call in at the Baths Hall on Avenue Road. The dancing was good and the girls' faces lit up when we arrived. I usually had the chance to take a girl home and arrange a walk the following day: no hanky panky in those days! Life was tough in the 1930s, so a number of us would use summer nights to walk the fields and bring home snared rabbits, mushrooms, berries, pheasants' eggs and a few bits from farmers' fields.*"

He loved cricket: a big hitter and wicket keeper in local circles, especially Broom Ley's Club. He scored many forties and fifties, but just one-century, coming in Italy in an inter-regimental match on a matting wicket just after the war had finished.

At work, after learning the finance side of the business, he moved onto the factory floor; this involved the manufacture of silk stockings, half hose, and all kinds of socks. In 1936, Jim met a lady that became the light of his life: Elsie Amy Cox. Amy, born on 11th February 1908 was the daughter of Samuel Edward and Eliza Agnes Cox. She lived with her Uncle Alfred and Aunty Rose Dennis in the house next to her siblings at 165, London Road, Coalville. Amy's Aunty, Francis Butler, ran the 'Fox & Goose' public house. The courting pair enjoyed the 'Pictures', concerts, dances and lengthy walks along the lanes and across the fields of Charnwood Forest. Amy, a talented violinist, was in frequent demand for a variety of

Jim and Amy Hill's Wedding Day, 2nd December 1939.

productions, particularly church festivals. They attended most chapel anniversaries in northwest Leicestershire. Jim:

"*War clouds rumbled, so some of the rugger lads joined the Royal Air Force Volunteers (R.A.F.V.R.) and received training at Desford and elsewhere. This*

*Jim Hill, mother and Amy at 301 Ashby Road. 1940.*

whetted my appetite but when I tried to enrol there were no vacancies."

After deep deliberation Jim and Amy decided to marry, considering that a short time together would be preferable to none; a relative's offer of a house to rent was welcomed. The couple married on 2nd December 1939 at Christ Church, Coalville.

*"The sun shone brightly through the chancel window as we made our vows to each other, and they were to last for nearly sixty four years!"*

Jim, called-up, March 1940, asked for the R.A.F. but their need was men for the Army.

*"Looking back it was a blessing because I lost some very good friends who were airmen. I reported to the 39th Signal Training Regiment of the Royal Artillery. My section was based at Swift's Hotel on the north bay of Scarborough. There were twenty of us for training. I chummed up with Jack, a professional rugby player with Castleford Town, and soon we were playing for the Regiment at weekends.*

*I learnt Morse code but foreign transmissions stopped when Dunkirk fell in early June 1940. For a while we guarded a bit of coast called Cayton Bay: a German invasion was expected. We had one 1914 Lee Enfield rifle for every four men and five rounds of 303 ammunition; we wouldn't have stood a chance! After a few weeks the defences were improved and we were posted to Nostel Priory, near Wakefield, Yorkshire."*

Jack and Jim travelled to nearby Castleford where Jim met his pal's family and the chairman of Castleford Rugby League. He played several times for the Club and made a small sum of money that came in use. I deem that but for the war his sporting talents would have lit-up even larger arenas. Jim reached the standard on the buzzer, lamp and wireless procedure

and also learnt to drive 15 hundredweight trucks and 500 cc motorcycles.

*"Jack, two others and myself had to report to the 3rd Survey Regiment at Coed-y-Brenon: out in the Welsh mountains near to Doogelau. Later we moved to 'B' Troop in the Elan Valley Hotel: near to the dams. It was the very cold winter of 1940, but I helped in the warm kitchen and did really well. As a lad Mam taught me to cook so that I could care for myself."*

Jim's Battery was named: 'Flash Spotters and Sound Rangers'. Their headquarters was in a nearby town and the Regiment numbered over five hundred men. When the prospect arrived he volunteered to do their cooking, and never looked back. Posted for a six-week training course at Rhyl, he returned with a pass mark of one hundred per cent: never before known! There followed an NCO course and three stripes; with assistants he cooked for nine hundred men and was a founder member of the Army Catering Corps.

*"I was given a week's embarkation leave, Christmas 1941, and then entrained for Greenock on the Clyde. I boarded the 'Arundel Castle', a large ship with about five thousand of us on board, and for the next three days everything was battened down, the ocean was very rough. We thought it a good thing, as it would deter the 'U'-Boats. We were part of a huge convoy and darting in and around us were destroyers and many other protection vessels. Saturday, 5th February 1942 we lay off Freetown on the west coast of Africa; it was called 'The White Man's Grave'. We docked at Cape Town for four wonderful days and were treated like royalty. We had maids running hot baths for us, ate good food and fruit, some of which we had not seen since 1939. Around the Cape of Good Hope we joined another convoy which had assembled at Durban, and by 15th March we docked at Aden."*
Disembarking at the port of Tewfiq they entrained for the desert camp of El Quassine, and were informed that they were part of C.M.F. (Central Mediterranean Force). Jim and other drivers had driving practise on sand and how to escape from quicksand.

*"We'd been sent to strengthen the Eighth Army that was rebuilding at El Alamein. On our right hand-side was the sea and on the other flank the Qattara Depression: a huge mass of quicksand. Our Battery, the 'Flash Spotters and Sound Rangers' had to get a bearing on the enemy artillery and forward the*

*information to our own guns. Our work was limited because the desert was quite flat and to build any sort of construction immediately drew fire from enemy snipers and heavy guns. 'Sound Rangers' worked alongside our frontline infantry and used microphones to pick up the sound waves and try to obtain a bearing. Most of my time was now on active service but I cooked when the need arose."*

Jim saw the steady build-up of men and resources. He says that lots of dummy obstacles, such as tanks and guns, were made from cardboard, and strategically positioned to confuse the enemy. On 23rd October 1942 all hell let loose:

*"That night a thousand of our guns started to fire and I have never experienced a barrage like that before or since. The flashing guns lit-up the desert and the shells screamed above us. Even so it was slow progress for our lads until 4th November, then, they made the final break through; the sappers had to lay a route through the minefields so that our tanks and infantry could get through."*

Sergeant Jim Hill just after El Alamein in October 1942.

After that pivotal victory the Eighth Army pushed across the Western Desert to Tunisia; during this advance the food supply was a constant concern: an army marches on its stomach!

*"Somehow we survived on dried pulses and eggs; I'd swear they were crocodile eggs, they were no bigger than a pigeon's; it took a dozen of them to make a decent omelette. In July 1943 we could feel that something was going to happen, especially when Field Marshal Montgomery appeared with his staff. He stood on his jeep and said that we would be the first troops to land in Europe. He wished us luck and drove off! I became one of my unit's first twenty-eight men to form an advance party; a major and a lieutenant commanded it. We boarded a ship at Alexandria and after eighteen hours we were given a booklet to read: 'A Soldiers Guide To Sicily.' On 10th July we landed near to the port of Syracuse, it was without incident apart from the occasional dive-bombing which was very frightening. We eventually crossed the Straits of Messina into Italy and then came a long slog through mountainous regions. We found no enemy at Regio as the R.A.F. had flattened it. All of the bridges had been smashed and so progress in vehicles was slow: our infantry were quicker! Malaria was rife, so we were told to wear drill trousers in the evening and a sort of veil across our heads as we slept; we also took two tablets daily of a drug called, Mepacream.*

*When the Italians surrendered in early September 1943, it only made the Germans more determined, and they dug-in on all the strategic points. Heavy rain and thunder went on for days and now only certain names come to mind like: Potenza, Isernia, Bari, Barletta and the Foggia Plain, the latter being very hazardous to say the least, being continually attacked by the Luftwaffe. Our unit was the only one of its kind in the Eighth Army, although there was another with the Fifth. As one Division took over from another we just slotted in, and so we never came out of the Line completely. I recall a fierce battle by the River Sangro: what with so much rain it was very deep and wide!"*

Jim and his companions sheltered in barns or any building during enemy barrages. On one occasion his barn took a direct hit and Jim ran out with his clothes on fire. He immediately stuck his hand into a 7lb tin of margarine and smeared it onto his face and arms whilst colleagues smothered the flames. He was transferred to a Casualty Clearing Station, given penicillin and had his face bandaged for six weeks. Everything turned out fine thanks to his speedy thinking: the margarine protected his skin and avoided scarring.

*Jim Hill, centre, with friends at Monte Cassino, Italy. May 1944.*

"*By June 1944, after many months of bitter fighting and heavy casualties, Polish troops did magnificently to take the Monte Cassino Line. Soon afterwards we entered Rome: it was declared an 'Open City', undefended to avoid damage. After a few weeks we left the beautiful city and crossed the River Tiber towards 'Reiti on to Terni'. The enemy was tough and used 88mm guns to good effect on our way to Perugia and Florence, but we spotted their flashes. I noticed sheep that had been killed and did no more than slice them up for food: we ate well for quite a while. For years after the war at reunions, Captain Pinney reminded me of eating lamb without mint sauce. Apart from lamb we also caught geese, turkey, duck, rabbit and found local wine. Christmas of 1944 was the best of the war for food!*"

Jim comments that during the Italian Campaign, letters sent and received could never be relied upon to reach their destination.

"*It was clear that the War would soon be over. Our final destination was outside Monfalconi at a place called Ronchi, and we took trips to the sea at Grado, also seven days at Venice.*"

After three-half years abroad, Sergeant James Hill was given a month's leave, travelling by train through the Gothic Tunnel into Switzerland, then across France, the Channel, and home.

"*It was lovely being back with Amy and son Stephen, who was born on 8th August 1942. It was the first time I had seen him apart from photographs. I took him a clockwork-train that I'd bought at Trieste and he loved it, but it didn't last long because all of his friends wanted to play with it (you couldn't buy toys in the U.K.). Amy and I went for a seven-day bed and breakfast holiday at Blackpool: we hadn't had a break together for six years!*"

Refreshed, he returned to Italy and caught a bug: but a drop of Grappa proved beneficial.

"*I was put to bed with a very high temperature/shivers: a typical bout of flu I said.*

*The lady of the house where I was billeted gave me some hot goat's milk laced with this Grappa: it came from the distillation of wine. It was amazing because the next day I felt fine.*"

Discharge papers arrived and with rail communication improved, Jim had a speedier journey: Calais, the Channel, and the Royal Artillery Depot at Aldershot.

"*I received a demob suit, £1 when I handed in my greatcoat, six week's paid leave, and a rail warrant to Leicester via London. I telegrammed Amy to let her know the time I was expected to arrive at Leicester's London Road Station. It was on time and we had a lovely reunion; I'll never forget it, the future was ours, but it took me a while to adjust to civilian life. Summing up my life in the Army: I enjoyed the camaraderie, my four days at Cape Town, the Pyramids, the Sphinx, and ten days in Rome. The lows were living with death and in particular the heavy casualties and destruction of Monte Cassino.*"

Life changed for Amy; she was able to resume her work with fashion houses in Leicester: sitting and passing her City & Guilds, and started playing her violin.

"*With rationing going on I didn't think it was the time to stay in catering. I met my old boss in the hosiery trade and he offered me my old job, I accepted after some thought. Our second child, Ian, was born on 11th April 1948, and I took an allotment to grow vegetables and fresh fruit. Life became difficult: Ian had his appendix removed at the age of two, and when he was six a vehicle knocked him down, breaking many bones in his body. A surgeon at Leicester's Royal Infirmary, Dr. German, my father's officer in the Great War, operated on our boy for the full night, eleven hours! With typical grit and determination he was back home after six-seven weeks. He'd have made a good prop forward.*"

Jim bought a Ford Popular and recalls happy holidays on the east coast of Lincolnshire and Devon. He was to be head hunted by Jaeger: a leading hosiery manufacture.

"*My old boss died and Jaeger, who had a factory in*

*1914-18 soldier, Roland Hill and his wife on their Golden Wedding day. 1951.*

*a nearby town, offered me a good job. We moved house to a grand village, Bushby, five miles east of Leicester. The house was one of twenty-five properties in a cul-de-sac, no numbers: just names, with ours: 'Homeland'. It had two acres of land and I turned it into a smallholding with a forty feet greenhouse, free-range hens, ducks and the odd goose. I got myself elected on to the Bushby Parish Council."*

*Ian, Jim and Amy at Bournemouth. 1958.*

The Hill family lived a good life with memorable holidays at resorts such as Bournemouth and in 1961, a tour of Brittany in France. The years passed and their sons left home, so Jim and Amy downsized and found a pretty little bungalow at Belton, six kilometres north of Coalville.

*"I was on Belton Parish Council for twenty-seven years, and joined the Belton's Royal British Legion, and after finding discrepancies with their accounts I offered to be their treasurer."*

Jim, always creative and proactive, was a key figure in raising finance for many good causes. At Belton, in 1991, the Parish Church had its Bell Tower restored, the three existing bells retuned and two new ones purchased. The roof of the village Baptist Church was also repaired and later, Royal British Legion bungalows were built on Wilson Court with the legendary fighter pilot, Johnny Johnson, assisting in the opening ceremony.

Moves were afoot in hosiery manufacture: Jaeger was taken-over by another firm and Jim was asked to re-deploy to London, but they decided a move to the big city was not for them!

*Wife, Amy congratulates Jim for his prize-winning vegetables.*

*"As Chairman of Belton Parish Council, and with my accountancy knowledge, I applied to Loughborough Urban District Council and received an appointment which turned out to be the happiest of my life. It was in the payments section: a very challenging job: I also became their Union representative."*

Meanwhile, Steven, a keen footballer and cyclist in his youth, married Mildred in 1968; having Dawn and Philip. Following a divorce he married Gillian and had Lisa, Jackie and Tony. Steven is now retired and is married to Annette. Ian played rugby for his school but could not progress due to injury. He married Rosemary in 1970 and had son, Michael who sadly died in 1987, only eighteen years. Ian:

*"After we lost Michael we adopted our niece, Anne, and moved to Cornwall in 1996. My dear wife died in 1998: only forty-seven years old! On 8th April 2006 I married Anne, a lady I had known for some years. The day and month is the same as when my grandparents got married in 1901, and I used Roland's wedding ring for the ceremony. For many years I was employed as a motor engineer, but when Rosemary died I was left as a single parent with an eight year old to care for. I was a British Water-ski Federation instructor for a time but now I am retired as a result of injuries sustained when I was a little lad."*

Retirement brought many years of happiness and contentment with Jim, remarkably active, often to be seen at Coalville Rugby Ground and Welford Road: home of the Tigers.

Great sadness and loss occurred when Amy died on 24th March 2002, after nearly sixty-four years of marriage; she lies in the Parish Church Yard: a short walk from their home.

*Amy's grave in Belton churchyard.*

*"My Ninetieth Birthday was celebrated at Broom Leys' Cricket Club, a wonderful day. Now, in my nineties I enjoy sitting in the armchair listening to some classical music. I turn all of the above thoughts over in my mind and thank my Maker for watching over me."*

*Jim relaxing in 2007.*

My gratitude to Jim, a man who is always available to assist others, a man whom initiates and supports worthy causes and a person that has accomplished so much in life.

After recording all of the above I was very saddened to hear of Jims death on 25th March 2008. He rests alongside Amy, once again reunited. God Bless them both.

I also thank Ian, who since his father's death has supplied additional material.

# GRENVILLE ROY HUDDLESTONE

Grenville was always called, Roy. His parents: Mr. & Mrs. Christopher Huddlestone came from Thorpe Satchville, a village five miles due south of Melton Mowbray in northeast Leicestershire, with Christopher employed in farming. On 24th September 1909, his wife gave birth to Roy, at Thorpe Arnold, just outside of Melton Mowbray. Soon afterwards the family moved to Stoney Stanton, a village fifteen kilometres (ten miles) southwest of Leicester. His father was bailiff for a farm owned by a Mr. Kendrick.

When Roy left school, around 1923, Stanley & Edgar Chamberlain's, a hosiery manufacturer at Burbage gave him employment. He trained as a knitter; subsequently, a pretty girl in the factory's warehouse took his eye, namely: Florence Emma Hill, always Emma by name. Emma was born at Stoney Stanton on 26th June 1906, and the couple married in 1927. Their first-born was, John: 22nd August 1928, the second birth, Dorothy, sadly died from pneumonia at ten months and finally, Derrick on 19th October 1931.

Roy was a very fine sportsman and played both cricket and football for Stoney Stanton. Emma's brother, John Charles Hill, featured in: 'Greater Love'. Enlisting in November 1914, he entered the Eighth Leicestershire Battalion.

*Private John Charles Hill..*

On 29th July 1915, the Battalion left for France, spending a week in the Kemmel Sector of Belgium: seeing frontline trenches near Locre, and marches to the Ypres Sector. On the first day of the Somme, 1st July 1916, they were at Bienvillers-Bailleulmont, and on July 6th marched south to support faltering attacks. On July 7th they marched to Mametz Wood and Bezentin-le-Petit; here they fought a hellish battle in an area of shell–scarred earth, decomposing corpses and lachrymatory gas. On 4th October 1916, the Battalion left for Bethune, and marched south to the Loos Sector, with its slagheaps. In January 1917, the Battalion was despatched to the Arras Sector, and on 3rd May 1917 they attacked at 'Fontaine Les Croisilles'. Large numbers of the enemy attacked from the left and right flanks and used bombs and guns to great effect! During this battle, Roy's future brother-in-law, Private John Charles Hill met his death on 3rd May 1917.

*A young Roy and his father. Circa 1920.*

In 1938, Roy and family moved to a house named: 'Faenza', 77, Coventry Road at Burbage (on the outskirts of Hinckley): sixteen kilometres northeast of Coventry. Roy continued with his sports and played cricket and football for Burbage; a friend and teammate was future 'Dam Buster' pilot: Flying

Officer Geoffrey Rice D.F.C., who lost his life in a later raid.

Neither Roy, who continued to work at Chamberlain's, nor his family ever forgot the dramatic Luftwaffe raid on the former city on the night of 14/15th November 1940. Roy's son, John:

*"My bedroom window looked out onto Bramcote Aerodrome and then beyond to Coventry. I lay in bed with my curtains open and heard the distant bombs exploding; the raid lasted all night and the sky was bright red. I'll never forget that night!"*

Roy was called-up on 19th March 1942, service number: 4868665, and posted to the 2/5th Leicestershire Battalion; in 1940 this Battalion fought in France.

*"Mother took us on Sundays to see him in the barracks at Leamington Spa; we were all sad when we waved goodbye when his convoy past through our village. He'd just had some leave to go abroad, only later did we know he was to fight in North Africa and elsewhere."*

Roy trained as a driver, qualified on 17th July 1942, and spent a period on battle training at Folkestone, Kent.

*Roy Huddlestone: 2/5th Leicestershire Battalion.*

On 24th December 1942, the 2/5th, as part of the 46th Division, steamed from Liverpool aboard the troopship: 'Derbyshire'. The seas provided a rough passage, but on 3rd January 1943 they arrived at Algiers, and after a few days entrained to a railhead at Ghardimaou in Tunisia. The 550 kilometres (350-mile) rail journey took two days and a night. On arriving the Battalion had a long night's march to the staging area from where, the next night, the rifle companies were driven in troop-carrying vehicles (TCVs), to positions allotted in the frontline near Sed Jenane in the northern sector. Over the months, Roy drove a colossal amount of miles, mainly in darkness, but always subject to enemy attack.

The Allied attack in Tunisia was overstretched; it ground to a halt opposite Bizerta and Tunis in the face of strong enemy opposition. The 2/5th was positioned in the northern sector, facing German positions on hills defending Bizerta.

There was a momentary stalemate while each side built up its resources. In the meantime, the German Afrika Korps, following defeat at El Alamein on 23rd October 1942, had been making an orderly withdrawal towards Tunisia. Suddenly, on 16th February 1943, without warning, Field Marshal Rommel launched a fierce Panzer attack against the American Forces defending the Kasserine Pass in southern Tunisia. The attack was aimed at the American railhead at Tebessa. **For a detailed account of the African and further campaigns**, please read Volume One 'Sons and Daughters', Major Peter Moore MC of the 2/5th Battalion.

So it continued for Roy, and when the situation demanded, drivers took their part on the frontline. Eventually, after great success but heavy casualties, the Battalion left Africa on 6th September 1943. **There follows a brief account based on Peter Moore's memoirs to illustrate Roy's campaign**.

The convoy steamed across the Mediterranean carrying Anglo-American troops: with the 46th Division part of the American 5th Army. The sea was stormy, but they sailed all day and all the following night, and on the 7th were in a bay near Palermo, Sicily. The island's fighting had finished in late August, so the troops had a twenty-four hours break before being told their destination was Salerno, on the Italian mainland (sixty-five kilometres southeast of

Naples). While crossing the Tyrrhenian Sea news came of Italy's capitulation; this was bad news because it now meant facing German troops: a far greater challenge.

On September 9th, just off Salerno, Roy saw a tremendous artillery exchange between the guns of our capital ships and those of coastal defences. The Luftwaffe was also present.

The Battalion's 'A' and 'B' Companies, under a smoke screen, were scheduled to land on the left flank, nearer to the town, however, cannon fire and bombs from the Luftwaffe forced them out to sea. Over the ship's radio, frantic calls could be heard from the beachhead, where the Hampshire Regiment was trying to take 'Green' beach, but had met Tiger tanks and heavy gunfire. Leicester's 'C' and 'D' Companies landed on the beachhead and helped push the Germans back, and soon received support.

The anticipated smooth Salerno Landing became critically complicated with the 3rd and 15th Panzer Grenadier Divisions greeting the invaders. The situation was so serious that thoughts of abandonment were considered, however, the British 8th Army thrust from the south and forced the Germans to retire to the *Gustav Line*. Naples fell on the night of 30th September 1943. Roy bought two postcards of Salerno and sent them home on 21st November 1943: wishing his family a Merry Christmas and all his love (see photograph).

The Division was taken from the frontline for re-equipping in Camp 21 at Hadera in Palestine. Eventually, they entrained for Port Said and returned to Naples. Its new task was to spearhead an attack intended to breach the '*Gothic Line*': the German's final defensive barrier across Italy. The Battalion encamped at Pignatoro, near Naples. After intensive training, they left Bastardo in Umbria on 20th August 1944, travelling north for the assault. The *Gothic Line* ran from Pesaro on the Adriatic coast to near Spezia on the west, with the central Apennines forming a defensive spine. The Line was twelve miles deep with extensive minefields and concrete fortifications. The Battalion would attack on the eastern front, facing a series of tall hills: one/two thousand feet high, with many river valleys. On the morning of 26th August 1944, 'A' and 'B' Companies attacked and met heavy mortar, artillery and machine-gun fire. They became pinned down, and the other two Companies attacked in the afternoon to relieve them, with support from Churchill tanks. Eventually, the Germans retreated along the entire front and fell back to their main defensive bastions twelve miles to their rear. The enemy was outflanked and men of the 2/5th had punctured a hole in the *Gothic Line*, but at a cost, 'C' Company was down to one platoon, with 'D' under strength.

The next target was the small hill town of Mondaino, and this they attacked at 10.00pm the following night.

The enemy troops were supported by Panther tanks and self propelled guns, but the furiously brave and tenacious efforts of 'A' and 'B' Companies, amid shellfire, mortars, grenades, and small arms fire somehow fought their way into the town! After lengthy and bitter hand-to-hand fighting the enemy was finally driven out. In twelve days of fighting, three German Divisions had been mauled as the Allies advanced twenty-five miles on foot across terrain ideal for defensive warfare. The 46th Division sustained a thousand casualties, including fourteen officers, and one hundred and forty nine men killed.

On the night of 13th/14th September 1944, 'A' and 'D' attacked the village of Croce, and after fierce fighting captured it. Next morning, 'B' Company attacked, in open formation with six Churchill tanks, the village of Poggio. The area had already seen action whilst the Battalion had taken two days rest, and all around lay dead British troops, tanks had crushed some and the stench of putrefying flesh was horrific. The village was on the top of a rocky ridge and dominated the Battalion's line of advance. Just as Peter Moore was about to order the attack a shell exploded near to his sergeant, Bill Taylor, who received a dreadful leg wound but survived the war. Peter led the assault under heavy artillery fire as well as mortars and Spandau; casualties were low due to stonewalls that provided good cover. With the aid of the three remaining tanks, 'B' Company stormed and captured the village by mid-afternoon. The Battalion then helped to attack the town of Cesena, took the village of Celincordia, about one mile further on, and also Abbadesse. On 28th November 1944, the Battalion was taken out of the Line and sent to Bari: on the heel of Italy. Bivouacking overnight on an airfield they were then airlifted to Greece where it took part in the fighting and remained until the Greek government was restored. It then returned to Italy and after the armistice moved into Austria, where it remained until disbandment.

Roy was awarded the Africa Star with the 1st Army Clasp, the Italy Star and the 1939-45 Star.

During Roy's Service, when the opportunity arose, he played cricket and football. While in North Africa he played alongside the England and Yorkshire bowler, Hedley Verity. The great man took 1,956 wickets at an average 14.87, and scored 5,603 runs averaging 18.13. Hedley was born on 15th May 1905. He was seriously wounded in the chest whilst leading an 8th Army's attack on German positions at Catania, Sicily. In darkness, Verity led his men, in a creeping barrage, for seven hundred yards against a strongly defended ridge. The barrage stopped as they closed on their objective through fields of two feet high corn. Suddenly, tracer bullets swept towards them and Very lights and mortars set the corn alight. He sent a party of men to attack a farmhouse, but on meeting growing resistance decided to withdraw; the last his men saw of him, he was on the ground by the burning corn, his head supported by Thomas Reynoldson, his batman. Verity died a hero on 31st July 1943.

Roy finished his service days in Austria and his demobilisation papers state: '*His military conduct was exemplary. A first class soldier and motor driver, exceptionally honest, sober, reliable, smart and clean. Very hard working and cheerful with it.*'

Roy returned to civilian employment and life, but not before he took Emma for a holiday at Torquay in October 1945 (see photograph). He returned to his former employment at Chamberlain's, however, an interesting account concerns his time in Greece; its shows the kindness that he felt for those in need. John:

Roy and Emma at Torquay, 1945.

"*My father befriended a Greek family by the name of Kurimetis; I'm not sure what he did for them but I recall him saying they were absolutely down-and-out as a result of the war. They had no more than the clothes on their back; father must have been very kind to them because at a later date, long after the war, the head of the family travelled to see him and to thank him once again for his kindness and charity.*"

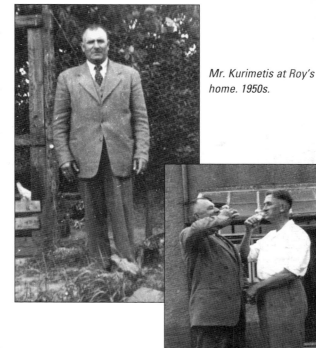

Mr. Kurimetis at Roy's home. 1950s.

Mr. Kurimetis toasts Roy.

*Jean with a photograph of her father. Dennis Hodges, one of the Famous Fifty.*

*John and Jean Huddlestone.*

Roy was a very keen gardener and also kept some fowls in his back garden. He remained at Chamberlain's until retirement: they treated their employees with respect and consideration. The old soldier passed on at his home with heart problems on 29th May 1974, aged sixty-five.

Emma lived on at Burbage until she died on 3rd December 1997 at the Leicester General Hospital, aged ninety-one years.

John Huddlestone worked on two farms during the later stages of the war, assisting 'Land Girls', and later with his father at Chamberlain's. He met his future wife on a blind date at Hinckley, and the couple tied the knot at Ebenezer Chapel at Coalville on 1st August 1953. His wife is none other than Jean (nee Hodgetts), daughter of Dennis Hodgetts, one of the Famous Fifty that features strongly in 'Fifty Good Men And True' and who's on the back cover of 'Greater Love'. Following marriage they lived with his parents, but Jean longed for Coalville. In February 1954, they did so at her grandparent's home: 234 Ashby Road, with Jean giving birth to Linda; in 1959 they moved to their present address on the outskirts of Coalville.

John worked for a subsidiary of Clutsom and Kemps at Market Bosworth: polishing blades for jet engines to a very high standard, but after six months switched to Ellistown Pipes, Bricks and Tiles Estates Ltd. Jean spent many years working for Grieves of Coalville, manufactures of hosiery needles.

John and Jean had two children, Linda, born: 1954 and Martin: 1961. Linda lived with Royston Howe, son of Roy Howe, whose account is in Volume One of 'Sons and Daughters', sadly Royston died in 2007, aged only fifty-six years. Martin married Tracy Sleath from Stanton under Bardon; they had two children, Robyn: aged eighteen and Connor: sixteen. Connor takes after his grandfather and is very interested in military history.

John remained with his Ellistown employer until retirement. His brother, Derrick, lives next door to his parents: 75, Coventry Road, Burbage, with his second wife. A fine singer, he had his voice trained for operatic recitals.

Once again I thank John and Jean Huddlestone for their assistance. As a result of diabetes, John has had his legs amputated, but his spirit and energy are as strong as ever. Many folk know of Battle of Britain pilot, Douglas Bader, an inspirational figure and John is equally inspiring, a brave and courageous man; Roy and Emma would be very proud of him! I know Jean and their family are; I certainly am!

# WILFRID JARVIS AND FAMILY

Thomas Jarvis, as a young man, moved from Wales to Ellistown, near Coalville and obtained employment at Ellistown Colliery. He was and remained the engine-winder at that colliery until the age of seventy years, and was highly regarded. In the 1890's, he met Whitwick girl, Mary Jane Oliver, who was working at T. & J. Jones: later Joseph Burgess and Son on Belvoir Road, Coalville. They married and settled-down at 184, Whitehill Road, Ellistown: next door to his mother (at 182). The couple had ten children of whom six made maturity: Percy William, born 1893, Ethel or 'Tiddy', Thomas Wilfrid born 21st June 1896, Maud, Olive, and Gwenfred. Shortly after the latter's birth the family moved next door to 182, and in 1911, Dorothy was born: her twin, Nora died at five months from a heart defect. Wilfrid was named after his father, Thomas, but used his second name: Wilfrid or Wilf.

All of the siblings attended Hugglescote Baptist School except Dorothy: attending a newly opened school in the village. Percy and Wilfrid furthered their schooling at the prestigious Ashby de la Zouch Grammar School, even though purse strings were tight! They studied beside future soldiers Jabez, William and Alfred Emmerson, Frederic Scott and Philip Bent. Percy progressed to Birmingham University, but Wilfrid: equally bright, accepted that his parents couldn't afford to send him to university too! Just before Percy sat his Batchelor of Arts degree, illness struck, and he passed later via a correspondence course. He moved to teach at Peterborough. Tiddy also passed for Grammar School, but died at the age of fifteen from pneumonia; she lies at Hugglescote Cemetery.

In 1914 both brothers enlisted, Percy at Peterborough into the Northamptonshire Regiment, whilst Wilfrid enlisted at Leicester: directly from Grammar School into the Fourth (1/4th) Leicestershire Battalion. Percy's qualifications were noted and he was selected for officer-cadetship; after training at Harrogate he was commissioned a 2nd Lieutenant. He served in the major battles on the Western Front and also in the Salonika Campaign, but in 1917 at Cambrai he was hit by bullets in the leg and had to crawl to his trenches. Hospitalised at Weymouth, he met his future wife, Elsie there. On returning home he applied for a grant to continue his studies at the University College

*Private Wilfrid Jarvis of the 1/4th Battalion, Leicestershire Regiment. 1914.*

of Nottingham. Percy and Elsie married and lived locally, having two children, Pauline and Philip. In 1922, he received a headmastership at Ravenstone Primary School and in 1930 he undertook the same role at Kirby Muxloe School, a village a few miles west of Leicester until retirement in 1958. He died in 1985: aged ninety-two years and rests in Kirby Muxloe Cemetery.

The bestial war never broke the bond of brotherhood, and they often thought of each other's whereabouts and safety. Wilfrid served with distinction at Ypres, the Hohenzollern Redoubt, Gommecourt on the Somme, Lens, Bellenglise, indeed all of the battles described in my earlier book: 'Fifty Good Men And True'. Following four years of devoted service his final stint was in Ireland; a short-term romance with a girl named Rose, from Tralee was always a source of in-family amusement. He left the Colours as a sergeant and was highly respected by the men both above and below him.

Wilfrid declined a grant to enable him to study at university because of a clause stipulating a commitment to teaching. His sister, Olive, read

Mathematics at Birmingham University.

He signed on at the Labour Exchange and had a number of jobs until settling for a position at Ibstock Brick and Tile Company, where he remained. Ultimately, he became a buyer for the company and managed the accounts' department.

Around 1920, he met Dorothy Fowkes from nearby Stanton-under-Bardon, and the daughter of George and Minnie Fowkes. In 1922, they married at Bardon Park Chapel, and for a few years lived with her parents until securing the tenancy of 46, Central Road, Hugglescote. Roger was born on 26th April 1928 and Gwenfred on 12th April 1932. Shell-splinters had damaged Wilfrid's knees and this resulted in a stiff-kneed walk, however, on work-days he walked several miles to and from Ibstock; his nickname: 'Jumper Jarvis' was taken with his usual good humour.

Soon after the war, Wilfrid became an early member of the Coalville Branch of 'Toc-H', and with old companions like Jabez Emmerson, assisted local veterans whom were still suffering from the effects of war; there were many! In the 1930s, 'Toc-H' organised visits for veterans and/or family to the battlefields of France and Belgium, etc; he revisited on a few occasions to pay respects to fallen comrades. On these emotive trips he bought a selection of books such as: '*Ypres And Its Surroundings: a Little Guide For Tourists*', also '*Ypres: Heros et Martyrs*', '*Tales of Talbot House in Poperinghe, Ypres*', '*Ruines d'Arras*'. Locally he bought: '*Ashby de la Zouch and the Great War: a Roll of Honour*', and others. His daughter, together with his medals keeps these treasured items safely.

In 1939, he was appointed an A.R.P. (Air Raid Precaution) Warden, and throughout the war spent many evenings checking the Hugglescote locality to ensure that no lights were visible to the naked eye, or rather to enemy aircraft! All such duties and added responsibilities were in addition to standard working hours at the place of employment.

Wilfrid and Dorothy's son, Roger, undertook the task of a messenger boy; based at The Adult School on Bridge Road, he travelled by bicycle to convey messages from different units of the Home Guard, etc. The pay was two shillings and sixpence a night: 12 1/2new pence. Others who may have had a similar duty include: Derek Bradley, Michael Pepper, Roland

*Wilfrid Jarvis, ARP Warden during World War 2.*

Haddock and Desmond Hart. Roger, an Ashby de la Zouch Grammar School pupil later studied at Jesus College, Oxford before emigrating to Canada in 1950. He worked for Canada's Atomic Energy Authority and married a Canadian girl.

Gwenfred Jarvis recalls the inky-dark nights of wartime when vehicles, with a very restricted amount of light, drove by their home:

"*Mother spent her war years as an ambulance assistant, not driving, but sitting in the back with the patient(s): caring and comforting them. And so, with my dad usually being on duty at night, I spent many evenings with my maternal grandmother, Minnie (nanny). I recall the sirens and sitting under the stairs with nanny. When not at school my playtime friends were Peter and Jennifer Tovell, their Uncle Archie was sniped in the Great War; I can also remember 'Titch' (Denis) Baker and Sheila Wortley from Forest Road. There were large numbers of evacuees from the 'black-country' in the village. Post-war my father received the Defence Medal for his contribution as Deputy Post Warden.*"

Gwenfred attended Hugglescote Primary School and Coalville's King Edward V11 Grammar School (a spell as deputy head-girl). At eighteen years she went

*Roger Jarvis.*

*Dorothy Jarvis, Ambulance Attendant during World War 2.*

*Gwenfred Jarvis.*

to Loughborough College of Art and Design, and continued the theme at The Royal College of Art, London. In 1959 she won the 'Design of the Year Award' for Liberty and Company.

Gwenfred met her future husband, Terrence: 'Terry' Shrives, whilst both taught at Coalville Grammar School. Terry's father, Arthur Shrives: born in 1908 at Kettering and educated at the town's grammar school, served with British Intelligence in the war. Mostly, he was stationed at Gibraltar and then Italy, but after its fall he finished with the Royal Corps of Signals, involved with codes and ciphers. Terry was born at Nuneaton and grew up in Warwick, and can well recall the night that Coventry was bombed. A science graduate he did his National Service as a flying officer with the R.A.F. The couple married at Saxon Mill, near Warwick on 2nd April 1960. Their son, Mark, a former Loughborough Grammar School boy, furthered his learning by reading Law at Downing College, Cambridge, and is now a practicing solicitor at Leeds.

Wilfrid Jarvis was steadfast in his support for the Boy Scout Movement; Lord Rowallen, who took over from Lord Baden Powell, presented him with the 'Medal of Merit'. In 1945, he received the 'Long

Wilfrid, Dorothy and Gwenfred Jarvis in the early 1950s.

Coalville Times announces Awards to Scout Leaders in 1955..

Service Ribbon' for being secretary to Ashby and Coalville Boy Scouts Association for thirty years. Percy, Wilfrid and their respective families regularly met for luncheons and spent annual holidays together. Gwenfred:

*"My father and uncle, when alone, spoke of their time between 1914-18, but all my father told me was that warm and dry feet and well polished boots were essential to well-being. Also, when his mother sent him a birthday cake it arrived in fragments, and so he mixed it with jam and made a Christmas pudding.*

*Finally, the carol: 'Silent Night', especially if sung in German, was very moving for him, a poignant reminder of Christmases in the trenches."*

Wilfrid, the old soldier, was informed during his retirement year that he had a terminal illness. He 'faded away' in November 1961, aged sixty-five. Cremated at Loughborough, his ashes were sprinkled on the Garden of Remembrance; in 1983 those of his dear wife joined him.

When I wrote of Percy and Wilfrid in my 'Greater Love' I was not aware that Gwenfred and Terry lived just one mile away from me at Quorn, and had done since 1970. On visiting them I very much liked their grand home: the 1905 architecture, enchanting gardens and extensive lawns. Terry said that in 1941 their house: 'The Towers' of Chaveney Road, was used as: 'HQ Y Signals ATS' for the girls from Beaumanor Hall, and later in the war as a billet for Beaumanor's officers. In earlier times an air-raid shelter was visible towards the bottom of the garden. Terry was my wife's (Beryl Hare) form teacher in 1964 at Coalville Grammar School.

Many thanks to Gwenfred and Terry Shrives for their help and additional information.

## Beaumanor and Garats Hay

The above was commissioned by M15, and, as War Office 'Y' Group it became one of the major stations serving Bletchley Park: home of the Enigma Code Breakers. The personnel consisted of officers from the Army, Royal Navy, Royal Air Force, Metropolitan Police, The Post Office and Foreign Office. Each of the above listened to the encoded messages of their enemy equivalent Service, and women of the Auxiliary Territorial Service, Naval Service and Air Force were trained as 'Special Wireless Operators'. They were so capable that by radio 'finger printing' they regularly knew which enemy radio set was broadcasting the encoded message and it was a cause of some amusement that they often received decoded messages before the intended receivers.

Beaumanor cared for security, censorship, interpreters/ linguists, photographic analysis and interpretation. Their original radio call sign was G3MBR. Wireless research workshops were based in the cellar, and around the widespread gardens operative-huts were constructed but disguised as farmhouses.

Beaumanor and Garats Hay's secretive role was a major key in the allies winning the war, and without their contribution the Enigma Code would not have been broken.

After the war, Beaumanor 'Y' Station became a GCHQ controlled civilian operation until 1970. The

*A.T.S. Wireless Operators tidy up their Nissen Hut, Forest Road, Old Woodhouse.*

County Council purchased Beaumanor Hall and it is now used for educational purposes, but Garats Hay remained intact until the late 1990s and was utilised to train radio personnel.

**It is of historical note to mention that the coded-signal of 'Nigger': sent by Guy Gibson's radio-operator to announce the breaching of the Mohne Dam, was received by War Office 'Y' Station, Beaumanor Hall at Old Woodhouse. The radio-receiver who did so was CSM Jessie Adams, who immediately forwarded the information to Bomber Command. See David Maltby.

*Beaumanor Hall.*

# LEICESTERSHIRE MEN OF THE ROYAL AIR FORCE

## A representative few including pilots who trained at Desford

In addition to the aircrew featured in my two volumes of Sons and Daughters, the following men left vivid vapour trials in the skies of World War 2. By 3rd September 1939, thirty-four R.A.F. Leicestershire Volunteer Reservists had received their Wings from Reid and Sigrist Training School, Desford and fourteen flew in the Battle of Britain.

**Eric Neal** was born in 1920, son of Mr.& Mrs. Arthur Neal of 4, Avenue Road, Coalville. A classmate of Harold Catlow and Les Kendrick at Bridge Road School; later employed as a clerk at Whitwick Colliery. Eric, an R.A.F.V.R. (Royal Air Force Volunteer Reserve) served as a sergeant-gunner on Blenheim bombers of Coastal Command. His name appeared on the front cover of November's 1940 'Billet'. The announcement reads:

'*Sergeant Gunner E. Neal of Coastal Command, whilst wounded in a turret jammed by enemy gunfire, shot down one of three Messerschmitts that attacked his aircraft. The action started with one fighter flying below their Blenheim with the others on either beam. The first burst from the German guns put his turret out of action, he could only fire on one side. Eric was able to fire a long burst at one of the fighters and it burst into flames and plunged to the sea.*'

Sergeant Eric Neal was admitted to hospital suffering from shrapnel and bullet wounds. The censors allowed him to give his account of the action.

'*We were out on patrol over the Channel. It was about 18.15pm and there was little cloud. The sun was shining and it looked very nice. Suddenly our observer saw a Nazi bomber going towards France. It was escorted by fighters, so being alone we didn't interfere. Continuing a little I spotted some fighters coming up behind us, at first I thought they were our Hurricanes, but as they got nearer I saw their guns fire. One in particular came right in and fired away; it jammed my turret by smashing the oil-pipe line to it and put the radio out of action, thus making it impossible to contact my pilot or observer. My guns were fixed in one position and so I couldn't fire at the ME 109. The fighter then came in really close and in doing so made a fatal mistake. He passed into my gun-sites and so I let him have it and the observer said that it went down in flames. The other fighters turned away into the clouds. I reckon the reason the careless one came alongside was because he thought I was killed! So we put our nose down and tore back to base. We were apprehensive all the time as our plane was damaged. On the way back I noticed blood on my trouser knee and a hole with blood around it on my flying boot. My leg was going numb. But we got back; shrapnel from explosive shells wounded the observer. I had two pieces of shrapnel in my knee and one in my foot, a bullet passed through the bottom of my little toe. We had the congratulations of the flight commander, the station commander and the air-officer commanding our group. I am in hospital but I am progressing. The wound is healing slowly but I wont be able to walk for some time yet.*'

Sergeant Eric Neal was the first man from Coalville to be decorated in World War 2; he was awarded the Distinguished Flying medal (D.F.M.). He married in early 1942 but later was reported as missing in action.

**Johnnie (James Edgar) Johnson** was born 9th March 1915. A personal friend, and the first verse of a dedicational poem in '*Epitaph For The Few*' says much about him.

'*Born at the heart of the country, Barrow-upon-Soar,
a favourite son of Leicestershire.
His father a policeman, however, it was another
'highway' Johnnie policed without fear.
A Loughborough Grammar School athlete, strong
runner and rugged rugby footballer.
Always believed in straight speaking, two of a kind
and best buddies with Doug Bader.*'

A Nottingham University graduate, he joined the R.A.F.V.R. and was called up at the outbreak of war. Johnnie, service number 83267, flew in the 1940 Battle of Britain with 616 Squadron, but his flying time was limited by illness. He became the Allies' top-scoring pilot with thirty-eight confirmed victories to his credit.

Retiring from the R.A.F. on 15th March 1966 as an Air Vice Marshal his honours include C.B., C.B.E., D.S.O. and two bars, D.F.C. and bar, Order of Leopold, Croix de Guerre, D.F.C. (U.S.A.), U.S. Air Medal and Legion of Merit. Johnnie passed away in 2001.

**Dennis Garth Ashton** was born in 1920 at Keyworth, Nottinghamshire. He joined the R.A.F.V.R. at Desford and learned to fly at the Reid and Sigrist Training School. Air Commodore Fulford commanded the School; Major Read owned the airfield and Lindsay Everard owned the Tiger Moth aircraft. Dennis, service number 741212, was commissioned in December 1939 and flew with 266 Squadron at Wittering during the Battle of Britain. Whilst engaged with the enemy over the Channel, near to Portsmouth, his Spitfire crashed in flames. His body was recovered and the twenty year old was given a sea burial.

**Sydney Wild** was born in 1920 to Mr.&. Mrs. Walter Wild of Green Lane, Whitwick. Educated at King Edward V11 Grammar School, Coalville, he obtained his pilot's license before the war whilst studying at Loughborough College. Called-up at the start of the war as a sergeant-pilot he was commissioned as a pilot officer in August 1940.The May 1941 edition of the Billet carried a front-page version of his crash landing:

*'I was returning home when I ran into clouds. I knew where I was upon entering the clouds but from there it was guess work to judge the position of my aerodrome. The cloud was two/three thousand feet in height and started at fifty feet from the ground. I travelled round and round and knew I must be over a town, missing a few tall chimneys. I was considering whether to climb for height and baling out, my wireless wasn't working, when suddenly, through the clouds came two Verey lights. I went as low as I dared towards the lights, about twenty feet, and saw patches of ground. I made a calculated approach, but what with the rain and failing light I realised I was about to land on a bomb dump! I opened the throttle, cleared the dump, and repeated the approach but cut it short and made a good landing, but I was too fast and my gunner and me were thrown from the aircraft. Within half an hour we were fine apart from a few bruises and we flew the next day.'*
In July 1941, he was posted as missing, but a few weeks' later reports stated that he had been wounded when his aircraft was shot down in flames by enemy fire over Germany. He wrote to his parents to tell them that he was all right: he had walked two miles to the nearest house and received drink and a cigarette before being taken to a hospital. Sydney was in hospital for eight weeks with bullet and shrapnel wounds. He was a German prisoner of war until 1945.

**Kenneth Maltby Carver** was taught to fly at Desford. Commissioned in May 1940, service number 79730, he joined 229 Squadron at Wittering on July 17th. A few months later, he had to bale-out from his burning Hurricane after an attack on a He111; taken to a hospital near to Maidstone, Kent, he was retained for four weeks with burns. Incidentally, his aircraft crashed on the Goudhurst Road, Kent; a holiday retreat in Kent widely used by the author and his wife. He rejoined 229 Squadron and while flying with 605 Squadron in 1944 was awarded the D.F.C. Ken left the Service as a squadron leader.

**Stanley Douglas Smart** was the first Coalville airman to be awarded the D.F.C. The son of Police Sergeant and Mrs. E. Smart of Bridge Road, Coalville. Educated at King Edward V11 Grammar School, Coalville, he won the Victor Ludorum and was captain of their football and cricket teams. On finishing his initial education he became articled to a firm of accountants at Derby, and whilst there played for Derby County F.C. colts. While living at Hugglescote, he played for Albion cricket team, Snibston Colliery and Coalville Rugby F.C. Trained to fly in Canada he was commissioned in 1943 and finished two tours of operations with the elite Pathfinder Force: flying deep into Germany. His most momentous day was when his aircraft was one of the first to open the 'D'-Day

Offensive on 6th June 1944. Three of his brothers served in the Forces, Edward in Italy, Reginald and Clifford. He left the R.A.F. as a flight lieutenant. One of Coalville's finest sons!

*William Davis is standing. North Weald, September 1940. His colleagues are Pilot Officers Meaker and Crossley. (Photo: Tom Neil).*

**William Davis** was a Hinckley man whose family owned a textile business. Trained at Desford he joined 249 Squadron and flew Hurricanes from Boscombe Down and North Weald during the Battle of Britain. He was shot down on September 11. An old friend of the author's, Wing Commander Tom Neil D.F.C and bar, A.F.C., A.E., recalls William: *"I returned to Dispersal to hear that Sergeant Davis had been shot down in flames over Kent. A nice lad, a bit of a P.G. Wodehouse character I thought."*

Commissioned in early 1941, William was shot down over enemy territory on 10th February 1941 and imprisoned for the duration of the war. 249 Squadron pilot, J.B. 'Nick' Nicholson, was the only pilot during the 1940 Battle to receive the Victoria Cross. On his release, William returned to the family business. He passed away in 1984.

**T. Holmes,** son of Mr.& Mrs. Holmes of 88, Silver Street, Whitwick, was a sergeant tail gunner when his squadron attacked Peenemunde in 1943. He came close to loosing his life:

*"We had just dropped our bombs and about to leave the target when we were attacked from the rear by two enemy fighters. I told our pilot and then the mid-upper gunner and I fired five bursts each. The enemy's fire smashed our turrets and all our controls but somehow we were unhurt. Our pilot dived to below one hundred feet and the fighters didn't follow, they must have thought they had done enough to finish us off. One engine caught fire but the engineer doused it and our pilot brought us home on three engines. The bomb aimer sat in the nose of the plane and advised the pilot when to climb to overcome chimneys and buildings. We flew on for three hours, thinking that every minute would be our last, and we saw our base just as we were running out of petrol, and our pilot did brilliantly to land on one wheel. After we landed most of the ground staff came out to greet us: no one could believe the amount of damage to the plane, and thankfully no one was injured, a real miracle.*

**Denis Crowley Milling** was born in Flintshire on 22nd March 1919 and educated at Malvern College. He was an apprentice at Rolls Royce and trained to fly at Desford in 1937. Denis, service number 78274, fought with 242 Hurricane Squadron in the 1940 Battles of France and of Britain. Whilst in 242 he flew alongside the legendary Douglas Bader. Denis destroyed four enemy aircraft, a half share and two probables. He was shot down over enemy territory in 1941 but escaped via Spain with the help of the French Underground. He retired From the R.A.F. on 29th June 1975 as an Air Marshal: K.C.B., C.B.E., D.S.O., D.F.C.

*Frank Hares' military headstone.*

**Frank Hares** of 26, Crescent Road, Hugglescote. Educated at King Edward V11 Grammar School and a keen member of their Air Training Corps. He was on the staff of Ellistown Colliery before joining the R. A. F. in 1942. A few days after being awarded the D.F.M. in early 1945, he was killed over northern Europe. His aircraft returned and the flight sergeant, aged twenty-one, was buried in Hugglescote cemetery.

**Henry Cox** was born 1920 and from Warren Hills, Greenhill. The flight engineer received the D. F.M. for great promptitude: his efforts saving the crew of his bomber. Pre-war he was employed as a gardener by Mr. J. Stenson Turner of Greenhill. His efforts were in 1944:

*'The aircraft was returning from a bombing raid over Hanover, Germany, when, a mere four hundred yards from base the two starboard engines stopped.*

*The airman, noted for his keenness and skill, promptly succeeded in re-starting the engines despite the petrol supplies being almost exhausted. His effort enabled the pilot to land the aircraft safely.'*

**Neville David Solomon** was born in 1914 and trained at Desford. He was manager of Lewis' Department Store at Leicester when he was mobilised. One of the Few, he flew Hurricanes with 17 Squadron, joining them at Debden on 19th July 1940. He was reported as 'missing' on August 15th: a Messerschmitt 109 shot him. He lies in Pihenles-Guines cemetery, France.

**Joseph Alfred Leonard Alldread D.F.C.** was educated at King Edward V11 Grammar School, Coalville. The son of Mr. & Mrs. J. W. Alldread of Vaughan Street, Coalville, and pre-war he was assistant scoutmaster of the 4th Coalville Troop.
During his period of military service his wife, Freda, and baby resided with his parents.
Joseph served and saw a lot of action with the Fleet Air Arm, mainly in the Far East. In early 1945 he was awarded the D.F.C. The citation reads:
*'With his strike leader stranded on the deck of their aircraft carrier with a damaged aircraft, Sub Lieutenant Alldread, who had already taken-off, took over command of the flight and continued the operation. The job was the bombing of the buildings in a Japanese town during a bombardment of the Sakishima Islands. The planes met with intense light flak, but Sub Lieutenant Alldread and his small force managed to drop bombs right across the buildings.*
*For this and previous exploits, during which he showed himself as an able leader, Lieutenant Alldread was awarded the Distinguished Service Cross. He completed eight sorties during three days of operations.* He served as a flight lieutenant.
Post-war Joseph and Freda: sister of Olive Reynolds, emigrated to Nova Scotia, Canada, but not before his headmastership at schools at Croft and Swaffam. (See Olive Poole's account).

**Sergeant Pilot Boothby** of Central Road, Hugglescote was also awarded the D.F.M. in 1940.

**Edward Murray Frisby** was born at Cropston in Leicestershire. After Desford training he joined 504 Hurricane Squadron in 1938 and was mobilised on 28th August 1939. Edward, service number 90507, fought with 504 Squadron throughout the Battle of Britain, and on September 30th, had to force-land his damaged aircraft at Yeovil. Edward, a flight lieutenant was killed on 5th December 1941 and is buried at St. Cuthbert's Cemetery, Great Glen.

**Eric Edward Lockton** was born at Ashby de la Zouch. A Desford trained pilot, he joined the R.A.F.V.R. in March 1937. On 3rd July 1940, the sergeant pilot, service number 74005, was loaned from Fighter Command to 236 Squadron (Blenheim light bombers) of Coastal Command. While on an escort mission on July 20th he was shot down by Hauptmann Neumann: a fighter ace. Eric and sergeant gunner H. Corcoran were lost. The gunner only joined the Squadron the previous day. Both are remembered on the Runnymede Memorial.

**William John Timms,** a Desford trained pilot who joined 43 Squadron on 1st July 1940. By the end of July, William, service number 74021, was on his way to Malta. He perished in combat on 11th January 1941 and is buried at Capuccini Naval Cemetery in Malta.

**Harold John Soars**, a Desford trained pilot, he joined 74 Squadron at Kirton-in-Lindsey on 20th August 1940. Harold, service number 134228, flew Spitfires with the famed 'Sailor' Malan and Glenfield's Arthur Smith (recorded elsewhere). A Messerschmitt 109's shot him down on November 1st whilst he patrolled Dover; he was admitted to Victoria Hospital, Folkestone. Commissioned in October 1942, he left the Service as a flight lieutenant in 1947. He continued in the R.A.F.V.R. from 1947 to 1955. This member of the Few died in a car accident in 1975. I last heard that his widow lived at Wigston.

**James Pickering** was born in Hinckley in 1915; he had a brother and four sisters. I spoke to Jim a number of times in 2003. He was educated at Wyggeston

School, Leicester, and then joined the family firm of Messrs. W. Pickering & Sons of Hinckley. Joining the R.A.F.V.R. he received his pilots licence from Desford in May 1937: one of the first to do so. Early in the war he was in a Torpedo Spotter Reconnaissance Flight and also trained for deck-landings on H.M.S. *'Argus'*. James, service number 117397, served for two weeks with 64 Squadron during the Battle of Britain; the Squadron lost twelve of its pilots during the Battle. James then embarked with the above ship for Malta: as a member of 418 Flight. On the 2nd August 1940, they flew-off to land at Luqa airfield and were amalgamated into 261 Squadron a few weeks later. Initially, they were armed with just twelve under-serviced Hurricanes and three ancient Gloster Gladiators: 'Faith, Hope and Charity', their bravery and sacrifice became legendary. They prevented the capture of the Mediterranean island, which in turn helped to deny the Axis Forces from taking the Suez Canal and the Persian oil fields. It was an air-war fought in a white-hot crucible of battle, the eye of a firestorm, staving off an overwhelming number of enemy bombers and fighters. Jim told me that twenty-two of his comrades, indeed brotherly friends, perished in those battles. Jim spent nine months on Malta and completed the maximum two tours. During that time he received a telegram from his childhood friend, Wanda, to say that she would marry him. Leaving Malta on 7th April 1941, he joined 80 Squadron in the Western Desert.

He left the R.A.F. as a flight lieutenant in 1945, but remained in the Voluntary Reserve until his sixtieth birthday: his flying career lasted for sixty years. The great aviator passed away on 6th April 2004, aged eighty-nine years leaving his wife at eighty-six years and children, Guthrie and Penny.

**Shirley Underwood,** of a well-known Whitwick family was educated at Coalville King Edward V11 Grammar School and Nottingham University; on leaving he was appointed to the staff of South Wigston Boys' School. Before the war he played football for Coalville Town and Whitwick White Cross. He

married the daughter of Councillor J. D. Smith, a Coalville magistrate. In the autumn of 1944, as a flight lieutenant, he achieved fame as a navigator/plotter who flew over the North Pole in a British built Lancaster Aries. The aeroplane flew all around the world in a navigational mission to the Pacific Ocean. The flight was made to study the behaviour of compasses, radar installations and automatic dead reckoning gear, and also to collect engine-handling performance, magnetic and meteorological data. The lieutenant sat at the navigator's table for nearly twenty-hours without a break: a flying distance of 17, 720 miles, and when he signalled to his base an estimated-time-of-arrival (ETA) the aircraft arrived forty-five seconds late. A remarkable achievement. At that time his wife and child lived on Ashby Road, Coalville.

**Geoffrey William Garton:** the Desford trained pilot was posted to 73 Squadron in early 1940, service number 67034. He fought in the Battle of France and claimed a Me110 fighter, and destroyed two more in the Battle of Britain. Posted to the Middle East he claimed two Ju87s and an Hs 126 in April 1941 and a Me202 in September, then a Ju87 and another Ju87 fell in October, also with several ground targets. Geoffrey commanded 112 Squadron and was awarded D. S. O. on 21st August 1945. The wing commander retired from the R.A.F. on 13th February 1962. He died in November 1976.

**James Richebourg Buchanan** was born in 1915 at Iden in Sussex. Living in Leicestershire he was a ground-staff engineer at Desford's Reid and Sigrist Training School. In 1938 he received his flying license and on the outbreak of war was posted to 609 Squadron. On 27th February 1940, he shared in the destruction of a He111 that was attacking allied shipping.

Over Dunkirk he damaged another one and shot down a Me109. On 27th July 1940, this one of the Few crashed in flames into the Channel just off Weymouth. He is remembered on the Runnymede Memorial.

*Barry Royce DFC, 1940.*

**William 'Barry' and Michael Royce**, born in 1913 and 1919 respectively at Pleasley Vale, on the Derbyshire borders. An old Charnwood family, both were pre-war pilots and called-up to 504 Squadron in 1939. They served in the Battles of France and Britain with Michael claiming a Do17 and a Bf110 in September 1940. He left the R.A.F. in 1945 as a squadron leader. Barry destroyed four enemy aircraft during the Battle of Britain, receiving the D.F.C., and left the Service as a wing commander in 1945. He died on 6th November 1979, leaving a wife, Nancy and two daughters, Nicola and Carolyn. Michael died in 1998 leaving a wife, Sylvia, and son Christopher, Richard and Judith. He is buried in the Isle of Wight.

*Michael Royce, 1940.*

**Frederick and William Cross,** sons of Frank and Bertha Cross of Coalville. Frederick George Cross joined the RAF at seventeen: service number 568279. Later he served with 209 Squadron, Coastal Command in the Shetlands, flying the huge 'Catalina' flying boat, one of which located the German battleship *Bismarck* in 1941.

*Fred Cross*

On 22nd February 1942, Frederick and his crew failed to return from a mission. Charles William Cross, joined the RAF determined to avenge his brother's death and passed his training in record time, service

*Bill Cross.*

number 1815434. Described as a brilliant scholar and navigator with 150 Squadron: Lancaster bombers, he took part in thousand bomber raids. On the night he died: 12th December 1944 over Essen, his mother said that it was a foggy and hoped Bill: "*was not out tonight!*" Next day a telegram arrived notifying her that her twenty years old son had been killed-in-action! My thanks to Sue Perkins (niece of the airmen.)

**Group Captain 'Dixie' Dean:** a former president of Ashby de la Zouch Royal British Legion. A famous Bomber Command pilot who flew on many missions over enemy territory.

**Thomas Holmes** of 88, Silver Street, Whitwick was a rear gunner with Bomber Command. On the night of 17/18th August 1943, his Lancaster, one of nearly six hundred, took part in a vital raid on the German Rocket and Aeronautical base of Peenemunde, on the island of Usedom in the Baltic Sea. The base, used to test the V1 '*Doodlebug*', was working on the potentially lethal V2 rocket, as well as other missiles and artillery projectiles. Sergeant Holmes' bomber had just released its load and was turning for home when two enemy fighters attacked from the rear. He spotted them, and after informing the pilot, he and the mid-upper gunner chose a target. They opened fire but the enemy replied with cannons and smashed the gun turrets and elsewhere, somehow, no one was injured. The pilot put the lumbering giant into a steep dive and only pulled up at the last moment; the fighters believed it was a death dive and left the scene. The return journey was at a perilously low level, with the bomb-aimer giving guidance to clear chimneystacks and tall buildings. An engine caught fire, but it was extinguished, the return flight lasted for three hours, with the crew believing every minute would be their last. Only excellent piloting stopped the Lancaster from rolling at landing: the starboard wheel failed and the petrol tanks were almost dry. Sergeant Holmes and the crew left the aeroplane and were told by the ground crew that it was a miracle for such a damaged Lancaster to return to base. The raid caused extensive damage and put the V2 developments back by a crucial four months: thus saving many allied lives.

**John Hannah V.C.** was born in Paisley on 27th November 1921. He joined the R.A.F. on 13th August 1939, and trained as a wireless operator/gunner, becoming sergeant on 27th May 1940. With 83 Squadron he was involved in bombing barges in enemy occupied ports that had gathered for an invasion of Great Britain. On the full-moon night of 15/16th September 1940, his Hampden bomber: P1355 *'Betty'*: one of fifteen, took off from R.A.F. Scampton to bomb Antwerp. Over the target they met searchlights and anti-aircraft fire; the pilot dropped to two thousand feet for greater accuracy. *'Betty'* shuddered when hit by shrapnel and bullets! Just after releasing her bombs, a shell entered the open bomb doors and set the fuselage alight. John saw the alloy floor dissolve under his feet and spare ammunition drums explode. He darted through the blaze to gain two fire extinguishers, emptied one, but near to suffocation leaned through the perspex cupola to gulp fresh air. Refreshed he used the other extinguisher, then his logbook and finally his hands to beat out the flames. He put it out in ten minutes and reported his efforts to the pilot, who was shocked by John's look. His face, where uncovered by his helmet was burned black, eyes puffed-up, eyebrows singed, both hands severely burned and his flying suit: burnt and ragged! In spite of his injuries, John helped the pilot to navigate back to base, arriving at 03.00am, but on landing was instantly taken to hospital. Guy Gibson, piloted one of the other aircraft on the raid, he later received fame and a V.C. as a 'Dam Buster'. On the 7th October 1940, shortly after leaving Rauceby Hospital in Lincolnshire, Sergeant John Hannah attended Buckingham Palace to receive the Victoria Cross: the youngest airman, at eighteen years to receive such an

award. The citation: *'He displayed courage, coolness and devotion to duty of the highest order.'*

John didn't return to operational duties. On 4th November, he reported to 14 O.T.U. at Cottesmore as an instructor, and met his future wife, Janet Beaver of Oakham, there.

On 4th September 1941, he joined No2 Signal's School at Yatesbury but his health deteriorated, and on 10th December 1942, Flight Sergeant John Hannah was discharged from the R.A.F. on a full disability pension due to tuberculosis. John and Janet lived at Birstall, just to the north of Leicester, and by the war's end they had three daughters. Unable to do a full time job he found it difficult to support his family, and the lung disease ended his short life at Markfield Sanatorium on 6th May 1967. The Leicester Mercury opened a fund to help support his widow and children. Later, as W.W.2 memorabilia became highly collectable, Jane turned down a sum of £3,000 for the medal.

On 6th May 1967, a memorial service took place in a hanger at Scampton, with crews of 83 Squadron (Vulcan bomber) being present. At the service, Jane Hannah presented John's V.C. to his old unit on permanent loan, and said: *"This is where it belongs."* It is still there.

**Robert Morley's** name appears annually in the Coalville Times: *'Treasured memories of our only brother who was killed in Italy while serving with the RAF on 31st August 1944. Time and years slip quietly by, but memories of you will never die. From loving sisters & families.'*

**Nicholas Alkemade** was very well known in the 1960s, mainly due to the 'Victor' comic of that time describing his miraculous escape from a burning Lancaster bomber. Born in Norfolk to a Dutch father and an English mother, the family settled down at Loughborough. In 1940, at seventeen, he joined the R.A.F. and served with Air Sea Rescue before Bomber Command as a rear gunner. On the night of 24th March 1944, his fifteenth raid, his aircraft was one of three hundred over Berlin. Just after setting a course for home a Junkers 88 attacked and set them ablaze; the pilot ordered the crew to jump. The fire prevented Nick from opening the doors to the fuselage to collect his parachute. His choice was death by fire or death from a fall of over fifteen thousand feet; choosing the latter he miraculously survived! Later he described his sadness while falling, at not being able to say goodbye to his fiancée and friends. He passed out before ground-fall or should it be tree-fall; on regaining consciousness at 3.20am he found that a thicket of interlocking fir branches covered with a blanket of heavy snow had cushioned his fall. Shaken and badly injured he furiously blew his emergency whistle, not wanting to freeze to death after such amazing good fortune. After a few hours he was located and taken to hospital with a twisted right knee, a deep splinter wound to his thigh, a strained back and a nasty scalp wound. After recovery he was taken to Stalag Luft 111, a hundred miles southeast of Berlin. At first the Germans doubted his story and took him to be a spy, but on examining his parachute harness they found the snap-hooks still in their clips and the lift webs still fastened to the chest straps. On finding the crashed Lancaster, four of the crew died, they saw the charred remains of his parachute just as he told them! German officers congratulated him on such an incredible escapade, with the senior commandant saying: 'a *miracle no less, what a story to tell your grandchildren!*' When the two hundred British, French and Americans prisoners of war in the camp heard there was uproar of delight! The German commandant wrote a letter of authentication and the senior British officer countersigned this in the presence of two NCOs. On his release in 1945, he returned to Loughborough and married his fiancée, Pearl, and

*Grandson Luke Alkemade in TV series.*

resided at 27, Linden Road in the town; the couple had two children, Valerie and Nick. He worked as a salesman in the town for many years, specialising in furniture until he retired to Cornwall. He passed away in 1991. In an old diary he wrote that he could only wonder why such a marvellous thing should have

happened to a man as ordinary as himself! The last I heard, Pearl was living in William Street, Loughborough, and that she was pleased when her grandson, Luke Alkemade, starred in a Channel 4 TV series called: 'Bomber Crews'; Luke played the part of a rear gunner and rightly so.

**Richard Colton Alexander,** pilot officer with 44 Squadron. Lost over France on 8th May 1944. Son of A.C. & J. Alexander of Queniborough.

**Thomas Eric Anstey,** sergeant with 110 Squadron. Lost on 27th December 1941.Son of Thomas & Agnes Anstey of Leicester.

**Reginald Albert Attfield,** sergeant with 61 Squadron. Lost over Germany on 8th December 1940. Son of Albert & Francis Attfield of Thornton.

**Francis Peter Bramley,** 622 Squadron. Lost over Germany on 15th February 1944. Son of Francis & Kate Bramley of Ashby de la Zouch.

**Ernest Albert Brookes,** sergeant with 7 Squadron. Lost over Belgium on 6th December 1942. Son of Ernest & May Brookes of Loughborough.

**Frank William Burdett,** flight sergeant engineer with 12 Squadron. Lost over Holland on 20th February 1944, aged 21 after raid on Leipzig.

Son of Mr & Mrs Rose Burdett of 17, Bassett Street, Leicester. Took-off from Wickenby, Lincolnshire. All of the crew buried at Harderwijk Cemetery, Holland.

**Obadiah Cave,** sergeant with 150 Squadron. Lost over Malta on 15th May 1943. Son of Mr. & Mrs. J.W. Cave of Stanton-under-Bardon & husband of A.E. Cave of Leicester.

**Walter Chester,** sergeant with 35 Squadron. Lost over France on 5th October 1942. Son of Walter & Sophia Chester and husband of Doreen of Leicester.

**Frank Cobley,** sergeant with 7 Squadron. Lost over Germany on 18th October 1943. Son of William & Florence Cobley of Leicester.

**Edward Patrick Deville,** flying officer with 7 Squadron. Lost on raid on 12th June 1943. Son of Theophilus & Emily Delville & husband of Helen of Loughborough.

**Stephen Nelson Dougan,** sergeant with 630 Squadron. Lost over Germany on 27th April 1944. Son of Jim & May Dougan of Loughborough.

**Eric Dwyer,** sergeant with 44 Squadron. Lost on raid on 2nd September 1941. Son of Harry & Edith Dwyer of Leicester. **AND**

**John Harold Dwyer,** sergeant with 106 Squadron. Lost over Germany on 2nd January 1944. \*\*The brother of Eric Dwyer.

**George Alfred Philip Edwards,** sergeant with 156 Squadron. Lost on raid on 22nd June 1943. Son of Alfred & Florence & husband of Marjorie May of Leicester.

**Douglas Archibald Eld,** sergeant with 104 Squadron. Lost over Romania on 8th May 1944. Son of Fred & Annie Eld of Leicester.

**Charles Stanley Field,** flight sergeant with 40 Squadron. Lost over Malta on 20th August 1943. Son of Arthur & Emily Field of Leicester.

**Lawrence Fitzsimmons,** sergeant with 103 Squadron. Lost over France on 25th October 1942. Son of Roger & Mary Jane Fitzsimmons of Leicester.

**Kenneth Joseph Fletcher,** sergeant with 214 Squadron. Lost over Germany on 6th November 1944. Son of Mr. J & Mrs. E. Fletcher of Leicester.

**George Norton Glithero,** sergeant with 76 Squadron. Took off from R.A.F. Holme and shot down near Paris on 3rd June 1944. Buried at Dreux Communal Cemetery, France. Son of John & Annie Glithero, Leicester & brother of John.

*George Norton Glithero*

**Alan Roy Green,** sergeant with 640 Squadron. Lost over France on 3rd June 1944. Son of Horace Dormer & Elsie Green of Ashby Magna.

**Samuel Robert Groom,** wing commander with 102 Squadron. Lost on 21st November 1940. Son of John Bax & Charlotte Groom & husband of Josephine of Foxton.

**Henry Theobald Hanbury,** flight lieutenant with 511 Squadron. Lost over Egypt on 20th November 1946. Son of Charles & Ethel Hanbury of Melton Mowbray **AND**
**Reginald Lewis Hanbury,** squadron leader with 254 Squadron. Lost on raid on 8th June 1944. \*\* Brother of Henry Theobald Hanbury.

**Donald Handford,** sergeant with 226 Squadron. Lost over Belgium on 27th April 1942. Son of William & Gertrude Handford of Coalville.

**Henry Hetterley,** flying officer and bomb aimer with 51 Squadron. Lost over Germany on 22nd November 1943. Married in May 1943. Son of a Mr & Mrs Hetterley of Coalville and nephew of Walter Handford: one of Famous Fifty of World War 1 fame.

**George Herbert Johnson,** flying officer. Lost over Holland on 25th January 1941. Son of John & Louisa Johnson & husband of Kathleen of Loughborough.

**Wilfred George Joy,** squadron leader with 141 Squadron. Lost on raid on 26th March 1943. Son Frederick & Bessie Joy & husband of Ivy of Stoke Golding.

**Richard Henry Julian,** sergeant with 106 Squadron. Lost over Germany on 23rd September 1944. Son of Leonard & Rosa Julian of Leicester.

**Thomas James Kelly,** sergeant with 462 Squadron. R.A.F.V.R. Lost over Libya on 12th October 1943. Son of Thomas & Edith Kelly & husband of Constance of South Wigston.

**Leslie King,** sergeant with 180 Squadron. Lost over Germany on 13th March 1945. Son of George & Ethel & husband of Joyce of Leicester.

**George Kenneth Kirk,** sergeant with 36 Squadron. Lost over Algeria on 4th March 1944. Son of George & Annie Kirk of Costock.

**Douglas Leatherland,** squadron leader with 97 Squadron. Lost over France on 21st April 1944. Son of Joseph & Edith & husband of Margery of Loughborough.

Philip **Frederick Lill,** sergeant with 40 Squadron. Lost over Sicily on 5th January 1942. Son of Charles & Nellie & husband of Doris Lill of Loughborough.

**Eric Edward Lockton,** sergeant with 236 Squadron. Lost on raid 20th July 1940. Son of Frederick & Annie Lockton of Ashby de la Zouch.

**Raymond Phillip Margetts,** flight sergeant. Lost on raid 16th April 1945. Son of Josiah & Ellen Margetts of Coalville.

**George Austin Marshall,** flight lieutenant with 264 Squadron. Lost 8th November 1944. Son of George & Priscilla Marshall & husband of Julie of Coalville

**Clifford William Morley,** flight sergeant with 12 (S.A.A.F.) Squadron. Lost over Italy on 31st August 1944. Son of Robert & Emily Morley of Swannington.

**Claude Ronald Nash,** sergeant. Lost on raid on 24th April 1942. Son of Claude & Lilian Nash of Loughborough.

**John Frederick Allen Neal,** flying officer with 69 Squadron. Lost on raid over Germany on 30th November 1944. Son of Edward & Eleanor Neal of Desford.

**John Edward Norman,** flight sergeant with 460 Squadron. Lost over Germany on 21st November 1944, aged 21. Son of James & Maud Norman of Glenfield.

**Joseph Thomas Owen,** sergeant with 83 Squadron. Lost overseas, aged 21, name on Runnymede Memorial. Grandson of Elizabeth Owen & husband of Betty Owen of Belgrave.

**Alan James Poulton,** flight sergeant with 158 Squadron. Lost over Germany on20th January 1944, aged 20. Son of James (MM.) & Emma Poulton of Leicester.

**William Powell,** sergeant with 83 Squadron. Lost overseas 1st November 1941, aged 21, name on Runnymede Memorial. Son of William & Florence of Loughborough.

**James Thomas Price,** sergeant with 9 Squadron. Lost over France on 8th July 1944, aged 21 and buried at Beamont-les-nonains Cemetery. Son of Osmond & Mabel Price of Hugglescote. ('Jimmy' was a good friend of the Hatter side of my family.)

**John Francis Anthony Rayns,** flying officer with 148 Squadron. Lost over Italy on 22nd November 1944, aged 21. Son of Alfred & Joanne Rayns of Loughborough.

**Norman George Reed,** flight sergeant with 626 Squadron. Lost over Germany on 5th April 1945. Son of George & Ethelwyn Reed of Bagworth.

**Samuel Ivan Rudkin,** pilot officer with 44 Squadron. Lost overseas on 17th August 1943. Son of Albert and Nora Rudkin of Leicester; his brother also died in the war.

**Ronald Shuttleworth,** sergeant with 77 Squadron. Lost over Holland on 27th December 1941, aged 21. Son of Thomas & Florence Shuttleworth of Donisthorpe.

**Norman Alfred Smith,** flight sergeant with 46 Squadron. Lost over India on 6th February 1945, aged

22. Son of Luke & Naomi Smith of Countesthorpe.

**Reginald Smith,** sergeant with 20 Squadron. Lost overseas on 13th April 1943, aged 21, name on Runnymede Memorial. Son of John & Elizabeth Smith of Loughborough.

**Basil James Thompson,** sergeant with 32 Squadron. Lost over Malta on 6th April 1943, aged 22. Son of Rev. John & Helen Thompson of Leicester.

**Neville William Gordon Thompson,** sergeant with 115 Squadron. Lost over Germany on 25th February 1944. Son of Neville & Harriett Thompson of Market Bosworth.

**Cyril Timms,** flying officer with 114 Squadron. Died on 9th February 1946 and remembered on Alamein Memorial. Son of John & Caroline Timms of Measham.

**Sidney Underwood,** sergeant with 223 Squadron. Lost over Italy on 15th October 1943. Buried: Cassino Cemetery. Son of Sidney & Mary & husband of Vera of Leicester.

**Graham Wale,** sergeant with 106 Squadron. Lost over Denmark on 2nd May 1942, aged 20. Son of George & Stella Wale of Leicester.

**Sydney Watkins,** sergeant. Lost overseas on 14th January 1944, aged 19, name on Runnymede Memorial. Son of John & Leah Watkins of Ellistown.

**William Derek St Clair Weeks,** flight lieutenant with 98 Squadron. Lost over France on 23rd July 1943, aged 22. Son of William & Julia Weeks of Leicester.

**John Edward Yarnell,** flight lieutenant with 246 Squadron. Lost over Azores on 14th March 1945. Son of John & Margaret Yarnell & husband of Mabel Yarnell of Leicester.

**Desmond Alert York,** sergeant with 150 Squadron. Lost over Holland on 30th July 1942, aged 22. Son of Thomas & Olive York of Leicester.

Most of the above belonged to Bomber Command, and from this random sample it is apparent just how youthful they were. Nearly 55,000 aircrew lost their lives between 1939-45: with an average age of just twenty-two years. The mainstay of Bomber Command was the Lancaster bomber; of the 7,377 that were built nearly 4,000 were lost in combat. In my book *'Epitaph For The Few'* I dedicated a poem to the above men, it is entitled: *'The Last Goodbye'*.

# WILLIAM JAMES HENRY LOCK

James John Seamer Lock married Selina Chalk on 30th September 1906 at St. Michael and All Angels Church in the Parish of Knighton, Leicester. James: aged twenty four years, was a gardener living-in at Park House, Aylestone Road, Leicester and Selina: aged twenty-two years, was living with her parents at 136, Knighton Fields. National Telephones employed Selina's father, Henry William Chalk as a 'Wireman'. For James to be a collier they moved to 54, The Green, Hugglescote, and William James Henry Lock was born on 4th January 1908. The surname, unlike most being Locke, has no 'e'; this together with the additional surname 'Seamer' carries a mysterious and intriguing history, along the lines of looted treasure from shipwrecks, and hitherto financial investments and possible gains for a certain few!

*(In 1800, John Lock fathered a child of the same name born at Crediton, Devon. He became a farm hand, then a general labourer in St. David's Hill, Exeter. By 1851 he was married and living on High Street, Crediton, but in 1852 they moved to Kittycot, Crediton.*

*The 1861 census shows John married to Thirza (nee Seamer: aged forty-three). John was described as a 'Common Carrier', possibly in the mining of slate or tin. They had six children: Ann (aged twelve years), John (ten), Elizabeth (seven), Emila (five), William (three), and James Seamer (eight months). The surname 'Seamer' has value: Thirza's father was Robert Seamer, a surname linked to a bizarre past! By 11th February 1880, James Seamer Lock, at nineteen years had left Kittycot to enlist into the 5th Brigade of the Royal Artillery: service number 5302. His first posting was as a driver at Woolwich Barracks. In 1881, with a number 4917, he served at Newcastle-on-Tyne. Records show he remained at Woolwich for quite a time, both as a driver and a saddle-maker in the Royal Artillery. On 16th May 1881 he married Jane Comerford, daughter of Thomas Comerford and had thirteen children: \*\*James John Seamer in 1881, Ernest, Mary, Elizabeth, Emma, Benjamin, Jennifer, Florence, Harold, Anne, Albert, Daisy and William. On leaving the Royal Artillery, James moved to Leicester to work down the mines. James' wife died on 29th April 1932, and he died in 1950.)*

William Lock's siblings were Albert, Ernest, Selina

From left: Benjamin Lock (son), Albert Lock (son), Sergeant James Seamer Lock (born 1861, father) and William Lock (son born circa 1896). Circa 1915.

(Lena), Nellie, Frederick, Florence, Elsie, another Nellie and the youngest, Beryl: born 1927. He was educated at St. John The Baptist Church, Hugglescote, and his first occupation was in hosiery, later a Building trade labourer, and then as a miner at Bagworth Colliery.

William married Fanny Faye Clarke, an Ellistown girl, on 21st April 1911: daughter of Joseph Henry Clarke. At first, they lived 19, Kendal Road, Ellistown, and later moved to 111, Ibstock Road in the same village. Whilst there they had two sons, Joseph James Seamer Lock: born 12th December 1934, and Barry: born 30th June 1936. Shortly afterwards, in 1937, his mother, Selina, died tragically! She had been to visit her grandson, Joseph, at Ellistown, and on her return bus journey got off at the stop, which was opposite to the gates of Hugglescote Cemetery on Station Hill. While crossing the road in front of the bus, she fell beneath its wheels and received severe head wounds: dying instantly aged fifty-two years. For

*William and Fanny Lock on their wedding day.*

*Sergeant William Lock, circa 1939.*

the youngest sibling, Beryl, it was an emotional time and she had to move into digs and work in the hosiery trade at Clutsom and Kemp, Coalville.

Around 1926 he enlisted into the 1/5 Territorial Battalion of the Leicestershire Regiment, service number: 4855253, and come 1939 was a sergeant in that Battalion.

The Fifth Battalion maintained its proud stature in the inter-war years, with men of the calibre of Lieutenant-Colonel (Dr.) John Jamie in charge between 1931-37, successors J.C. Barrett V.C. and Guy German putting the icing on the cake. It was rated one of the best in the Territorial Army; hence the decision to post it to Norway in 1940 as part of the 148th Infantry Brigade, and to help the Norwegians to resist a German invasion.

The Battalion spent Christmas 1939 at Raby Castle, County Durham, with intensive training continuing until entraining in April 1940 for Rosyth on the Firth of Forth, Scotland. Shortly before evacuation William had been on furlough, and while at Coalville

*William, Fanny and Barry Lock at Coalville Railway Station, early April, 1940.*

Railway Station to return to his unit a photograph caught him kissing and embracing his wife, and son, Barry.

Later, maybe incorrectly, the press spread this photograph on most front-pages of newspapers to improve the country's morale; all will be revealed.

On 16th April 1940, the Battalion's 'A' and 'D' Companies departed from Aberdeen on the anti-aircraft cruisers: H.M.S. 'Carlisle' and 'Curacao' for a 640 kilometres (four hundred miles) voyage. On 18th April, Companies: 'B' and 'C', left in 'S.S. Sunniva' and 'St. Magnus'. They faced a tempestuous North Sea as well as a 'U'-Boat threat: one of their convoy: 'S.S. Cedarbank' was torpedoed and sunk. (See Les Bishop on H.M.S. 'Repulse'). The sea was so rough that virtually every person in the convoy suffered from acute seasickness.

The Expeditionary Brigade's initiative was countered by a pre-emptive German strike; army units ably supported by their airforce, invaded Denmark and Norway during hours of darkness on April 8th/9th. They rapidly commandeered most of the strategic locations, while Herr Hitler absurdly claimed that he had invaded the Scandinavian countries to prevent Great Britain from adding them to her empire. Earlier, on 11th April, Mr. Churchill had promised the Allies would aid Norway: "To the best of their ability." Royal Air Force bombers raided the enemy occupied aerodrome at Stavanger: damaging aircraft on the ground, and earlier the Royal Navy, led by the battleship 'Warspite', caused havoc at Narvik Fjord. (Marine H. Davenport of 126, Crescent Road, Coalville was on the battleship and featured in this attack, saying: "It was all very exciting".)

On April 18th, a forward team led by Lieutenant-Colonel Guy German, landed at Aandalsnes: standing at the head of the Romsdals Fjord. Commanders of the Norwegian Army met him and specified that unless he offered immediate support they would surrender to the Germans. British tactical plans were scrapped, and together with French units they joined them in trying to stop the enemy's advance on Oslo. Undeniably, the Nazi seizure of Oslo was the epitome of treachery. Unknowingly, for months, enemy agents had schemed with Norwegian traitors led by Major Quisling; he wittingly fouled communications, ordered forts not to fire, and arranged for fjord mines to be disconnected.

*British troops prepare to disembark at Norway. April 22nd, 1940.*

When the 5th Battalion's 'B' and 'C' Companies arrived on April 22nd, they realised that 'A' and 'D' were fighting, not just the Germans, but also deep snow. Irresistible enemy troops forced 'A' and 'D' to retire by train, and the Battalion regrouped at Tretten. Issued with unsuitable khaki battledress, the soldiers were sodden and bitterly cold, and 'Stuka' dive-bombers attacked them. The Battalion commandeered civilian lorries and drove for the coast, but their progress was hindered by the weather and a lack of local maps. They endured difficult times and saw poor morale when sections of the Norwegian Army threw away their rifles! The Leicestershire Territorials bayonet attacked and cleared a pathway, but superior numbers counter-attacked with tanks, mortar bombs and additional Stuka attacks. Platoon Sergeant Major John Sheppard took part in this ferocious battle just south of Lillehammer, and destroyed two enemy tanks on St. George's Day, 23rd April 1940. The tanks were the first to be destroyed in the war by British fire, and his actions delayed the enemy's advance by two hours, allowing many senior officers and men to escape. John was awarded the Distinguished Conduct Medal (D.C.M.) for his bravery but was captured and spent five years as a prisoner-of-war in Poland and Germany. John, now in his nineties, lives at Rothley.

The Tigers fought valiantly to evade capture, especially as most had not eaten or slept for thirty-six hours. The Tretten road to the coast was pot-holed and shell cratered, and Me109 fighters strafed the convoy of lorries: troops had to surrender. Moving at night, sections of the Battalion reached Aandalsnes and were evacuated by the Royal Navy, whom lost three destroyers and a sloop. Others found alternative routes to the coast and requisitioned fishing vessels to return to Scotland. The Luftwaffe's bombing Aandalsnes,

Aandalsnes being bombed, early May, 1940.

Trondheim, and Namsos hindered the evacuation, which started on May 2nd.

Only six officers and one hundred and fifty-five other ranks managed to return to Battalion Headquarters at Loughborough. That figure increased slightly as a number managed to evade capture and crossed into neutral Sweden. William's photograph was headlined 'Escape from Norway'

Evacuees from Aandalsnes aboard a British warship.
2nd May 1940.

After internment in Falan Camp they were repatriated, with Hitler, as propaganda, offering a prisoner exchange of one German to four British prisoners.

Most of the 'Falan men' returned in late 1940, one such was Lieutenant Reginald Coleman, son of the owner of the retail hardware business at Coalville.

Sergeant William Lock escaped from Tretten in a bus with Joe Rawlinson, who lost an eye during the expedition. Colonel Guy German of Ashby de la Zouch spent five years as a prisoner-of-war and was Senior British Officer at the infamous 'Colditz'. He was awarded the Distinguished Service Order (D.S.O.) for his leadership in Norway and Colditz.

The Fifth Battalion regrouped and refitted at Hawick, in the Scottish Borders, and posted to Northern Ireland where it became an officer cadet training battalion. William was hospitalised in Ireland with a kidney complaint; being in his mid-thirties, he was honourably discharged. For the remainder of the war he repaired 'Defiant' fighter/bombers at nearby R.A.F. Desford. After the war he returned to Bagworth Colliery. Though promoted to a deputy, poor health resulted in him conducting on Midland Red buses, and then to the Springfield Centre at Coalville. (Ex: Stableford's). He loved his recreation and played lawn-bowls for Ellistown, the National Coal Board and Grieves' Needle Manufacturers, being chairman of the latter.

William James Henry Lock died suddenly at 111, Ibstock Road, Ellistown from a heart attack on 28th November 1964, aged just fifty-seven years. His second son, Barry, lives with his wife, Betty (nee Fairbrother) at 34, North Avenue, Hugglescote, and he served with the R. A. F. during his two years of National Service.

The eldest son, Joseph (Joe) James Seamer was educated at Ellistown Church School and Hugglescote Secondary Modern. Joe recalls his time, as a lad, in Leicester during the city's blitz. "I wasn't far from the City Football Ground, Filbert Street, when the sirens started. Before I arrived at the shelters I looked up and saw this aeroplane with crosses on its wings."

Joe is proud, and rightly so, of serving with the 1st Battalion of the Royal Leicestershire Regiment, service number 23265337, during his National Service as a lance corporal in the serious Cyprus conflict. The campaign (1955-58) was against the EOKA terrorists under the former Greek Army officer, Colonel Grivas, after violent protests broke-out against British rule. Joe maintains strong links with the Tigers and the Cyprus Veteran's Association, and earlier was a

*Lance Corporal Joseph Lock.*

*Angela Witham aged 18 years.*

battalion commander with the Church Lads' Brigade. He attended night school at Loughborough College and qualified in plumbing and heating, and, after his retirement, received several management qualifications. Joe deserves credit for his book about fixing leaky pipes and dodgy boilers entitled: '*Above The Water Line.*' Beryl Lock, his father's youngest sibling, married Maurice Hatter, son of Charlie Hatter, one of the 'Famous Fifty'.

On 26th July 1958, Joe married Angela Alice Witham at St. John The Baptist Church, Whitwick. Angela, born 21st December 1939, lived with her father, Frederick: a coalminer, mother, Beatrice (nee Thirlby), and brother, John Rex Witham at 72, Leicester Road, Whitwick. Angela once managed Benson Shoe Shop on High Street, Coalville. The couple live happily at Ibstock, and have a son, Steven: born 25th February 1959, Ruth: born 18th March 1963, and David: born 21st April 1969. Steven was a regular soldier with 2 Para: R.A.F. Regiment, and lives at Newarke, Nottinghamshire. Ruth is married to Gary Storer and lives on Chapel Street, Ibstock, and has two children. David was a regular soldier with the Royal Artillery, like his ancestor (and at Woolwich), until retiring on health grounds. He lives with his wife, Cheryl, and three children.

*Steven, Ruth and David Lock.*

Angela's roots run deeply in Charnwood: paternal great-grandfather, William Thirlby lived from 1809-1847, while grandfather, George Thirlby (1864-1942, born at Whittle Farm, Beaumanor was an auctioneer's assistant for cattle sales at Coalville and district. Angela's mother, Beatrice (1896-1974) married Frederick Witham (1900-1967). Two of her uncles, William Thirlby (1886-1953) and George Thirlby (1888-1958) served in W.W.1; George had emigrated

*William Thirlby in 1916.*

to Canada but returned to *'fight the good fight for liberty and freedom.'*

Angela was in the St. John Ambulance Brigade and a Sunday school teacher. Aunt Edith Thirlby married Thomas Catlow, one of the 'Famous Fifty'.

Her elder cousin, Harold Catlow, served in India during W.W.2 and he used to send her letters and cards, and once he sent her a beautiful doll. Angela has inherited the Thirlby's talents: highly skilled at designing, pattern cutting and made her daughter's wedding dress.

*George Thirlby of the Canadian Rifles.*

In November 2000, a local newspaper did an article on William and Fanny's emotional farewell sixty years before.

Fanny said: *'I remember the emotional day when I said goodbye to William, and the terrible feeing of not knowing whether he would return from the war. William was on his way to Norway at the time and I remember the Leicester Mercury photographer coming up and asking if he could take our picture. I* *have seen the photograph in the Leicester Museum.'* (See colour section). Fanny passed away on 26th June 2003, aged ninety-two years, and is buried with her husband at Hugglescote's Station Road Cemetery.

## Albert Lock MM

Another son of **James John Seamer Lock was Albert Lock. Born in 1913, he enlisted in 1934 as a regular soldier with the 1st Leicestershire Battalion. He served in India for two years and also fought on the Northwest Frontier for one year. Following the invasion of Malaya by Japanese troops (see Leslie Bishop), Albert fought in the campaign from beginning to end, and was at Singapore when it fell. The following is a synopsis of an account that appeared in The Billet of January 1943. At this time his father was living at 11a Hotel Street, Coalville:

*'After the fall of Singapore we were told to lay down our guns, which we did to our annoyance. A few Coalville pals were in my section including Private John Beeson* (the singer), *Harry Davis and Fred Cockerill. We were all so exhausted and battered that we went to a hut and fell asleep on the floor. I planned to escape and at 3.30am on 26th February 1942 my opportunity came. In the darkness I crept out and went to the harbour: a mile and a half away. My every limb shook with nerves: knowing that if caught I'd be killed. On the shore I found an open rowing boat and saying prayers and thinking of freedom at Coalville I started to row.* (Albert had not been in England for seven years). *All I had with me were the clothes I wore and I followed the stars at night and the sun with the hope of making Java. Sharks frequently visited me but they didn't attack. I drifted with the tide a lot and after three days I saw land; it was a small island but it had fresh water and some food and feeling more confident I put to sea again. I rowed and drifted, rationed my food and drink; days passed and on falling into a deep sleep I knew no more until I was picked up by a British Cruiser. I heard that I was about six hundred and fifty miles south of Ceylon.* (Sri Lanka). *I was given every attention by the surgeon who eased the pain I was suffering from two bayonet wounds inflicted by the Japanese. By the time we reached Colombo I felt much better and after reporting to the authorities I was sent home. The Malaysian Campaign cannot be imagined; there are vast forests of rubber trees with thick*

*undergrowth holding all sorts of terrors, swamps, mosquitoes and all sorts. During the day it was almost as dark as night-times and so you can imagine what it was like looking for the enemy! In our section, ten Coalville Militia lads covered the entire Battalions withdrawal and impeded the Japanese advance for over an hour; I have never served with better fighting men than those and I was the only regular soldier amongst them. They fought like hell, knew no fear and were all 'Mentioned in Despatches!' The Billet is a real comfort to me, my only link with Coalville: a real Godsend.*

*I was sad to hear that my mother had died while I was serving on the Northwest Frontier.*

Sergeant Albert Lock received the Military Medal for his bravery and determination. He was one of very few to escape the clutches of the Japanese. Upon returning to Coalville on leave, he decided to celebrate and went out with his brother, Frederick to Ashby de la Zouch. A local newspaper reported that the 'war hero had been taken ill' (Albert Lock) and taken to hospital. The brave soldier wasn't ill, he was drunk - but who could possibly blame him! He remained a regular soldier after the war, married, had children and passed away around 2003.

Frederick also served in World War 2, again a sergeant, he lives at Scoon, Perthshire, Scotland. All of his male siblings fought in the war.

My thanks to Joe and Angela Lock, and my dear Auntie Beryl Hatter.

# DAVID JOHN MALTBY D.S.O., D.F.C.

had just completed the feature regarding Clement Culley of the Pathfinder Force, when his son, Brian Culley, told me that the son of a Dambuster pilot lived in Quorn. I didn't know this but quickly took note. The son in question, John Maltby: is a director of a business in Meeting Street of the said village, and the following relates to his father.

David's father, Ettrick Maltby, was born on 12th August 1885 at Aspley in Bedfordshire, but came from a line of clergymen from Nottinghamshire. He attended Keble College, Oxford and then taught at a preparatory school in Kent. On 28th July 1914, Ettrick married Aileen Hatfeild (spelt ei): she came from a prosperous family at nearby Margate. Both were good at sport and under her husband's tutorage, she played hockey on several occasions for England in the 1920s, indeed, her eldest brother, Eric, played cricket for Kent until his wartime death in France. Their first child, Audrey was born on 26th June 1917. In 1918, Ettrick became joint-headmaster at Hydneye House, a school at Baldslow near Hastings in Kent. David was born there on 10th May 1920 and Jean on 30th December 1924. Apart from 1940-45, when the army acquired Hydneye (the school moving to Witherdon Manor at Germansweek, a village in Devon) it was the family home for thirty-seven years.

*Hydeneye House Boy's Preparatory School.*

After Hydneye House, David was educated at Marlborough College, and in 1938 decided to study as a mining engineer: spending time in the south Yorkshire collieries. In 1939, he applied for aircrew: being called-up to the R.A.F.V.R. on 20th June 1940, travelling to R.A.F. Uxbridge. From there he was posted to Initial Training Wing at Paignton, and then flew the Tiger moth at the Elementary Training School

at Ansty in Warwickshire. Further training at Grantham: flying an Anson bomber, he received his 'wings' and the rank of pilot officer. His first posting, 5th June 1941, was to 106 Squadron at R.A.F. Coningsby in Lincolnshire, and near to Woodhall Spa where his future wife's sister: Betty and her husband, 'Woody' Walter lived. The Squadron was in the process of changing from Hamden bombers to the new but unreliable Avro Manchester.

*David Maltby at the controls.*

His first operation on June 11th was the bombing of Duisburg in the Ruhr valley, and two weeks later he was transferred to 97 Squadron: still at Coningsby. Between August 6th to 18th he flew on six operations but when on leave at his parents in Devon, took his girlfriend, Georgina (called Nina: born 31st May 1919) Goodson: the sister of Betty Walton at Woodhall Spa: twelve kilometres southeast of Lincoln. The same arrangement applied for his Christmas leave. In early 1942, the revised Manchester bomber: now with four engines and called the Lancaster began to arrive at the airfields. Nina's parents owned a fruit growing business in eastern Kent. During the Battle of Britain, Nina, saw a parachute land in their field. He was a badly burned German pilot; Nina nursed him until he died a few minutes later.

On 18th February 1942, Flying Officer D. Maltby had his first outing in a Lancaster and later went on 'gardening' missions: mine-laying operations just off Germany's coast.

*David Maltby in the cockpit.*

*The wedding day: Nina's sister, Betty, Nina, David," Woody" Walton, Betty's husband.*

*David Maltby at Woodhall Spa, Spring 1942.*

Flying Cross, awarded on 11th August 1942, he was approached to join a new squadron: possibly by the legendary Wing Commander Guy Gibson. It was to be a new squadron and formed for a very special and top-secret purpose. In the late winter of 1942-3, Bomber Command laid plans for a dedicated and concentrated attack on Germany's industrial centre around the Ruhr.

The river served navigational needs, also, on its upper reaches stood about a dozen reservoirs that stored water for drinking and industrial use, notably steel manufacture. The two most important being on the Mohne: a north bank tributary of the Ruhr and the Sorpe: a south bank tributary.

The missions clocked-up. While flying Lancaster R5553 over Stuttgart on the evening of 4th-5th May 1942 his aircraft was damaged. On his return to base the hydraulics failed and David landed without the use of the flaps; the aircraft was written off but all of the crew survived. A lengthy overseas trip on April 27th was from Lossiemouth in Scotland to a Norwegian fjord in an attempt to destroy the enemy pocket battleship: 'Tirpitz'. The latter escaped by its location near overhanging cliffs, but soon he was approaching the magical end of a tour of duty.

At 1.45 pm on Saturday 30th May 1942, David Maltby and Nina Goodson married at St. Andrew's Church in the enchanting village of Wickhambreaux in Kent.

David bombed Essen on June 8th: it was his twenty-eighth and the last of his tour before changing squadrons. His father wrote in his diary: '*David off ops - God be praised.*'

Now a flight lieutenant and with a Distinguished

*David Maltby.*

The largest dam was at Hemfurth on the river Eder: a hundred and sixty kilometres to the east of the industrial Ruhr. All three dams were well-constructed, dominant structures, and until Dr. Barnes Wallis developed the 'bouncing bomb' were rated as unbreachable to conventional aerial bombing. From the famous 1955 film: 'The Dam Busters', readers know of an explosive charge detonating on the lower inner surface of a dam's wall, thus using the constrictions and power of the surrounding water to compress the shock wave and break the structure! It was assessed that the damage caused by breaching such dams would have a massive effect on Germany's industrial war effort and morale. The reservoirs were at their highest levels in mid-May; the moon was at its most suitable on the night of May 16/17th.

On 28th February 1943, Arthur Harris: Commander in Chief of Bomber Command, passed command of No5 Group (Lancasters) to Vice-Marshal the Hon. Ralph Cochrane, and asked him to form a new squadron. The Vice-Marshal appointed Wing Commander Guy Gibson D.S.O. and Bar, D.F.C. and Bar, with a hundred and seventy-four operational sorties, as squadron commander. It is believed that he, in turn, assisted in picking elite pilots for the new: 617 Squadron. Around the 25th March, the pilots teamed up with their crews at Woodall Spa and moved to R.A.F. Scampton, eight kilometres northwest of Lincoln. There came a period of extensive training, mostly long distance, low level night flights. In essence this necessitated the finest of crews for the practice of correct approach speeds, heights and distance for releasing bouncing bombs for targets in question. None of the crews knew of the intended mission. Meanwhile, Doctor Wallace continued to refine the structure of the bomb and its means of rotation. David's son, John Maltby:

*"Father piloted for Barnes Wallace on test flights over the Kent coast near to Reculver, and mother, a talented amateur artist, used to paint various logos on the side of the aeroplanes."*

Later, dummy towers were precisely positioned on Derwent Water to mimic those on the Mohne, so that the bomb aimer, by using a triangular device, could locate the towers against the device's two nails and so know the distance from the dam and when to drop the bomb.

On the morning of 15th May 1943, with favourable weather forecast, the decision was made to begin the operation: codenamed 'Chastise'. It involved a total of nineteen Lancasters from R.A.F. Scampton in three separate waves. The first wave of nine aircraft in formation, led by Guy Gibson, would attack the Mohne, and if breached any aircraft with unused bombs would target the Eder. A second wave of five aircraft, flying singly and taking off first, would use a more northerly route and attack the dam, whilst a third wave of five Lancasters would take off two hours later and act as a mobile reserve.

At 21.30pm on May 16th the second wave took to the air: shortly followed by Guy Gibson's formation; the latter including Lancaster ED906/G AJ-J for 'Johnnie': flown by Flight Lieutenant D.J. Maltby D.F.C. David's crew consisted of Sergeant W. Hatton (flight engineer), Sergeant V. Nicholson (navigator), Sergeant A. Stone (Wireless Operator), Pilot Officer J. Fort (bomb aimer), Sergeant V. Hill (front gunner) and sergeant H. Simmonds (rear gunner). Guy Gibson's wave headed for The Wash and then flew over Southwold. They crossed the sea at very low level to avoid the German radar on the Dutch coast. An aircraft was lost to flack over the Rhine at 00.15am. Once over the Mohne, Guy Gibson led the first attack, with a planned three minutes between each aircraft to allow the water to resettle near the dam. The gunners in the dam's twin towers opened up with a stream of fire. Each pilot, flying at 230 mph, had eleven seconds to position himself for the dam and less to drop the bomb. Gibson's bomb bounced three times and there followed a massive explosion: but the dam remained intact. The second aircraft was hit on its approach run and the bomb bounced over the dam: the aircraft crashing. The third aircraft was hit and its bomb hit side mudflats and well short of the dam: which remained intact. Aircraft number four released its bomb and it bounced perfectly to explode in position: but no breaching.

Guy Gibson called David Maltby to attack and as he approached he could see the dam's parapet under stress, his bomb bounced four times and when it exploded it was clear that the dam was breaking-up. A radio message was sent to Number 5 Group with the codename: 'Nigger' meaning that the Mohne had been breached. Guy Gibson ordered David Maltby and

*The breached Mohne Dam.*

another to return to base (flight time 5 hours 20 minutes), there job well done, whilst the remainder headed to the Eder. Guy Gibson directed the raid at the Eder, and when the final Lancaster (Pilot Officer L. Knight) dropped its bomb at 01.52 pm, the pilot saw a huge explosion and a hole punched in the side of the wall which rapidly saw the dam collapse. The Sorpe was attacked and damaged but remained unbreached. Operation *'Chastise'* was an undoubted success and considered as one of the finest displays of bravery and flying skill in the history of the R.A.F. The human cost to 617 Squadron was considerable: eight of the nineteen crews failed to return! Of the fifty-six aircrew posted as missing only three survived. Wing Commander Guy Gibson was awarded the Victoria Cross, with the remaining surviving pilots the Distinguished Service Order.

David Shannon, one of the surviving pilots, said that David Maltby made a perfect run to the Mohne, and that it was his bomb together with that of Squadron Leader H. Young's that did the damage by getting their bombs in the right place. David Maltby said:

*'Our load sent up water and mud to a height of a thousand feet. The spout of water was silhouetted against the moon. It rose with tremendous speed and then gently fell back.'*

Guy Gibson said that David Maltby came in fast and dropped his bomb within feet of the exact spot.

Harry Humphries, the Adjutant for 617 Squadron, remembered David Maltby landing at 03.11am and asked him how it went. David replied that it was absolutely marvellous; that he had never seen anything like it and that there was water everywhere: *'wonderful, wonderful!'* Harry also said that David asked if he had buried 'Nigger', Guy's dog that was killed just before the mission, as superstition plays a part. David always took his service hat with him on missions, even though it had become covered in oil and grease.

The B.B.C. announced the following: *'This is London. The Air Ministry has just announced the following communiqué. In the early hours of this morning, a force of Lancasters of Bomber Command led by Wing Commander G. P. Gibson DSO DFC attacked with mines the dams at the Mohne and reservoirs. These control over two thirds of the water storage capacity of the Ruhr basin. Reconnaissance later established that the Mohne dam had been breached over a length of one hundred yards, and the power station below had been swept away. The Eder dam, which controls the headwaters of the Weser and Fulde valleys and operates several power stations, was also attacked and reported as breached. Photographs show the river below the dam in full flood. The attacks were pressed home from a very low level with great determination and coolness in the face of fierce resistance. Eight of our Lancasters are missing.'*

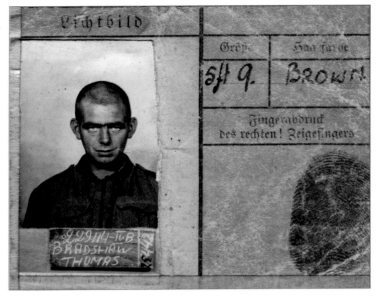

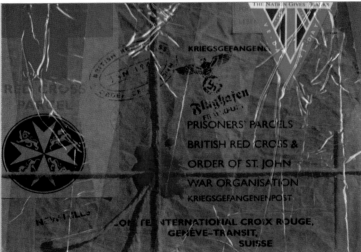

Top left: Tom Bradshaw's I.D. at Stalag IVB. Above right: Anne Bradshaw holds a Swastika flag that her husband retrieved from Germany.

Left: A Red Cross parcel as sent to P.O.W.s.

Left: Arthur Smith's identification tags and the bracelet he wore around his neck. Above: Arthur Smith's original wings that were worn during the Battle of Britain and his terrible crash.

The wreath that lay on Les Bishop's grave.

*Doug Bacus, second from left, with Normandy veteran pals. Circa 1990's.*

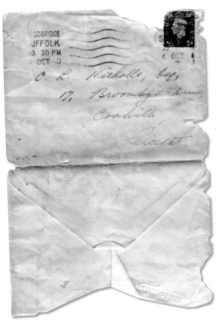

*Left: Bert Black's letter to his cousin Cyril Nicholls.*

*Below: Commemorative Book, tie and signatories in 1970, the Thirtieth Anniversary of the Battle of Britain.*

*Jack Pearce at Changi Cemetery in 1995. (40th Anniversary of P.O.W.s release)*

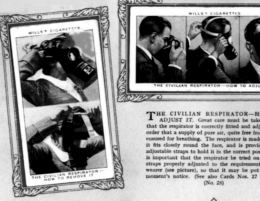

Les Bishop's ship: H.M.S. 'Repulse' taken from a fag card.

Fanny Lock in 2000 recalls the 1940 photograph of her husband and herself on Coalville Station. The image was used on a Leicester Mercury supplement.

A page from Denis Baker's 1940' Air Raid Precaution' fag card collection.

Below: Jim and Amy Hill in 1990.

From left: Roy Howe, Ron Gilliver and Len Taylor on 11th November 2006.

ALL PALS TOGETHER

Top left: Horace Bird's campaign medals: 1939-1945 Star, Africa Star, Italy Star, War Medal and Defence Medal.
Above right: A selection of postcards depicting scenes around Sorrento, Naples and Capri. Horace was very familiar with the area.
Left: Horace Bird made these recordings in a record booth in Florence.

The group to the right are the three medals of Warrant Officer Clement Culley: a proud Pathfinder with the R.A.F. Below is his Pathfinder's badge.

Joe Cavendish's Medical Board Grade Card: 12th June 1940.

EDWARD CAVENDISH 1915-1985

Edward, brother of Joe Cavendish.

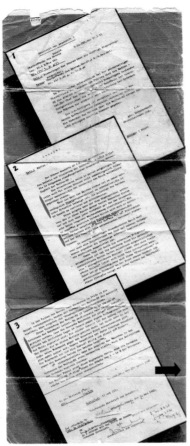

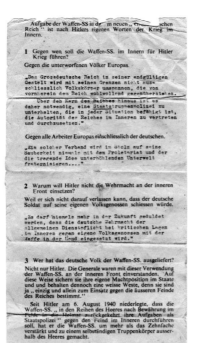

*Joan Allen's National Fire Service Badge.*

*This propaganda leaflet was given to Daisy Bird, Horace Bird's sister by Thelma, a girl from Coventry then evacuated to Coalville. The leaflet was dropped during a bombing raid.*

*Left: Harold Catlow in 2007 with his collection of memorabilia.*

*Bottom: A letter sent by Harold Catlow in September 1944 to his young cousins, John Rex and Angela Witham.*

*Above: A Christmas card sent to John Rex and Angela Witham.*

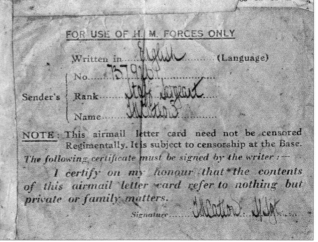

*Indeed, an amusing war*
— FOR-THE AMERICANS

By the way, old chap, did you ever think it over why the "inexhaustible reserves in man-power" of America have not turned up yet in this war? Possibly the statement contained in the news bulletin broadcast by the B.B.C. on 25.3.44 might give you an idea. It ran as follows:

"It is beyond doubt that the Germans have concentrated crack troops at Cassino for whom only the very best allied troops can be a match. For this reason the U.S.-units have been recently withdrawn from the main fighting line in order to be temporarily employed at quieter sectors."

This is not exactly a compliment to your American pals — but London ought to know how far they can rely upon them. It is a fact that until to-day 70% of all Americans who came across are still in England, where they are being "trained" — as is officially stated.

How this training looks like, Corporal Richard C. Rogers of L Coy. 3rd Bn. 350th Inf. Regt. 88th U.S. Inf. Div. is able to tell you. He had just arrived from England and was unlucky enough to be taken prisoner West of Minturno on the 16.3.44. In his wallet he had a slip of paper with the following anecdote:

Two English women met on the street in London one day. Said one, "Do you know Americans?" "Do I know Americans, says you," replied the other.

"Why just the other day the old man sent me over to the Pub for a bucket of beer, and when I was coming out who should I meet but a blooming American.

"Before I could say Trafalgar Square, he grabs me by the Ass, shoves me under a tree, ups me, outs me, wipes his tallywhacker on me petticoat, drinks me old man's beer pisses in the bucket, and walks off whistling, 'God save the King', and you ask me, do I know Americans?"

He was proud about this joke, old Corporal Richard C. Rogers, and boasted he knew many more similar ones with which he could prove that the Americans were "quick workers".

Definitely, it is a story that makes one laugh; it might be a little exaggerated, but surely, there is something true in it. But, on the other hand, would you still laugh if you considered that your sister, your girl or your wife at home might be the aim of the exploits by these "quick workers"?

Obviously, the "blooming Americans" are much braver in England than at the front where you, poor devil, have got to fight German crack troops along.

No wonder they are looking upon the war as something quite amusing.

*This propaganda leaflet was carried by Horace Bird in his wallet for the remainder of his life.*

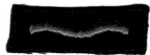

*James Hatfield's Goldfish Club cloth badges.*

WOMEN'S · ROYAL · NAVAL · SERVICE

join the Wrens

AND · FREE · A · MAN · FOR · THE · FLEET

APPLY TO DIRECTOR W.R.N.S. ADMIRALTY S.W.1.

It might be YOU!

CARING FOR EVACUEES IS A NATIONAL SERVICE

*Colourful period poster art.*

MAKE-DO AND MEND

says Mrs Sew-and-Sew

*Membership Card*

This is to Certify that
Sgt. J. Hatfield
has qualified as a member of the Goldfish Club by escaping death by the use of his Emergency Dinghy on September 19th, 1942.

Signed
CHARLES A. ROBERTSON
Hon. Secretary

*James Hatfield's Goldfish Membership Card.*

THE GOLDFISH CLUB
GOLD FOR THE VALUE OF LIFE · FISH FOR THE SEA

CHARLES A. ROBERTSON, HON. SECRETARY
BEEHIVE WORKS, HONEYPOT LANE
STANMORE · MIDDLESEX

TELEPHONE: WORDSWORTH 4521 - 4530
TELEGRAMS: 'BECOW' PHONE, LONDON

CAR/MJ

17th May, 1943

1196249 Sgt. J. Hatfield,
Sgts. Mess,
R.A.F. Station,
Moreton-in-Marsh,
Glos.

Dear Sgt. Hatfield,

Many thanks for your application received by me a few days ago. As a result of the brief details contained therein, I am pleased to advise you that you have been elected a life member of the above Club.

Please accept my congratulations on getting away with a ditching in the Bay of Biscay. This was certainly a good show considering the whole crew got away unhurt. Although I have fortunately never experienced the sight of a dinghy circumstanced as you were, I can well imagine your feelings.

I enclose your Club Badge which will be followed by your official illustrated membership card as soon as I have it back from the processors.

With my best wishes and good luck on all future ops.

Yours sincerely,

C.A. Robertson.
Hon. Secretary

This Club has been made possible by the courtesy of P. B. Cow (Queensbury) Ltd. in appreciation of many gallant airmen.

*Letter from the Goldfish Club to James Hatfield.*

BRITISH GOVERNMENT

To all Arab Peoples - Greetings and Peace be upon you. The bearer of this letter is an Officer of the British Government and a friend of all Arabs. Treat him well, guard him from harm, give him food and drink, help him to return to the nearest British soldiers and you will be liberally rewarded. Peace and the Mercy of God upon you.

*The British High Command in the East*

*James Hatfield's' Goolly Chit'. They were issued to Allied aircrew who travelled over the Middle East following reports of unfriendly Arabian tribes emasculating crew members.*

The surviving Dambuster pilots: From rear left: W. Townsend, J. McCarthy, H. Wilson, Guy Gibson, J. Munroe, David Maltby and K. Brown. Front left: C. Anderson, G. Rice, H. Martin, D. Shannon and L. Knight.

After the investiture: David Maltby, Guy Gibson, E. Johnson and H. Martin.

The newspapers led with the story and, this, following success in North Africa improved home morale enormously. David was promoted to Squadron Leader and given command of 'A' Flight, and when Guy Gibson was on leave in early June he took temporary command of 617 Squadron. After the dams raid they returned to Coningsby but continued with special operations, but soon without Guy Gibson, who accompanied Winston Churchill to Canada.

At 10.45pm on 1st July 1943, John Goodson Maltby was born at Woodhall Spa, much to the joy of his parents and family.

On the night of 15th-16th July 1943, the Squadron attacked the power stations of Aquata Scrivia and San Polo d'Enza in northern Italy. Squadron Leader G.W. Holden led six crews and Squadron Leader D. Maltby a further six. The latter headed for San Polo D'Enza near Bologna, but neither target could be pursued due to a thick mist covering the area. The Lancasters continued their flight and landed at Blida near Algiers to refill and refuel, the refilling was by the crew who enjoyed exotic fruits, good food and wine.

The Dortmund-Ems Canal was a vital and heavily used traffic route between the Ruhr and the northern ports. Bomber Command, without success, had tried to breach the canal banks and the flak was notoriously bad. On the night of 14th/15th September, eight Lancaster bombers captained by G. Holden and including David Maltby took off, but over the North Sea they ran into bad weather and the radio informed them that the area had become blanketed by low cloud. The mission was aborted, however, during the return manoeuvre David's aircraft may have flown into the slipstream of another; his wingtip struck the sea and the giant bomber crashed. Only David's body was recovered.

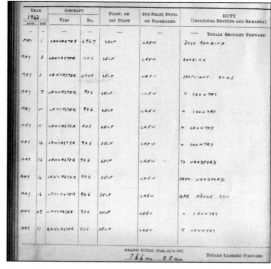

David's Logbook: note 'spotlight runs' on 28th April 1943 and Guy Gibson's signature.

David's Logbook: note 'spotlight runs' and 16th May 1943' OPS' Mohne' Dam.

S/Ldr. D. J. H. Maltby, D.S.O., D.F.C.

Cuthbert Orde's sketch of David Maltby: a Dambuster.

David Maltby's grave, Wickhambreaux, Kent.

John Maltby:

"On the Fortieth Anniversary of the raid I was invited to a gathering at a London Hotel. I was approached by one of the pilots, David Shannon, and he said he could tell I was David Maltby's son: that I looked just like him. He then said that my father was too good a pilot to have made such a mistake, and that there was more too it!"

Research suggests that a Mosquito bomber of 139 Squadron may well have collided with David's aircraft in the inky and cloudy darkness. The next night the Squadron pressed on to the canal but had little success: losing five out of eight aircraft. The two nights cost forty-eight lives including twenty of the dam buster survivors. Leonard Cheshire then took over the Squadron.

Squadron Leader David John Maltby's D.S.O. D.F.C. grave is in the graveyard of St. Andrew's Church at Wickhambreaux in Kent, indeed the very church where he and Nina got married. For many years now on the anniversary of his death, members of East Kent branch of the R.A.F. Association lay a wreath to his memory.

On returning to this country, Guy Gibson obtained permission for a few more operations, on his fourth whilst flying a de Havilland Mosquito on a raid over Bavaria his plane crashed in Holland and he and the navigator were killed.

My thanks to John Maltby, who has lived in the area for thirty-five years, for loaning me his father's photographs and the above information. John holds a pilot's licence and has flown for many years.

Also, recommended reading: 'Breaking The Dams' by Charles Foster.

**Jessie came from Coventry where her father was a florist; she married George F. Reeves who owned a butcher's shop on Maplewell Road at Woodhouse Eaves and remained in the village for the remainder of her long life. With thanks to John Maltby and Gordon Ambler MBE. *(See Jessie Adams on page 139)*

# LESLIE ARTHUR MERCHANT

Arthur and Rosa Merchant owned a grocery shop at Swadlincote in Derbyshire: close to the Staffordshire border. The largish village was, until recently, situated in the heart of a coal-mining community, fifteen kilometres northwest of Coalville and six kilometres southeast of Burton-on-Trent. The Merchants, by name and profession, lived at Grendon House at Swadlincote, and that is where 'Les' was second born on 20th July 1909; having a sister, Muriel, three years his senior, who later attended Burton-on-Trent Grammar School.

Following the Great War, the 1920's were fated to become a decade of economic depression, and matters came to a head in 1926 when the Trades Union Congress called a General Strike. The strike was in support of the colliers, a fraternity of very hard-working men who suffered the most appalling and dangerous of working conditions for paltry wages. There followed a worldwide economic plunge: the Great Depression of 1929-34, and financial circumstances for all but the wealthiest were very difficult!

It is apparent that Arthur and his wife were fine people: kindly and generous, and during those hard times allowed many customers the opportunity to have groceries on the slate. They struggled along and encouraged Les to join the business; being appointed the manager of his parent's second shop at nearby Midway, but he did not enjoy life in this section of the retail trade. His consuming love belonged to the mechanics of road and flight transport.

When Arthur died in his forties, around 1932, the shops finances had to be addressed, and sadly customer accounts were badly in arrears; many customers owed a lot of money and were unable to repay. Rosa therefore divided Grendon House into two properties and rented them out for income.

Meanwhile, Les had married Evelyn May Yeomans: born 14th October 1906 on Coronation Street, Overseal, a few kilometres south of Swadlincote and educated at Ashby-de-la-Zouch Grammar School. Les and Evelyn thought it best to leave the area and purchased 8, Scotlands Drive, Coalville, they had two children: Jean Alison, born 19th October 1930 and Ruth, born 19th January 1942.

Les took a job in engineering and as finances improved continued a very active interest in vehicles,

Les in his car, circa 1930's.

Evelyn in the 1930's.

Les, in the light suit, outside the Railway Hotel, Coalville. 1938.

and eventually achieved his dream: the position of sales manager at Forest Road Garage, once located on the corner of Forest Road and London Road, Coalville.

Les' love for flying developed in the mid-1930's, joining a private flying club and often flew from Rearsby airfield; it is uncertain whether he possessed a private licence.

*Les and Evelyn at Skegness in the late 1930's.*

A 1938 photograph shows him standing with a leading group of Coalville businessmen outside of the Railway Hotel; he was well known and highly respected, the future looked very rosy.

At the outbreak of war he volunteered for the Royal Air Force, only to be rejected until such time that his high-blood pressure was controlled. Several months later he applied again and was accepted for aircrew. He asked to be a pilot, but this was denied on age grounds, thirty/ thirty-one, and possibly health wise. Training took place at various locations including Sutton Bridge, near 'The Wash' and postings were to the Isle of Man and ultimately to St. Eval: just inland from the coast of north Cornwall. This posting was to 407 'DEMON' Squadron: Royal Canadian Air Force (R.C.A.F.). They used Lockheed Hudson twin-engined

passenger aircraft converted for bombing and including a gun turret. Flight Sergeant L. A. Merchant was wireless operator/air gunner with R.A.F. Coastal Command.

*Flight Sergeant Les Merchant. Circa: late 1941.*

To enable the aerodrome to be built, the hamlet of St. Eval had to be demolished, apart from the church, and the St. Eval Station was officially opened on 2nd October 1939. DEMON Squadron was formed on 22nd May 1941, and it quickly built up an awesome reputation, with newspaper articles regularly relaying the amount of enemy ships they were sinking. One account describes how a bomber from Demon (in bold print) Squadron attacked a ship at very low level, with Pilot Officer C. W. Taylor and Sergeant J. D. Banting stating that the mast of the ship tore off their trailing aerial! Proof of its success was borne out in January 1941 when the Luftwaffe raided St. Eval and killed twenty-one service men and women.

Les's daughter, Jean, recalls:

*"Father told me that the last object they saw when*

*A converted Hudson of 407 R.C.A.F.*

The photographs are striking, one shows Les with members of the same crew, another with him having written, missing in action, while two show badly damaged aircraft that had limped home to base. There's also a series of cuttings reporting accounts of the squadron's success in sinking enemy shipping in the Channel and the Bay of Biscay; on how Hudson bombers dive low to bomb the enemy vessels in spite of their Ack-Ack. Various pilots of the squadron receive impressive decorations like a D.S.O. to Wing Commander H. M. Styles and Flight Lieutenant Robert Christie, with a D.F.C. to Pilot Officers Frank Paige and Frank Kay.

*taking-off was the church spire, and the first object they saw on returning from a flight was the same. I think it must have been comforting for the aircrew. While father served at the aerodrome he used to send photographs and paper cutting home for me to paste into a scrapbook.*"

"*Father sent me a cutting on which a poem was written by a leading aircraftsman of 407 Squadron.*

### *Ode to a WOP/Air gunner.*

*If I must be a gunner*
*Then please Lord grant me grace,*
*That I may leave this station*
*With a smile upon my face.*

*I may have wished to be a pilot*
*And you along with me,*
*But if we were all pilots*
*Where would the Air Force be?*

*It takes guts to be a gunner*
*And sit out in the tail*
*When the Messerschmitts are coming,*
*And the slugs begin to wail.*

*The pilots just a chauffeur,*
*It's his job to fly the plane,*
*But it's we who do the fighting*
*Though we may not get the fame.*

*But we're here to win a war,*
*And until this job is done*
*Let's forget our personal feelings*
*And get behind a gun.*

*If we must be air gunners*
*Then let us make this bet,*
*We'll be the damn best gunners*
*That's left this station yet!*

During the squadron's first year of existence (Les was probably a founder member), it chalked up an unsurpassed operational record and added to the laurels of the R. C. A. F.

A gala party was held on its first anniversary (Friday May 22nd 1942) with Air Commodore Curtis and other senior officers attending a very successful evening.

The squadron proved to be the bane of enemy shipping, and was generally conceded to be the most consistently successful squadron of Coastal Command. A special photomontage impression by 'Daily Sketch' artist, George Mottram, shows a Lockheed Hudson climbing away after scoring a direct hit on a supply ship. Another bomber releases a torpedo while an enemy fighter crashes into the sea.

*Left: Tom Grains, Les Merchant, Alan Kiel and Moses Zumar.*

Les, wireless operator/rear gunner, was one of the crew that mostly flew in Hudson 'PRF', indeed, one photograph shows this aircraft with a badly damaged (by flak) tail. The pilot was Moe Zumar, a twenty-five year old Canadian from Ottawa. One of Moe's brothers, Harry, was stationed at St. Eval, being with an Air-Sea Rescue squadron, while another, Reuben (wireless operator), served with an R.A.F. torpedo-bomber squadron, also in Cornwall and not far from St. Eval. With Les was Flight Sergeant Tom Grain, a Leicester man who became engaged in October 1942. The other member was Canadian, Alan Kiel.

It was always difficult to obtain leave, however, Les Merchant and Tom Grain were lucky and with a twenty-four hour pass decided to travel home in Les' Morris 8. Since the threat of invasion, the journey of

over nine hundred kilometres (600 miles return), had no signposts and involved mainly winding country lanes. Les dropped Tom off at Leicester and then drove to Coalville. Next day they completed the return journey, and soon after arriving at base had to change into flying gear for an emergency mission. They must have been tired, but such were the unforeseen circumstances of war! Les and the crew composed themselves as Moe Zumar accelerated along the runway and took to the skies, glancing at the church spire, and as normal said a few prayers.

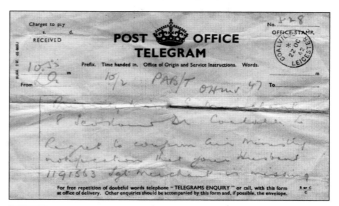

Jean passed the eleven-plus, and in August 1942, began studies at Coalville's King Edward V11 Grammar School. One dinnertime, she strolled the five-minutes to her home. Jean:

*"On 22nd October 1942, I came home from school for lunch to find mother weeping while making the open fire. That morning a telegram had arrived informing us that father was missing whilst on active service and offered the deepest sympathy! There was no counselling in those days; I ate my meal, kissed my sobbing mother and returned to school. Later we heard that they had taken off and set course for the Bay of Biscay to bomb enemy shipping.*

*No one ever knew what happened, nothing was ever found; the pilot's brother, Harry Zumar, was with*

*R.A.F. Sea-Rescue and he flew out to see whether he could find any wreckage. There was nothing! Life was difficult for Mother, Ruth and myself; we only received a small widow's pension, and that was smaller than it should have been because father was awaiting a commission when he died."*

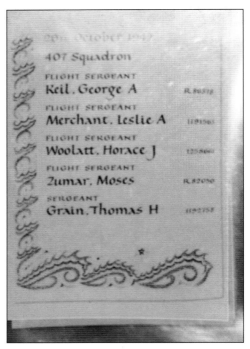

*The Telegram was delivered to the house on the left: 8, Scotlands Drive, Coalville.*

*The name of Les Merchant and his crew at St. Eval.*

The two-page telegram reads:

*'Priority Mrs. E. Merchant. 8 Scotland Drive. Coalville. Regret to confirm Air Ministry notification that your husband is missing on operation on afternoon of October 20th-stop. Letter following giving particulars known- stop. My deepest sympathy. Officer Commanding 407 squadron RCAF.'* Jean:

*"Mother could drive, it was quite a rare occurrence in those days, and for the rest of the war she used to drive around Coalville and district collecting insurance monies for Britannic."*

One of Jean's acquaintances at the grammar school was Victor Kendrick, who later joined the R.A.F., achieving the senior level of Group Captain.

In 1949, after three years of sixth form, Jean studied at Nottingham University, graduating in physics with a BSc (Hon). While there she met her future husband, Kenneth Brittan, ex: head boy of Gateway School at Leicester: he qualified in the same subject as Jean. They married on 9th June 1953 having the one daughter, Yvonne. They moved to Cambridge, with Yvonne attending the High School and Jean teaching physics to 14-16 year olds.

In the 1960s they returned to Coalville and Yvonne continued her education at Coalville Grammar School, the same school name as her mother, but it had been resituated on Warren Hills, on the edge of Charnwood Forest and overlooking Coalville. My future wife, Beryl Hare, was in the same year.

Yvonne passed her GCE 'A' levels at seventeen years (normally eighteen) and studied Economics at Loughborough University under Professor Swan (a friend and neighbour of the author). She later took a degree in tourism at Guildford University, studied at Amsterdam, and whilst at Oxford University researched socio/legal studies. Yvonne lives at Oxford and runs her own company: 'The Other Oxford Company'.

Evelyn, moved closer to her daughter, first to Snibston Grange, and then 11, Broomleys' Road and finally to a bungalow at 62, Blackwood. In 1975, Jean's grandmother, Rosa Merchant passed away in a Leicester hospital at the premature age of sixty-nine years, never having fully recovered from the loss of her husband.

Yvonne married Yiannis Vlachonikolis, a Greek national and future professor, who died in 2004 and George is their son. A dynamic young man, he studied for a BA and MA at Sheffield University before joining the Army, and recently left Sandhurst Military Academy. George was in '*Alamein*' Company, the same as Princes Harry and William, and so the Queen was present at the Passing-Out Parade.

Jean's younger sister, Ruth, married Richard Randle, once of Randle's Shop in Coalville Precinct, and they have three children: Sally, born 20th August

*George Vlachonikolis, Sally and Yvonne Brittan at Sandhurst.*

*Yvonne and George at Sandhurst.*

1962, Lucy, born 21st July 1965 and Timothy, born 6th October 1973. Ruth lives at Whitwick. Sally lives at Donisthorpe and is married to Colin Davis, a racing motorcycle engineer. Lucy married Leicester City F.C. and Burnley footballer Neil Grewcock, a fine left wing footballer. They have two children: Evie, 11 years and Charlie 8 years. Timothy lives with his partner at Whitwick and is a driver.

Jean's husband, Ken is a professor and spent most of his working life in industry, once a director of the Rank Organisation. He enjoys his retirement working with classic cars.

My thanks to Jean Britton for the information and photographs.

# DENNIS & DOREEN NUTTALL

Dennis and Doreen have been friends and neighbours for over two decades. On several occasions I have listened, with enormous interest, to their memoirs of life as a young boy and infant girl in wartime England. After many requests they finally agreed to document their early years for present and future generations.

## Dennis

*"My father, Alfred Nuttall, was born at Garstang, about twelve miles northeast of Blackpool. He'd been a career soldier, and my mother's name was, Florence (nee Poessinouw), of Dutch stock. I was born on 24th January 1935 and when war was declared I was living with my parents and younger sister, Beryl, at Highgate in North London. Father, still a reservist, was called-up almost immediately into the Signals, and left with the British Expeditionary Force for France. Nothing much happened for about six months, it was called the 'Phoney War', but in quick succession came the German Blitzkrieg of Holland, Belgium and France: father managed to get away two days before the Dunkirk evacuation proper of late May 1940.* (The Dunkirk evacuation took place from 26th May to 4th June 1940). *He told us that he spent three days walking, sometimes through enemy lines, to get to the French coast."*

Next: the 'Battle of Britain', the September day bombings of London and the Night Blitz.

*"We heard of the Few, the Hurricane and Spitfire pilots that fought over Kent and Sussex. Then, from early September, in daylight raids, we saw the white contrails of aeroplanes as they battled in the sky. I remember the sirens wailing and bombs whistling their way to earth and exploding; of mother with my two-year-old sister being pushed out of the way by people running to air raid shelters in a blind panic. Despite what people say it wasn't always orderly. Mother, my sister and I were evacuated to Leighton Buzzard in Bedfordshire. We had to find lodgings and ended up in a rickety old summerhouse at the bottom of someone's garden, and all I can remember is the bombing, on or near, the Vauxhall Bedford factory at Luton. My mother couldn't endure this and so we returned to London at the height of the Blitz. As the weeks passed the bombing was mainly at night, and it remained until 1941.*

*It was on a bright late September morning when mother told us that father was coming home on leave. On his first night at home he decided we would spend the night in an air raid shelter about a quarter of a mile away. The shelter, it smelt awful, was made of double or triple coarse brick-concrete and had a domed roof with a blast screen; only by a direct hit could it be destroyed. The shelter stood at the junction of three roads and we slept on the floor. In the night there was an enemy raid and bombs started falling all around us, it was very alarming. Suddenly the shelter seemed to go up into the air, or at least that is how it felt to me. The sirens sounded the 'all clear' and father went outside to have a look around: we went back to sleep. When daylight came I couldn't believe my eyes, we were in the middle of a bombsite. All around people were lifting bricks and peering into holes to try and find survivors; were we pleased to get home because in the shelter we had no lighting, water, nor toilets. It was just a refuge, Thank God!*

Dennis, father Alfred and sister Beryl.

*Father was stationed at Catterick Camp on the North Yorkshire Moors, and because of the raid, which he thought was as bad as the old Western Front, he would evacuate us. He finally got us to York, a beautiful city, and we spent three years there, in the attic of a tiny house in Bishop Hill Senior (see photograph). Our mother, sister Beryl, newly born sister, Anne, father (when he came on leave) and I lived in that small room. We had no internal heating and only an outside toilet. The owner of the tiny house used to sell newspapers just inside the door and they occupied the ground and middle floor and slept in the attic as well.*

The arrow points to a tiny house wedged between taller and larger buildings in Bishop Hill Senior, York. Dennis and his sister occupied one room in the loft from 1940-1943. There was no internal heat and only an outside toilet.

The same house in 2005.

Mother worked days in an ammunition factory just opposite to where we lived, and the River Ouse ran behind our house. I recall taking my socks off to place my feet in the river, and then spotting that my socks were floating away with the current. Mother was furious because I only had two pairs: one in the wash and one for wear.

We only saw one air raid there between 1940-43; a 'Baedeker' raid in 1942 and they made a mess of inner York.

But in 1943 relatives persuaded us to return to London, it appeared as though the war was virtually over. So we 'upped sticks' and together with baby sister, Anne, boarded a train to London: we had one suitcase between us. London had been badly knocked-about, particularly the city and the docklands, but everyone seemed buoyed-up because we were winning on most campaigns and when 'D'-Day arrived in early June we thought 'its all over!' Then - BANG the Doodlebugs arrived. By this time I was nine and Beryl seven, old enough to be evacuees on our own. Before we bussed to Paddington Station we had to assemble at our school, where we were checked to make sure we had our gas masks and a small case each. We waved goodbye on the platform but had no idea where we were travelling. Eventually we arrived in south Wales, feeling dirty and tired, and it was getting late. Taken to a school hall I noticed that people spoke differently from us. Our evacuation was to Llanelli, to be precise. We were given a drink and told to make ourselves comfortable on the floor and go to sleep. The floor was dirty and I can still recall the horrid smell. Next morning we had to line-up in rows, and these people with strange accents walked up and down tapping the heads of some of us while a teacher wrote down the parent's names on a clipboard. Slowly but surely the hall began to empty and soon there was only me and twelve other boys remaining. Beryl had gone without saying goodbye, and then a Mr. Lloyd, his face covered in coal dust, said he'd take me. He took me in his coal truck to a house in Sandy Road, and on arrival his wife and son, John, greeted me. After a few days of rest I was sent to a village school where there was one teacher in the room and the desks were in lines. After the trauma of the previous days I was told we were going to chapel. We duly departed to this rather bleak looking brown building, and as we approached I was so pleased to see, Beryl. She was with a Mr. Thomas, a skinny man, and his wife: a red haired, large bluff woman and their teenage daughter. On approach I smiled and called to my sister; Mr.& Mrs. Thomas sharply said: "Don't you dare come any closer!" Despite this I regularly saw my sister as she lived just opposite on Sandy Road, however, when Mrs. Thomas saw me she used to chase me away with a broom. I have no idea why, and can you imagine this happening today?

Through the war we had no toilet paper, we cut newspaper into squares, but had to be careful of colour magazines as they were pinned together. Ah! The pain! Four months passed and with the Doodlebug menace fading we returned to London—-

only for the V2 to rear its head.

By now father had been discharged from the Army, and when he had heard that we were not being fed enough he accompanied us to South Wales. It seems our former hosts were being paid four shillings and sixpence (twenty-three new pence a week) to take care of us, and yet I can recall that one meal was a plate of runner beans and gravy! Generally, Londoners were not welcomed; I got into fights with lads, had a few battle scars but never lost and also argued with Mrs. Thomas. The locals said our accent was odd, and many thought that all Londoners were flea-ridden paupers capable of no good. During my stay I picked-up a Welsh accent and so when I returned home I was picked on yet again!

When I sit and reflect I realise that World War 2 was a turbulent moment in history: a benchmark for future generations and mine. For example, I met a Czech boy who had an Auschwitz number tattooed on his arm and a bullet wound from his hip to his kneecap; that takes some appreciating even by today's standards. I witnessed Spitfires and Me109s in dogfight combats and saw crashed aeroplanes of every possible sort. Our playgrounds were bombed-out buildings and water-tanks; all very dangerous but so exciting, and with wooden wreckage we built scooters and trolley-carts. I have seen Doodlebugs at rooftop height; also a V2 ballistic rocket in flight and not many people have seen that, but it is true.

During the war and immediately after there was an aspect of life that we, as children, knew nothing about. Only recently have stories of the 'Black Market' come to the surface; it seems that many, if not most people, were involved to a lesser or greater degree. If caught the punishment was extremely severe!

An ex-employee of mine, an insurance agent in Camden Town, North London, was paid by one of his clients (an employee of a large North London bakery) by way of pilfered goods, namely the firm's tea towels. He put them in the saddlebag of his pushbike with the intention of selling them to another client. The police stopped him and when he was found guilty of 'black-marketing' he was sentenced to two years of penal servitude. Because he was literate he was given a job in the prison library: there was no remission!

My children say to me that it must have been awful; it was but we were all in it together! No one was better off than his or her neighbour. But they then say that I must have been unhappy; I reply that I was, especially when the sweets went on ration!"

## Doreen

"I was born on 13th June 1937 into a large Italian/Irish family, and lived in North London, about a quarter of a mile from the main London to Scotland railway-line. My father's name was Guiseppe Burzio and my mother's name was Annie (nee Farrell).

Doreen's father, Guiseppe Burzio. 1930's.

I was one of the 'lucky' ones meaning that I was not evacuated, mainly because schools arranged the evacuations, and when the war started I was only two years old. By the time I reached school age the general attitude was that the war would soon be over (I'd say it was wishful thinking), and so I remained in London and started school in the normal way.

Our school was an old Victorian building with large, bare classrooms and a coal-stove on one side of the room. The teacher had to rotate the rows of children every week to allow each child the opportunity to sit in the warmth: no central heating for us! The toilets were outside and quite a walk from the classrooms: they were freezing and the roof leaked. I must add that my classroom was full, so I conclude that since evacuation was not compulsory many parents decided against sending their children away. Possibly some had returned from evacuation for reasons such as Dennis outlined, as well as home sickness, bullying or general unhappiness.

I recall bombs dropping all around us; the enemy bombers must have been after the railway line. A flight of three bombs narrowly missed our house; the first bomb exploded near to our underground station. Very little damage was done to the station, which was a relief, because many people took refuge in the Tube stations at night. Yes, people actually took their bedding, blankets, warm drinks, etc, and slept on the concrete platforms. The second bomb hit a public outdoor swimming pool and the third fell on waste ground near to the railway line.

Many is the time I recall walking the mile to or from school and hearing the sirens wail their warning call: meaning a raid was imminent. I literally had to run for my life to a shelter, and the best sound you wanted to hear was the 'all clear', only then could you relax. I mentioned I wasn't evacuated but my two brothers: Dino and Frank, and two sisters: Lina and Kathleen were. They went to a small town called Kelveden in Essex, half way between Colchester and Chelmsford. I also had three brothers in the Army, my eldest, Joe, served in Holland, Jim served in Italy and later John went to India.

I heard some harrowing tales about evacuation from my brothers and sisters. Siblings were not always kept together; my brothers were often bullied and became homesick while my sisters faired a little better. Their host mother, Mrs. Abbott, kept a spotless home and she was kind but could also be very strict. Mother took me to visit them, but travelling costs and perilous wartime conditions meant it was kept to a bare minimum. When I did see them they took me to their school, an improvised village hall, were they were taught by their teachers who had come with them. They found having familiar faces around very comforting, but before long they returned to London. My sister, Lina, said that they were then placed in local schools. My two sisters were away for five years, apart from one or two visits during school holidays. This was a

Doreen and siblings at Kelveden 1940/1.

Back row left: Host mother, Mrs. Abbott, Annie Burzio (mother) and Kathleen (sister). Middle row: Maria Burzio (sister). Front row: Doreen and Lina Burzio (sisters). Kelveden, Essex. Circa 1940/41.

long time to be separated from parents and siblings.

Lina, who was two-and-half years older than me, mentioned there was an American air base close to Kelveden, and that they gave parties for local children and evacuees. I remember attending once during a

Lina and Doreen, 1944.

visit, and we recall our astonishment at being served, what we thought, was a dish each of raw eggs.

We were horrified, and then relieved when told that they were tinned peaches, something we'd never seen before. Lina also recalls that when the war was over school children were given a small bar of chocolate: what a treat!

Evacuees from deprived city areas found it difficult to fit-in to new surroundings and on arrival were subjected to bullying and ridicule because: 'they talked funny!' To compound the problem, when, after several years, they returned to their natural homes they were again tormented because: 'they talked funny!' "Just when we thought the bombing had finished then along came the V1 Doodlebugs; they were pilot-less aeroplanes that looked like a rocket and had a motorbike sound to its engine. It was packed with explosives and when it ran out of fuel it crashed with a deafening roar. One night, from my bedroom window, I saw a red light in the sky and heard the 'whur-whur' of an engine; it went quiet and I shot under my bed and prayed. It crashed some distance away. We were fortunate to have an Anderson Air Raid Shelter built in our garden. The government offered and installed them, either an outside one or one constructed indoors, usually beneath the staircase. Ours was at the bottom of the garden. First, a large trench-like hole was dug to about four by three metres; secondly, liquid concrete was poured in as a base, with extra forming side supports to waist level and finally a corrugated domed roof was fitted. The roof was covered by turf or soil and to enter you had to use a small stepladder: the bunk beds were on either side. Adults, what with no lighting, heating, and rather cold and damp during winters, didn't like them, but for children it was an exciting time.

We had lots of fun singing songs, drinking mugs of hot cocoa and keeping warm with our hot water bottles. When the raids tailed-off people returned to their homes and took delight in their warm beds.

We were more fortunate than most, as we had a large garden and father kept chickens; he replaced the flowerbeds with vegetable plots, and we also had fruit bushes and two mature apple trees. Father also had two allotments and he grew anything from cabbages to cucumbers and rhubarb to radishes. I recall helping him with 'Digging for Victory'. A lot of trading took place with friends and neighbours: swapping two fresh eggs or a bag of fruit for a few clothing or sweet coupons. We were a bit worried about the factory just behind the allotments because it was building wooden frames for our Mosquito fighter/bomber and an obvious target if the enemy knew of its existence.

When it was Victory in Europe Day (V. E. Day), we were given the day off from school.

There were flags flying from houses and bunting along the streets; mother had a flag and photographs on the front door saying: 'WELCOME HOME' to my brothers in the Army. One-day crates of oranges were delivered to the schools, and we were asked to line-up so that our teacher could give us one orange each to take home. Also, word got around that bananas were for sale in the shops; after buying one I took it home and slowly ate that 'exotic' fruit.

Somehow we survived the bombs, rationing (which went on long after the war finished), powdered egg and Spam, long queues outside shops, bus and train queues, the blackout (which meant no lights of any sort on streets, pushbikes and certainly not from houses), and a general shortage of most items that nowadays we all take for granted. It was an unusual childhood for a young girl, but I learned a lot from my experiences in wartime Britain and treasure a good deal of them. Of course you always remember the good things, and not so many of the bad. Finally, after all we had experienced during the war it was a very sad day in January 1946 when my father suddenly died from a massive heart attack: he was only in his early sixties.

My thanks to Dennis and Doreen. It is important, especially for children and youngsters of today, to realise that earlier generations had a lot to contend with, and to their credit they emerged all the stronger for it.

# FRANK PARKER

Alfred Parker, a collier, was married to Jane (nee Spencer) and they lived on North Street (now Central Road), Hugglescote. On 5th March 1896 came the birth of Frank (senior), father to the above man. He attended St. John the Baptist Church and School and therefore knew most, if not all, of the Famous Fifty. In the autumn of 1914, he enlisted at Coalville into the Eighth (Service) Battalion of the Leicestershire Regiment. There followed a similar training agenda, location, and war campaign to that of the Sixth, Seventh and Ninth Battalions: 110 Brigade, which has been documented in 'Greater Love'. On the 19th July 1915, nineteen years old Frank married Sarah Eagle, aged twenty, a laundry worker of 85, North Street (Central Road), Hugglescote. Her father, Joseph Eagle, was employed as a shoe-hand. On the Wedding Certificate, Frank's rank is described as: '*Private, 8th Battalion, Leicestershire Regiment, Perham Down Camp, North Tidworth in Hampshire*'. Local men who served with him include James Bancroft of Thringstone, Robert Berrington, Bill Cooke, Arthur Johnstone and John Price of Whitwick; Len Brown, James Crooks and Fred Parker of Coalville.

*Sarah Parker (nee Eagle).*

*Private Frank Parker Senior, 1915.*

A photographs shows Frank just after enlistment in his 'Kitchener Blue' outfit, another as a sergeant later in the war, and a third sent by his wife to Sergeant Frank Parker, 7 Company, 24 Camp, N.C.D. Ripon, Yorkshire, possibly in 1919. The card reads: '*To my Dear Husband with Love XX*'. Another interesting feature is his sergeant's whistle: used to alert the men under his command and which 'saw' plenty of ferocious fighting!

Frank Parker, the subject of this essay, was born on 23rd March 1921, at 12, North Street, (now 197, Central Road), Hugglescote. He had two sisters, Ivy: born 24th August 1918, who is still fit and well, and Doris, who passed away aged four years from appendicitis. He was educated at his father's old school: St. John The Baptist Church School, and on leaving in 1932 also went to work for a shoe manufacturer, at Leicester, but returned to Coalville to train as a florist at 'Holdreds' on Belvoir Road. Later he was employed by the Co-Operative Slaughterhouse, and remained there until his call-up.

*Middle row, second from left: Sergeant Frank Parker and friends, circa 1917.*

*Frank Parker's World War One whistle.*

On 9th May 1942, he married Dorothy Hodgetts of 205 Ashby Road, Coalville, and she stayed with Frank's parents until he returned post-war. The couple met on a 'monkey walk' (some know it as 'monkey parade'); a former local tradition whereby teenagers strolled appointed pathways and roads knowing they would meet members of the opposite sex and thus form friendships, viz: a courting procedure!

Frank signed-up on 1st October 1942 into the Royal Artillery, and Gunner Parker, service number 14303605, trained as a driver/mechanic. His main responsibility (with 'R' Battery) was to transport heavy (field) barrage guns to positions behind the frontlines. He served with the Eighth Army in the Western Desert and Italian Campaigns. On the reverse side of Frank's 1942 photograph he has written: *'To my ever-loving wife from your ever-loving husband, Frank. With all of my love and kisses darling XXXXXXX.'* Another photograph of Frank in North Africa, 1943, he writes: *'Yours forever-darling wife, Dot. Frank XXXXXXX.'*

On 9th January 1947, at Woolwich, he was demobilised (with release leave expiring on 13th March 1947. His military conduct rating was *'exemplary'*; his officer wrote the following:

*'An extremely good chap. Very reliable and a first class driver. Always very smart in appearance; a thoroughly clean and trustworthy type.'*

The couple had one daughter, Denise:

*"I have always been proud of my dad's efforts during the war, it must have been far from easy driving for hundreds of miles along very poor roads in soaring tropical temperatures. The enemy aircraft were always keen to strafe enemy convoys; in fact he was blown off a road, breaking a leg and his collarbone and confined to hospital! My maternal grandfather was Dennis*

*Gunner Frank Parker. Summer 1942.*

*Frank Parker in North Africa. Circa 1943.*

*Dorothy Parker, 1942.*

*Hodgetts, one of the 'Famous Fifty'; he must have been a very brave man.*

*I am also proud of what grandad achieved during the 1914-18 War, however, he died in a most dreadful accident!"*

Arthur William 'Dennis' Hodgetts served for four years with the 1/5th Leicestershire Battalion and suffered no serious injuries; indeed, post war he played for Coalville Town Football Club.

On 21st December 1921, he married, at Coalville's Christ Church, Ethel Mary Hoden: see William Ogden Hoden in 'Greater Love' and John Charles Hoden in Volume 1 of: 'Sons and Daughters'. Dennis and Ethel lived at 205, Ashby Road, Coalville and it was there, on 13th December 1923 that Dorothy was born. On 2nd March 1932, Ethel gave birth to a second daughter, Jean; three days later Ethel died from complications. Dennis was distraught, but the family sadness was not to end there. He was an electrician by trade, and by 1938 had a vast amount of knowledge and experience. Whilst strapped to the top of a pole correcting a fault on some wiring, with the power turned off, a dreadful error occurred when a lever was pulled and the full electrical power passed through Dennis' body. The incident happened near to the corner of Market Street, Coalville. The very brave war veteran died instantly.

In the years to follow, happiness flooded into the Hodgetts' household; first Dorothy, who was educated at Bridge Road School, married Frank on 9th May 1942, and later Jean married Burbage born, John Huddlestone on 1st August 1953 at Ebenezer Chapel, Coalville. (Please read Grenville Roy Huddlestone in this book.)

*Private Dennis Hodgetts.*

Frank returned to the Co-Operative slaughterhouse after the war, but in his middle years he was made redundant and relocated to Grieves (needle manufacturers) of Coalville. He retired at the age of sixty-three and enjoyed sixteen years of contentment with his family, allotment and floral gardening. Denise reflects on earlier years:

*"Mum was a wonderful wife; she often said that dad was the love of her life and I could not have had a better or more loving mother. She adored her home, liked to potter and tend to her garden and was a very keen dressmaker but suffered ill health for the last six years of her life. My dear mum passed away from cancer on 15th March 1978, aged only fifty-five years. I was just twenty-one at the time!"*

Frank was an excellent coarse-fisherman, so good that he regularly represented his country in the 1960's: having tours to Ireland and Denmark. Local friends who represented England were Jerry Colver, Rodney Marlow and Ivan Marks of Leicester.

*"Dad kept an allotment and so we had wonderfully fresh vegetables nearly all year round. He loved the countryside and God's wildlife too; he was always the first in the family to hear the cuckoo. Dad would think nothing of walking ten miles before lunch, and he really appreciated the blooms of spring and summer and the rustic nature of autumn. I couldn't have had better parents!"*

Frank died unexpectedly and suddenly of a heart attack on 12th October 2000. The old soldier was seventy-nine years of age.

*Dorothy and Frank Parker at Great Yarmouth, 1952.*

Denise: *"Mum and Dad are buried together in Blackwood (Broom Leys') Municipal Cemetery, Coalville. They have a headstone shaped like an open book and this bears the inscriptions."*

Many thanks to Frank's daughter, Denise for the information and photographs.

*Frank and Dorothy's daughter, Denise, with her Auntie Jean Huddlestone.*

# JOHN ARTHUR PEARCE

*Jack Pearce in 1941.*

Ernest James Pearce was born on 20th June 1890 on Thornborough Road, Coalville. He married local lass, Elsie: born in May 1896 at nearby Shepshed and the couple lived on Albert Street, indeed, under the shadow of Whitwick No6 Colliery, where Ernest worked.

John, who prefers to be called 'Jack', was born at Shepshed on 25th June 1918, one of four siblings with Stanley, Leonard and Marian. Jack was educated at Coalville's Christ Church School, and passed to attend Broom Ley's School, however, times were hard, money scarce and so he went to Bridge Road School. He left at fourteen years of age, and with local jobs scarce found employment in a shoe-manufacturing factory at Leicester: (12/6d a week or 62 ½ new pence). He cycled the forty-eight kilometres (thirty miles) round trip each working day from 1932-37.

*"Father bought me a new B.S.A. bicycle at 2 shillings and six pence a week."*

Jack was not alone in cycling to and fro from Leicester, my father and many others did so. A friend obtained a job for him at another shoe-factory—where he worked, and so the two cycled together: both living on Albert Road. The bicycle came in handy when Jack and three friends decided to cycle to Hunstanton, on the Norfolk coastline: a hundred and thirty kilometres as the crow flies each way (eighty miles). They sent the tent, pots, pans and primus stove, etc by rail. This was their very first holiday and their first sight of the sea! Jack said they were a bit saddle sore, and with the tent being a low bivouac they had to lie down to put-on trousers. They had a similar adventure two years later, cycling to Skegness: about the same distance. On arrival, they found they only had half an old penny between them, but Jack said such hardship stood them (him) in good stead for the war years. Just before that time the foursome took the train to Blackpool and with a little more cash to spare. Jack:

*"When I was about sixteen I began my football ' career'; I loved the game and began by playing for Oaks in Charnwood (Reserves) in 1934, and then joined Thringstone House. By this time I decided to get a job nearer home, and succeeded with one at 'Greens' shoe factory in 'The Lant' at Shepshed. A worker there persuaded me to play for Whitwick Holy Cross and played for them until going into the army in 1939."*

In June 1939, men between the ages of twenty to twenty-one had to register for military service, and Jack signed on the June 3rd.

*"Three of my pals were in the Royal Navy, and naturally I wished to do the same, but could do so only on a twelve year engagement. This did not go down very well with my parents so I decided to take potluck in the Army. I joined the Colours at Bradford in Yorkshire."*

Jack entrained to Sheffield, met a party of similar lads, and officers took them to Edmund Road Drill Hall.

*"I was in 122 Field Territorial Regiment of the Royal Artillery and stationed at Bradford.*

*Arriving at Valley Parade Barracks we found very little preparation had been made for us. After a reasonable meal we were taken on a tour of sleeping quarters and billets; we had no beds and had to sleep on the floor, but after seven days we were given palliases and shown a pile of straw with which to fill them."*

Jack found the food 'wholesome' but found washing eating utensils difficult with just one small Dixie for over a hundred men; also they discarded the palliases on health grounds and they slept on the floor. Later, camp beds were provided and ten weeks of disciplinary training; the high spot being entertained by the cast of 'Mother Goose', who were appearing at the town's Alhambra Theatre; Albert Modley had the starring role.

*"I had seven days privilege leave a fortnight before Christmas and so returned a week before festivities began, such as they were in wartime. On Christmas Day the officers waited on us (as is customary) and we had an enjoyable time, however, some heavy snow and sharp frost made guard duty rather unpleasant."*

On 8th January 1940 he was posted to 278 Battery at Halifax, still in the same regiment, but another unit: 280 Battery, still at Bradford. The men were 'billeted' in the Alexander Hall, a pre-war venue for dinner/dances; they slept in the plush balcony seats and food was good.

*"We had many route marches and also became familiar with a World War 1 eighteen pounder gun. I was stricken with tonsillitis and 'hospitalised' in the Hall's cloakroom. After eleven days we returned to Bradford, billeted in empty houses on Manningham Lane, and on one occasion fed by a local restaurant called 'Bushleys'. The weather was cold and for a while we had to sleep on the floor again."*

In February 1940, Jack was singled out to be a signaller; not to his choosing, but an officer 'persuaded' him to undertake the role. After a T.A.B. inoculation, a vaccine for fever, his body reacted strongly to it and was excused duty for two days. Two weeks later he had a second T.A.B., and given seven days' furlough. In mid-March, the Battery started night-drill orders on the Yorkshire Moors. Invariably the men were rain soaked, but with only one battle dress they had no option but to remain indoor to dry-out.

*"At Whitsuntide 1940, there were big fears of an invasion following the Dunkirk withdrawal. We were confined to barracks, sleeping fully dressed and so ready for any emergency, and if necessary to aid the civilian population (Civilian Aid Precautions). We were allowed one night in every six off duty, and had to take bayonet and rifle drill."*

During June and July the signallers held a variety of posts, such as communication personnel at Lonesboro Hall, and manning telephones linked to headquarters in remote areas, etc. On the 20th July their task was to guard an aircraft factory making Blackburn Skuas, Rocs and bombers at Brough, only eight kilometres east of Kingston upon Hull (Hull).

*"Our billets were unfinished housing and food was supplied by a local factory canteen: we ate with their workers. We were grateful when two other troops, about sixty men in each, arrived to ease our burden. We had been constantly manning the machine guns: four men to a gun, and also patrols for stints of twelve hours. While there we were bombed by enemy aircraft; Hull was an important port and targeted by them."*

On August 9th, a move a few kilometres northwest to South Cave, under canvas, but pleased to be served by a good N.A.A.F.I., a small cinema and a helpful Women's Voluntary Service; there was also a bus service into Hull. Early September saw them under canvas again, this time at Aldbrough, near the coast and sixteen kilometres northeast of Hull.

*"Our task was to dig gun pits and lay telephone lines to an observation post that had been hacked into the cliffs. Quite a few wrecks of aeroplanes were spotted and collected by the R.A.F. for identification, and a person was constantly involved in sweeping the horizon with binoculars in case of sighting an invasion force. The post was then in contact with French 75mm guns that were situated in a farmyard a few miles beyond. Two signalmen: Westbury and Kelly cooked our meals, they were quite tasty."*

Mid-October saw a reduction in daylight bombing raids, although more at night. They were posted to Wolsingham, twenty kilometres southwest of Durham. Considerable time was used packing equipment; they were issued with 4.5 inch Howitzer Guns, new wagons and extra signal equipment.

*"We had extensive lectures, twenty mile marches to make us fit: I was only fit to drop afterwards. Our billets were very old almshouses at first, and then the upper room of a Methodist Chapel. We bathed at Willington Colliery, making sure we looked good for when dances were laid on for us at Crook and Bishop Auckland. The locals were friendly and hospitable, and we frequented their public houses, two fish and chip shops and Y.M.C.A."*

Jack received seven days privilege leave in November, and on returning was given ten day's embarkation leave following Japan's attack on America's Naval Base, Pearl Harbour. Christmas arrived, the officers served the men, and: *"The Army cooks did us proud!"*

On 3rd January 1941, they packed their kit and entrained for Glasgow Station. Jack recalled that it was cold and frosty. They arrived at the Docks, and after standing on parade for two hours boarded the 26,000 tons and aptly named, *'Empress of Japan'*, a converted passenger liner of the Canadian Pacific Line.

*"Sleeping accommodation was at a premium with thirty thousand troops on board. Our choice was between a hammock or mattress on the floor, I chose the former but found it so uncomfortable that I slept on a mess table. We left at midnight on January 11th and passed the dark silhouettes of Greenock and waved farewell to our homeland, but for how long?"*

The ship's first port of call was Freetown on the Western coast of Africa; having picked up supplies they sailed south to Cape Town. Jack said the four days spent there were most pleasant, with the warm climate being ideal after the winter weather of England.

*"The locals were most friendly; a kindly couple took my mate and I to visit Table Mountain, the view from the top was breathtaking. Time quickly passed and we embarked once again: destination Bombay. We were given a day's shore leave. It was smelly, none too pleasant and we were pleased to get back on board, and within a few days we docked at Singapore Naval Base on 11th May 1941.*

They were billeted in attap roofed huts, quite adequate, and fitted with beds, white bedding and mosquito nets. They also received a change of shirt and shorts for every day, but what was to come? They travelled north and spent six weeks digging gun pits and slit trenches, and returned to Singapore. Jack thought the city was quite interesting with various eating-houses and cinemas, and noted the population consisted of many races. Noticeably so, tension rose as the Japanese Army marched into Indo China.

*"It was no surprise to us, when from our barracks, we saw the arrival of two battleships: H.M.S. 'Prince of Wales' and H.M.S. 'Repulse'. They were both sunk in the near future. Being on guard duty at the barrack's main gate I was able to watch the initial bombing of*

*Singapore; this was the first day of many! On 13th December 1941 we entrained from Singapore Railway Station for northern Malaya, whilst there we saw action at Kroh, Kampar and other places, their names elude me."*

Jack Pearce at Cape Town, 1941.

In early 1942, Jack was back at Singapore (island) with their guns firing from Pasir Panjang, the observation post being in the Law Courts, with their backs to the sea.

*"The order came to cease fire and to make our way to Changi. We commandeered a truck, not realising that the Japanese had forbidden this, lucky us! Life was not too bad at Changi, although all we had to eat was rice. Concerts were organised, football matches: I was selected to play for an England X1 against a*

*Scottish X1, so perhaps I can claim to be an 'international footballer?"*

Jack was placed into a 'work party', clearing rubble and repairing war damage. He was also in a party of troops that marched thirty miles to build a memorial to both Japanese and Allied troops killed in action. When he returned to Changi by lorry he found that a number of men from his regiment had been despatched (*we later found out*) to Korea.

On June 26th they were despatched to slave on the notorious Burma/ Siam '*Railway Of Death*'.

*"We left Singapore in freight wagons, thirty two men to a truck, and after four dreadful days we arrived at Ban Pong. We all had grave fears about contracting highly contagious cholera with its excruciating death."*

Within hours the water-borne parasite that causes the disease awakens in the warmth of the human gut. Victims rapidly dehydrate from vomiting accompanied by severe stomach cramps, and they have a fear of water. The pulse slows and arms and legs turn dark blue, viz it's other name: 'Blue Death'! (See essays: Les Kendrick and Harold Smalley in Volume One).

*"I was fortunate that two friendly Japanese soldiers, Payma San and Canya San, wangled me a pair of boots: I was very grateful. Also, on leaving for Burma they came to say goodbye to all in our tent, which goes to prove there are good and bad in all races."*

After Jack slaved on the appalling 'Wampo Viaduct', together with other jungle campsites along the railway line, he arrived at Konquita, near to the 'Three Pagodas Pass' where Burma crossed to Thailand (Siam). In October/November he went by rail to Takanun, where the Japanese were pressing for prisoners to travel to work in Japan.

*"I thought it couldn't be any worse than slaving on the railway, surviving another monsoon period or being bombed by allied aircraft (the marshalling yards at Non Pladuk), and so took a chance. I left Takanun, with a party, aboard railway wagons in February 1944 and arrived at base camp, Chungkai."*

On 12th March 1944 the party left by rail and stopped just outside of Non Pladuk, with Jack praying that it would not be bombed during his stay. He said there was a big Dutch camp nearby, and they shared whatever food was available: it was always inadequate. The party left on June 8th and arrived at Singapore five days later.

*"After a stay at a transit camp we boarded a five thousand ton old crate called: 'Asaka Maru'. It was built in Great Britain in 1898, and just before departure a German 'U'-Boat passed by with their crew standing on deck in smart white uniforms. We must have looked a decrepit lot: if they even bothered to look at us! After saying goodbye to Clifford Pier and Singapore we sailed on 4th July 1944."*

Before lifting anchor, the prisoners were brutally forced below decks (enemy rifle butts being rammed into skeletal frames), as they were herded into the holds. There was little ventilation and several men lost consciousness. Jack's officer, who spoke a little Japanese, asked the captain if some could sleep on deck, and Jack was one who did so.

The 'Asaka Maru', as part of a convoy, arrived at Muri on the South China Sea coastline of Borneo, and took aboard supplies and water, etc, before steaming for Manila on the coastline of the Philippine Islands.

*"We arrived on July 17th and just as the convoy was entering Manila Bay it was hit by a stream of torpedoes from allied submarines, probably Americans. All hell was let loose but I wasn't in a position to say how many ships were lost."*

On August 8th, the remainder of the convoy took a northern bearing into the Pacific to continue their voyage to Japan. The convoy was hit by a typhoon and the 'Asaka Maru' lost all of its cooking facilities (stored on the top deck) and most of its food as heavy seas washed the precious items overboard.

*"I was sleeping on deck and faced several squalls; we packed our blanket into our kitbag and sat on it, using our groundsheet to cover over us. When we were hit by the typhoon we forced ourselves under the fo'castle until we ran aground on August 15th, the engine room being flooded, due to a section splitting and allowing sea water to flow in. The wooden boxes that we used for toilets were washed away, so we had no facilities whatsoever. We found a store that was packed with rice chippings (the residue of burnt rice that clung to the sides of the kualies and was being returned to Japan for feeding pigs and chickens). We ate some of this and as far as water was concerned it was at a premium, whatever we collected from the now infrequent showers."*

On the early morning of August 17th two Japanese destroyers 'hove to'. One stayed and the other departed. During the afternoon the prisoners were ferried to the destroyer, a tricky operation in a turbulent sea; fortunately no one was lost. The destroyer steamed off and Jack said that no one was sorry to see the back of the 'Asaka Maru'. The following morning, after spending the night standing on deck, the party saw the coastline of Formosa (now Taiwan) and the ship dropped anchor there.

*"We were taken aboard the 'Hakusan Maru', a former pleasure cruiser that had been used as a troopship. We were given a hot meal and bedded into the holds, of course. On August 22nd, and after the convoy was again attacked by American submariners, we were allowed on deck to take ten minutes of fresh air. We saw a tanker hit by torpedoes and the guards quickly ushered us below decks."*

Finally, the convoy arrived on 26th August 1944 at the port of Moji, situated on the northern tip of the most southern of the islands that constitute mainland Japan. After debarkation the prisoners were deloused and their cloths fumigated (returned to them in a damp condition), and the next day they were taken in a coal barge across the Shimineseki Straits to Ube.

By November 17th, Jack was working down the coal mines, volunteering after hearing that by doing so one received an extra two-hundred grams of food a day as against one hundred and thirty only for working at the P.O.W. camp.

*"I worked for ten hour shifts in a ten day week and had the eleventh day off; using this day for washing, cleaning, etc. The billets were clean but the bed bugs were a pest to say the least.*

*On Christmas Day we were issued with an American Red Cross Box each, on the 'Railway of Death' it was one box per twelve men. We had a concert and a full stomach for a change; the cooks had been keeping some rations back for an extra treat."*

Jack and his fellow prisoners were not aware of the progress of the war, however, they knew that the allies had not been defeated due to earlier experiences. The New Year (1945) was pleasing in an indirect and double-edged way; American Super Fortresses (B24 bombers) were becoming regular visitors, now being able to fly from captured aerodromes. One heavy incendiary raid left the neighbourhood around the camp a blazing inferno: fortunately the camp remained unharmed.

*"During the raid we were marched to a nearby beach and there stood a covered lorry. We feared the worse and word got round, 'Lets get the bastards before they get us!' After the raid we were marched back to the camp and we felt someone must be watching over us."*

The raids became more numerous and Jack saw American Naval planes, having taken off from aircraft carriers, sweeping in low and machine gunning and bombing. The mine where he worked was a target; fortunately there were no casualties.

*"On August 15th we were on our way up from the mine, and usually, we met the next shift going down. When we got to the surface everything was at a standstill and we were informed that there was great interest on the radio in the Japanese's office. Rumours were rife that the war was over and all work ceased.*

On 17th August 1945, Captain Petrovsky and Lieutenant James (who spoke Japanese), and following an interview with the Japanese commandant, informed us that they believed the war was over. At 10.00am some of the 'prisoners' went down the mine to recover stacks of Red Cross parcels that had been denied them.

*"There was great elation all around, men were crying with emotion, it appeared that after three and a half years we were free: no longer slaves. Three days later we retrieved some more Red Cross parcels and also some medical supplies."*

Dates and quotes from Jack's 1945 memoirs:

**August 23rd.** *All Japanese staff was turfed out and the British took over mounting our own administration. First meat for six months arrived, basic rations increased to 1,450 grams as from August 25th. Told to paint letters 'P.O.W.' on roof of camp.*

**August 26th.** *An American B29 flew low over the camp and dropped foodstuffs, clothing, cigarettes, chocolates, everything to meet our needs. They dropped them in large oil drums that had been welded together. Included was a letter from one of the aircrew writing: 'We are glad to help', and pinned it to our notice board. There was also a letter from the Swiss Red Cross saying they were doing everything to ensure a speedy evacuation from Japan.*

**August 30th.** *B29s again dropping supplies over our camp. One container fell though the roof of our cookhouse, another unfortunately fell on and killed five civilians.*

**September 3rd.** *Supplies now becoming a headache; no one allowed out of the camp except for fatigue duties, order rescinded the following day.*

**September 5th.** *We went on a trip by wagon to another P.O.W. camp and met a Coalville lad called Ken Ward from Owen Street. He told me that he had heard rumours that we were going home via America. (This rumour, for a change, was correct.)*

**September 6th.** *Train trip to Moji.*

**September 8th.** *Trip to Yamaguchi and had a good time. On our return we went to Ube Town Hall where beer was being consumed quite freely.*

**September 9th.** *Nothing happened of importance, patiently await our homeward journey.*

**September 10th.** *Heard on the radio that General McArthur said that all prisoners are to stay put: "We know where you are and will get you out as soon as possible. Sad day: learned that five of my best mates were drowned on the way to Japan in the same convoy that we were in.*

**September 12th.** *Trip to Motoyama.*

**September 13th.** *Orders came at 12.10pm; given ten minutes to prepare to move, entrained at Ube for a thirty-six hour trip to Wakayama, then handed over to the American Eighth Army.*

**September 15th.** *At approximately 4.00pm we arrived at Wakayama to be met by a New Zealand ship's band, one of many allied warships lying in the bay. Had another medical and taken to the Beach Hotel. After being deloused and discarding our clothes we were issued with American naval kit and given a good meal. Eventually, as a C3 medical case I was ferried to the hospital ship: U.S.S. 'Consolation', put into a bunk with clean white sheets and pillows. Female nurses attended to all our needs. It was hard for me to comprehend my situation after being a prisoner for so many years and being away from the good things of life for so long. I thought I was dreaming.*

**September 16th.** *Still in bay, we were to sail at 2.00pm but a nearby typhoon prevented us from doing so. I was now discharged from being 'bed down' and went to many of the film shows on the ship, that is, in between squalls, rain, etc.*

**September 17th.** *On the ship's journey the captain welcomed us aboard and said our destination would be Okinawa, an island six hundred miles south of Japan's mainland.*

**September 18th.** *Sailed at 11.30pm into pitching and tossing seas. I sent a telegram home.*

**September 19th.** *Nothing happened of great importance, the sea is quite calm and with the moon shining on the water it looked so peaceful after seeing it at its worst so many times.*

**September 20th.** *At 11.30 am we arrived in Okinawa Bay, the amount of warships lying in the bay is tremendous. We were met by a destroyer, passing lots of aircraft carriers on the way. .*

**September 21st.** *Woke up this morning to find we were already anchored on the other side of the island, and at 11.00am personnel started to go ashore. About 2.00pm I got as far as the gangway and was sent back as I was C3 (obviously a mistake had been made.)*

**September 23rd.** *At 11.30am a party of us were ferried ashore by boat, boarded an ambulance, arrived at a camp, and were told we would be flying to Manila.*

**September 24th.** *Awoken at 3.45 am and told to pack our kit. Left camp and arrived at an airfield three hours later. At 9.ooam left Okinawa in a B24 Liberator to arrive at Luxon in Philippine Islands at 2.00pm. Stayed night at a camp before leaving on September 25th in a C36 Dakota, eventually landing in Manila (Clark Field) and taken to Camp 5th Replacement.*

**September 26th.** *Nothing much doing; had a medical examination, a kit issue (American), interrogation, then a grand welcome by the Red Cross.*

**September 27th.** *My pal, Claridge, left today for home, also met Ken Ward again and lots of other lads who came to Manila by boat.*

**September 28th.** *No sign of moving; drafts of P.O.W.s still coming in.*

**September 29th.** *Seems to be plenty of mail, but none for me. The fact is I haven't had any mail since I became a prisoner. Rumour that we are going home in aircraft carriers.*

**September 30th.** *Went to the post office regarding some mail and after being allowed to go through bundles of parcels, nothing doing.*

**October 1st.** *Quite a few lads of the Regiment arrived today. No sign of moving.*

**October 2nd.** *Nothing of great importance except a draft from Korea arrived with a lot more from 122 Field Regiment.*

**October 3rd.** *I went to the post office, no mail for me, obviously communication difficulties.*

**October 4th.** *News came round of a show about Danny Kaye. Who is he? I did not bother.*

**October 8th.** *Rumours of moving on the 9th. Greatcoats issued, also berthing cards.*

**October 9th.** *Rumours were right and we left camp by wagon, arrived at the docks, and boarded the Liberty Ship 'Marine Shark'. Rumour that we are sailing at 7.00am tomorrow.*

**October 10th.** *At 1.30pm we set sail from Manila for a fourteen-day trip to San Francisco. The boat is rather crowded as they say there are 3,500 aboard, but we seem to be pretty well organised and everything points to a good trip. Here's hoping!*

**October 11th.***Nothing untoward; sea is calm and things are beginning to go with a swing.*

**October 12th.** *Had our first boat drill, saw a cinema show on dock at night.*

**October 13th.** *At 12.30pm we passed the Marshall Islands (seven thousand kilometres or four thousand miles due east of Manila) on the starboard side. Another boat drill, nothing of great importance occurred, went to another cinema show but was rained off due to a sudden squall.*

**October 15th.** *We are finding the Americans quite friendly, all with different tales to tell us; like us they are glad to be going home.*

**October 16th.** *Told we are staying at Honolulu for eight hours and could write letters home, presumably to be posted from there.*

**October 17th.** *Been sailing eight or nine days and the voyage is getting rather monotonous. We get two Fridays this week as we crossed the International Date Line on the 20th.*

**October 18th.** *Seas rough and very strong wind.*

**October 19th.** *Various tales of what we will do when we get to San Francisco; kit issue, and rumour that we will cross America by train. Found out we have been running on one engine, consequently we will arrive later than expected, about October 23rd.*

**October 20th.** *We've been told that since 12.00pm last night, the engine we have been running on ceased to function and that we have been drifting for 9-10 hours. They have now got it going again and we are travelling at 10 knots.*

**October 21st.** *Seem to be travelling a little faster tonight, the moon shining on the water presenting a wonderful sight. We will probably arrive on the 23rd as; according to the ship's log we have about 550 miles to go to Honolulu.*

**October 22nd.** *Expect to arrive at Pearl Harbour at 10am tomorrow morning. Cinema show.*

**October 23rd.** Arrived at Pearl Harbour at 10.30am and docked, it looks to be a lovely place' all that it's cracked up to be. Unfortunately we are only staying for 24 hours and there is little chance of us going ashore (shame); any amount of naval craft to'ing and fro'ing, sailing in and out of the docks, as there is to be a 'Navy Day' on 27th. Needless to write that our engines are being worked on. Strolling on the deck, everything looks so peaceful in the moonlight.

**October 24th.** *Left Pearl Harbour at 3.30pm with the girls in their grass skirts swaying to the music, lovely sight. On leaving the harbour we found the sea rather rough but all set for the four-day journey to San Francisco.*

**October 25th.***The weather is a little cooler and the need for warmer clothing is evident.*

**October 26th.** *More rumours that we will not arrive at San Francisco until 30th, controversial. Notices posted for the disembarkation procedure, FEPOWs are to be first.*

**October 27th.***The sea started to be rough during the night and has remained so all day. Gigantic waves keep pounding the bay of the ship and we seem to be making little progress; the wind is blowing with gale force ferocity. Told over the ship's tannoy that our destination is now to be Seattle. We do not know why the sudden change.*

**October 28th.***The sea is a little calmer today, have just learned we have done 350 miles in two days; the ship certainly seems to be crawling along. A lot of conflicting rumours as to the day of arrival, let's just wait and sea. Battle blouses issued in the next compartment.*

**October 29th.** *Issued with pullover and tunic today and we are told over the tannoy that, once again, our destination will be San Francisco, to arrive at 10.00am on November 2nd. The sea is still rather rough and we have been pitching and tossing all day; night settling down.*

**November 1st.** *Arrived at San Francisco about 2.45pm and escorted under the Golden Gate. An all girls military band were playing San Francisco. We boarded a ferry and arrived at Fort MacDowell on*

*Angel Island. Have been told we are leaving at 1.00pm tomorrow. In the evening we were issued with battle dress, greatcoat and all the necessities to do with the British Army as we were wearing American navy issue. From Fort MacDowell we could see Alcatraz Prison and what a foreboding place it looked.*

**November 2nd.** *Left Fort MacDowell and ferried to Oakland, then boarded a hospital train which was the last word in luxury. Given a bunk and lay looking at the passing countryside; sheets white, clean, and nurses in attendance. They are Pullman coaches, a far cry from the wagons on the railway in Thailand. Everything seems set for a 26-hour trip to Seattle.*

**November 3rd.** *Still travelling: our destination is now Tacoma: arrive there at 12.30am.*

**November 4th.** *Fort Lewis is our billet; we have been told that we will stay for about 4 days. Had a look around Tacoma.*

*November 5th. Had another trip into the city, had the misfortune to lose or be pick pocketed of my wallet and had to get a sub.*

**November 6th.** *Another trip into the city and went to a cinema, got back aboard at 12.00pm and told we were leaving at 7.00am on 7th.*

**November 7th.** *Boarded a Pullman coach (only the best it seems). Passed through Seattle and told we would cross the American/ Canadian border at 6.30pm. Stop at Vancouver for Red Cross officials to get on board.*

**November 8th.** *Passed through the Rockies covered in snow and looked very beautiful. Due to pass through Edmonton tonight, weather very cold.*

**November 9th.** *Passed through Saskatoon and were allowed off the train for 30 minutes to stretch our legs. Told the temperature last night was 17 degrees below zero.*

**November 10th.** *Passed through Winnipeg in the early hours of the morning; told there was a reception to be held for us but we arrived too late!*

**November 11th.** *We seem to have passed out of the cold region and the weather seems quite mild. The coach windows are no longer frozen-over and no snow at all; expect to reach New York sometime tomorrow afternoon.*

**November 12th.** *Reached New York about mid-day, boarded a ferry and transferred to the 'Queen Mary'. After being led to our bunks it was said that the 'Queen*

*Mary' had been ferrying American troops at something like 5,000 a trip, we had ample room (only 3,000 of us) to explore the ship. My mate and I decided to go down the gangway and onto the docks, but we were not aloud outside the docks, being stopped by military police. We tried to board the 'Missouri' but we were soon told "no way soldier", because they were holding a reception for naval big-wigs who kept on arriving by taxis. We were helped by a friendly taxi driver who told us after he had dropped his passenger off, to wait near to the pillar at the main gates. This we did and met his taxi at 5.00pm; he took us on a tour of New York. First call was the Empire State Buildings, which we ascended, but could not see the view because of fog. We went to Radio City, 42nd Street, Broadway, Coney Island and then took us back to the ship which was due to sail at midnight. Sailed at noon.*

**November 13th.** *Set sail, we were on our way to England, passed the Statue of Liberty on our starboard side. We were scheduled to dock at Southampton on Sunday morning, the 18th. Told there was some mail to be had at the post office (formally the swimming pool) and received my first letter for four years (no mention of what was to come). Crossing the Atlantic was quite good, it being on its best behaviour, food was good and we busied ourselves by playing games and some physical activity; all very light hearted.*

**November 18th.** *The cry suddenly went up: "The shores of England". At last we had made it after nearly five years away. It was without doubt emotional, especially as the view gradually unfolded itself as we neared Southampton Water. Someone more knowledgeable said it was the Isle of Wight. We were shepherded in by tugs to Southampton and eventually docked, the gangway was let down and we went ashore (many to be met by relatives.) When my turn came I bent down and kissed the ground of 'Old England'. I was not alone in doing this!*

**November 19th.** *Reveille at 7.00am. Breakfast at 8.00am. We were then told to go to the transport office to collect our leave passes and railway warrants. Wagons took us to the railway station and I caught the train to Leicester, arriving in the dark at 4.30pm.*

*Prior to leaving Southampton I sent a telegram giving the time of my arrival there, but there was no welcoming party, because the train had pulled into Central Station and not London Road Station. Of this I was not aware. Sitting rather forlornly on my kit and not quite knowing what to do, a gentleman approached me and asked if I was a FEPOW who had arrived on the last train. He explained the situation and suggested we go to London Road Station, and this we did. Waiting there was Uncle Wilf, Aunt Gert and Stan. After saying goodbye to them the gentleman offered to take me to where I wanted to go. He set off and as we approached Markfield, I asked Stan how Mum was. I was stunned when he told me she had passed away in 1942, not knowing whether I was dead or alive! Still, although home would not be the same, I knew that Dad and Marian would be waiting to greet me. The welcoming helped to ease the feeling I had for Mum, she had been the spur that had kept me going during many terrible moments, in which I could have given up all hope. When I arrived at home, 12, Blackwood, Coalville, I was welcomed with open arms and we all shed tears; the feeling of being 'home' was beyond description. The following morning I noticed the flags had been put out and a big: WELCOME HOME, JACK' sign had also been erected. Now I can honestly say, after a trip around the world, I have had the flags put out for me!*

*12, Blackwood, Coalville. Home of Jack Pearce.*

Jack remained at 12, Blackwood, living with his father and stepmother, and worked in a cobbler's shop (repairing shoes) on Belvoir Road, Coalville. He later moved to Quorn (living with his sister in her home near to Rawlins School), and finally to Shepshed, where he still lives, aged eighty-nine years. Since the war Jack has played a leading role in many Royal British Legion events and taken great pleasure in retaining contacts with regimental friends.

After the war, Jack's sporting interests extended into cricket, and he not only played for Coalville's leading local club, Broom Leys', but also captained them as well as later being on the committee and chairman. Jack is indeed a very brave and resourceful man to have survived such terrible ordeals.

Many thanks to Jack Pearce, also to John and Pauline Hoden, who of course have an excellent presentation in 'Greater Love'. Jack and John met while playing for Broom Ley's Cricket Club. Pauline contacted me to say that Jack had passed away on 26th February 2008 at Charnwood Oak's Nursing Home, Shepshed, aged eighty-nine years.

*"He had a lovely disposition and a beautiful singing voice. He often regaled us over the years and his memory will remain with us for ever."*
God bless, Jack.

Some folk may remember Harry Sparham from Battram (near Ellistown); he too was a Japanese prisoner of war.

# TONY GARFORTH PICKERING

## Mentioned in Despatches

Tony Pickering was born on the 25th August 1920 at Foxton, a village sixteen kilometres southeast of Leicester and five northwest of Market Harborough. He went to the prestigious grammar school of the latter town and in 1937 joined Thomson Houston and Company as an apprentice engineer.

Some of Tony's earliest memories are of his grandfather, Henry Pickering, talking of the 1815 Battle of Waterloo. Henry, as a boy, often sat neath an old oak tree in Foxton to listen to the tales of ageing veterans from that battle, and these he told to his grandchildren. Henry and his wife, Mary, enjoyed a very long and happy life and saw past their golden wedding. Their son, Harry (born in 1880s): Tony's father, joined the Royal Navy directly from school and as a Warrant Officer served in Admiral Beatty's Cruiser Squadrons during W.W.1. Harry's wife, Lily (born in 1880s) was the daughter of a manager of British Glues and Chemicals. Harry's military discipline imbued to his children, and Tony says it was a wholesome advantage as they matured to adulthood. Tony was taken by modern technology; upon hearing aeroplane engines his eyes turned to the sky. He knew the designs and performances of them all and sensed that his destiny lay in the realms of flight.

The 1914-18 post-war generation knew of the reverberations that followed that war. Tony recalls watching the film: 'All Quiet On The Western Front'. A Lewis Milestone low-key, but deeply felt screen adaptation of Erich Maria Remarque's novel. It starred Lew Ayres who played a teenage German soldier: the film reflected the full horrors of warfare.

*"I watched this film and it made me think deeply about my future."*

By 1937 it was apparent that another war was on the horizon, and Tony and his youthful companions chatted about the issues of the time, even to discussing the branch of the armed services they would rather serve in. In that year, the R.A.F. realised the ever-growing power of the German Luftwaffe, and set a drive to train pilots and to build more aircraft. Tony: *"A fellow apprentice, Bryn Willis, told me that a friend of his was flying Tiger Moth aircraft at weekends, and paid two shillings an hour for the pleasure. My pay as an apprentice was paltry, but to be taught and to be paid to fly was of definite interest to me."*

Tony joined the R.A.F. Volunteer Reserve. On 29th July 1939 he was taken into the skies by Flying Officer Morris; going solo on August 26th from Ansty (Coventry R.A.F.V.R. airport.)

*"Before my first flight the future agenda was explained; I climbed into the cockpit and was informed of the controls and then an instructor took us into the skies. I loved every minute, and after a few trips I was allowed to take over the controls and taught various manoeuvres and how to take-off and land. It was wonderful when I went solo: to see what was going on below and to be paid to do it! We all knew we were being prepared for war and now I knew that the R. A. F. would be my destination."*

Tony needed flying hours and secured some at 15: Elementary Flying Training School in a Miles Magister, and from 22nd November 1939 to 26th April 1940 his flying time increased to 46.40 hours (duel) with 39.00 hours solo. Then to 5: Flying Training School at Sealand (just northwest of Chester) in a Miles Master. The Commanding Officer at Sealand reported that Tony was *'slightly over-confident'*. Tony: *"I felt at ease within the R.A.F. and very pleased to be selected for Fighter Command. We were all in it together and would fly and fight for each other as comrades. We felt confident that we could hold the Luftwaffe."*

Towards the end of July 1940, early days in the epical and pivotal Battle Of Britain, Tony, a teenage, raw combatant, was sent to 32 Squadron, but the commanding officer believed that he had insufficient experience. The frontline squadron, flying Hurricanes, had fought well during the springtime Battle of France and knew their requirements.

*"With two other sergeant pilots, Ray Gent and Tony Whitehouse, I arrived at Biggin Hill in Kent.*

*Squadron Leader Worrall asked how many hours I'd spent in Hurricanes and wasn't too happy when I hadn't even sat in the cockpit of one. Pilot Officer John Flinders showed me the controls and I did a few circuits, and was told that next day I was to go into action. I was number two (wingman) for Flight Lieutenant John Proctor (later Wing Commander D.F.C. and bar), and told to formate ten feet behind his tail at all times, especially in combat and not to put my gun button onto 'fire'. After some days in combat I became enlightened to this instruction."* (Later the

The Royal Air Force crest.

Tony Pickering in 1940.

pair met in the Middle East.)

32 Squadron scrambled at 9.00am, and twice more during the day, but Tony was soon to leave the Squadron: he was considered too raw. On 3rd August 1940, Sergeant Pilot Tony Pickering and two other recruits went to Sutton Bridge, 6: Operational Training Unit on the flatlands near 'The Wash' of East Anglia. Within twenty days his logbook showed 31.55 hours in a Hurricane, and they returned to 32 Squadron, only for a few days. The Squadron had moved for a rest to Acklington, Northumberland, and the commanding officer told them they were not entitled to a break. On August 27th, the three pilots were posted to 501 Squadron at Gravesend on the Thames estuary, in Kent. The Squadron was confident with pilots of the calibre of Paul Farnes, Henry Hogan, John Gibson, 'Ginger' Lacey and Ken MacKenzie. Tony and his pals replaced Flight Lieutenant George Stoney and Pilot Officers John Bland and Pawel Zenker: killed in action on August 18th and 24th respectively.

*"Squadron Leader Hogan was a first class man, he could understand our differing outlooks and managed us accordingly, a very good leader of men."*

While at Gravesend, Tony, nor any pilot put on weight because the food from the Army was dreadful.

One day he visited a nearby hotel to satisfy his hunger. The food was wonderful, but his stomach couldn't take it and so it proved an expensive regurgitation!

The 1940 Battle was at a crucial stage. Hermann Goering, head of the Luftwaffe, demanded victory over the R.A.F. as a prerequisite for land invasions of Kent and Sussex. On August 30th, Tony took-off and saw action and wrote in his logbook that he damaged a Dornier 215 bomber. The Luftwaffe was doing its utmost to devastate Fighter Command's airfields, and looking at Tony's logbook it is clear that he had a very busy eleven days from August 31st to September 10th: recording twenty-five operational flights. The first, a 7.50am scramble to intercept a German air-fleet approaching Gravesend (some bombs exploded on their airstrip.) Sergeant pilot Antoni Glowacki was injured and forced to bale out over the airfield after combat with a Me109, and later that day the Squadron intercepted a large force over Ashford.

Friendships could be fleeting; on September 2nd, Flying Officer Arthur Rose-Price joined them in the morning, immediately did a patrol and during his second in the afternoon was shot down and killed at 4.30pm over Dungeness. He was the brother of Dennis Price, the actor.

*"We met the bombers head-on with our attacks, going in at three abreast in a formation about fifty yards apart. The meeting speed was about five hundred miles per hour, so timing was all-important and we fired our guns as we went through—-and then got the hell out before the Messerschmitt fighters collared us. We were doing three or four patrols a day and it was getting a bit much, very tiring."*

Another ace with 501 was Russian born Pilot Officer Stanislaw Skalski. He flew for the Polish Airforce in 1939 and downed four enemy aircraft. On September 5th, he was shot down at 10.00am over Canterbury, and hospitalised. (He totalled 24 of the enemy.)

There came another scramble at 2.50pm; Tony landed at 4.00pm and at 4.20pm was ordered up again. Life was hectic! September 6th saw no let up with an 8.40am scramble to meet one hundred plus over Ashford. Tally-Ho, Tally-Ho! The Hurricanes tore into the bombers with the Me109s doing likewise into them and at 9.00am (within one minute) three pilots lost their lives: Pilot Officer Hugh Adams crashed near Elham, Sergeant Pilot Oliver Houghton near Charing and twenty-one years old Sergeant Pilot Geoffrey Pearson near to Hothfield, Kent.

*The esteemed 1940 fighter pilots of the frontline Few.*
*Survival as probable and ethereal as the morning dew.*
*Young and zestful and with no shortage of panache.*
*Sporty airforce blue uniforms and a rolled moustache.*

*They defended the many by displays of bravery and sacrifice.*
*Utterly outnumbered with fatality being a toss of the dice.*
*Endless summer of nineteen-forty saw young flyers grow tired.*
*As fading heavenly shooting stars their life-light soon expired.*

*Everyone recognised our aircraft of Hurricanes and Spitfires.*
*Always remember the pilots who fell on England's sad shires.*
*Pretty village churchyards and forget-me-nots where they lie.*
*Pilots in a mantle of deathly black in a clear pastel-blue sky.*

*Scroll dedicated to the Few.*

On 7th September 1940, Hermann Goering switched tactics from the total destruction of Fighter Command's pilots and airfields to the bombing of London. At 4.00pm RDF (radar) stations on the south coast picked-up large enemy formations circuiting Calais. The Few took-off and were vectored to protect their bases but the enemy were not to be seen! A German juggernaut of nearly one thousand aircraft, a third bombers, the remainder fighters, were following the Thames! Cargoes of high explosive and incendiary bombs rained down upon the capital city as civilians took cover in shelters and tube stations.

*"We took-off at 4.30pm and saw four waves of bombers with a heavy Me109 escort. It was tough going and I eventually returned at 5.50pm, but within five minutes I was up again. The R.A.F. shot down forty-one Hun aircraft, but we lost twenty-eight.*

On the afternoon of September 10th the Squadron moved to Kenley to offer greater cover for London. Tony says that the food and accommodation, compared to Gravesend, were superb as were the teenage W.A.A.Fs. The next day, as most of that eternal summer, was beautifully clear and sunny. Tony, one of eleven of 501 Squadron plus a full complement of Hurricanes from 253 Squadron, called a Tally-Ho at 3.20pm, over Maidstone as they peeled off against a large formation of bombers and fighters.

*"We hit them head on at 18,000 feet, but as I closed in on my target there was a horrible bang and my plane shuddered. My Hurricane had taken enemy fire in the sump and so I turned over and went into a vertical dive to escape further damage. My aircraft was finished with, so I switched off the fuel and the ignition switches and opted for a forced landing at Kenley. I dropped to 3,000 feet and was about to lower my wheels when flames started shooting out of the engine, and then down the side of my cockpit. My cockpit was open so I pulled the pin on my harness and stood up: the slipstream sucked me out and then pulled the parachute cord. Upon landing I was approached by two Irish Guardsmen but they hadn't seen my aeroplane and I was just in a shirt and slacks. They viewed me in an untrusting manner with bayonets to the fore, but once I established my innocence I was taken to Kenley. I was then a sergeant pilot, but three years later, as a flight lieutenant and travelling on the Irish mail train from Euston Station to Rugby, two men*

*asked me if I had been shot down over Caterham military camp. They were very upright, dressed in civilian clothing, but clearly military types. When I answered in the affirmative they told me they were the two Irish Guardsmen who had apprehended me. What a coincidence, they were travelling to Southern Ireland!"*

Fighter Command Records show that a Me109 shot down Tony's Hurricane P5200 over Maidstone at 1545 hours, but Tony insists he was attacking and firing at the bombers.

*"Had a Me 109 joined in and had been attacking me I am certain that it would have followed me down, because my Hurricane was pouring smoke and would have been an easy target."*

Twenty-nine British fighters fell that day, seventeen pilots died, six wounded. September 13th was unlucky for 'Ginger' Lacey, a pilot in double figures for aircraft kills.

He baled out over Maidstone after attacking a Heinkel 111 bomber and was unhurt, doing so again on the 17th over Ashford following combat with a Me109. Tony was non-operational on the 15th when the Squadron was in several dogfights with Pilot Officer Van den Hove d'Ertsenrijck's Hurricane exploding in mid-air. The R.A.F. lost thirty fighters: twelve deaths, nine wounded, with the enemy losses at sixty! On September 17th Tony lost a good friend:

*"Eddie Egan and I were the same age, we enjoyed a quiet drink and the company of a couple of W.A.A.Fs. We were scrambled in mid-afternoon, gained height and peeled off to go through a bomber formation over Ashford: our guns firing all the way. I was with Eddie and waiting for Squadron Leader Hogan to call us when four Me109s came up behind to target Eddie, why not me I thought? I went after them but they were too fast. Eddie didn't bale out and his Hurricane hit the ground. They didn't find Eddie until September 1976, in a wood at Bethersden, Kent; his parachute riddled with 7.9mm bullets. It was only when they unearthed his aircraft in November 1979 and confirmed the number plate that the Ministry of Defence accepted it was Eddie. He rests in Brookwood Military cemetery and in addition to basic details his sister has added: 'In Treasured Memory of a much Loved One of The Few'.*

The next day a 9.10am scramble resulted in

Sergeant Pilot Cyril Saward being attacked by Me109s over Tonbridge at 9.35am; he baled out and the aircraft crashed at Staplehurst. Cyril and Tony had known each other and were friends from pre-war Coventry days. Squadron Leader Hogan, had to do likewise at 12.30pm over West Malling.

*"We were certainly taking punishment and were tired, but I don't think for one moment we thought we were going to lose. Typically British, but we had a good CO."*

The Battle continued and Tony was becoming a seasoned pilot, between mid-September to the 30th, he flew on twenty-four patrols. It had become a battle for survival! On September 27th a wounded Sergeant Pilot Victor Ekins baled out over Godstone, Surrey; he was taken to Sevenoaks hospital and recovered. Pilot Officer Edward Gunter was 'taken' by Me109s while attacking a Dornier 17, he baled out at 12.25pm: his parachute failed to open. The R.A.F. lost twenty-nine aircraft, twenty deaths, five wounded. The enemy lost fifty-five.

*"I probably shot down a Me110. We were attacking a number of them head on and mine peeled off with smoke pouring from it as it went down. I couldn't stop to look because Me109s were on to us and I'd taken evasive action. Our guns tore strips off many an enemy frame but we left it to the experienced pilots to do the finishing off and claiming, it was all team work."*

September 28th: seventeen fighters lost with ten deaths and three wounded. The Squadron had Pilot Officer Everett Rogers shot down over Deal at 10.10am: baling out safely whereas at the same time Me109 cannon shells ended the short life of Pilot Officer Frederick Harrold.

By the end of September 1940 the Squadron had lost twenty-two aircraft with eleven pilots killed or wounded. The Battle of Britain was indeed a very intense affair.

*"With October the days grew shorter, so we could get up later and enjoy ourselves a little more in the evenings. We'd go to the pub, the WAAF girls were great, and what with Kenley and Biggin Hill being badly bombed those girls had to take it, quite a few were killed, we respected them enormously."*

By October 1st, the R.A.F. had lost 1,653 aircraft; it was looking as though it would not be an invasion for that year, but air-action continued. On October 7th,

*Commemorative book, tie and signatories for the Thirtieth Anniversary, 1970.*

a *schwarm* of Me109s was intercepted over Ashford: Pilot Officer Nathaniel Barry, a twenty-two year old Cambridge University student being killed. The cannons of a Me109 hit him over Wrotham at 10.40am, he baled out but when found at Wilmington had died from wounds. After further actions during the month, on October 29th, Tony saw a Me109 on his starboard side and about one mile ahead, he wrote in his logbook:

*'I closed to 300 yards and saw it was yellow with large black crosses on the upper surfaces of its wings. I immediately opened fire from dead astern and he went into a dive, turning and twisting to evade my fire. I followed him down firing short bursts and when he was at about 500 feet and diving for the ground, I gave him my last bursts which set fire to his starboard petrol tank and he dived into the ground at the corner of a wood and immediately blew up. The pilot did not bale out. The aircraft crashed at Ham Street, approximately 15 miles northwest of Dungeness.'*

Tony felt no compassion for his fallen enemy. He had lost many friends during the Battle and it had become par for the course: defending his country and trying to reduce civilian deaths.

By October's end the Luftwaffe having turned its attention to night bombing. (It had lost far too many aircraft and crews during the summer months). 501 Squadron had lost eighteen young men. Tony's logbook shows ten operational patrols in the first seven days of November, and nine patrols in the first twelve days of December. He, and two others were posted to 601 Squadron at nearby Northolt, to replenish numbers. It was a time when experienced pilots were reposted to O.T.U.s, both for respite and to pass on knowledge. Tony was posted to 57: O.T.U., Hawarden (just west of Chester) on 14th February 1941, and subsequently became a test pilot after completing the Chief Flying Instructor Test on March 13th. Over the year his logbook displays 675 flights, including 154.20 hours flying Spitfires.

Tony says that the Hurricane was a good old workhorse and could take a lot of punishment, whereas the Spitfire was like a well-bred racehorse. On 13th December 1941 he was promoted to pilot officer. By 19th February 1943, Flying Officer (acting flight lieutenant) T. Pickering was posted to 131 'County of Kent' Squadron at Castletown as flight commander of 'B' flight. After a few months, Tony began practise for landing on a ship; his logbook shows that he completed four deck landings in a Seafire (converted Spitfire) on H.M.S. 'Argus' and assessed: 'above average'. Tony undertook this training so that if losses necessitated a swift move, he could be transferred to the Mediterranean where aircraft carriers were in regular use.

With 131 Squadron, Tony was regularly involved in escorting American Bomber formations conducting daylight air offensives over Western Europe. In the second half of the year the Squadron also participated in fighter sweeps into enemy air territory, attacking land targets and shipping, and for his achievements received a **Mention in Despatches.**

*"We didn't get too close to the American bombers for obvious reasons, and we flew under an umbrella of Johnnie Johnson's Squadrons in Spitfire 1Xs, so we didn't see too much action."*

Typical of the action is recorded in Tony's logbook dated, 3rd August 1943.

*'At 1925 hours the Exeter Wing took part in 10 Group *Circus No49. They were acting as part of the target cover for Whirlwind bombers attacking Brest/Guipavas aerodrome. The Wing flew in three groups of 8 aircraft arriving over the target area at 20.27 hours, stepped up from 10 to 14,000 feet. They orbited for a few minutes while the Whirlwinds went in and bombed, and then started back home. About 8 to 10 FW190 fighters and at least 23 Me109s were encountered on the way back between the target and 10 miles out to sea. Individual combats resulted during which Flight Sergeant Parry probably destroyed a FW109. It was last seen going down steeply at 500 feet with much black smoke coming from it after having been hit on three occasions by bursts from the Spitfire cannon and machine-gun. Also 5 FW109s were damaged by the Commanding Officer, Pilot Officer*

*Luckoff (2), Flight Sergeant Turnbull and Flight Sergeant Tate. But against these claims, gratifying as they are has to be set the loss of Flying officer E. Smith. (Australia).'* * (Circus: code for escorting bombers.)

Tony says that Earl Smith became a prisoner-of-war, being reunited with his brother, Flying Officer Cyril Smith, who also flew for 131 Squadron. They were shot down within a few days of each other. He maintained contact with the two brothers after the war, visiting them during a business trip and also on a holiday after Tony's retirement. Tony completed his last flight for 131 Squadron on 7th January 1944. His logbook reads:

*'Off for a rest from flying duties after 4½ years continuous flying.'* The Squadron ORB recorded: *'Flight Lieutenant Pickering, 'B' Flight Commander, is posted to Exeter for Controller's duties. He joined the squadron 11 months ago, when he commenced his second tour of operations.*

*He was an experienced fighter pilot and a good instructor who organised his flight extremely well. He was popular with the whole squadron and will be missed by all who came into contact with him.'*

On arrival at Exeter it was thought that he would make a fine sector gunnery officer, having been on a gunnery course and with a good assessment. Later he was posted to Colerne, to the northwest of Bath. At Colerne, Roy Watts, an old friend and comrade of Tony's from the 1940 days, was commanding a Wing including 616 Squadron, flying Meteors. Tony also knew the flight commanders and they would chat in the officers' mess. They asked Tony if he would like to return to action and fly in the first 'jet' squadron. Tony reminded them that Fighter Command had issued strict orders that no one was to use any influence to join this squadron. Roy insisted that he could 'work it', and so Tony nodded; it was like offering gold, no pilot could turn down such an opportunity! Something went badly wrong because within two days Tony received a telephone call from a WAAF officer simply informing him that he had been posted to Egypt.

No reason given! On arrival at Cairo he realised no one expected him; happily, he met Wing Commander John Proctor, the pilot from 32 Squadron days. He arranged for Tony to join R.A.F. 'El Ballah' where, as a squadron commander, he trained pilots for Hurricanes and Spitfires, and stayed there until November 1945.

*Squadron Leader Tony Pickering in 1945.*

*Chris and Tony Pickering with Josephine Smith, wife of the late Arthur Smith. 2005.*

*Tony Pickering and the author in 2006.*

Records of 25th June 1945 show that Squadron Leader T. G. Pickering development as a fighter pilot as '*exceptional*'. Tony never knew why he was ushered to Cairo and can only assume that Fighter Command outgunned Roy Watts. Returning to England in early December 1945, he was released later that month to rejoin his old trade. Tony embarked on a successful career in that industry: designing and selling steam turbines and travelling all around the world. He married his first wife, Stella, in December 1940. Their son, Michael, has recently retired after headmastership at a Skipton school. Daughter, Pauline, is married to a professor at Southampton University, and is also a teacher. Stella lives at Rugby and enjoys life with her children and grandchildren. There are nine grandchildren and four great-grandchildren, the latest grandchild being 'Lotte', born December 2006.

Tony has a very happy retirement with his second wife, Christine. Both are regular members of the Church of England, and as campanologists have rung church bells in many cities, towns and villages of Great Britain, also Australia and New Zealand. Christine, a keen 'rambler' has completed lots of famous British walks, such as Hadrian's Wall as well as on Cyprus.

I asked Tony to reflect on memories of when our nation s endured traumatic and crucial days, and feared an invasion and all that involved. He modestly replies:

"*I was young, and I feel proud to think that youngsters of my generation came forward to ensure our freedoms. It wasn't just the pilots, there were fitters, armourers, and everyone who kept us in the air; all of my comrades in the Battle of Britain Fighter Association would agree that it was down to the people who kept us airborne. Those WAAFs, particularly the young girls, they did a magnificent job. We just flew the aeroplanes, they were the ones who were bombed, not us, it was all down to a team effort! I must also say on behalf of my comrades that we will always remember the heavy losses of Bomber Command, and all services that contributed to the war effort. We don't want glamour, we just did our best.*"

I asked Tony for a final reflection:

*"Looking back on the war years, I feel that the comradeship existing between the Services, the support of the civilian population and the encouragement offered by Winston Churchill, will never exist again. In real terms we have never recovered from the severe losses sustained to the cream of British manhood during our two most bloody wars."*

There is very little I can write after Tony's completion other than to thank him for his time and friendship.

*Statue of Lord Dowding, Marshal of the Royal Air Force: outside the church of St. Clements, London.*

# KATHLEEN 'OLIVE' POOLE

Having advertised for a member of the Women's Land Army to appear in this book, progress was only made when I met old friend, John Cowley. I could not have chosen better than to write about, Olive: as she likes to be known. Olive, a lady of grace, resides at the excellent Coalville Care Home, Albert Road at Coalville; my mother and mother-in-law were well looked after there by Kim, Janet and company.

Sarah Ellen Cowley (born 6th April 1893), from an old Hugglescote family, married Alfred Edwin Reynolds (born 1891) of 49, Forest Road, at the village's St. John The Baptist Church on 20th October 1915. Sarah was the sister of Joseph William 'Bill' Cowley, one of the 'Famous Fifty', who sadly lost his life on 8th May 1916 at Vimy Ridge, just twenty years of age. (See Fifty Good Men & True).

*William 'Bill' Cowley, 1914. One of the Famous Fifty.*

Alfred: service number 94815, served as a corporal cook with the West Yorkshire Regiment from 13th April 1916 to the end of the Great War. Eventually, the couple settled at 7, Breach Road, Hugglescote, and had three children, Hilda: 9th October 1916-1982, Freda 6th January 1921-2006 and Olive: born on 7th June 1922.

*7 Breach Road.*

Freda, a keen girl guide married Coalville's Flying Officer Leonard Alldread D.F.C. of the Fleet Air-Arm. Post-war they emigrated to Kentville in Nova Scotia, Canada, but not before his headmastership at schools at Croft and Swaffam. (See Leicestershire Men of the R. A. F. in this book.) Olive went to St. John The Baptist Church School, where many of the Famous Fifty attended, including her uncle Bill Cowley, and passed for Broom Leys' School. Olive:

*"I had a lovely childhood with so many relatives and friends around. Michael, I can remember your grandparents, Charlie and Hetty Hatter, and their children, Betty and Maurice, they were about my age, and Maurice walked with me to Broom Leys' as well. I can also remember your red-haired father, Les; he sang in the church choir."*

On leaving school, Olive travelled to Leicester to work in the offices of Wolsey, in King Street: opposite to New Walk and the De Montfort Hall. In June 1940, when aged eighteen, she had to decide how best to help the war-effort.

*"I have always loved the countryside, walking and the open air, and didn't fancy factory work, but I had seen posters asking for volunteers for the Women's Land Army."*

In 1917, during World War 1, the country found itself with only three weeks of available food. The Minister of Agriculture, Roland Prothero, appointed Dame Meriel Talbot to enlist women to 'work the land' as replacements for the thousands of male farm-workers who had either perished or were fighting for King and country. Twenty-three thousand women had enrolled by 1918. On 1st June 1939, undeceived by Hitler's promises at Munich, 'The Women's Land Army' (W.L.A.) was formed and by September a thousand volunteers had been trained and ready for deployment. So rapidly did the W.L.A. develop, that by December there number was 4, 544. It was part of the Ministry of Agriculture and Fisheries, and the honorary director was Lady Denman D.B.E., and her home: the baronial Balcombe Place was the headquarters. The entire organisation was staffed and run by women.

*"I was interviewed and enlisted in Leicester and was soon kitted out with a uniform"*

The issue was: 2 green jerseys, 2 pairs of breeches, 2 overall coats, 2 pairs of dungarees, 6 pairs of stockings, 3 shirts, 1 pair of ankle boots, 1 pair of shoes, 1 brown felt slouch hat, 1 overcoat with shoulder titles, 1 oilskin or mackintosh, 2 towels, an oilskin southwester, a green armlet and a metal badge. After every six months of satisfactory service she receives a half-diamond to be sewn to the armlet and after two years a special armlet and another after four years.

*"In no time at all I found myself with nineteen other girls in a hostel at Long Whatton, six kilometres northwest of Loughborough. The hostel was really a few old cottages opposite the Parish Church and owned by Lord Michael Crawshaw with bare stone floors."*

By December 1940 there were just 172 girls working in Leicestershire and Rutland.

On arrival at hostels, the girls produced their Medical Cards and advised to be placed on the local doctor's list as soon as possible. A warden cared for their needs and the Ministry of Works supplied a First Aid Kit: farming could be dangerous; she also kept sickness records and forwarded them to headquarters every six months.

Whatton House.

*"When we came back from work we only had the one bath, so we put it by the fire in the living room and climbed in one after another. Lord and Lady Crawshaw owned Whatton House, and during the war it was used first for evacuees and then as a maternity*

Return from a hard day's work.

*centre. My best friend was Hazel Hutchinson, she was from Sheffield, and kindly allowed me to sleep on the bottom bunk."*

The girls had a kit box each, two shared a wardrobe and a chest of draws and every girl had a drawer that could be locked to safely keep personal possessions.

*"I remember a farmer called Mr. Tolly and another named Mr. Ken Blood, he was originally from Shepshed. I enjoyed the long, warm days of harvest the best. Our set hours were 8.00am until 5.00pm, but they often varied especially during harvest-time when we'd do twelve-hour shifts and get paid the overtime after working fifty hours per week, forty-eight in winters. After the threshing machine had done its job, we collected the hay and stacked it into bales for it to dry out. Later though, when we came to load them onto the wagons, we'd disturb many a rat's nest, but men set their dogs to catch and kill them, but they were very fast. We tucked our dungarees into our socks to prevent them from running up our legs; one person forgot to and was horrified by what happened. There was a nice lady, a Mrs. Carden, who used to run the small local store where we could buy a few provisions."*

Olive said the twenty girls always worked together as a team, and generally got on very well together, saying their job was important. They had replaced many of the male farmhands who had joined the armed forces, and what with many food ships being lost in Atlantic convoys, the need to grow even more food was paramount.

In all hostels the girls were encouraged to form their own 'House Committee': responsible to the warden for recreational activities and disciplinary matters. Such committees encouraged: dances, Whist Drives, Make and Mend classes, First Aid, and lectures

Threshing time.

Hay making.

on general health, child welfare and current affairs.

"*We worked in all weather, but we were never really cold because we were given such good clothing. Where possible I stuck to my low shoes, but we also had Wellingtons and boots. I had long hair and so rolled it up and tucked it under a scarf. The farmers paid us, our normal pay was £2.00 per week, working Monday to Friday, but when we left to travel home on a Friday night the farmer always gave us some bacon and eggs to take with us.*"

From that weekly wage was deducted board and lodgings, but girls of eighteen years or over who worked 48 summer hours or 50 winter hours, was to receive in cash no less than 22s 6d (112 and half new pence).

By the end of December 1941, there were 627 girls working in Leicestershire and Rutland.

The girls could take various proficiency tests, which would allow them to progress after the war: milking and dairy work, general farm work, poultry, tractor driving, fruit work, and pest control. Added examinations allowed a girl to progress to a forewoman.

"*The Land Army gave us bikes, and I used to bicycle home to Hugglescote, about ten miles, in rain, snow, sunshine and darkness: a lot of the journey was through open countryside, but there was no trouble in those days!*"

For those girls working more than twenty miles from home a free rail warrant card was provided. From around 1941 onwards the girls received assistants from an unexpected source.

"*German and Italian prisoners-of-war from nearby camps, one was on a hill at Nanpanton (near to Loughborough), came to help us. The Germans in* particular were very polite, and when we had mucked-out the cowsheds they insisted on wheeling the heavy load and spreading it on the land: everything was recycled.*"

The work for the Land Army girls was physically demanding, but it had its rewards.

"*We were well fed at the hostel, plenty of good farm-food and we always took a big piece of cheese and large chunk of bread with us for a snack during the day.*"

The girls' duties sometimes involved helping in clearing forestland: timber always an important requirement in military and industrial manufacture.

"*Farmer Ken Blood wanted some woodland cut down. The Italian prisoners-of-war felled the trees, and we attached chains to them so that they could be dragged away and loaded for despatch to the mill at Loughborough. We tidied the mess that was left; the Italians weren't as polite as the Germans, and one of them stole my lunch, but my best friend, Hazel, shared her lunch with me.*"

When it came to bagging the potatoes the girls developed a few extra muscles.

"*We were taken to the farm on the back of a horse and cart, but for some reason, every time the horse passed a large log at the side of the lane it bolted and the farmer said: "Hold onto your hats! We filled lots of sacks with potatoes and then carried them on our back to load them onto a truck, it was heavy going but it kept us fit.*"

*Muck spreading.*

*Hoeing.*

In fine weather, harsh weather, sun, snow and wind they worked; in seas of golden grain and quagmires of winter bleakness, but it must also be remembered that farmland had its dangers.

*"Farmer Staniland at Grace Dieu Farm was killed when he was attacked by a bull, and even cows had off days. When I bicycled home I used to pass the ruins of Grace Dieu Priory, often in darkness, there were lots of rumours about ghosts and I was pleased to pass that spot."*

Being in the countryside didn't deny the Luftwaffe: on three occasions the area was bombed, mainly because they were after Castle Donington airfield. One raid saw the old vicarage damaged and the death of a maid there, another cratered some fields and finally, on the night of 10th February thirty incendiary bombs fell in the grounds of Whatton House. In 1941, heavy snow and blizzards prevented access to the village other than by foot, freezing and dangerous times if out in the inky darkness.

On one particular Saturday night in 1943, Olive met Cedric Norman Poole, the local milkman, at the Progressive Hall at Coalville (was behind the Liberal Club). Olive liked to dance, often at the 'Baths', but they arranged to meet again under the Co-Operative clock in Marlborough Square, and invariably took long strolls. They enjoyed following Hugglescote brook and also walks to Heather and district were not uncommon. *"We got married on 23rd December 1943 at Ashby de la Zouch Registry Office, but by then my husband was*

*serving with the Royal Engineers (R.E.M.E.). He was on the tanks at Millhill, London, but also travelled to Egypt and Jerusalem."*

Cedric's parents, from Ellistown, were William Henry Poole and Jane (nee Oxford), and he was born on 9th October 1922. As a family they lived at 156, Ashburton Road, Hugglescote, and for a while after marriage that is where Olive and Cedric lived.

*Olive and Cedric Poole on their wedding day.*

*"I left the Land Army in early 1944 and started work at Dunlop, on Bridge Road, Coalville. Dunlop built aeroplane engines and was where the old Technical College stood. I worked nights but after a while I had to leave because I couldn't stand the smell of paraffin or night work."*

As mentioned earlier, Olive was born at 7, Breach Road, and her parents informed her that the house next door was for sale: No 9.

*"It was too good an opportunity to let slip, so we moved there, and our children were all born at Coalville Nursing Home on London Road. Janet was*

*born on 30th September 1945, she is married to Gordon Mugglestone and they live at Ellistown. Vivien was born on 23rd August 1948, she is married to Alan Howson and they live at Hull, while Lynne, born 11th May 1952, is married to Bagworth born Paul Goacher and they live at Hugglescote."*

*Nearest the camera, 9 Breach Road.*

After the war, Cedric returned to the Co-Operative, but, using his engineering knowledge, was then employed as a mechanic in their garage on Owen Street. On leaving Breach Road, they lived at 16, Bakewell Street for a short time, but found greater happiness at 51, Wentworth Road: living there for fifty-three years.

Olive's father died at Markfield Hospital on 23rd May 1959; her mother, Sarah in February 1979. When Cedric retired, he and Olive had a splendid time: walks in Derbyshire, etc, ballroom dancing, supporting and loving their enlarging family: *"I love all of my family, they mean the world to me!"*

Cedric also loved watching football, cricket, and all forms of sport. Olive suffered a 'stroke' in November 2003, and while awaiting a bungalow at St. Mary's Court, lived for a spell with her daughter, Lynne. They lived contentedly until Lynne found her father; he had passed away on 2nd May 2006 and is buried in Hugglescote Cemetery.

Olive, looking at least a decade younger than her age is very well cared for and recently received her commemorative medal and citation. The medal: awarded to those who served in the 'Women's Land Army and Timber Corps', was minted by 'Firmin & Sons Ltd (1677), appointed to the Queen. The citation,

signed by Prime Minister Gordon Brown:

*'The Government wishes to express to you its profound gratitude for your unsparing efforts as a loyal and devoted member of the Women's Land Army and Women's Timber Corps at a time when our country depended upon you for its survival."*

*Olive and daughter, Lynn.*

The Coalville Times of 15th August 2008 carries a picture of a gathering of local ex-W.L.A. girls. They had listened to David Taylor M.P. give a moving speech about their fine W.W. 2 efforts. Two of the local girls: Olive Watkins from Heather and Eileen Callaghan from Ibstock said it was just like old times. They had worked together as threshers on Cattow's Farm, and expressed their delight at the recognition. Olive, aged eighty-four, said that they worked very hard and would cycle around to various farms to work. They often worked from 7.00am to 8.00pm, and then the farmer would come out and say: *'Come on you dozy mares, you can go now.'* Olive says that there was a great spirit between them all and that's what kept them going. Olive continued by saying: *"Its lovely that we're now receiving some credit but its also a bit sad that other Land Girls who have now passed away can't receive this recognition."* Eileen Callaghan adds: *"There wasn't a fat lot to do back then, not like it is for younger people now, so we didn't really mind. We'd save our pennies from the week and take a bus into Burton to watch the movies at the cinema. They were wonderful times considering what was going on."*

A slightly earlier edition of the Coalville Times featured Coalville's Mrs. Jean Brauer of Verdon Crescent. Jean enlisted at the age of eighteen into The

*David Taylor and Land Girls in 2008.*
*(My thanks to the Coalville Times).*

*Mrs. Jean Brauer as she was in 1946.*
*(My thanks to the Coalville Times).*

W.L.A. in 1946 and was stationed in a farm at Melton Mowbray. *"I earned £2 per week and worked alongside German prisoners-of –war, even though the war was over. We were up early and did all general farm work, fetching and milking, whatever farmers wanted us to do."*

Mary Crowson (as World War 2) from Thringstone was another W.L.A. girl.

With special thoughts for Olive Poole and other Leicestershire W.L.A. girls I now print their W.W.2 song: it was written by W.L.A. girl, P. Adkins and the music by W.L.A. E. K. Loring.

Many thanks to Olive Poole and her daughter, Lynn Goacher for their assistance.

### Back To The Land

Back to the Land, we must all lend a hand,
To the farms and the fields we must go.
There's a job to be done, though we can't fire a gun
We can still do our bit with the hoe.
When your muscles are strong
You will soon get along,
And you'll think a country life's grand.
We're all needed now
We must all speed the plough,
So come with us back to the Land.
Back to the Land, with its clay and its sand,
Its granite and gravel and grit,
You grow barley and wheat
And potatoes to eat
To make sure the nation keeps fit.
Remember the rest
Are all doing their best,
To achieve the results they have planned.
We will tell you once more,
You can help win the war
If you come with us back to the Land.

# THE SCOTT FAMILY DURING WAR & PEACE

Readers of my earlier books will be aware of the above family, but for the unfamiliar I will digress a little. The story begins with Walter Vernon Scott, Station Master of Coalville East Railway Station. He had four sons with his first wife, Kate, and two with his second, Elizabeth. First born was: Walter (1887-1962), then Len George (1889-1946), who emigrated to the United States of America but returned to fight for his country. Frederic (no K.1893-1918) was educated at Cambridge University and won the Military Cross in the Leicestershire Regiment; Captain F. Scott was captured in May 1918 and died in captivity. Clifford Ernest (1895-1915), one of the 'Famous Fifty' lost his life in Flanders during an enemy artillery bombardment. Robert (1900-1977) served under-age on minesweepers in the Royal Navy Volunteer Reserve, and finally William (Bill) Franklin Scott (1905-1994).

On 26th December 1923, Robert Scott, relief Station Master at Coalville East Railway Station, married Lillian (Queenie) Gwendolyn Underwood. In 1925, he became full Station Master after his father's retirement, and happily, Doreen, their first child, was born 24th August 1927.

His parents had retired to Southsea, and when his father informed him that the fine job of landlord of 'The Eastney Tavern' was in the offing, he immediately applied, got the job and moved to the south coast. The Tavern stands on Cromwell Road (near to the Marine Barracks). On 29th January 1932, Anthony (Tony) was born, and one year later on 12th July 1933, Barrie. In 1936 Robert Scott and family

moved to 7, Jubilee Road at Portchester, seven kilometres inland and on Portsmouth Harbour.

The Tavern was in the 'Portsmouth News' newspaper in May 2003. It published a photograph of the 'famous shell wall' at the rear of the public house. Roy contacted the newspaper and informed them that it was his uncle, Robert Scott, who had positioned the thousands of decorative shells. Still in fine condition, the shells were gathered from Southsea beach.

## Who built the shell wall?

On the *Pictures from the Past* page for February 23, we published a photograph of the famous shell wall at the rear of Eastney Tavern in Cromwell Road, Southsea. The sender, Mr RS Marsh, of Cardiff, said it was built by his grandfather, Mr H Davies, of Eastney.

Roy Scott, of Southsea, says this is not so, and that the shell wall was built by his uncle, Robert Scott, a former licensee of the Eastney Tavern.

Roy has provided this photograph of Robert Scott and the wall with a cutting featuring it in an early 1930s copy of the *Portsmouth Evening News*. Evidently, Mr Scott had help in building the wall from his father, Walter Vernon Scott, who was the creator of the shell gardens.

Roy's cousin, Mrs Doreen Collier, of North Yorkshire, the eldest daughter of Robert Scott, believes her father possibly engaged Mr Davies for further work in the garden.

The shells came from Southsea beach.

*Robert Scott by the shell wall that he made in the early 1930's.*

Robert, educated at Coalville Grammar School and Cambridge University (like his elder brother), took employment as an estate agent and life for the family was idyllic, especially so for the lads. Tony and Barrie played all around Portchester Castle and the Creek, they were inseparable, and also enjoyed the concerts that Doreen performed in the garage and, in later years, continued on a larger amateur stage.

*Barrie and Tony Scott in the rear garden of the Tavern. Circa 1935.*

1939 saw dramatic changes: especially for the children. First, Grandfather Walter Vernon Scott died: he rests in Milton Cemetery, Portsmouth. Secondly, everyone was provided with a gas mask, much to the

*The Eastern Tavern at Southsea. Robert Scott was Landlord in the 1930's.*

Queenie with Barrie (middle) and Tony on the right, also a girl cousin. Porchester, 1937.

amusement of the siblings who used the masks to make rude noises.

It was anticipated that Germany would direct air raids over Great Britain, and nowhere was considered to be safe from bombing. As a precaution some neighbours on Jubilee Road were provided with fire buckets and stirrup pumps, although some buckets contained sand. The contents were to be used to smother incendiary bombs, and the said houses possessed such gate signs as: 'S.P. HERE'. For greater security the majority of folk dug reinforced shelters in their gardens, namely: 'Anderson shelters'.

Central: The home of Robert, Queenie, Tony and Barrie: 7 Jubilee Road, Porchester from 1936 - 40. Photograph taken in 2004.

I am told that one neighbour refused to have her decorative garden ruined by any such action and often declared: *"Those wicked bastards!"* That same lady insisted on having her alcoholic evening beverage in spite of the situation; her hapless husband had to venture out even amid raids to fetch her Guinness from an off-licence. There were no streetlights and potholes were aplenty on the unadopted road.

Robert and Queenie Scott instructed the children never to pick up anything from the streets; there was always the possibility that even innocent objects, such as pens or pencils, could be booby-trapped! Barrie and Tony continued to go to the local school, although much of their school-time was spent in air-raid shelters. The horror and realism of war became fact during a surprise low-level raid when they witnessed some of their friends machine-gunned and killed in the school playground! They also saw other children machine-gunned as they ran home from school. During one raid a German bomber crashed onto the school grounds. Upon hearing the explosion from the safety of her home-shelter, Queenie ran all the way to the school to find out if her children were safe.

Officials tried to stop her but she ignored them, and only took cover on seeing that they were safe and secure. Ironically, after raids, children ran and try to locate incendiary bombs, simply because they were given two old pence for each one by Air Raid Precaution (A.R.P.) officials. As a precaution against an enemy sea-borne invasion the harbour front was blocked-off from the general public, also, anti-aircraft guns became a common sight: some were dummy guns made from camouflaged entrenched telegraph poles.

Robert, with no requirement for estate agents, was helping the war effort by working at the Ordnance Depot at Portsmouth.

A suburb of Southsea in August 1940. Note the safety of the Anderson Shelter that stands firm despite the bomb damage.

Throughout the Battle of Britain (July 18th - end of October 1940), the Scott family spent many hours living and sleeping in their Anderson shelter.

Dogfights, a term used to describe the R. A. F's Hurricanes and Spitfires as they intercepted the massive enemy bomber and fighter formations, were a regular daytime occurrence. The Luftwaffe also came over at night, primarily to bomb the docklands of Portsmouth and Southampton, however, targets were never easy to identify and civilian casualties began to rise rapidly. Barrie Scott describes some scenes: *"In our shelter you could hear the whistle of the bombs as they came down; then the loud explosions and the ground around us used to shake! You could hear the blasts from our Ack-Ack guns, and we were proud of them fighting back for us. During periods of relative quiet either Dad or Mum would rush into the house to prepare meals or drinks. Then, following a spell of heavy rain our shelter became flooded and so we had no alternative but to go into our house and shelter under the stairs. It was a very frightening time to hear the bombs and later see all the devastation."*

There were some lighter moments, especially when neighbours were so united and helping each other, and they also helped themselves to something of a military nature, and who could blame them! Barrie:

*"I recall an occasion when a large silk barrage balloon: they were used to keep enemy aircraft from flying low, became disconnected from its wire cable, and the sea breeze snared it onto the house opposite. When the police and the R.A.F. men came to collect it they found most was missing: neighbours had cut chunks of silk off to make under-clothing."*

In the later summer of 1940, amid fears of a German invasion, our government decreed that where possible children should be sent overseas for their own safety. Winston Churchill was against it, yet, within three weeks over two hundred thousand parents applied. This meant a hazardous ocean journey and the dangers of enemy submarines. The scheme was swiftly discarded when torpedoes sank two ships carrying evacuees to Canada. All three hundred and twenty aboard: 'Volendom' were rescued, but seventy-seven children aboard: 'The City of Benares' drowned! Among those who successfully went overseas were Shirley Williams, Elizabeth Taylor and the missing or late Lord Lucan.

A pregnant Queenie Scott showed admirable common sense in disallowing her children from travelling abroad, but did stress that it was time to move to a safer Leicestershire. In late 1940, they moved-in with her parents (Underwood) at Coalville, and Anne was born on 22nd July 1941. Robert initially obtained employment at a local munitions factory, soon becoming an inspector, and then joined the office staff of R. J. Kemp, an electrical firm.

He then rented a house for his family in the Market Place of Whitwick, with the children attending 'St. John The Baptist Church of England School and Bible Class'. Soon Barrie and Tony were choristers, and remained so for several years.

Robert, intelligent and talented supported the: 'Three Crowns P.H. Forces' Comfort Fund', by writing poems under the pen name 'Blue Orchids'. These excellent poems were printed and sold heavily in support of the fund. In addition dance-band nights were arranged with his lads helping to sell tickets. Also, after junior school lessons, the two lads, together with schoolmates, helped to dig for potatoes on the Whitwick Park allotments, picked rose-hips and got involved with 'Dig For Victory' events: general fund raising for the war effort.

Tony Scott.

In June 1950, Tony volunteered for national service with the R. A. F. and altogether served for nearly five years, finishing in January 1955. He was stationed at Wellesbourne, about five kilometres east of Stratford-on-Avon, Warwickshire. In his later years he was involved with Whitwick Scouts and Youth Club. Barrie dreamt of being in the Marine Corps; regrettably, he suffered a life-threatening illness in his late teens and could no longer achieve the high physical requirements. He married the delightful June Irene Gee on 28th May 1955.

*Doreen Scott.*

Doreen's husband, Terry Collier, was stationed in Malta for his national service commitment.

Queenie died on 13th May 1959, aged only fifty-five years, and Robert married again to Clarice Goddard. They shared many years of happiness until he died in 1977, aged seventy-seven years. Clarice died in 1986.

William Franklin Scott (Bill), youngest of the six brothers was born at Coalville in 1905. He married Gladys Chambers in 1927 and they had two children, Alma and Roy, before moving to Southsea, later having another daughter, Wendy. Bill was a professional and successful musician with his own orchestra. One day, a colonel with the local territorial battalion sought out his professional services. Bill joined the battalion and when it mobilised in 1939 he was drafted into the Medical Corps. In 1940, he suffered severe head injuries in an accident and was invalided out of the Corps the same year. Bill's family,

with the exception of Roy, returned to Leicestershire, settling at Blaby, about five kilometres south from the capital city. He worked for Power Jet at nearby Whetstone, and before long set-up a dance-band that eventually played at numerous county venues: so improving morale and brightening the gloom of the war years.

As mentioned, Roy stayed at his grandparent's house with his grandmother, Elizabeth Scott. The house: 33, Fordingbridge Road, Eastney is right on the southern tip of Langstone Harbour and opposite to Hayling Island, in the thick of the war, but Roy was intrigued by the heroics and skill of the Few, as they defended their mother country. During the war his grandmother billeted sailors and marines. In 1942, Roy, understandably so, joined the R. A.F. and became a fighter pilot, flying Spitfires in both the Middle East and the Far East. During that time his father carried Roy's photograph (as seen in this book) in his wallet: safe and secure.

*Roy Scott: serving as a fighter pilot in the Far East in 1944.*

In 1947, Bill, Gladys, and their two daughters returned to Southsea. Roy lives there to this day. Alma married and emigrated to Australia, Roy remained single and Wendy married an officer in the Royal Navy. Barrie and June took a delightful two-week honeymoon at Eastney.

Bill Scott died in 1994 aged eighty-nine years, Gladys departed in 2000.

Knowing the Scott family have suffered such tragedies in times of war; I have to convey that since writing: *'Fifty Good Men And True'*, tragedy has spilled over in times of peace. David Andrew Scott: born 1st May 1965, the elder son of Barrie and June, loved his motorbikes. He knew their styles and powers, and everything about them enthralled him.

*David Scott and motorbike at his parent's home: 16th August 2003.*

He was very well known within the 'biker fraternity', they knew him as Scottie. He loved taking part in biker activities, often for charities, and was always part of the swell that attended race meetings at Donington Park and other venues. He was a caring person, for instance, if he didn't see his parents for two days he had to ring to check they were well. He was loved as boy and adult, and known as someone who would always help others; he being in St. John's Ambulance Brigade as a teenager illustrates this. David married Mandy in July 2005, and two weeks before their first Anniversary he was killed on the way to work at Caterpillar, Desford.

He was one minute from his workplace when a car pulled-out from a side-road into his pathway; David died within minutes after suffering massive internal injuries, aged forty-one years. At his funeral, which was attended by many bikers, his wife said: *'Having met and married David, I now know that nice men still exist!'*

I am indebted to June and Barrie Scott for the information and photographs. The quality of the storyline reflects the obvious quality in two very fine and brave people. The Scott story started in the nineteenth century and continues into the twenty-first, and long may it last. God bless David, his latest family recruit. Suddenly, Tony Scott passed away on 22nd May 2008.

*The grave of David Andrew Scott. 1st May 1965 - 16th June 2006*

*' A smile for all, a heart of gold, one of the best this world could hold. Never selfish, always kind, what a beautiful son to have to leave this world behind.'*

# OUR JACK'S DIARY
## The diary of Jack Rowland Simpson
### Edited by his nephew: Brian Simpson

*'John' Simpson.*

Brian Simpson:

"*The following extracts are taken from a tiny notebook: only four x five inch when opened; very faded, pages missing and sometimes with ink running. I have copied the parts not relating to family news and personal details, and alongside are explanatory notes for readers who may not understand military and World War 2 references. It was against orders to keep diaries, however, my uncle decided to. He was much younger than my father, indeed, I was called-up in 1945 into the Queen's Bays and 1st Dragoon Guards. Jack originally enlisted into the South Staffordshire Regiment, not the Staffordshire Yeomanry that represented the Tank Unit. Uncle was a brilliant wireless-operator and was transferred to the 13/18th Hussars (Queen Mary's Own), with whom he went to France on 'D'-Day. His unit was among the first to land: going ashore in DD tanks, which 'swam' (propelled) themselves onto the invasion beaches. Uncle finished the war as a sergeant and passed away in 1991. When his wife followed in 2000 the Diary was* passed onto me. I contacted Mr. Pat Hennessey of the 13/18th Hussars and also Nancy Langmaid, a researcher at the Tank Museum. A copy of what follows is now in the Tank Museum Archives."
(Comments by Pat Hennessey 'P.H.', those by Nancy Langmaid 'NL'.)

**Jack's Diary**
**19th January 1944. Wednesday**. *Mobing started.*
(P.H. We mobilised at Fort George at Inverness in January. Very cold and the barracks were ancient: once home of the Seaforth Highlanders. Every morning bagpipes played Reveille).

**20th January. Thursday.** *Transferred to Recce Troop as guard*.
(N.L. Reconnaissance or scouting troops are always at the front: looking for trouble).

**21st January. Friday.** *Going on a course called Stuart Course on Monday.*
    (P.H. The '*Stuart*', a U.S.A. Tank M5, also known as '*Honey*', was smaller and lighter than the '*Sherman*', but similar in shape. Introduced with the '*Grant*' into Desert War in late 1941. By 1944 it was used almost exclusively for reconnaissance and was popular with the troops).

**23rd January. Sunday.** *Moved to Fort George.*

**24th January. Monday.** *Left camp at 1900 for Bridlington and stayed at Carlisle overnight.*
(N.L. Bridlington: many seaside resorts became training areas in the War).

**25th January. Tuesday.** *Changed at Leeds, arrived by train at Bridlington at 1600.*

**2nd February 1944.** Wednesday. *Moving back to Fort George tomorrow.*

**3rd February. Thursday.** *Left Bridlington at 11.55 got as far as Edinburgh by 21.15. No trains till morning so stayed at Y.M.C.A.*

**4th February. Friday.** *Left Edinburgh at 0845, changed at Perth, arrived at Inverness at 16.00. Wait until 18.00. Snowed very heavily. Arrived camp 19.00. Clean up, inspection tomorrow.*

**5th February. Saturday.** *Inspected by General Montgomery C in C. Very cold day. Preparing and loading for exercise 'Crown'.* (P.H. On parade very early and ground was marked out with white tapes to ensure our lines were straight when we fell in. Our regimental sergeant major was very active and concerned. When Montgomery arrived he didn't even look at us, but climbed onto bonnet of his jeep and asked us to gather round).

**6th February. Sunday.** *Reveille 05.00. Breakfast 06.00. Left 07.00. Loaded on LCT at 11.00. Gale blowing, sea very rough. Spent all day on boat. Too rough to carry on, disembarked at 17.00. Exercise postponed for 24 hours, so start again tomorrow as per this morning.* (LCT is a Landing Craft Tank).

**7th February. Monday.** *Weather still as bad, so exercise is postponed for another 24 hours.*
(P.H. This exercise continued at Invergordon; the hard training at sea went on until March. It is described in my book: 'Young Man In A Tank' page 48).

**8th February. Tuesday.** *Weather improving. Standing by to load up some time today, we finally loaded at 19.00 and set sail. Weather turned rough again but we carried on. Many seasick, I was O.K. but felt a bit queer.*

**9th February. Wednesday.** *'H' is 08.28. Due to land at 'H' plus 40. DD Tanks had a rough landing: two sank, others damaged, crews saved. One man run over and killed by tank. Several infantry drowned. No casualties in our unit. Fought our way inland, captured our objective and harboured for the night.* (N.L. 'H' hour stands for time of invasion, so twenty-eight minutes after eight. 'D' stands for the day of the invasion; hence 'D' Day plus 6 is six days after the event. 'DD' Tanks

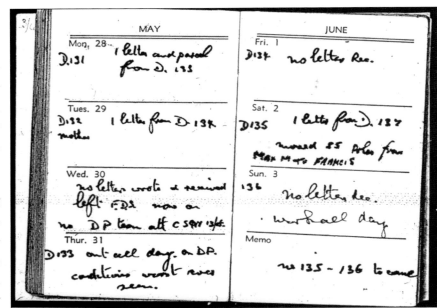

Pages from John Simpson's diary.

means 'Duplex Drive': tanks capable of switching the power from 'tracks for land' to 'propeller for water'. They had heavy canvas screens all around, held to the top of the gun turret by hydraulically inflated tubes, and so could operate as boats. The top of the tube just showed, and the tank commander could view from his turret; once on land he dropped the screen. Most DD's were 'Sherman's', but the design was British, another of Hobart's 'Funnies'! The Americans did not use DD's or Flail tanks).

**10th February 1944. Thursday.** *We were counter-attacked at dawn, beaten off, our advance continued. Exercise ended at 13.00. Went back, camped by road, arrived teatime, very tired.*

**11th February. Friday.** *Maintenance work all day.*

**12th February. Saturday.** *A lecture of French coast defences. French maps. Maintenance work. Ex: Anchor due to start on 22nd.* (P.H. Models were made of the Atlantic Wall and all aspects of the German defences that we knew of. Pre-war holiday snaps and Michelin maps were sought to give information to our invading troops, but weren't told of the point of invasion).

**15th February. Tuesday.** *Appointed Acting Unpaid Sergeant from 8th February.*

**16th February. Wednesday.** *Guard Duty.*

**18th February. Friday.** *Final sealing for*

*waterproofing tank; done with rubber pieces and Bostik laced with small explosive charges, so seals can be blown off when on dry land. Done for 'Operation Anchor'.*

**19th February. Saturday.** *Moving to Clachnaharry Point for loading. Rained all day. Left Fort at 15.00 and arrived at Box 107 at 19.30.* (Box: defined military area).

**20th February. Sunday.** *Remained in Box all day: maintenance.*

**21st February. Monday.** *Reveille at 3.30. Left Box at 5.55. Loaded on LCT 107 at 08.15 and spent all day on boat.*

**22nd February. Tuesday.** *Weather turned very rough. Sea Rough: seasick. Landed at 09.40. Joined RHQ and spent all day with them.* (P.H. RHQ: Regimental Headquarters: a troop of 3-4 tanks with commanding officer and adjutant).

**23rd February. Wednesday.** *Scheme ended. Convoyed D. Drive tanks down to beach to load on LCT. Went back to camp by road and arrived afternoon.* ((Scheme: military exercises).

**Diary pages for 24-28th missing.**

**29th February. Tuesday.** *DD Squadrons exercises.* (P.H. Squadron: 4 troops of 3 or 4 tanks each, usually about 15 tanks. Jack was in a reconnaissance troop with RHQ Squadron. The *'Sabre'* Squadrons were 'A' 'B' and 'C').

**1st March 1944. St. David's Day. Wednesday.** *Squadrons landed in a blizzard, two tanks lost, one man lost, others survived but injured. The first man to be lost in our regiment.* (P.H. Two tanks sank: one commanded by Corporal Sweetapple/ other by Corporal Underhay (drowned).

**8th March. Wednesday.** *Watch naval demonstration from destroyers and LCT.* (P.H. The LCT fired about 1,000 rockets simultaneously, very dramatic on 'D'-Day.

**10th March. Friday.** *We watch Exercise 'B' vehicles. Poor show!* (N.L. 'B' vehicles delivered petrol, water, food, ammunition, ambulance, fitters, etc, to serve *'Sabre'* squadrons. Went onto battlefield at night because they had no armour. 'B' echelons were a very brave people).

**11th March. Saturday.** *Ex PHILCO operation for 'A' Squadron leaders.*

**13th March. Monday.** *Left camp at 13.00 for Tain. Snowed all the way. Very cold journey and landed at 18.30.* (P.H. Tain: an R.A.F. station in the north of Scotland where we stayed for two days. Surprised to learn that airmen had sheets on their beds: we had two horse-blankets each. Also at reveille a soft, female WAAF voice spoke: *"Good morning boys, time to get up."* What a difference from the shouting of an angry orderly sergeant).

**14th March. Tuesday.** *Spent all day on gunnery ranges, snow and very cold.*

**15th March. Wednesday.** *Same as yesterday, but got stuck in the mud, it is very bad. Nearly got shot up by a 75mm gun!* (P.H. The main gun of a Sherman tank).

**16th March. Thursday.** *Turned a lot warmer. Stunt* ended *tonight.* (Stunt: an exercise)

**17th March. Friday.** *Left for Fort George at 09.00 and landed at 13.30. Maintenance all afternoon, bath and bed early.*

**18th March. Saturday.** *Going on leave today: left Fort George at 14.30 and Inverness at 16.20.*

**19th March. Sunday.** *Arrived Nuneaton at 07.30 and at home (Hinckley) for 09.00.*

**28th March. Tuesday.** *Last day of leave. Very sorry. Left Nuneaton at 14.00 and arrived at Crewe 16.00. Left Crewe at 17.30: train over one hour late.*

**29th March. Wednesday.** *Changed Perth at 13.30 and arrived at Inverness 19.30 Very tired and fed up. Had letters from Tom and Henry.*

**30th March. Thursday.** *Guard duty. Wrote to Henry Rhodes (trooper 5050940), 'A' Squadron, 46 RTR CMF.* (N.L. Central Mediterranean Forces. 46 RTR was the Tank unit at Anzio).

**31st March. Friday.** *Warned I'm to go with an advance party to (can't say).*

**1st April 1944. Saturday.** *Left Fort George at 07.00 and arrived at Wishaw (Glasgow) at 18.30, stayed night.*

**2nd April. Sunday.** *Set off at 08.00, moved all morning and nearly all afternoon. Raining. Arrived Preston at 19.00.*

**3rd April. Monday.** *Set off at 08.00, moved all morning and most of afternoon. Arrived at Lutterworth at 06.30, only ten miles from home and very disappointed that I can't get there!*

**4th April. Tuesday.** *Set off at 08.30 and left in convoy. Arrived at Guildford at 15.00 and onto Petworth Station to pick up rail party. Found camp just over two miles from Petworth.*

**5th April. Wednesday.** *Checking and taking over camp, same for 6th. Jeep arrived on 9th.*

**10th April Monday.** *Troopers Wheals and Hind smash up the jeep with Hind taken to hospital and Wheals put under arrest.*

**14th April. Friday.** *Left camp at 13.00 to fetch tanks and stopped at Stevenage for night.*

**15th April. Saturday.** *Picked up tanks at Hatfield, very surprised, they are M3 A1s and don't think much of them.* (P.H. American M3 'Grants' had a small turret cannon with a machine-gun and 75mm gun in a sponson in the hull: so main gun has some elevation but no traverse).

**16th April. Sunday.** *Arrived safely back at camp just after tea. Tired and ready for bed. Troopers Wheals and Hind both fined £4.*

Gap in Diary until 2nd May.

**2nd May 1944.** *Went out on Ex FABULOUS.* (P.H. Exercise Fabulous was one of many exercises we undertook. Having trained very hard for our seaborne landing in Scotland, we now trained as a normal tank regiment fighting on land).

**8th May. Monday.** *Left camp to go firing at Lydd (Kent). Stayed out all night.*

**9th May. Tuesday.** *Arrived at Lydd 15.00, and fired all the following day.*

**11th May. Thursday.** *Fired up until 17.00 and then set off for camp.*

**12th May. Friday.** *Arrived back at camp 13.00.*

**14th May. Sunday.** *Left camp again for Brigade Workshops for modification.* (P.H. Usually three Regiments to a Brigade. In this case: 13/18 Hussars, Staffordshire Yeomanry and East Riding Yeomanry formed 27th Armoured Brigade. Hussars later transferred to 8th Brigade).

**26th May. Friday.** *Camp is sealed.* (P.H. No person allowed to enter or leave, no post at all, no telephones: fear that 'D'-Day secrets may be leaked).

**29th May. Monday.** *All tanks have sealing completed and ready to move.*

**30th May. Tuesday.** *Left camp at 13.00.*

**3rd June 1944. Sunday.** *Left assembly area at 16.00. Loaded on LCT 323 at Newhaven in Sussex at 19.00.* (P.H. Jack embarked from Newhaven; the two DD Squadrons: 'A' and 'B' left from Gosport (Hampshire). 4th June. Sunday. *Still in harbour.* (Jack has placed a four-leaf clover in his diary).

**5th June. Monday.** *Left harbour at 10.00 for (can't say). Sea is very rough. Very seasick.*

Back row. Sergeants Bennett, Martin, Richards and SQMS Pack. Front row. Sergeants John Simpson, SSM Cooke, Sergeant Partlow and SQMS Lymm. Sergeants Mess at GOCH. March 1945.

**6th June. Tuesday. 'D'-Day.** *Landed in France at Lion-sur-Mer at 10.00. Opposition slight except for shelling.* (Gap until 11th June)

**11th June. Sunday.** *RTU* (Returned to Unit) *and went to Brigade Workshops for repair to power traverse* (for turning turret).

**16th June. Friday.** *Back with Unit from LAD* (Light Aid Detachment: repair team). *Turret removed* (shell blasted off), *Penny killed, Pimblet and Beattie injured.* (P.H. Trooper J. Penny killed at Douvres-la-Delivrande. Trooper Pimblet was one of twins, twin recently died).

**17, 18, 19th. June.** *Shelled.*

**20th June. Tuesday.** *Went to DZ Area. Shelled.* (P.H. 'Drop Zone Area', probably used by 6th Airborne Reconnaissance Regiment on 'D'-Day when they parachuted/gliders into the Area and took Pegasus Bridge. 6AARR included glider-borne tanks).

**21st June. Wednesday.** *Went to LAD for modifications.*

**22nd June. Thursday.** *Mod completed and RTU.*

**1st July 1944.** *Joined Gordon Highlanders at Longvil.*

**3rd July. Monday.** *Left the line for our first rest.*

**4th July. Tuesday.** Arrived at Luc-sur-Mer for rest.

**7th July. Friday.** *Left Luc-sur-Mer at 23.00 for front. Arrived 03.00.* (P.H. I'm surprised at no mention of the massive R.A.F. air raid on Caen that we witnessed from Luc-sur-Mer).

**8th & 9th July.** Saturday & Sunday. *Battle for Caen lasted until late on 9th.*

**17th July. Monday.** *Big attack for Falaise by 3 Corps. Not a success. We took 96 other ranks and six officers as prisoners.*

**27th July. Thursday.** *Took out of line for refit and rest.*

**29th July. Saturday.** Gone back into line!!! *Moved up to attack Evrecy.* (N.L. Evrecy must be a village in the locality of Tilly-sur-Seulles in Normandy where the regiment was attacking.

**30th July. Sunday.** *Attack started, I'm in reserve with 'B' squadron. Hit by shrapnel in right hip and taken to hospital.*

**31st July. Monday.** *In a field hospital, being taken home tomorrow.*

**1st August 1944.Tuesday.** *Left France on 'Duke of Rothsea' at 10.00. Landed at Southampton at 18.00. Taken to Canadian General Hospital at Farnborough. X rayed. Everything O.K?*

**2nd August. Wednesday.** *X ray shows chip of bone, very painful.*

**4th August. Friday.** *Left Farnborough.*

**5th August. Saturday.** *Arrived at Broad Green Hospital, Liverpool.*

**8th August. Tuesday.** *Derris* (his wife) *came to see me, very pleased, stopping for a few days. Happy again. Ma and Dad also came.*

**14th August. Monday.** *Moved to Wrexham by bus, very rough ride. Still not allowed to get up.*

**25th August. Friday.** *Went under operation, had seven stitches in my side.*

**2nd September 1944.** Saturday. *Took out 3 stitches.*

**15th September. Friday.** *Arrived at MCD, Trentham Park Camp, SOT.* (P.H. Military Convalescent Depot at Stoke-on-Trent).

**5th November 1944.** *Went to Brancaster Ranges (Norfolk).*

**9th November. Thursday.** *Back from Ranges and going on 14 day embarkation leave on 11th.*

**26th November. Sunday.** *Leave ended, very sorry, had a grand time. Left Nuneaton 19.20 and train late. Arrived at camp at 00.03 on 27th.*

**27th November. Monday.** *Woken up with orders (07.20) that I was on a draft and had to be ready to move at 08.20. Scale 111 France and big shock when told I was going by air. Left Newmarket Aerodrome (Suffolk) at 15.00 and landed at Brussels at 16.30. Staying night.*

**28th November. Tuesday.** *Still at No2 ARU, Vilvord.* (Armoured Reinforcement Unit).

**29th November. Wednesday.** *Left Brussels for 265 FDS Hoousbrook.* (Forward Deliver Squadron. They took replacement tanks up to the frontline). *Arrived at 15.30.*

**30th November. Thursday.** *Still at 265 FDS, Hoousbrook.*

**1st December 1944. Friday.** *Left 265 FDS to rejoin Unit. Reached it at 20.30, back with Reconnaissance troop.*

**3rd December. Sunday.** *Regiment out for a rest.* (Minimal diary reports until February 1945.

**5th February 1945. Monday.** *Rained most of the day, advance party set for Eindhoven.*

**7th February. Wednesday.** *Left at 13.30, raining all afternoon, reached Eindhoven at 23.59.*

**8th February. Thursday.** *Tank broke down, stayed with it all night, no food. Got going at 13.00 and reached unit at 15.00, very tired and hungry*
.

**15th February. Thursday.** *Night scheme. Foggy all day.*

**22nd February. Thursday.** *Sunny and warm all day. R.A.F. busy.*

**1st March 1945. Thursday.** *Advanced party went to Geldern.*

**7th March. Wednesday.** *Moved to Germany, Geldern, no warning.*

**15th March. Thursday.** *Move to Goch, feeling ill, worked till dark, went to bed at 20.30. Sleeping in cellar, not bad.*

**16th March. Friday.** *Feeling a little better. Started with instructions again, worked till dark.*

**17th March. Saturday.** *Feeling a lot better.* 18th March: *Feeling well again.*

**21st March. Wednesday.** *Weather grand. R.A.F. busy.*

**22nd March:** *Still grand, Eindhoven.*

**23rd March. Friday.** *Weather still grand. Big news expected.* (Family: baby on the way. In those days pregnancies were rarely mentioned except obliquely).

**24th March. Saturday.** *The Rhine crossed at 21.00 yesterday. Saw airborne army pass overhead, fine sight.*

**25th March:** *Moving again, left behind on rear party.*

**1st April 1945. Sunday.** *Waiting for lorries until 18.30. Not moving until morning? We crossed Rhine but weather poor, cold and wet.*

**2nd April. Monday.** *Conditions poor, sleeping rough, weather bad. Guard with Ord sergeant.*

**16th April. Monday.** *Moved again, long journey, 110 miles from Bremen.*

**21st April. Saturday.** *Rain most of day. Schools packed up, worse luck!* (Teaching new crews).

**23rd April. Monday.** *Went to pictures for the first time since coming out here.*

**28th April. Saturday.** *Guard duty. Moving out tomorrow. Had an accident, 2nd finger left hand badly damaged and nail to come off!*

**29th April. Sunday.** *Moved to outskirts of Bremen and feeling ' all in', finger very painful.*

**8th May 1945. Tuesday.** *V.E. Day, no holiday for us.*

**9th May. Wednesday.** *Took off fingernail.*

**11th May. Friday.** *Guard duty. Very hot day.*

**20th May. Sunday.** *Warned to move at 21.30.* 21st May: *Reveille at 05.00.*

**21st May. Monday.** *Started moving at 07.30. Picked transport up after about 15 miles and held up by bridges. Stayed on the road all-night and arrived at Hanover just after dinner.*

**25th May. Friday.** *Moved again but only a short distance. Very good billets.*

**30th May. Wednesday.** *Left FDS for DP team attached 'C' Squadron 13/18th.* (P.H. 'Displaced Persons': there were several million at war's end, needed to be fed, deloused and stopped from taking vengeance on the German population until they could be reunited).

**31st May. Thursday.** *Out all day on DP, conditions are worst I have ever seen.*

**10th June 1945. Sunday.** *Worked late repairing a wireless set.*

**26th June. Tuesday.** *Baby daughter, 61/2 lb.* (Brian's cousin, Pauline).

**29th June. Friday.** *Letter from mother telling the long awaited news, that I'm now proud father of daughter. God bless Derris.*

**1st July 1945. Sunday.** *Moved some Italians.*

**8th July:** *Going on leave tomorrow.*

**9th July. Monday.** *Set off at 11.00 for 42 RHU* (Replacement Holding Unit), *Hanover. Truck to Osnabrook.*

**10th: July. Tuesday.** *Left Osnabrook at 11.00, train for Calais and arrived at 06.00.*

**11th July. Wednesday.** *Waited for boat until 12.30, landed at 16.00. Finally arrived home at 21.00 and had a glorious leave.*

**21st July. Saturday.** *Leave due to end but have 48 hour extension and very happy about it. 'Pauline' is Christened. Disappointed and unhappy to go back.*

**23rd July. Monday.** *Going back, downhearted and sorry to leave the best two people in the whole world. Left Nuneaton 18.45. Left London 21.30 to arrive at Folkestone 01.30. Stayed till 08.20 then got boat to Calais. Train left there at 17.00.*

**25th July. Wednesday.** *Arrived at Hanover 15.00. Went to 42 RHU and reached Unit at 19.00.*

**26th July. Thursday.** *Went back to HQ. Bags of Bull.*

**28th July. Saturday.** *Brigade Sports and Regiment won.*

**2nd August 1945. Thursday.** *Working like hell all day, again. Tanks inspected by Co, all OK.*

**3rd August. Friday.** *Handed 4 tanks to 4/7th DG. Visited by Prince Regent of Greece.*

**9th August. Thursday.** *Football match in afternoon. Beat 113 WFA 14-3.*

**15th August. Wednesday.** *Jap War has ended. Roll on Civvy Street. Squadron photograph.*

**20th August. Monday.** *Ceremonial Parade through Hanover. On Military Guard for 24 hours.*

**31st August. Friday.** *Credit of £17/17/00.* (Undrawn pay usually held for going on leave).

**12th September 1945.** Wednesday. *Out on firing range all day near to Belsen.* (The concentration camp was next to the military training area of Bergen).

**22nd September. Saturday.** *Swimming all afternoon. Opera at night, Carmen.*

**23rd September. Sunday.** *Regimental Church Parade. On guard at Hanover prison 24 hours.*

**26th September. Wednesday.** *Went to Football match, Wolves v Combined Services X1.*

**27th September. Thursday.** *Took over job of Mess caterer in Sergeants' Mess.*

**16th October 1945. Tuesday.** Farewell party. (For men going home on demobilisation).

**30th October. Tuesday.** *Took over Mortar Troop.*

**15th November. Thursday.** *Set off on leave. Arrived Hanover 33 RFU at 12.00.*

**16th November. Friday.** *Left 33 'Replacement Holding Unit' at 01.00. Train to Hanover 03.00, arrived Hook of Holland 16.00.*

**17th November. Saturday.** *Landed at Harwich 08.00, London at 10.00 and home 14.00.*

**29th November. Thursday.** *Left home at 10.00. Nuneaton at 11.00. London at 13.30. Harwich at 16.30, and boat at 19.00.*

**30th November. Friday.** *Hook of Holland at 08.00. Train at 10.00. Back at camp for 16.00.*

**1st December 1945.** *Left Hanover at 13.00. Back at camp 16.00.*

**3rd December. Monday.** *'Got a house!'* I'm Acting SSM. (Severe housing shortage after the war: the house was in Hinckley. Acting Squadron Sergeant Major).

**4th December. Tuesday.** *SSM returned. Back with troop, start training tomorrow.*

**5th December. Wednesday.** *At Eindhoven. SSM sick. ASSM again now.*

**7th December. Friday.** *At Hoenbruck. Still snowing.*

**8th December. Saturday.** *Eindhoven. Very cold and still snowing.* See Harry Wortley and Dedication to Tank Crews in Volume 1.

The Diary ended in December 1945.

A poignant memento of how our Armed Forces had to live with the stresses of training and ultimately, warfare! After 'D'-Day, Jack fought his way across France, Belgium and into Germany, and apart from one instance, does not mention the fierce and horrific fighting he took part in. Also, it is clear to understand the raw emotion when he has to return from leave. (Author)

Footnote from Brian: *'Jack's newly formed Armoured Brigade wore a new arm badge that depicted a golden sea horse on a royal blue shield; I am proud to say that I have just received Jack's battered and faded badge from his son: my cousin, Keith. Five of the 13/18th tanks were lost on 'D'-Day: two of which were hit by landing craft.'*

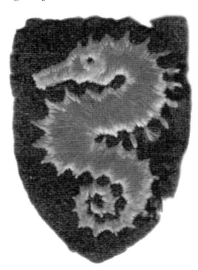

Brian Simpson told me the amazing story about Lawrence Brooksby from Loughborough. It is extracted from the book: 'Tank Warfare in W.W.2', published in 1998 by Constable & Company and printed by kind permission of the author Lieutenant Colonel George Forby.

## The Last Prisoner of War

*'Lawrence Brooksby, ex-3 RTR tank driver from Loughborough in Leicestershire, now lives in Stuttgart (still does in 2008) and describes himself as being: 'The Last British Prisoner of War Left In Germany', but he is not complaining, as he told me: "In December 1944 I was with 3RTR in the Ardennes, and after a short stay at Poperinghe, near Ypres in Belgium, we changed our 'Sherman' tank for a much better tank, the 'Comet'.*

*A few months later we came to Flensburgh, Germany, where I met and later married my German wife. Our two children were both born in England. After living at Flensburgh for twenty years we moved to Stuttgart, where I came into contact with the N.A.T.O. Sergeants' Club, and have been a member for the past seventeen years. I am also a member of the Afrika Korp's Stuttgart Old Comrades' Association, and the RTR Old Comrades Association in England.*

*On my seventieth birthday I received the 'Rommel Medal' in silver and in May 1997 the Bar to the medal. I think I can say I am the only Englishman to have received such awards. Last year, with two German colleagues, Afrika Korps, Stuttgart, sent me to lay wreaths on both German and British graves at Poperinghe and at Cannock Chase, not far from Birmingham. We also laid wreaths on the Blackpool War Memorial during the RTR Reunion in May 1997. As you can imagine I am very proud to have been awarded these medals, so I am a very happy 'prisoner'!'*

My thanks to Brian for all of the above information and photographs. Brian is checking on his ancestry to see if he and my wife, Beryl, are related. Beryl's grandmother, Jane Simpson, came from the Stoney Stanton area but died while giving birth to Beryl's mother, Jenny.

# ARTHUR JOSEPH SMITH
## (Taking off the Gloves)

'Twas on a warm summer's day in 2001: I was with Arthur and his wife, Josephine, as they nostalgically flicked through photographs depicting Arthur's 'ages of man'. An emotive picture punctuated their sighs and pauses; it was taken just before the 1940 Battle of Britain. It displayed the pilots of 74 Squadron (The Tigers), with a certain 'Sailor' Malan, and other heroic men such as Harbourne Stephen, John Mungo-Park and Derek Dowding: son of the magnificent Lord Air Chief Marshal 'Stuffy' Dowding. Arthur pointed to a teenage figure: himself, and then to John Freeborn, a straight-talking Yorkshire-man who flew more combat hours than any other pilot in the 1940 Battle. I interjected by saying that Bob Cossey had recently published an acclaimed book: 'A Tiger's Tale' about John (an old friend of mine), to which he smiled appreciatively. With tongue-in-cheek, I raised the topic about a little known member of the Few: Flight Lieutenant Arthur Smith. Just half a dozen lines and no picture in Kenneth Wynn's: *'Men of the Battle of Britain'*. A modest man, Arthur, and so I asked if it was a time for 'taking off the gloves.'

Sadly, Arthur has now passed on, but Josephine remains a good friend, and only now will Arthur's memoirs be released to the wider public; it is my great honour to do just that.

*Arthur Smith aged three/four.*

*Arthur at the wheel.*

He was not of Leicestershire birth, but over four decades within our county and marriage to a northwest county born wife, justifies entry into this book. Arthur was born on 8th November 1920 at the *'Duke of Lancaster'* public house, New Barnet, where his father, also named Arthur, was the landlord. I shall refer to his father by his nickname 'Joey', a physical training instructor at Woolwich during the Great War, attached to the Royal Horse Artillery. That war ended his boxing career, but what a tremendous career: *'Lightweight Champion of Europe';* his only two defeats were against future world champions. Pre-war he boxed three hundred professional contests, loosing just the aforementioned two on points. Joey was a hard man in the ring, knocking-out most of his opponents, and labelled a box-fighter: very skilful with a big punch and a combination puncher par excellence! It was his trade, yet outside of the ring was amiable and fun loving. His wife, Daisy Rosa Smith (nee Winters), had a dynamic personality, was capable, and very attractive. She held the distinction of being the youngest woman to hold a public house licence in London. Intelligence was also inherent; an elder sister had been headmistress of the City of London School for Girls.

After a few years, Arthur was taken to Woking in Surrey, a fine looking commercial hotel / public house called: *'The Red House Hotel.'* Arthur remembered a striking old building, resplendent in rich red Virginia creeper. At the age of eleven he passed for King Edward V1's Royal Grammar School, and later joined the Scouts, becoming assistant scoutmaster. The summer-term form report for 1934 shows excellence

*A sketch of Arthur's old School, King Edward VI, Guildford.*

in English composition and Literature, the Sciences and Gymnastics. His form-master wrote: '*An efficient form captain, very reliable in work and behaviour,*' and the headmaster: '*A very good worker.*'

Arthur's younger brothers, Norman and Eric wrote: '*Arthur was virtuous and law-abiding, an exemplary student who also watched over the two of us, just like a second father."*

The middle sibling, Norman, admitted to being a wilful, non-conformist and a bit of a handful during his schooldays, adding: "*Arthur was reasonably competent at Maths, Chemistry, Physics, and had tolerable capacity to master the English language. He could not master French and that was to prove an obstacle later in 1940*". As a child, Eric was thought of as being a little vague—living in a world of his own, but his intelligence and diligence enabled the young man to qualify as a general practitioner.

As a youngster, Arthur was a fine all-round sportsman, moreover, being trained by his father he specialised in boxing. Indeed, he was superb and was never beaten in the ring: tall for his age and with a long reach, very agile and possessing sharp reflexes. He won the school's boxing championship when only in year two, defeating an older and two stone heavier opponent in the final!

He developed pneumonia and pleurisy in his last year at school: before the discovery of penicillin. Seriously ill and in hospital, Arthur battled for weeks to survive, the doctors suggesting that his recovery owed much to his excellent physique. Concerning his durability, shortly afterwards he passed a stringent physical examination to enter the Royal Air Force on a short service commission: 1st June 1939. The interview-board considered his boxing as a real plus: '*Someone with guts who could look after one's self in a fight!*'

Of the thirty applicants only Arthur and one other were accepted. Arthur: "*On joining the R.A.F. at eighteen I looked forward to and soon received flight training. I knew a war was coming because Mr Hitler had already entered Czechoslovakia. I just wanted to fly and if I was to serve my country then let it be in the air.*"

Arthur attended No9 and No3 Flying Training Units and trained on Avro Cadets and Harts.

"*I was then sent to Sutton Bridge, by the Wash in East Anglia, and had ninety minutes duel control of an American monoplane, the Harvard. Later, I was nervous when asked to go solo in a Hurricane, but I enjoyed it. It's a lovely aeroplane and much easier to fly than the Spitfire (which he flew in the Battle of Britain), because its wheels are spaced wider apart, and so on landing you could plonk it down, whereas with a Spitfire and it would turn over, you had to treat that with more respect.*"

*Pilot Officer Arthur Smith, 74 Squadron 'The Tigers'. 1940.*

On 13th April 1940, aged eighteen and a pilot officer, he was posted to 'The Tigers': No74 Squadron, at Hornchurch. Squadron Leader, Francis White, swiftly arranged for Arthur to travel by boat and train to Arras, France, because pilots were urgently needed to offset losses during the 'Battle of France'.

"It was a two-day journey; whilst at Amiens staging post, just short of Arras, the troop-train was bombed and many were killed! Stuka dive-bombers did the damage. Five other pilots and myself were in a carriage and the next one carried our kit; this received a direct hit and shattered the windows of ours! On climbing out of the train the Stukas returned and strafed us with machine-gun fire, leaving dead and dying folk all around. We had no means of burying them so we took their identification discs so that their next of kin could be notified.

Another pilot and myself walked into Amiens: all we had were the clothes we were wearing. We reported to the R.T.O. (Rail Transport Officer) who was at a loss to know what to do, saying that Arras had already fallen to the Germans. He advised we travel to Poix airfield, seven miles away, but it was a case of walking, as no transport was available. On arrival at Poix we found the airfield locked-up and deserted. My schoolboy French was awful, and so, with some difficulty, I attempted to find the best way of evading the German Forces. We trudged wearily onwards for two days, sleeping in woodland, ditches and fields, but only for short spells: trying to cover as much ground as was physically possible. Oh! An R.A.F./Army Co-Operation unit came along with two trucks; we'd 'got lucky'. At first the officer was highly suspicious and spent an age checking our papers, and then at long last asked us to climb aboard. They took us to Cherbourg, but we had to wait as the Luftwaffe was bombing the port. As we travelled through the smoking ruins an old tramp steamer pulled alongside the dockland; planking was arranged and with glee we climbed aboard, and went below deck."

Arthur has often told Josephine of the 'silver-service' they received:

"Having just spent two days on the road I looked and felt very rough. I was not hungry: I was simply ravenous! Soon an immaculately dressed steward approached and welcomed us. He bade us a good afternoon and then in turn enquired what we would like to eat (Sir). Anything, I replied, thinking such etiquette was more typical of being off Brighton pier. The steward then impressed upon me that there was a menu, and again asked what would I like to order (Sir). I pointed at something and following a pause he asked: one egg or two (Sir). I politely asked for two, and with

stomach rumbling, thanked him! The old steamer, the very last boat to leave Cherbourg, chugged her way contentedly across the English Channel to the relative safety of England. I entrained to Uxbridge, was fully kitted out, and rejoined 74 Squadron at Rochford, which was Hornchurch's satellite airfield."

Tiger Squadron saw plenty of activity over Dunkirk. Squadron Leader Francis White shared in the destruction of an Hs 126, but was hit by return fire and crash-landed at Calais-Marck airfield. On 22nd May 1940, Flight Lieutenant James Leathart, who flew a Master to Marck and returned under the cover of two Spitfires, bravely rescued him. James Leathart became an ace in the Battle of Britain and later reached air ranking. Arthur:

"I had the immense good fortune of having 'Sailor' Malan as my mentor and flight commander. He was a South African, quietly spoken and fairly easy going when not flying, but in flight was tough and demanding: expecting every man to give of his best."

Malan adjusted the focal-concentration of the Spitfire's eight machine-guns from 200 yards to 50 yards, thus requiring precision flying and shooting: he argued that possessing only 30 seconds worth of ammunition, then every bullet had to count!

"Shortly afterwards over France, I made an attack in tandem with Malan. Nervously I held my finger on the gun button for too long and expended every bullet. A minute later we dived for another attack and I was too afraid to tell my leader, so produced a mock attack against an enemy bomber."

Flight Lieutenant Malan claimed a He111 on the 21st May (unconfirmed), but by the end of Dunkirk had destroyed or damaged ten enemy aircraft: being awarded the D.F.C.

On the 27th May 1940, the Squadron was posted to Leconsfield for a short respite, and Arthur had the happy task of piloting 'Sailor' and his dog, Peter, there. He flew a Miles Magister: a light, training monoplane of wooden construction. On June 6th the Squadron returned to Rochford and became the first to receive the latest Spitfire 11's. It was at this time that the classic, aforementioned squadron photograph was taken. Soon afterwards, on the night of 19/20th June, the pilots were amazed to hear of Malan's achievement. It was during a night raid over Kent, a waxing moon saw Malan roar down a dark runway and

*74 Squadron 1940: Arthur Smith is on rear row, fourth from left. 'Sailor' Malan is first left on the middle row.*

reach the stars, he shot down two enemy He111s and received a bar to his D.F.C.

Arthur believed that he and every other sane pilot were afraid during the course of the battle, and spoke of battles over Kent, Sussex, and the fear when intercepting enemy air-fleets.

*"It was a question of concentrating my guns on an enemy aircraft in the knowledge that a series of multi-barrelled machine guns were focussed on me, trying to kill me! Yes, I was frightened, sometimes very frightened. I often thought I might not get back, but I had to cope with it, it was our responsibility, but when Malan led us I felt safer, he never led us into stupid situations. He was a great and inspirational leader and felt I could follow him to the end of the earth. I was nineteen and most of my time entailed being a wingman: covering the tail of a more experienced pilot, and the Tigers had plenty of top men. I must say that all the pilots during that Battle were volunteers. There were no conscripts at that time. It was a 'live for the day attitude', especially when friends or colleagues failed to return from action."*

Jimmy Young was shot down over the Channel on 28th July 1940, the same fate as to Harold Gunn three days later. On the 31st, Fred Eley went down in flames near Folkestone pier, and on August 11th, Don Cobdon and Dennis Smith disappeared while on convoy duty off the Essex coast. Arthur respected his inspirational friend, twenty-years old John Freeborn. A tough Yorkshireman with Scottish ancestry, he was born in Middleton, Leeds, and was one of 74's youngest pilots. His coolness, maturity and sharpness in combat made him a wonderful role model for many pilots. Most colleagues consider him to be one of the top pilots of the Battle of Britain. Harbourne Stephen was in his mid-twenties and another fine pilot; he worked for Allied Newspapers before the war. The same can be said of Wallasey born, John Mungo-Park.

As the Battle of Britain drew to a victorious close in late October, Arthur spent a few months in air-ferrying duties. After promotion to flight lieutenant he became a test pilot, and flew a wide range of aircraft until disaster struck on the 9th April 1942. Flying in Scotland on a test routine, he had just taken-off when his engines cut out and he crashed into treetops that bordered the airfield! Arthur was rushed to hospital; the doctors feared the worst and sent for his parents and brothers.

Months passed-by and gradually the will power and strength that had saved his life four years earlier

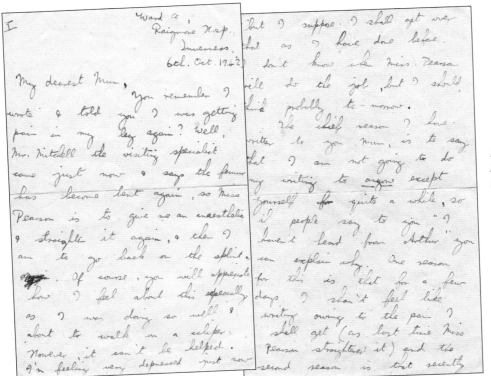

*Letter from Inverness hospital dated 6th October 1942.*

*Arthur Smith recuperating from his horrific crash. Circa 1943/4.*

*Pain shows on Arthur's face, his mother's gaze says it all. 1943.4.*

resurged. After numerous operations to repair serious injuries, one leg was found to be 2 ½" longer than the other, and so had the same measurement removed from his goodish leg. Once a six-footer, however, he was now shorter than his brother, Norman. How Arthur was teased about being cut down to size! An inquest established the cause of the crash was by accident. A mechanic had mistakenly failed to replace the fuel cap and the petroleum had become contaminated with rainwater. For Arthur, whose ambition it was to become a long-term R.A.F. pilot, the dream was lost. However he did have the satisfaction of spending a period as a training instructor before being released from the service in 1946.

*Flight Lieutenant Arthur Smith leaves hospital. 1944.*

*Norman Smith.*

**Norman Smith** was eighteen when he volunteered for service in The Tank Regiment: trained as a wireless operator/gun loader. He was posted to 'B' Squadron, 5th Royal Tank Regiment, famed as 'The Desert Rats' for their fighting ability in North Africa. He had a very unpleasant incident at 'Gold Beach', Arromanches, on 'D'-Day plus 1 (7th June 1944). A Royal Navy Skipper advised his tank commander that it was safe for their Cromwell Tank to leave the landing craft, even though it was over sixty yards from the Beach! The tank sank in the heavy seas, fortunately Norman and the crew survived and subsequently fought in the mighty battle of Caen. In Norman's 1989 book: 'Tank Soldier', he describes the events of 1944-5 in France, Belgium,

Holland and Germany. He writes of his confrontations with mighty German Panther and Tiger Tanks, of being bombed by the Luftwaffe, and facing enemy artillery whilst at 'point' during an advance. During that campaign well over a thousand allied tanks were lost, 164,954 troops, with another 538,763 wounded and 78,657 missing or taken prisoner. After the war, Norman, always a bit of a maverick, specialised in interior design, often having publications regarding furnishing of period houses for 'Period Home' magazine. He passed away on 7th May 1997. (See Dedication to Tank Crews in Volume One).

During Arthur's many months in hospital after his near fatal crash, he had been particularly impressed by the skills of an osteopath/naturopath. This Canadian practitioner had been of tremendous help in aiding his recovery, and also taught Arthur the benefits of a healthy diet. After deep consideration Arthur decided that his immediate future lay in studies at The British School of Osteopathy, London. The R.A.F. was prepared to offer a retraining grant, but on hearing the study-course, refused. Osteopathy was then considered a 'fringe medicine'.

*Arthur Smith, his father Eric and Norman Smith. 1950's.*

Unperturbed, Arthur financed his own four years of study, and after subsequently qualified and took up a practice in Leicester. Shortly afterwards he opened a two-day a week practice at Derby, buying a little car that was suitably fitted with clutch, brakes and accelerator, all attached to the driving wheel. By the 1950's he was married with sons, Neil, Bruce and Guy. He pioneered treatment for racehorses and became President of "The Osteopath Association of Great Britain".

A gathering of 'The Few'. From left: Jack Tombs, Ken Wilkinson and Arthur Smith. Circa 2001.

Josephine and Arthur Smith. 1970.

Josephine scatters her husband's ashes on the Garden of Rememberance. Biggin Hill.

Arthur and his second wife, Josephine, spent many years at 123, Station Road, Glenfield, with lots of friends, especially at Anstey Tennis Club, where he played doubles into his eighties. An excellent poker player, hobbies included reading on a variety of subjects, correspondence, and time spent on a dance floor: using hand and arm movements to entertain. A huge part of his time involved generosity of spirit and funding, as a member of 'The Leicester Round Table' and 'The Rotary Club'; holding the record with over forty years membership with each. The couple contributed in raising cash for The 'Battle of Britain Historical Society': to build a Memorial to the Few. Prince Charles unveiled the magnificent Monument on the Victoria Embankment, in September 2005. Sadly Arthur passed away suddenly on the 22nd December 2004. I feel honoured to compile this presentation about a friend and one of 'The Few'. My thanks to Josephine for her assistance in providing details, photographs, etc.

# SAMUEL AND BERYL SMITH (ROBINSON)

*Beryl and Samuel Smith.*

My dear mother, Betty Kendrick, is cared for in the 'Meadows' at Thringstone; many is the occasion when visiting I have also spoken to residents like Jim Cooper, a cricketer with Leicestershire in the 1950-early 60s, and Beryl Robinson. I was delighted on one such occasion to meet John and Shirley Cantrill whilst they were with Beryl. Shirley is Beryl's niece (her sister Freda's daughter), and while John and I chatted I heard a sad but interesting story concerning Beryl. I feel it should be remembered.

Samuel Bartholomew Albert Smith, or Sam as he was known, was born at Osgathorpe in 1919, and by all accounts was a very brainy fellow. In 1939 he was serving as a regular Coldstream Guardsman, service number 2616076, and posted to France and Belgium with the British Expeditionary Force. With being a career soldier in an elite regiment, he would certainly have been at the forefront of countering the overwhelming German Forces and in checking their advance to allow the 1940 'miracle' evacuation from Dunkirk.

The first indication that Sam had returned to England was a letter sent to his fiancée, Beryl Siddons (born October 1920) on Main Street, Osgathorpe, and stamped 3rd June 1940. He wrote from 'Somme Barracks' at Sheffield, Yorkshire:

'*Dear Beryl,*

*Well darling I arrived in England safely from Dunkirk; I suppose you have read all about it in the papers. I might add we had a hell of a time. We had to swim with our clothes on to the boat. I don't know how Lloyd has got on, whether he has pulled through or not, I don't know, I hope he has. Well, we have to go to London and then I think we get a spot of leave. I will write back straight away - may know more tomorrow or Wednesday. Love, Sam. Xxxxx*'

The couple married and looked forward to a happy life together in a world of eventual peace. Sam, after noting the events of the 1940 Battle of Britain, asked to

The letter from the previous page.

telegram informing her that her husband had been killed. A letter typed out on the same date from Squadron Leader Michael Beytagh stated:

*'Dear Mrs Smith,*

*You will have received my telegram informing you of the sad loss of your husband Sergeant Samuel Bartholomew Smith as a result of an aircraft accident. The Squadron was doing practice formation flying, and when over the sea off the Lizard (Point) your husband's aircraft collided with another aircraft. Unfortunately, the tail of your husband's aircraft was damaged causing him to go down spinning into the sea. Your husband must have been killed instantly when he hit the sea. Your husband's body was found by a Naval boat and has been taken to R.A.F. Station Portreath. I have just had a phone call from Doctor Jarry and am arranging to send your husband's body to Osgathorpe. I enclose a pamphlet, which gives particulars of arrangements for funerals.*

transfer to the Royal Air Force for training as a fighter pilot. His wish was granted and in due course served with 602 Squadron, flying Spitfires. In early 1940, *'The City of Glasgow'* Squadron, fought in some of the earliest battles of the war as the Luftwaffe attempted to bomb Scapa Flow, the Royal Navy's base for its 'Home Fleet'. In the summer of that year, 602 Squadron was

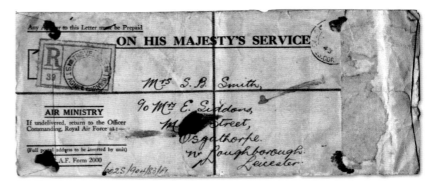

at Westhampnett (near Tangmere in Sussex) and saw a great deal of action. After a refit in Scotland, receiving Spitfire 11s at Ayr in May 1941, they flew south to Kenley and took on Spitfire Vs for cross-Channel operations. Sergeant Samuel Smith, service number 657263, joined the Squadron in July 1942; they had just been posted to Peterhead in northern Scotland. They flew south to use R.A.F. 'Biggin Hill' in Kent as a base to cover the disastrous Dieppe Operation of August 19th. The air battle was a massive affair, and Sam did well to survive before returning with 602 to Peterhead. In January 1943, the Squadron transferred to Perranporth in Cornwall to provide cover for that area. 602 Squadron's code letters on the fuselage were LO.

On the 24th January 1943, Beryl Smith, living with her parents on Main Street, Osgathorpe, received a

*Your husband's effects are being attended to and it is laid down they have to be forwarded to the Standing Committee of Adjustment, Colnbrook, from whom you will be hearing.*

*May I now express the great sympathy which all of us feel in the sad loss you have sustained. Your husband has been with us since last July and his many friends will also miss him.*

*Yours sincerely, M. Beytagh, Commanding Officer.*

*No 602 Squadron. R.A.F.*

Irishman, Michael Beytagh D.F.C. was a flight lieutenant with 73 Squadron during the Battle of Britain, and remained with the R.A.F. until 10th January 1946, retiring as an 'ace' and a wing commander.

Sergeant Samuel Smith was duly buried at Osgathorpe with an R.A.F. presence. A large brass

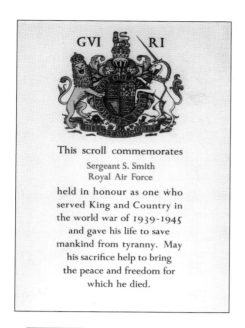

This scroll commemorates
Sergeant S. Smith
Royal Air Force
held in honour as one who
served King and Country in
the world war of 1939-1945
and gave his life to save
mankind from tyranny. May
his sacrifice help to bring
the peace and freedom for
which he died.

IN MEMORY OF
SAMUEL BARTHOLOMEW ALBERT SMITH
SERGEANT PILOT
ROYAL AIR FORCE
KILLED IN ACTION
JANUARY 23ʳᵈ 1943
AGED 23 YEARS
BURIED AT OSGATHORPE

WE WILL REMEMBER THEM

THIS TABLET IS ERECTED TO HIS MEMORY BY
HIS RELATIVES AND FRIENDS IN OSGATHORPE

*Memorial to William Dalby of the 1/5th Leicestershire Battalion.*

death, Hilda found employment at Loughborough's College of Art and Technology.

Beryl's second husband, Alan Colin Glover Robinson (his mother: Ethel Elizabeth Robinson) also served in World War 2. Alan's 'Certificate of Service' states that he was born on 4th August 1924 at 36, Swannington Road, Ravenstone. At five feet eleven inches tall with green eyes and fair hair he was employed as a 'motor driver'. Called-up on 21st March 1943, he joined the Royal Navy in that capacity and among others served aboard: H.M.S. 'Royal Arthur', 'Mercury' and 'Victory'. His Port Division was Portsmouth and his service number: J.X. 455150. On release on 12th August 1946, his character was described as 'Very Good' and his efficiency rating as 'Satisfactory'.

plaque hangs on the wall of Osgathorpe Church, and a tablet was erected in his memory by relatives and friends.

Beryl's mother, Hilda Siddons, also lost a husband in warfare; his name was William Dalby. He was born at All Saints, Loughborough and around 1914 enlisted into the Fifth (1/5th) Territorial Battalion of the Leicestershire Regiment. (See my book: 'Fifty Good Men and True'). He served in France and Flanders before marrying in 1916-1917, but was killed shortly after returning to the frontline. Private William Dalby, service number 240539, was killed on 16th June 1917. On 13th June 1916, the Fifth Battalion left Lens in France for the short trip to a line of trenches opposite Fosse 3, an old lag heap providing the Germans with a defensive redoubt. William was killed before the main attack and my conclusion is that he was sniped: all too common in trench warfare! Following her husband's

Alan and Beryl married on 30th March 1954, and had no children, but Beryl's sister, Freda had a daughter: Shirley. Alan retained his links with the Royal Navy via the H.M.S. Royal Arthur Association. I was fascinated to read his *Proclamation of Crossing the Artic Circle*' and to flick through pamphlets such as: 'Care and Maintenance of Mechanical vehicles (wheeled)' and 'Motor Car Fuel ration Books'.

My thanks to John Cantrill and his wife Shirley of Church Gresley for telling me such a moving story.

# DESMOND STARBUCK

*John Harold Starbuck in 1914.*

**D**esmond (Des) is the son of John Harold Starbuck, who featured in: 'Greater Love', a signaller with the Argyll and Sutherland Highlanders who was awarded the Military Medal during the Great War.

Des, born on 1st April 1923, grew-up on Ashburton Road of Hugglescote, firstly at number 145, then at 190: next door but one to Fred Briers of 'Famous Fifty' fame. He was educated at the Council School on the same road, and at the age of eleven passed for grammar school; but persuaded his parents to allow him to remain with his old school-friends.

On leaving school his father accompanied him into Leicester; he applied for a clerical position at Hilton's Footwear on Freeschool Lane. He was offered the job starting on the bottom rung, so allowing, Leslie Kendrick, my father, to take a step up the promotion ladder. Des' days were long; what with two nights a week at the '*Underwood School of Commerce*' at Leicester, learning shorthand, typing and book-keeping. Later, he obtained a job nearer home at Ellistown Brick and Pipe Works.

On 3rd September 1939, Des sat with friends, Cyril Blanchard, Bernard Gamble and Ernest Beal, around a radio, listening to Prime Minister Neville Chamberlain's Declaration of War. He was sixteen years of age, and immediately afterwards he and his pals jumped onto their bicycles and made for Reid and Sigrist's Desford Aerodrome. They found all the Tiger Moth aircraft neatly tethered in one corner of the airfield; a sitting target for enemy aircraft! They noted that the surrounding roads were stacked with tins of camouflage paint, with men hastily daubing the aircraft hangers. The 'Phoney War' became increasingly tense with friends apt to disappear as they were called up for duty. In the spring of 1940, newspapers printed dramatic events of the invasion of the Low Countries, the Air War over France and finally the Dunkirk Evacuation. Des recalls:

*"The Battle of Britain raged, notably in southern England, but sirens sounded in Coalville and bombs were dropped. By this time Winston Churchill was in power and talk was of a German invasion. An early precaution was the formation of the Local Defence Volunteers (L.D.V.), later called the Home Guard. The call was for anyone over the age of seventeen to come forward and report to the local police station. I volunteered and training consisted of two hours, 7.00pm - 9.00pm, each Tuesday and Thursday at Hugglescote's Church School, under the tutorage of W.W.1 veterans. Our main duty was to watch for enemy parachutists at a posting at Snibston pithead bank between 6.00am-8.00am and 8.00pm-10pm. I am not sure what would have happened if the parachutists had chosen a different timetable."*

Des transferred to 1188 (Coalville) Squadron of the Air Training Corps, based at Bridge Road School, becoming a founder member and staying with them until call-up on 31st July 1942.

*"Prior to this I had registered with the National Service Act, and so when I attended the Leicestershire Regiment's Headquarters at Ulverscroft Road, Leicester, I stated a preference for R.A.F. Air Crew. After a mix up with my medical grade, an R.A.F. recruiter had me as Grade1: my papers stated Grade 2, Dejectedly, I had to settle for 'ground staff'. I requested preference for work on aircraft as an*

*armourer, and this was provisionally accepted."*

Des' father was far from happy with his son's grading and enquired for the critical reasons. He was told that the minimum weight for Grade 1 was 100lbs: Des only weighed 95 1/2lbs.

Early morning on the 31st July 1942, Des caught the train at Coalville Station: destination No1 Recruit Centre, Penarth, a few kilometres south of Cardiff.

*"The first bewildering day was spent being issued with a knife, fork, spoon, plate and towel and then marched to numerous centres for a myriad of tests. At the end of the confusion I realise I'd lost my towel, and oh dear! In the next four days I was fully kitted-out and posted to No14 Recruitment Centre at Weston Super Mare in Somerset. A corporal met us at the railway station and set about allocating us to civilian billets. Just prior to our arrival the town had been subjected to a 'hit and run' daylight raid by enemy aircraft, and rubble lay in the streets and tarpaulins covered many a tiled roof. Corporal George, an ex-Loughborough College student, took great delight in pointing out the damage.*

*That night the sirens went and with no advice we stood in the street and watched the German bombers unload their cargo of death on Bristol. Soon after we*

*had kit inspection in a local park, everything was set out accordingly except my missing towel. The inspecting officer halted at my display, looked long and hard, and said: "Where is your button stick?"*

*After a pause I remembered that I had left it in my billet and explained as such. That brought a lecture on 'kit safety' but escaped further punishment, buying a towel from stores quickly."*

Des should have had eight weeks of 'square bashing' at Weston Super Mare, fortunately for him, tradesmen were in short supply: he passed after a mere five weeks. He was posted to No11 School of Technical Training at Credenhill, near Hereford, spending six months on an armourers' course. He was excellent with the final examination and was ensured promoted from AC2 Group V (GD) to AC1 Group 11 (Armourer, General).

*"Rumour was rife with talk that 140 men were required for overseas postings. A batch of us used delaying tactics by volunteering for the 'Fitters Course', at Kirkham, near the fleshpots of Blackpool! We undertook the course but afterwards were ordered back to Credenhill to prepare for another six-month stint. Things carried on much as before and at the end,*

*Des Starbuck: centre front row at Weston Super Mare in 1942.*

*with not such quite good results, I became an AC2 Group 1 (Fitter Armourer, General). As the AC2 Group 1 pay was less than previous I continued to draw Armourer's pay of 6/9d per day. Alas, by the end of the course there were no alternatives regarding postings."*

§In September 1943, AC2 (Group1) Desmond Starbuck reported for duty at No5 Personnel Draft Centre, Blackpool. Every morning all personnel attended Blackpool's Football Ground, Bloomfield Road, where names were called out and draft numbers given. Along with many others, Des, waited, but in between time visited the Pleasure Beach, which had extended its season in view of the high number of military visitors. Soon they were all broke, with many even volunteering for work in the orderly room. After two weeks and with no imminent postings, they were temporarily posted to various British stations to await recall (PWR- preliminary warning reserve).

Des and an airman from Leicester were given double rations and handed travel warrants to No: 32 MU, R.A.F. St. Athan in South Wales. This was a huge Maintenance Station and comprised of 19 MU (civilian manned) and 32 MU (R.A.F. & Women's Auxiliary Air Force).

*"The camp's perimeter was around forty-two kilometres (twenty-seven miles) and contained three railway stations. Waiting for major servicing were 600 Lancaster bombers and 1,000 Beaufighters; wherever one looked - spinneys, farmyards and barns, all you could see were aircraft. I checked into my billet and met an old pal that I'd trained with. He warned me not to get lumbered with a job in the Hispano Cannon workshop; needless to say, that is where I was placed! The camp had a reputation for very long working hours, hard graft and an oppressive standard of discipline. To illustrate: eight weeks later I was ordered to the orderly room to undertake an overseas posting, and by the time I had walked there thirty other personnel had volunteered for the posting. Two days later I was on the move to No: 2 PDC Morecambe."*

Des arrived at Morecambe at 11.00pm and in the pouring rain. With some urgency he was marched to a disused Woolworth's store and issued with a second kit bag and blankets; then onto a civilian billet where two spinsters had to be roused from their sleep. Next day he received tropical kit and a rifle; the issuing armourer being none other than Jimmy Springthorpe of

*Des Starbuck at Hereford in 1943.*

Ellistown, formerly a painter with the Co-Operative. Later he entrained to Gurrock, boarded 'SS Siberjak': late of the Dutch East India service, and subsequently awoke to find himself in grey rolling seas and part of a large convey under the protection of two Royal Navy corvettes. Not only was it very choppy in the Bay of Biscay, enemy aeroplanes also caused the odd scare until entering the Mediterranean at the second attempt, via the Straits of Gibraltar.

*"Our convoy was only the second through since the fall of North Africa, and we were joined by Royal Navy destroyers and ships fitted with barrage balloons.*

*A low- key Christmas was spent aboard, and after a ten-day voyage we disembarked at Port Said on the 1st January 1944. I then entrained to No: 21Personnel Transit Camp at Kasfareet, within the Suez Canal Zone. After a short spell at Kasfareet, absorbing the sights and smells of the Middle East and adjusting to the higher temperatures, I was posted to No: 78 OTU at Ein Shemer in Palestine. It took a seventeen-hours over-night train journey, and what an experience, to reach what was a new station and they were unprepared to receive us. There were no aircraft, the food was very basic, but over a few weeks Wellington bombers arrived and also the food quality improved. I was attached to the Station's Armoury, and within that routine I continued until the end of the European war.*

*There were hiccups: I had sandfly fever and was confined to sick bay and then No: 3 R.A.F. hospital at Televinski."*

*Des Starbuck at Ein Shemer, Palestine, with his dog Sheila. May 1944.*

Des also had an attachment to No: 1 Fuel Transportation Company to provide a service for the sea bombing range at Athlit. During his stay at Ein Shemer he met several pals from back home; Peter Thomas of Hugglescote arrived for a short break during a flight in a Liberator bound for the Far East. On the station were Bagworth's Ken Smith (with the Fire Section), Eric Harrison of Coalville training for aircrew, and Coalville's Arthur Underwood with the Army at Pardas Hanna.

*"I had a few uneventful leaves, but had a two-week break in Egypt: visiting Alexandria and viewing amongst other sights Pompey's Pillar and the Catacombs. At Cairo I visited the Sphinx, the*
*Pyramids, the Dead City, Memphis and Sakkhara."* Returning to Ein Shemer he passed a trade test and was promoted to AC1 (Fitter Armourer).

With the European War finished the military attention was focussed on the Far East conflict, with Des being posted to No: 1675 Heavy Conversion Unit at Abu Sueir, near to Ismailia in the Suez Zone (another long over-night train journey). Arriving for his new posting on the 14th August 1945, he was delighted when the next day 'Victory over Japan' was announced. Liberator aircraft were serviced and polished prior to being returned to the Americans as part of a Lease/Lend agreement.

*Des spent many a day working on the Liberator bomber (the American B24).*

Another posting at the end of September: No: 160 MU at Aqir in Palestine, meant working in the main armament workshops but desperately looking forward to home life. Trouble flared-up as nationals attempted to drive the British from the Middle East, but the nature of Des' work meant that his release was delayed.

*"We were all living on our nerves; the Irgun Gang raided our armoury and took three hundred weapons and 250,000 round of ammunition (later recovered). Somehow I found time to take another trade test and got promoted to LAC (Fitter Armourer) and eight shillings and a penny a day. I started an R.A.F.Association club with over one hundred members, and for the armourers an ' Animal Club', with all members being given an animal nickname to accord with their particular characteristics."*

In late September, Des made his way to Port Said and embarked on the 'SS Clan Lamont' for a five-day voyage to Marseilles, southern France. A night there and then a twenty-four hour train journey to Calais, and over the Channel in the 'SS *Daffodil'*.

*"I recall the wonderful white cliffs of our homeland; had a meal at Dover Castle, then a train to glorious home and twenty-eight days disembarkation leave (with a warrant to return to R.A.F. Silverstone)."*

Des arrived at Leicester Station in the middle of the night and decided to walk, with full pack, the twelve miles home. Having been away for three years he couldn't wait for the morning train. (My father, Les Kendrick, had a night's walk from Leicester to Coalville for Christmas 1940). Des arrived at home fifteen minutes ahead of the morning train at Coalville Station, and also found that his father had a car in his garage!

*"That leave passed all too quickly and by the end of October 1946, I received a telegram informing me that R.A.F. Silverstone was closing down, and instead to report to R.A.F. North Luffenham, Leicestershire. On arrival late one evening I was told not to unpack but to report to the parade ground at 10.00am.*

*I was taken by lorry and conveyed to No: 17 OTU Swinderby, Lincolnshire. Once again I was to work on Wellington bombers, and in early December 1946, my demobilisation number came up. I'd be home for Christmas. I reported to the orderly room only to be told that I couldn't be demobbed, as my documents hadn't been forwarded from the Middle East.*

*I was fed up, and started a campaign of harassment by practically living in the orderly room. This paid off as I was issued with temporary papers, but they were too late for me to be released for Christmas, although I did spend Christmas at home. Later, I reported to No: 107 Release Centre at Warton, Lancashire on the 1st January 1947, and next day passed through the 'machine': I handed in my kit, received civilian clothing and a three month leave pass. I completed four and a half years in the R.A.F. and felt that I had done my bit towards the war effort."*

Des received the standard 1939-45 War medals plus the Defence Medal and Palestine Medal, and proudly so. On returning to Civvy Street, Des rejoined his pre-war employers: Ellistown Brick and Pipe Works.

Mr Joe Morton, with his wife, Doris, left their hometown of Blackburn in Lancashire, for him to become manager at the Coalville Branch of Lloyds Bank, Marlborough Square. Their daughter, Audrey

Mary Morton: born on 1st March 1925, accompanied them. Time and Tide: Desmond and Audrey became smitten and the happy couple married on the 21st September 1949 at Coalville's splendid Christ Church.

*From left: Harold and Elsie Starbuck, Denis Taberner, Des and Audrey Starbuck, Joe Morton, cousin Valerie Shorrock, brother Joe, Doris Morton (mother) and auntie Muriel.*

Initially they lived with his parent's for about a year, then in a flat above Harry Blunt's Tailor Shop, Coalville (now a Ladies Hairdressers). Their first child, John, was born in 1952 in the residence above Lloyds Bank at Coalville. Later they purchased 72, Blackwood, on the outskirts of Coalville, living there for a decade. Illness necessitated a move to nearby 139, Greenhill Road, to take care of Audrey's father.

Desmond's career blossomed, and following a move to the Clay Works Division of the National Coal Board at Newbold Worthington, he returned to his former employers when the head of the Clay Works took over there in 1964. Later employment was with a London Timber Importer until retirement.

Desmond and Audrey had three children. John: born in 1952 is employed by H.S.B.C., whilst David, born 1956, is a general practitioner at Lancing in Sussex. Kate, born 1970, is a police sergeant with Nottingham Constabulary.

A terribly sad feature in a very happy and successful life was the death of Audrey in 1989 at the age of only sixty-four years.

Des is always busy, still very keen on anything and everything to do with the Royal Air Force and is rightly extremely proud of the success of his children. My thanks to him for supplying a wealth of valuable information and photographs, both of himself and his father. I look upon Des as a very fine friend.

# LEONARD TAYLOR

Ernest and Ellen (nee Oxford) Taylor of Ellistown were born around 1896. Ernest, on leaving school joined Ibstock Colliery; he became a deputy, and, ultimately proved to be the last person to leave at the colliery's closure. He relocated to Whitwick Colliery and subsequently gained promotion to overman viz: assistant manager. Following their marriage they lived at 'Ten Row': 6, Midland Road, Ellistown, almost in Hugglescote. Len (Leonard) was born on 7th October 1917 and attended Ellistown Primary School: excelling in his studies; indeed, he passed a scholarship for Loughborough Junior College one year ahead of schedule.

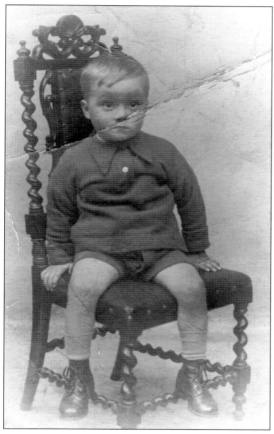

*Len Taylor at the age of three years.*

His parent's were very proud of him and saved money to buy his uniform and books. Len, aged ten years, caught the train from Hugglescote to Loughborough. He was doing especially well, but when he was fourteen and saw friends obtain jobs and have money in their pockets, he was tempted. He left school at fifteen: a year early, foregoing the prospect of a university place. His parent's were dismayed, and Len firmly regrets his decision to this day.

"*My first job was at George Ward's: a footwear manufacturer at Barwell. I cycled the round trip of thirty-two kilometres (twenty miles) on five/six days a week, and for the next eight years worked as a skilled lasting-room welt-sewer.*"

Len's elder brother, Leslie, born in 1914 and again a clever lad, passed as a surveyor at Whitwick Colliery and joined Leicestershire County Council in a similar capacity. From late 1939, he converted buildings, mainly factories for armament production, and upon completing this role joined the Royal Engineers. After a posting to the Middle East, based at Cairo, he was given a 'C-Class Release' from the Army to permit him to assist Sir Thomas Gibbs Company, who were phosphate mining in the vicinity: a vital ingredient in the production of explosives. He remained in the Middle East until 1945, and on his return to Great Britain, still with the same company, received a position in Scotland involving Hydro-Electric Power. He then went to Persia (now Iran) to organise an extensive irrigation programme that involved tunnelling waterways through hills. Leslie became a personal friend of the Shah of Persia. His next project, despite stating his concerns to Sir Thomas Gibbs, was to conduct an experiment in Kenya called: 'The Ground Nut Scheme'. The plan involved growing vast quantities of nuts to crush to provide oil: it was a dismal failure. Leslie, after a highly successful career succumbed in 1983, aged sixty-nine years.

Len also had a sister, Irene: 1923-2004, she had a happy marriage to Harold Woolley of Whitwick and they had two sons.

In 1939, a six-month's conscription period began as fears festered of a European War. By late August the family was living at 6, Kendal Street, Ellistown, and when Len's mother heard that war had been declared she immediately burst out into tears. Len:

"*Father was an overman at Whitwick Colliery and he offered to get me a job with a reserved occupation. I told him I couldn't live with that, but promised not to enlist; I added that if I were called-up I'd do my best for our country, anything other would rest on my conscience. Soon my call-up papers arrived and said my preference was the R. A.F., hopefully as a rear gunner, but was turned down after a strenuous medical.*"

Lenny ended up as a gunner but with the Royal Artillery, and set-off to war with several local lads, one being Jack Walker of Heather.

"*I took the train to Oswestry (twenty-four kilometres south of Wrexham) to report to the Royal Artillery, they had a large training establishment and barracks there. I was with a party of recruits and this sergeant major said: "You're the worst shower of men that I've ever had the misfortune to see, but I'll knock hell out of you until you became good soldiers." I was given the service number: 1534580. Our first meal in the barracks was terrible: potatoes and cabbage, it looked an odd colour. The next day we collected our uniforms: the only piece that fitted was the boots, and they weren't comfortable. A few complained but the sergeant major said it was their fault: they were deformed! We were given a short haircut and sent back if it was longer than a crew-cut and then we experienced our first parade, followed by some heavy physical training.*"

Len Taylor in early 1940.

Inoculations and injections were given, and after three gruelling months they passed-out for a posting at Tywyn: a cliff-top location sixteen kilometres south of Barmouth on the Cardigan Bay of west Wales. Here they were taught to use anti-aircraft guns, and how crucial this training would prove to be!

"*First we had to stand in a gun-pit and watch another team fire the 3.7inch gun so we could accustom ourselves to the severe blast and jolt. Some lads couldn't stand the sound and left the course, but I got used to it and soon a sense of competition developed between each gun to see who was the fastest and the most accurate. I was a gun-layer, operating a wheel to adjust the gun's angle of fire, and when it did my whole body shook with the blast. I was part of 330 Battery, 105th Regiment. I had been regularly writing home to the girl of my dreams, Gladys, and asked her if she would marry me: but pointed out all the problems of warfare, she was eighteen years old. After the course we were given seven days leave, and I couldn't wait.*"

Gladys and Len. Circa 1938.

Len had met the slim and attractive Gladys while working at Barwell. She lived with her parents at 29, Hinckley Road, Ibstock; her father was the steward of Ibstock Working Men's Club. Len arrived in Ellistown on Saturday night.

Gladys. A photograph sent to Len in early 1940.

"Next morning I cycled to Ibstock and asked Gladys' father for permission to marry his dear daughter, and he happily consented. No one knew how long the war might last, but we were in love and felt the need to finalise matters whatever the consequences. We walked to St. Deny's Church and asked the vicar how we could obtain a special licence. On Monday morning we caught the bus to Leicester and met the Bishop who told us the licence would cost £4-ten shillings, as against a standard seven shillings and six pence (37&half new pence). We paid and on Wednesday 21st August 1940 were married. Just before the vicar conducted our ceremony the sirens started: we asked him to continue and afterwards said how pleased he was that we hadn't let Mr. Hitler spoil the occasion. We may not have had bells peeling but a siren set the occasion. Gladys and I were thrilled to be man and wife and we had a beautiful few days before I caught the Saturday morning train to Towyn."

Len was told to change at Birmingham Station; a special train had been requisitioned for the Battery. Arriving at Towyn they were ordered to stay on the train! Their kitbags, which had been packed for them, were thrown aboard; the locomotive raced south, and the gunners of 330 Battery were soon to witness history in the making.

From 18th July 1940, mostly over southeastern England, a massive air war raged between the German Airforce: the Luftwaffe, and the Royal Air Force. The enemy's intent was to destroy the R.A.F.: air superiority a prerequisite before sea-borne invasions of Kent and Sussex. The 'Few', mainly Hurricane and Spitfire fighter pilots, though greatly outnumbered did their utmost to destroy the invading air-fleets. On the consequential night of 24th August 1940, sticks of bombs were dropped inside Greater London; the R.A.F. retaliated with Hampden bombers causing fires in Berlin! An enraged German Chancellor proclaimed that his bombers would totally destroy London.

By September, seven Anti-aircraft Divisions were operating throughout the country of which the First Division was responsible for the Metropolitan area. Len:

"We were told we would be part of the First Anti-Aircraft Division and our task was to defend the capital. One of my earliest memories of this time was taking over a gun site on London's southern outskirts and seeing these 3inch naval guns, much smaller than we had trained on and so thought the firing blast would be less. What we didn't know was that the smaller the gun the louder the crack; with the largest gun it was more thundery but with these the crack really hurt the ears, some of the lads ears bled, and from then onwards we stuffed our ears."

3.7 inch Ack-Ack gun.

That afternoon they fired at three Stuka (Ju87s) dive-bombers that were targeting factories.

"We had four guns and they were situated on an arc so that each gun was equidistant from a command post. Information was passed to us by height and range finders so that we could angle the gun and set the shell to explode at a pre-determined height. To start with we only had daylight raids and what a sight they were and

*4.5 inch Ack-Ack gun.*

*what a sound they made. They came in massed formations, literally hundreds of bombers with fighter escorts.*

*We had a set plan to work with our fighters; our guns were set for a ceiling: the height of the bombers, around 15,000 feet, and our Hurricanes flew around these formations like sheep-dogs to a flock of sheep, intent on keeping them together. This allowed our Spitfires to dive and shoot at them from above, but both types of fighter new the ceiling we were firing and so kept above it, where possible!"*

In September 1940, the First Division, commanded by Major-General F.L.M. Crossman, had only two hundred and thirty-five guns; the figure for the whole country was just 3,744 heavy guns (4,410 light guns: Bofors and Hispan).

Another integral part of country's defences, as in the Great War, was reliance on the men who crewed Barrage Balloons and Searchlights. In September, London was defended by four hundred and fifty Barrage Balloons flown from mobile winches; they were designed to keep the enemy aeroplanes above five thousand feet. At sixty-two feet long and inflated with nineteen thousand cubic feet of hydrogen, most were fitted with a double parachute link cable that could snap the wings of ensnared aircraft!

There were several thousand Searchlights in the capital and proved a valuable aid to gunners, but they had limitations, particularly so on cloudy or full moon nights; the same when aircraft operated over twenty-

five thousand feet. At sixty inches in diameter they carbon projected five hundred and ten million candlepower, with their movement controlled by radar. A master-light illuminated the enemy and then two others in the same section homed in to form a cone for the awaiting gunners. It was felt in some quarters that the location of searchlights helped the Luftwaffe to identify top targets.

Len said that it was always worrying to be on a Tube train under the Thames, knowing that if a raid started the line was closed and the flood doors shut.

*"If you were caught you'd be sacrificed to prevent all of the Underground being flooded! Lots of people took shelter down there, more so as the Blitz developed and especially in May 1941 when it was at its worst with millions of incendiary bombs!"*

The Battery was frequently moved around London and Len saw some terrible sights resulting from carpet (intensive) bombing. Some Battery's had 3.7inch guns, a successful weapon, while others possessed the heavy 4.5inch: efficient at higher targets but not so much against craft flying a lower ceiling or dive-bombers.

*3.7 inch guns open fire in 1940.*

*"The grumbling roar of the massed bombers overhead; the shrill whistling of the bombs as they fell; the massive fires and putrid smoke; the crack of the*

A 4.5 inch gun. The soldier is a predictor.

Len with the Dornier shield and a tea plate from the Blitz.

*guns and shrapnel flying though the air; we knew history was in the making! We also knew that no one was safe from sudden death: the machine gunners on the enemy aircraft targeted us gunners, and we lost some men. We wore a special shoulder flash that displayed a Dornier bomber with a sword passing thought its middle. Whenever we had a bit of leave and went into a London pub we were always treated to free drinks and cinemas let us in free: they knew what the flash represented and we were proud to defend such grand folk.*

Len: a bombardier (corporal) was in charge of his gun and team and responsible for the gun's maintenance and efficiency.

*"We shot a Dornier down and it crashed in Wimbledon, so a little later we found the site and with consent removed a few items. We used these to make a metallic Dornier shape with a slice of metal passing through it, just like our emblem. We mounted it on a wooden shield as a memento: it hangs on my wall."* See photo.

Len was off-duty one night, having a beer at the 'Robin Hood' on the Anerly Road, near to where Crystal Palace stood, when a bomb exploded just outside and blew the front in.

*"A tremendous crash and glass, debris and dust flew everywhere; a tea plate narrowly missed my head and fell on the floor, only chipped on the underside. I picked it up as a keepsake and have it to this day. I heard recently that the 'Robin Hood' is still in existence: I occasionally feel guilty about my 'steal'.* See photo.

Losses in the Luftwaffe were becoming serious; our fighters claimed many and the excellent anti-aircraft gunners had victims too, but their primary role was to keep the enemy high.

This prevented enemy bomb-aimers from cherry picking targets, as they did to great effect on mainland Europe. Such losses necessitated a tactical adjustment and they reverted to night raids composed of three waves of aircraft with short intervals between each.

*"Sometimes a small neighbourhood had as many as sixteen heavy guns firing most of the night with the locals in their Anderson Shelters. Next morning they'd open their front doors and sweep out the plaster that had fallen from walls and ceilings because of our guns' vibrations! But they'd wave and thank God that they still had a home to go to."*

Len's Battery set-up a secret, camouflaged site at Wallington: fairly near to Croydon Airport (used as a fighter station during the summer battle).

*"They built an imitation version of the Airport near*

*to us with planes, tankers and buildings made of canvas. The idea, called 'Starfish', meant starting fires on the runways just before a night raid: hoping to mislead the bombers into bombing ground that had a lower population. It worked well, but we felt sorry for the people of Carlsholton as they became a constant target. After the raids we'd go and help civilians put out the fires and clear up the debris. Night raids were frightening but very atmospheric. The sirens were wailing, searchlights crossed the sky like the fingers of a giant hand; there was often a mist in the air as well as a lot of smoke and all the activity of aerial warfare. We had many lucky escapes and one I recall well: a bomber approached our Battery and dropped three bombs. The first exploded a hundred yards short of us, the second fell into the gun-pit next to ours and didn't go off but tipped the gun nearly on its side and the third exploded a hundred yards beyond us! What an escape, we would have died if No2 had exploded! One night in particular was hell on earth; it was 29th December, later called the 'Second Great fire of London', with St. Paul's Cathedral rising triumphantly above the flames; what a night!"*

After the raid they took turns in carrying 56lbs-a-round of ammunition from the damaged site and awaited the Army Bomb Squad to remove the UXB. They defused a 500lb and took it for detonation elsewhere. (*"It didn't have our names on it!"*) The bad weather in January and February 1941 reduced the size and frequency of raids, and so the film industry 'made a visual record of events as they had occurred'.

*"They asked us if we would like to be extras, and we agreed. On one occasion I was one of a crowd of wounded Dunkirk evacuees climbing from a train; other times I was in the army and fighting against some of our lads dressed as German soldiers in mock battles. It was very authentic, the star of the film was Jimmy Handley; we didn't get paid for it but it was light relief for us. The film was called: 'The Peoples' Army'. In spring 1941 the enemy stepped up the bombing with incendiaries and for a few nights in particular it looked very bad. "*

Relative peace came to London with lighter night raids as the enemy turned its attention to Liverpool, Hull, Plymouth, Portsmouth, Southampton, Clydeside and Belfast. Also, the R.A.F. gained impressive night successes by installing radar into their Beaufighters and Defiants. From 7th September 1940 to16th May 1941, London received, on night raids alone, seventy-one major attacks during which well over eighteen thousand tons of heavy explosive was dropped, almost one-and-half times the aggregate that fell on other cities in Great Britain.

On Saturday 10th May 1941, with the Blitz having seemingly wound-down, sixty thousand fans gathered at Wembley stadium for the Football Association's Cup Final. At the same time, just over the Channel in France, over four hundred enemy aircraft were being loaded with bombs. That evening eleven thousand houses were totally destroyed, also the House of Commons, Westminster Abbey, Waterloo Station and the British Museum were damaged.

In the early summer of 1942, the Luftwaffe engaged on violent 'Baedeker' raids that seriously damaged some of our most historical town centres, such as Exeter, Bath, York, and Norwich.

I firmly believe that the personnel of Anti-Aircraft Command, the First Division in particular, never received the credit they richly deserved. Perhaps, and naturally so, the focus was too much on those forces that took the war to the enemy, thus neglecting ground defences and their role of damage limitation.

In my view our Ack-Ack batteries, as frontline troops, did a magnificent job whilst exposed to bombs, machine-gun fire, shrapnel and entrapment by fires. Another example: on Len's site near to Wormwood Prison a gun fired '*a premature round of ammunition*', a shell exploded on leaving the barrel and killed several gunners!

Others to whom we are indebted are: The Fire Brigade, The Observer Corps, and A.R.P. Wardens for their outstanding contributions.

330 Battery left the sector and returned to its base for additional training in preparation for a proposed 'Second Front' against the Axis Forces. Len was granted leave during this time as his wife gave birth to a son, Melvyn, in 1943.

*"We were taught how to operate our heavy guns against ground targets such as tanks, and to prepare for operation as a coastal battery firing at enemy ships. The training took us all over Great Britain until finally we knew of the forthcoming 'D'-Day. Just before the 6th June we were ordered to waterproof everything to stop seawater from attacking vital parts*

*of our equipment. We had just finished when we were told to remove it, a dreadful and filthy job. Not knowing why, we were rushed to the southeast coast. British Intelligence had just heard of the German's pilot-less bomb that would be sent to crash onto London, it was called the Doodlebug or V1. After a few days other Batteries relieved us and we headed for Normandy."*

The U.S.A. troops were low on artillery, and so, 330 Battery and others embarked on board an American 'Liberty' ship that dropped anchor just off 'Utah' beach, Normandy.

*"The sea was choppy and it made it very difficult for us to lower our equipment onto landing barges, and later we waded waist deep in seawater to the beach. In time the heavy guns and lorries got away and we travelled along the coast road to the cliffs overlooking Cherbourg: only taken after a fierce battle with many G.I.s loosing their lives. The harbour was unusable; the enemy had purposely filled it with all manner of sunken ships and train carriages, etc. Care was needed around there what with land mine and the occasional rifle shot after dark."*

They received improved rations and food from the Americans, and their tobacco ration was doubled. In August 1944, the Allies launched two set-piece offensives down the Caen-Falaise road, the aim, to encircle and capture an entire German Army. Two thousand aircraft and seven hundred and twenty guns supported eighty-five thousand British, Canadian and Polish troops. They faced 1 SS Panzer Corps and part of the fanatical Hitler Jugend; the resulting allied victory brought the end of the war a little closer. Soon, Len rejoined British Forces.

*"As a Bombardier I was chosen to skirmish ahead with the advance party to chose suitable sites for our guns, and also to clear any land mines. Caen was a real mess, it was just a ruin and many civilians lost their lives: the tragedy of warfare! Falaise Gap was choked with battered enemy armour and trucks, we felt the war was definitely going our way and we thought our fighter-bombers had done a great job with their rockets and cannons."*

Like so many of our troops, Len was overwhelmed by the reception from the Belgium people when they returned freedom to their country.

*"I'll never forget it, the roads were strewn in flowers and we were kissed and hugged by the women-folk and on buildings banners read: 'WELCOME TOMMY'. It was really wonderful."*

It took the Regiment a week to catch up with the advance party and on doing so they were allowed into the centre of Brussels.

*"About eight of us visited the 'Au Ballon Hotel' and had a meal, but the waiter didn't want to accept our issue of new notes until the manager arrived and eventually agreed. A local couple, only later did I find out he was a film director, had witnessed all that happened and asked to see my new notes. I offered him a free note, but he said he was only prepared to do an exchange by giving me the equivalent amount in a Belgium note. We chatted away and on leaving he gave me his card; later I visited their home and we have remained friends to this day. I hope to see him soon before we get too old!"*

When the Division moved into Holland, Len obtained some leave.

*"I got leave by the luck of the draw and I boarded a special train from Antwerp to Calais.*

*The train was draped with British Liberation Army posters and for every Belgium and French town we went through received wonderful welcomes.*

*We got on board a ship and you can imagine the huge roar when we first spotted the white cliffs of Dover; it brought a lump to my throat and I was so proud to be British."*

A special train was laid on at Dover for London, again it was draped with posters and the welcoming crowds were just as warm. Len had a great time but all too soon had to return, but received an extra day due to bad weather in the Channel.

*"On the return journey the memory of the sight I had seen when travelling to Antwerp to catch the train returned to me. I had passed a spot where an earlier battle had led to bodies from both sides being placed in a mass grave. They were being dug up, wrapped in sheeting and piled onto lorries for reburial at a military cemetery. It made me think of how fragile life was and how very easily I could have been one of those fallen men!"*

The winter of 1944/45 was one of the worst on record; they had to ensure that the guns were kept to a serviceable standard even though they had no shelter: Len says that evening tots of syrupy navy rum helped

*A photograph sent to Len's sister. May 1945.*

*Bombardier Len Taylor. Hamburg, 1946.*

to keep the cold at bay. The Battery guarded the famed: '*Arnhem Bridge*' (A Bridge Too Far) crossing and all was fairly quiet until the enemy launched a Panzer led counter-attack through the Ardennes over the festive period of 1944.

*"We were brought back to Belgium during this attack which was called: 'The Battle of The Bulge'. It was very cold with thick snow and poor visibility, and the German advance against the Americans was rapid, but it gradually ground to a halt; a little later we were attacked by the first jet aeroplane to go into action: it went before we could take any readings."*

Len took a short leave when Paul was born in January 1945. When the European war ended he was stationed at Hamburg and thought he'd be posted to the Far East, but having served our country for five years he was overjoyed upon hearing of the Japanese surrender.

*"Hamburg was a shell of a city, I can't describe what horrors must have taken place there during our air attacks; it must have been far more severe than London. One of our first jobs was to ship out thousands of German soldiers that had surrendered, many going to Denmark.*

*There were also loads of displaced persons, some in a terrible state having just been released from concentration camps."*

Len was in a party guarding the bridge over the River Elbe: the Allies were on one side of the river and the Russians on the other: he sensed an uneasy and suspicious tension, which later developed into the Cold War. He spent the next year at Hamburg engaged in training new recruits who were gradually replacing some of the seasoned veterans.

*"I was offered promotion to sergeant, and also a doubling of the annuity that had accrued over my war years, to stay one more year. I believe that the top brass felt that we were losing too many battle-experienced troops, and felt the Russians had sensed a shift in power, but I turned the offer down. I had already been away from my wife for six years and I had only seen my eldest son for five times and my youngest son for just once."*

Soon his demobilisation number: twenty-eight, came up and he left the Royal Artillery as a bombardier with a welcomed gratuity of £250.The train halted at Coalville Railway Station, Len opened the carriage door and stepped onto the platform as a free man. Mr.

*Len Taylor in the 1950's.*

to continue playing golf in his ninety-first year. Their sons: Melvyn married Carol Hill and Paul married Avril Noon. Len has four grandchildren with one granddaughter married to Dorian West, the famous Leicester Tigers and England Rugby footballer.

*A spot of golf for Len.*

& Mrs. L. Taylor settled at 29, Hinckley Road, Ibstock, her parent's home, but they lived-in as stewards of the Working Men's Club. With a wife and two young children to support financial issues were always a concern, and to this end Len took a variety of jobs. First, a storekeeper at Cascelloids, then as a bus conductor with Midland Red, and after six months of study a carriage inspector on the railways. He had a spell on the sales staff at 'Ford's Garage' on Hotel Street, before being recalled to the Colours during the Korean War. After three months in training with the Fourth Battalion of the Leicestershire Regiment, learning to fire lighter guns like the Boffers, the government decided not to send any more troops to the battle area and Len was demobilised. He spent four years inspecting railway carriages until in the swinging Fifties and Sixties, Gladys and he became stewards of the 'West End Club' on Ashby Road, Coalville. They moved to Heather in 1961, and Len still lives there, sadly Gladys passed away in February 1998. He often reflects of his time in the war years, and annually visits 'Utah' beach, at Normandy: usually shedding a few tears.

Len played cricket until the age of sixty and hopes

For about fifteen years I have chatted to Len at Remembrance Day parades and various other ceremonies. He is a very fine man, typical of an excellent generation who endured a good deal during the war years to ensure our freedom. Thank you Len, you are indeed a good friend.

*David Taylor M.P. with veterans at Coalville on Rememberance Day 2006.*

# LANCE WYKES

Lance, born in 1899, was the son of Alfred Wykes, who featured in 'Greater Love'. In 1914 Alfred received news of the outbreak of World War 1 with mixed emotions. As a devout Christian he believed in turning the other cheek, also, he had many German friends as a result of the Adult School National Council's pre-war inter-change movement. However, his nationalistic ideals surfaced when he read of German atrocities to Belgium civilians, and so enlisted into the 1/4th Leicestershire Battalion; soon he was in Flanders: on the Western Front.

*Lance Wykes and his dog. France 1918.*

In early 1918, Lance pursued his dream of becoming a pilot and enlisted into the Royal Flying Corps, soon to become the Royal Air Force.

During this latter course of the war, Flying Officer L. Wykes clocked over three hundred flying hours over the Western Front, fifty hours of which were during the lonely hours of darkness. He adored flying the Sopwith Camel, but flying was in its infancy, no parachutes, and life for a fighter pilot could be somewhat short. Lance did extremely well, although he suffered some horrific experiences, leaving a few mental scars for a number of years. He was far from alone in this instance!

Before the war he was educated at Rawlins School at Quorn, a pretty village midway between his Rothley home and Loughborough, and after leaving the R.A.F. studied mechanical engineering for three years at Birmingham University.

*Lance Wykes in 1918.*

The conditions were appalling, but he took great solace in writing letters to his family at the village of Rothley, near Loughborough. The dear love for his wife, Sarah Anne, and children Lance and Dorothy was clearly apparent, as was the fondness for his home and the emerging beauty of his garden in springtime 1915. Before the war aeroplanes fascinated Lance, he spent carefree hours making wooden models of his favourites. While Alfred sat in the cold, damp trenches his eyes often turned skywards to admire those very same aircraft in flight, often engaged in dogfights. He wrote to Lance and described the skill, daring and bravery of what he witnessed.

*Stella Wykes at home with Margot and Bob. Late 1930's.*

He married Stella Moore and they were blessed with two children: Margot and Robert (Bob), and lived in the delightful setting of Cliffe House at nearby Barrow-on-Soar.

The family home at Barrow-on-Soar.

Lance became a highly successful businessman, and by 1938 was managing director of Crowthers Ltd, engineering works at nearby Thurmaston and making machinery for the vibrant textile trade. He was often referred to by his nickname: 'A-L'. Naturally he was a keen member of a local flying club, and enjoyed exploring the serene castles and canyons of vaporous

Lance, wife Stella and son Bob. Late 1930s.

cloud. Whilst flying over his beloved, sunshine bathed Charnwood Hills; he recalled the pleasure of making model planes: perhaps he could venture into the manufacture of aeroplanes. He took time off from Crowthers on half pay and drew up detailed plans for the scheme: covering finance, factory space, as well as local aerodrome facilities at Ratcliffe and Rearsby.

In 1938, Lance travelled to the United States of America to negotiate a licensed agreement to build an American designed light-aeroplane in England. Whilst there he also purchased fifty Lycoming 0-145-A2 engines, and acquired details of the various components required. He contacted his uncle, Percy Wykes, at Leicester and asked him to buy all of the necessary equipment for the manufacture of the aircraft. He also posted the engineering drawings, with

Herbert Thompson using them to construct jigs and necessary components for production.

On 21st November 1938 the new firm: '*Taylorcraft Aeroplanes (England) Ltd*' was registered, with Lance ('A-L'), uncle Percy and boyhood friend Frank Bates as directors. The address was Britannia Works, Thurmaston.

Auster pilot Toni Strodle.

Manufacturing started in February 1939; the American design had to be adjusted and refined to comply with stringent British aeronautical standards. The personnel involved were Albert Coltman, together with ground engineer, Albert Codling, did the test flying; Mr. Herbert Thompson, chief development planning engineer, Gus Morris, tool controller and part time test pilot. The latter two and George Potterton started building the aeroplane. The fuselage and wings were then taken by lorry to Sir Lindsay Everard's Ratcliffe aerodrome for fitting, rigging and test flights.

The latter gentleman was president of the Leicestershire Aero Club and M.P. for Melton Mowbray. The first aircraft was completed on 24th April of that year; and piloted by Mr. G. Wynne-Eaton on 3rd May 1939. Lance was overjoyed and immediately took his uncle onto the airways and looped the loop. The aeroplane was marked as Taylorcraft Plus Model 'C', and priced at £500, and

*Women engaged in war-work involving the construction of Auster aircraft at Thurmaston. Circa 1941-2.*

soon production was one aircraft per week. Initially Lance delivered the aeroplanes to the customers, but later a glamorous young Danish lady, Toni Strodl, took on the role. The first test flying was held at Ratcliffe, but in 1940 was moved to Rearsby, Les Leetham being a prominent test pilot.

*Auster test pilot Les Leetham marrying Kath Watts on 6th December 1941.*

In 1939, Lance and John Hardy-Smith (Junior) of Quorn were celebrated in newspapers when they flew to Paris on 2/3rd August. The reason, a certain Oxford University graduate was striving to fly to Paris and back for a measly fifteen shillings (75 new pence). He was to become very famous during the war, won the Victoria Cross whilst flying for Bomber Command, a household name: Leonard Cheshire. The newspaper declared:

'*Two Leicestershire men have achieved in the ordinary course of travel what an Oxford graduate is striving to do for a bet, that is to go to Paris and back for 15 shillings.*

*Mr. A. L. Wykes of Barrow-on-Soar and Mr. Hardy-Smith of Quorn arrived back at Ratcliffe Aerodrome after an air trip to the French capital, which cost them 15 shillings each in petrol, oil and landing fees. They flew a Taylorcraft machine, leaving Ratcliffe aerodrome at 9.10am, calling at Lympne in Kent to clear customs and then on to Villacoubley. The reason for the trip was to allow representatives of the French Air Ministry to assess the Taylorcraft aeroplane. They were suitably impressed and the twosome were dined in the famous' George V' hotel and taken to the Folies Bergere in the evening. The following day they left Paris at 11.15am, landed at Boulogne-sur-mere to clear the papers and onto Lympne. The weather over the Midlands was horrible so they flew eastwards across the Thames and set course for Leicester. The weather became severe and map readings impossible in such conditions. Eventually they came down through cloud, read the signpost for Rushton Station and followed the railway line to Syston, eventually landing at Ratcliffe. I then went by car to home!*

*The return journey was a bit rough, as you can guess," commented Hardy-Smith. He also said for the cost of the journey it amounted to 30 shillings, of which 6 shillings were for landing fees. He quoted that the petrol consumption for the trip was about the same as for an ordinary motor car.'*

As World War 2 approached, production levels increased; in August, twenty-three of the latest 'Civil Plus Cs' left the production track: the first aircraft lettered G-AFNW. One of the early Civil Plus Cs was fitted with a 90HP Blackburn Cirrus Minor 1 engine and was supplied to the R.A.F. for trials marked as T9120. The War Office was assessing Airborne Observation Posts (A.O.P.); the Westland Lysander that was currently in use had good high lift devices but was heavy and lacked manoeuvrability. A Captain Bazeley and several other R.A.F. and Army officers journeyed to Leicestershire to check out the Model 'D' (G-AFWN). They were delighted in what they saw and asked for small changes regarding extra transparent openings and an improved vision to the rear.

On 13th December 1939, an interesting 'stage-run' took place with a Spitfire attempting to 'shoot-down' the Taylorcraft Model 'D'. The latter performed extremely well.

The French government wanted to improve their A.O.P. agenda, and sent representatives to Ratcliffe. The day before they arrived the area was covered in the deepest snow of the winter - disaster? Readers can no doubt appreciate Lance's qualities by now; he did no more than to ask for skis to be fitted to a model 'C' aeroplane within twenty-four hours. The results were spectacular; the visitors were delighted apart from feeling that the rear view needed to be improved. Before a batch of aeroplanes could be ordered, the Germans invaded France in the spring of 1940: it was checkmate! Great Britain was under threat of invasion: all private aircraft production and private flying ceased, and Taylorcraft Aeroplane Ltd undertook repairing aircraft for the Ministry of Aircraft Production.

Soon Tiger Moths arrived in large numbers, they were repaired at the Britannia Works and a converted barn at nearby Syston. So successful was the enterprise that extra floor space had to be sought: acquiring a sheet metal shop at Mountsorrel. Damaged Hurricane fighters from the Battle of Britain arrived, and they were repaired at the County Flying Club at Rearsby, an extra hanger being built for this purpose.

In June 1941, an Air Ministry official visited the company; he asked Lance if he had any aeroplanes in storage for communication duties, etc. He also asked him to trace as many pre-war Model 'C's as possible, to repaint them and deliver them for service within the R.A.F. The resulting aircraft were delivered to Old Sarum, where sufficient pilots had been trained to form the nucleus of 651 Squadron, under the command of Squadron Leader E. D. Joyce.

One of the problems encountered in early A. O. P. duties was the inability to prevent the enemy from tuning in to pilot to gunner transmissions. In September 1941 wireless trials were conducted at Farnborough to devise a suitable screening device. The following year, Lance and his highly motivated work force contributed further development designs and improvements. Soon afterwards, Taylorcraft was awarded a contract (No1995) for one hundred Model D1 aircraft, with the prototype listing as the AUSTER A. O. P.1; it was the birth of a legendary aeroplane. The name Auster dates to Roman times: 'A warm, dry, south-westerly wind.'

The R.A.F. designated the Auster to the role of intelligence gatherer: flying high over the battlefield and relaying vital information such as enemy troop movements and accuracy of allied artillery, etc. Also, communication was a key factor, dropping messages to troops or 'underground forces', cable laying and transportation of light supplies. Such was the noted reliability of the Auster, that King George V1 was flown from Radda to Sienna in Italy in July 1944.

Taylorcraft endeavoured to improve the aircraft; a new engine, the D.H. Gipsy Major was fitted (130 HP), as were split flaps, a cabin heater and improved visibility for the latter.

During the war 1,630 aircraft were produced for service with twelve A. O. P. squadrons. They served in France, (including 'D'-Day plus 2), North Africa, Sicily, Italy, Austria, Belgium, Holland, Germany and the Far East. Five hundred and ninety-four men were trained to pilot Austers, and as testimony to the

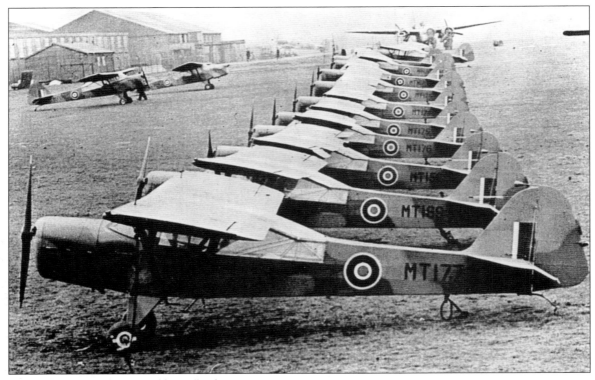

*Auster AOP 4s at Rearsby awaiting collection.*

strengths and reliability of the craft, only sixty-one pilots were killed; one hundred and eighteen received bravery awards!

An Auster is on display in the Imperial War Museum in recognition of its contribution towards success in the war effort. Lance ('A-L') possessed a dynamic personality together with the qualities of perseverance, initiative, and a determination to succeed. Before war's end he had plans drawn-up for a post war sale of civilian aircraft to all parts of the world. The future appeared to be golden.

*Lance Wykes climbing into his Auster aircraft shortly before his death in 1944.*

a beautiful spring morning in 1944 and she was not aware of breaking any house-rules. Margot was told to return home on the very next train, no other explanation other than there had been an accident. As she sat in the railway carriage, opposite to her was a man reading a newspaper; a headline revealed a devastating story!

14th May 1944 was warm and sunny; several thousands of folk had turned out at Abbey Park Oval to watch a Home Guards' Assault competition and a flying display. The occasion, to raise funds for the National War Saving's Campaign (a Salute the Soldier Parade took place in the city on the day before), saw Lance Wykes and Geoffrey Edwards piloting two Auster 4s at eight hundred feet. The Auster 4 prototype

*Lance with Margot and Bob. Easter 1944.*

Lance's daughter, Margot (now a friend living in the same village), was attending a boarding school near to Pontefract in Yorkshire, when she was asked to report to the head-teacher's office immediately! It was

was chosen to illustrate its incredible powers of manoeuvrability. An ultra-modern Hawker Typhoon dive-bomber then zoomed above them to contrast their different speeds. Geoffrey Edwards, chief test pilot for Taylorcraft, saw Lance suddenly stall and dive vertically into the ground. A black plume of smoke rose into the air!

Amid the expectant crowd in the park were Stella Wykes and Sarah Anne, Lance's mother.

Before climbing into his Auster, Lance had complained of feeling unwell; he was advised to postpone the event, but that was never part of his personality, he said he would be fine, and besides he had no wish to disappoint the large crowd or the Savings Campaign. He started the engine and set course for Leicester. It was reported that 'A-L' gave a brilliant display of flying and enthralled the huge crowd with twists, turns, loops and dives, etc.

Walter Hutchinson worked for Taylorcraft and shortly after watching the proceedings explained what happened:

*"He had just done a roll by the Blackbird Road railway line embankment when suddenly he dipped to the right and then dived into the ground. I could easily see the goggled pilot as he descended and he never moved, I think he had a heart attack! He only crashed about sixty yards from me, the aircraft burst into flames."*

Austin J. Ruddy in his excellent book: 'To The Last Round' researched the following:

*'First on the scene was Home Guard J. S. Matts, who made a gallant attempt to rescue the pilot, but he was driven back by the flames. When the fire died down, the deceased was seen to be pinned down under a wing. Matts lifted the wing and two other men named Lee and Orton dragged Wykes clear: he had been killed on impact. The police had great difficulty trying to control the large crowd that gathered near the crash. All that remained was the framework of the burnt-out tail plane reared into the air.'*

In a crazy formula of events, Stella Wykes was inexorably linked to the harsh realities of two world wars; her brother, Leslie Moore, a lance-corporal in the 1/4th Leicestershire Battalion was killed at the 1915 Battle of the Hohenzollern Redoubt. Stella looked upon the burning wreckage of the Auster but all she could remember were the flames that licked skywards.

Sir Stafford Cripps, Minister for Aircraft Production wrote to Mrs. Wykes:

*'It is with the greatest regret that I heard of the accident, a splendid job for the country, most sincere and deepest sympathy.'*

Mr. E. Etheridge of the same Ministry wrote:

*'He seemed to possess something of the explorer spirit, always ready to venture along new and untried ways.'*

Margot beside her parent's grave. October 2007.

Lance was buried at Barrow-on-Soar Cemetery. His Epitaph reads: *'Write of me as one that loves his fellow men.'* Aged 45 years, died 14th May 1944, and in memory of his wife, Stella Elizabeth who died July 27th 1995: 91 years.

Following Lance's death his old boyhood friend and business partner took over as managing director. As young men they adored flight and fast motorbikes! In March 1946, Taylorcraft was renamed: *'Auster Aircraft Ltd'*, and the Auster J/1 Autocrat became the first post-war civil light aircraft to go into production: four hundred were built at just over £1,000 each. Numerous variants of the Auster were designed and built for pilot training, tourist's tours, observation, crop spraying, military and racing. A grand total of 3, 868 aircraft were built and for over twenty-one years the firm was the mainstay of British light aircraft manufacture. L951 Austers were in action from 1952 in the Korean War. In 1960, the company was absorbed into the British Executive and General Aviation Ltd (Beagle). Eight years later design and development of the Auster ceased; it was the death of the brainchild of (Flying Officer) Mr. L. Wykes.

I began this essay with Alfred Wykes, a soldier of the Great War, who sat in his craggy trench and in pipe dreams thought of home. He envisaged Lance making his model planes, and from that small seed so a little empire was built. The subsequent 'oak tree' did much to ensure that our country won through between the years 1939-45.

Alfred and Sarah Anne Wykes never fully recovered from their son's death; a vibrant flame had been extinguished. Alfred died in 1947, Sarah Anne nine years later. Their daughter, Dorothy, was a teacher at Anstey Martins School for many years, passing away in 1983.

Lance's son, Robert (Bob) served some time with the R.A.F., and just like his father became a successful businessman; founder of: 'Airtools and Compressors Ltd' of Loughborough.

Bob let it be known, and rightly so, that from day one 'Taylorcraft' made a profit; when in 1960 and as 'Beagle', from day one it made a loss!

Lance's daughter, Margot (Brookman), is happily married and living at Old Woodhouse, a few kilometres from Quorn.

"I was stunned when I read the newspaper and read that my father had been killed; I have so many happy memories of him. He took me to Sutton on Sea one day, and also said that he would fly me around the world." There is no doubt that Lance Wykes contributed enormously to the Allies war effort, indeed in both world wars, but notably so by his lead and entrepreneurship in the latter war. His were the qualities that made our country great, and I feel we have a shortage in that department now. Several years ago I visited his old school at Quorn to enquire as to whether there was a plaque in his memory and/or recognition of his brilliance. No! What a role model he would make for today's youngsters? Time has not meandered, the problems within society do not decrease; and still there is no recognition of one of its very finest 'old boys'!

My thanks to Margot and her husband, David Brookman.

Beatrice Nurse in 1938.

**Postscript:**

In 1938, a glamorous lady, Beatrice Nurse, became the first woman in Leicestershire to hold a flying licence. Born in 1916 she lived with her parents on St. Stephen's Road, Leicester. After training as a typist she saved her wages to pay for flying lessons and eventually became pilot number 21 of Rearsby's Flying Club. In the late Thirties, Beatrice spent many hours in the air flying to and fro from France and southern England: a particularly brave and exciting hobby for women of that time. Unlike Amelia Earhart, she survived the 1930s decade, and many others! In 1997 she recalled taking her flying test:

"I flew in an open-cockpit Taylorcraft and was supposed to land in a circle marked on the ground at Ratcliffe Aerodrome. My heart sank when I landed but couldn't see the circle, then someone pointed out that I had come down in the exact centre of it.

I certainly travelled; on one flight from Leicestershire to the Isle of Wight I marked the route on the map with lipstick, navigated with a compass, and leaned out of the cockpit looking for landmarks and copses. I flew over the Channel coast hotel where my friend's mother was holidaying and she came out and waved to me!

At the outbreak of war Beatrice hoped to join the Air Transport Auxiliary, but had to stay at home to look after her ailing parents. She also loved fast cars, and ran a secretarial business until her seventies. The amazing Beatrice Nurse passed away in Crown Hills Nursing Home, Leicester in October 2003, aged eighty-seven years.

# A DEDICATION TO THE DESERT RATS

This dedication draws inspiration from the words of Prime Minister Winston Churchill, as spoken on 3rd February 1943: *"When the War is over it will be enough for a man to say that he marched and fought with the Desert Army."*

The 'Desert Rats', the most famous British Field Army of World War 2, were named after the desert rat or jerboa: the emblem of the 7th Armoured Division. The Eighth Army's fame grew, and with the 7th Division part of that Army, so the name encompassed the Eighth Army.

The Western Desert Campaign began in September 1941, although in 1940 the Allies planned to remove the Italian presence in North Africa, and launch an offensive in the Balkans to secure the Romanian oil fields. Following the Battle of Britain, the Mediterranean became the principal theatre of the war, and remained so until Germany invaded Russia in June 1941.

In 1940, the British Desert Force numbered just thirty-six thousand troops together with two hundred and five aircraft, and the 7th Division with three hundred tanks and armoured cars. Their role was to defend Egypt and the crucial Suez Canal passage. Facing them was an Italian Army of a quarter of a million troops: admittedly with aging guns and obsolete tanks.

The Desert restricted warfare to a lengthy coastal plain of nineteen hundred kilometres (twelve hundred miles). This plain was hemmed in by high ground/steep salty depressions that extended from Tripoli in the west to Alexandria in the east. Also, this mobile war on sandy wastelands required food, drink and military supplies to be delivered swiftly

Italy declared war on 11th June 1940. On 13th September they advanced to Sidi Barrini: ninety-five kilometres (sixty miles) into Egypt, and built fortifications. The British Forces were at Mersa Matruth, ninety kilometres due east, and recently strengthened by thirty-one thousand motorised troops, two hundred and seventy-five tanks, one hundred and fifty aircraft (with Hurricanes), plus field guns and Ack-Ack guns. Included were the 4th Indian Division and three Brigades of the 6th Australian Division. Churchill intended to defeat the Italians and boost morale on the Home Front.

On 9th December 1940, General Wavell, Commander in Chief Middle East, launched the offensive: *'Operation Compass'*. Surprising the Italians they recaptured Sidi Barrini within two days, captured forty thousand prisoners and pushed the enemy back into Cyrenaica. Advancing, they besieged the fortified coastal town of Bardia on 3rd January 1941: capturing forty-five thousand troops, and on January 22nd took Tobruk, eighty miles westward, with twenty-seven thousand captured. The assault, over fifty-eight days, was a resounding victory for the Commonwealth troops; the Italian Tenth Army was destroyed and one hundred and thirty thousand prisoners, nearly four hundred tanks and thirteen hundred guns captured. Circumstances prevented the capture of the port of Tripoli, if it had the North African War would have been over; it was two long years before Tripoli eventually fell!

In early 1941, British Intelligence knew of a build-up of German Forces in the Balkans, sent to support Italians with their incursion into Greece. To counter this, sections of the Desert Army and Air Force were despatched as *'Force W'*. The Army was further weakened by essential refits to the 7th Armoured Division and the 6th Australian Division: replaced by the raw 2nd Armoured and 9th Australian Divisions on frontline screening duties.

On February 12th, Lieutenant-General Erwin Rommel (later Field Marshal) arrived at Tripoli with elements of the legendary Deutsches Afrika Korps (DAK). The Force contained the 5th Light and 15th Panzer Divisions: troops with battle experience throughout Europe. The tactically brilliant Rommel was arguably the premier officer of World War 2.

He believed that British strength in Cyrenaica would recover, and so launched an attack on 24th March 1941 towards Agedabia. With Luftwaffe support he took the town in two days against the weaker screening force and pushed towards Egypt. With two Italian Divisions in support, on April 13th, the Axis Forces surrounded and laid siege on Tobruk. The siege lasted for two hundred and forty-two days with a sustained aerial and artillery bombardment, but loosing Cyrenaica meant that Malta was exposed to German air attack.

Also, Axis Forces claimed Yugoslavia and Greece: *'Force W'* was evacuated on April 22nd.

Winston Churchill urged Wavell to drive Rommel

back, after a convoy to Alexandria brought considerable reinforcements in tanks and infantry. 'Operation Brevity' started on 15th May 1941, but was a failure and coincided with the loss of Crete. Another attack to relieve Tobruk failed with the lethal enemy 88mm anti-tank gun claiming many allied victims. Stalemate followed with both sides lacking numbers to achieve victory.

July 1941: General Claude Auchinleck succeeded Wavell. He received reinforcements and on 26th September 1941, the *Eighth Army* was officially formed. In that same month, Rommel received considerable additions both in troops, armour and fuel. 'Operation Crusader' began on November 18th, another attempt to liberate Tobruk and there were initial successes, but Rommel's armour counter-attacked powerfully and both sides suffered severe losses! British naval and air power in the Mediterranean meant the Axis Forces ran low on fuel. This foiled Rommel's plans to remove the British near Tobruk, and subsequently on 6th January 1942 the siege was ended.

When Japan entered the war on 7th December 1942, British and Australian units had to be sent to the Far East, while Rommel was strengthened by increased 'U'-Boat and Luftwaffe activity in the Mediterranean: receiving Ariete and Trieste Panzer Divisions. Poor radio security allowed the enemy to become aware of Auckinleck's depletions and supply problems. He struck at Mersa Brega on January 21st and advanced to take Benghazi on January 29th. The Desert Rats retired to Gazala-Bir-Hakeim and built fortifications that were too strong for the Germans: who had also outstretched their supply columns. Again, a lull descended upon the Desert. Rommel laid plans to regain Tobruk, push on to the Suez Canal, control the Desert and later the oil fields.

Auckenleck had dug in at the 'Gazala Line'; it consisted of defensive 'boxes', artillery and sixty miles of minefields stretching from the coast to the fortress at Bir Hakeim. On 25th May 1942, the Luftwaffe bombed the area and two days later Italian troops attacked north of Trigh Capuzzo; Rommel led his Armoured Divisions, ten thousand strong, in a wide sweep further south to outflank the Line and cut off supply lines. At 9.00pm on the 26th, at Bir Hakeim, Rommel swung north-eastwards and caught the defenders by surprise;

very fierce fighting ensued! The Axis armour was repulsed and Rommel was forced to establish a defensive location in the region of Sidi Muftah. On May 31st, with the battle in the balance, Italian and German Forces threw everything into the 'Battle of The Cauldron'. The British 150th Infantry Brigade was annihilated: three thousand men and one hundred tanks lost. Auckenleck countered on June 5th, but was thwarted by a pincer attack that threatened the entire Line.

On June 8th, Panzer Divisions with Stuka bombers tried to trap a Free French Force at Bir Hakeim, but failed, and three days later they thrust towards El Adem: on the road to Tobruk. Churchill ordered that Tobruk must be held! On June 21st, after weeks of intense fighting Tobruk fell: some of its defences had been removed for the 'Gazala Line'.

On June 22nd, Auckenleck withdrew to Mersa Matruh in order to regroup and reorganise, but with Rommel advancing he further withdrew to the partially constructed 'El Alamein Line'. The Axis Forces attacked in a series of engagements from July 1st to 27th in what became known as 'First Alamein': and continued in an operation known as the 'Battle of Alam Halfa'. On August 30/31st, Rommel used armoured formations to swing into a wide attack around the British southern flank, but was funnelled towards strong British positions on the Alam Alfa Ridge. He was met by anti-tank guns, tanks in dugouts, and also bombed by the Desert Air Force, with some of the action extending to the Qattara Depression.

There followed an orderly retreat, but Rommel had been stopped and from then onwards his fortunes changed: he now had a very long and endangered supply line.

He had been close to an ultimate victory while the German Campaign in Russia was reaching a pivotal point. When Auchinleck refused Churchill's request to instantly counter-attack, the Prime Minister decided upon fresh blood.

On August 6th, he appointed General Harold Alexander as Commander-in-Chief Middle East and Lieutenant General Bernard Montgomery as General Officer Commanding the Eighth Army. Montgomery informed his subordinates that he would not countenance retreat from El Alamein. Making numerous visits to those under his command he

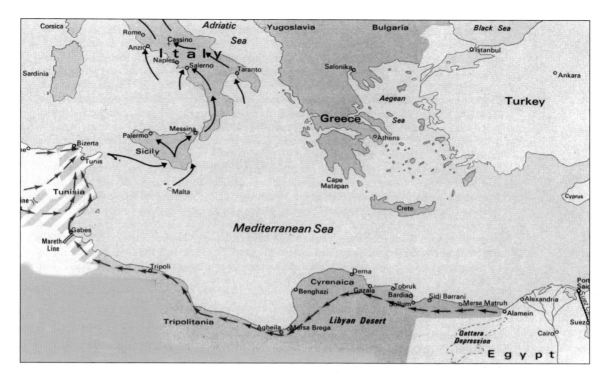

inspired his men and instilled a new spirit. Extra training was put into practice and eventually a date for a new offensive was announced: the night of 23rd October 1942. For four days prior to that date the Air Force attacked enemy airfields, and at 9.40pm, October 23rd, Montgomery's artillery opened up: the largest barrage since World War 1. The infantry left their foxholes at 22.00 hours, but many fell to mines and booby traps. Next day sappers and pioneers created corridors for them to pass through, but progress was slow. On the 25th, Montgomery ordered the 9th Australian Division and 1st Armoured Division to thrust north and prevent Axis Forces from retreating along the coastal road. A salient was formed, and in spite of a continual two-day's barrage along the frontline and other forages, a halt was called. The Germans followed with an unsuccessful counter-attack.

Montgomery planned 'Operation Supercharge', he intended, once and for all, to breakthrough and push the enemy across Libya and into Tunisia. As a preliminary, on October 30th, a barrage covered an infantry attack around Tel el Aqqaquir, while the 9th Australian Division renewed its push for the coastal road. With chess-like tactics, 'Monty' exploited weaknesses made by Rommel's shuffle to support the coast road! 'Supercharge' began at 1.05am on 2nd November 1942. Eight hundred guns laid a barrage along an enemy frontage of two and a half miles, and British and Australian infantry rapidly penetrated deeply into Axis territory. The armoured attack was assigned to the 9th Brigade. Montgomery told them that if necessary to accept one hundred percent casualties; they had to breach the enemy's artillery and anti-tank screen. It proved a sacrificial attack: loosing seventy of its ninety-four tanks, but Rommel lost thirty-five tanks, many guns and additional failings along his frontline. Further British armour exploited these weaknesses under cover of artillery fire. Rommel attacked in desperation but was subjected to air attacks: over a hundred German and Italian tanks lay wrecked on the battlefield. Rommel ordered a ninety kilometre (sixty mile) withdrawal along the coastal road to Fuka. Herr Hitler prohibited further retreats and ordered 'victory or death'. The Eighth Army attacked the southernmost section of the Line and four Italian Divisions were rounded up and imprisoned. In Germany, Field Marshal Kesselring consented to a retreat: Tripoli fell on 23rd January 1943. It was a considerable victory for Montgomery and his men who had pushed the enemy eastwards for over three thousand kilometres (two thousand miles). The Eighth Army stopped at Tripoli for vital supplies.

They suffered 13, 560 casualties, representing a quarter of its infantry, as well as five hundred tanks and nearly a thousand aircraft. On 8th November 1942, an Anglo-American Army landed in Morocco and Algeria. Their role in 'Operation Torch' condemned Rommel to a war on two fronts and necessitated him to fall back into Tunisia, where he was reinforced by an extra quarter of a million extra troops and equipment.

The Allies' attack on Rommel's defensive 'Mareth

*Line'* was launched on the evening of March 20th; the main thrust intending to punch a gap through defences near to the sea to allow armoured divisions to pour through. Simultaneously, a New Zealand Corps attacked near to El Hamma, a flanking movement to pin-down the enemy's reserves. The main thrust failed and the 1st Armoured Division supported the Kiwis: a stalemate. My Uncle Maurice, son of Charles Hatter, one of the 'Famous Fifty' was badly wounded in the Green Howards' infantry attack. RQMS Hatter was taken by hospital ship from Tunis via Alexandria to the 5th South African Hospital at Cairo where he spent several months. See Major Peter Moore's Tunisian Campaign in Volume One.

Apart from the warfare the conditions were entirely alien to British troops. The conditions were exacting: soaring daytime heat, freezing nights, sand storms, lacking food and water and plagues of flies that cultivated dysentery. On occasions hot, bone-dry winds breezed from the blistering Sahara Desert; they swept into and dehydrated the troops: men were seen to drain radiator water from damaged vehicles to satisfy their thirsts.

Colonel David Stirling founded the Special Air Service (SAS) during the Desert War in 1942. His elite troops worked in small, highly trained teams, usually under cover and many miles behind enemy lines. Rommel referred to Colonel Stirling as the 'Phantom Major'. (See Jack Cooper and Edward Cavendish under The Cavendish Family At War).

The Desert Rats' war continued in the mountains of Tunisia and the battlefields of Sicily and Italy: distinguishing itself repeatedly. Winston Churchill commented: *"Before El Alamein we never had a victory, while after Alamein we never had a defeat!"*

A future chairman of North West Leicestershire Council, Sergeant Stanley Southworth MM (later Major) of the 42nd/15th Light Artillery Regiment, showed outstanding ability and bravery on more than one occasion when firing at enemy aircraft attacking mechanised supply columns.

Apart from the Lount man, many Leicestershire men were 'Desert Rats'. Other locals lads: Harold Garrett** (killed in France in 1944), who saved my uncle's life (both Tigers then Green Howards), as was (Sergeant) Ronald Concannon: killed in Belgium on 10th September 1944 (leaving Gert and son, David). Howard Richards, Reg Carter, well known Coalville boxer: Billie Lowe, Jack Shaw, Maurice Cornford, Walter Clamp, Arthur Rabone, Ernest Moore, Archie Beniston, Herbert Cotterill, George Bunce, Sam Smedley, Gordon Stacey, Norman Green, Leslie Boot (son of one of the 'Famous Fifty'), Herbert Dalby, Ron Ball (one of the five famous rugby playing brothers), Norman Abell, Sydney Button, Kitch Beale, George Mason, Frank Spiby, Bernard Smith, Ernie Mee, A. Cowley and W. Bradford to name just a representative few. In 1942, local man, Peter Pittam wrote an enchanting little poem that allows us to read his innermost thoughts of that time:

*'When the golden sun goes down in this eastern land,*
*I lie and dream of you: whilst gazing o'er the sand.*
*I picture in my memory those happy days we knew,*
*Before I sailed across the sea to a land out in the blue.*
*I left England's fine shores to a land of sand and sun,*
*To do my bit in England's cause, till victory is won.*
*Then I'll sail back home to you, the home that I adore,*
*To England's green and lovely land, to stay for evermore.*
*And when we sit together dear, as soon as work is done,*
*I'll tell you how I missed you, in that land of sand and sun.'*

*"When the War is over it will be enough for a man to say that he marched and fought with the Desert Army."*

••Harold Garrett served with the 7th Battalion of the Green Howards. Born in Dennis Street, Hugglescote, Harold was a great friend of my Uncle Maurice Hatter. Harold rests in the War Cemetery at Hottot-Les-Bagues; fifteen kilometres from Bayeux in Normandy.

# THE END OF THE LINE

Not too long ago, on January 27th: 'Holocaust Memorial Day' I visited Beth Shalom Holocaust Centre, Laxton, in Nottinghamshire. I presented a copy of my poem and listened to Doctor Martin Stern describe his family background and boyhood years. Below are details of the aforementioned, and with his consent, I am honoured to dedicate this essay to the memory of all Holocaust victims.

German nationals Rudolf Stern and Elfrieda Letz met and fell in love in Berlin during Hitler's persecution of those with Jewish blood. Nazis classification covered a person with two or more Jewish grandparents. Rudolf, from an affluent family, was an architect, but he was also Jewish! In 1938, they fled to Belgium and married before settling at Amsterdam in Holland, and it was there that Martin was born.

Martin's father.

Martin's mother

Their happiness was short-lived: Germany occupied that country and those of Jewish blood had to register at a censor office. Enforcements meant that Rudolf could only shop between 3.00-5.00pm and needed a permit to use public transport; also his bank account was frozen. Unable to work and fearing deportation to a 'labour-camp', he sought refuge on farms in rural areas. He was finally captured and taken to Auschwitz, and Buchenwald, near Weimer, where he died. Nothing was said to Martin concerning his father's departure!

In late 1942, family friends, Joseph 'Rademakers and his wife looked after him while his mother gave birth to Erica; his mother died within days of a fever. The Rademakers were not Jewish and aware of the penalty for harbouring one: death! Nevertheless, they treated him as their own, and he attended school and played outside: he was not old enough to wear the distinguishing Jewish Star. He lived and played very near to where Anne Frank and her family lived in their secret annexe! In the summer of 1944, while at school, two men arrived and told the class to line-up against a wall. They sharply asked if Martin Stern was there. The female teacher said loudly that he wasn't, but the unwitting five-year-old stepped forward.

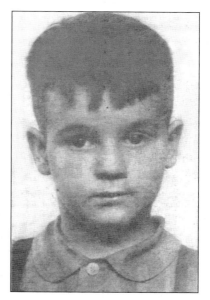

Martin as a boy.

Martin said he would never, ever forget the look on his teacher's face! He was taken to an office and questioned by a man in a German uniform, then led into a small poorly lit room where all he could see was a man with his back to him. When the man turned round he could see that it was Mr. Rademakers, and instantly called out his name. Such is the irony of life that the innocence of a child unwittingly betrayed the goodness of his guardian! Joseph Rademakers' head bowed and Martin was then shocked when two German guards forcibly grabbed Mr. Rademakers and led him away. Joseph, clearly a very brave and upright gentleman died at Neuengamme Concentration Camp: along with fifty-five thousand others! Incongruously or wickedly so, that Camp sent his spectacles to his distraught wife, Cathrien.

# Auschwitz

*(Arbeit Macht Frei-*Work will set you free)

Auschwitz was the end-of-the-line for a million human beings.
Settlers eyeing new eastern horizons? Simply double-dealings!
Onwards by train: Dutch and Poles, Slovaks and French to name
A few, all of Jewish blood, condemned and yet beyond blame.

A cortege of cattle-trucks rolling to the active Auschwitz abattoir.
Stripped and herded into 'showers' those born of David's star.
Mothers and fathers, sons and daughters, all within the camp-fold
For a short stay, a long stay, males and females, young and old.

Showers locked: crystals solved the final solution in gas chambers.
The Devil's Nazi workshop: eager aids that later filed disclaimers.
Bodies rendered to ash, not dust; specs and gold-fillings are spared
With cases and bags, hats and hair while shoes remained paired.

Frail fingers, five-by-two, hooked on barbed wire: will never fall.
Skeletal slaves were those who dug graves for death's timely call.
Bodies with tattooed numbers: filed, reviled, even the living-dead
At Auschwitz concentration camp, and all for want of a little bread.

The Final Solution should have been the Final Resolution.

Michael Kendrick.
2005

The 60th Anniversary of its Liberation